MICROSOFT® ACCESS® 2013
Instructor's Guide

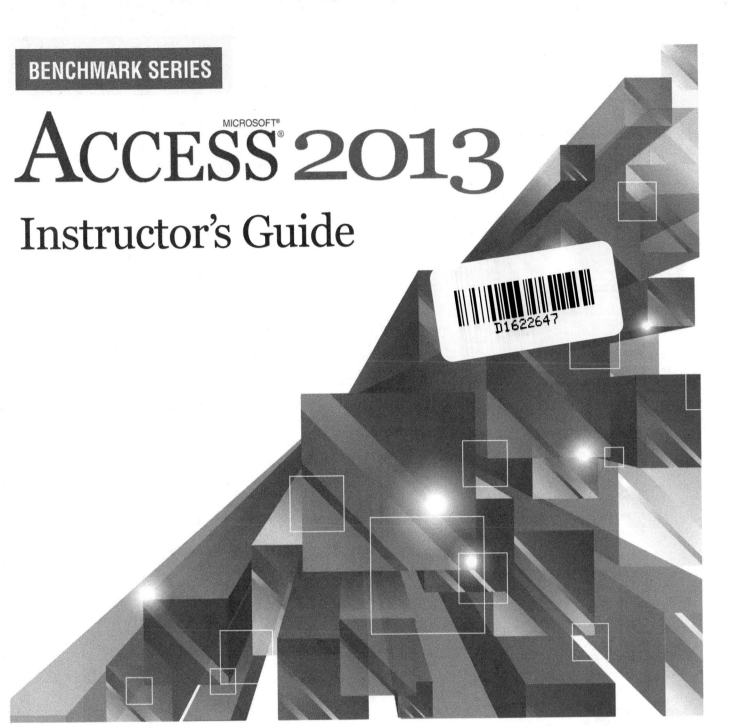

NITA RUTKOSKY
Pierce College at Puyallup
Puyallup, Washington

DENISE SEGUIN
Fanshawe College
London, Ontario

JAN DAVIDSON
Lambton College
Sarnia, Ontario

AUDREY ROGGENKAMP
Pierce College at Puyallup
Puyallup, Washington

IAN RUTKOSKY
Pierce College at Puyallup
Puyallup, Washington

Paradigm PUBLISHING
St. Paul

Director of Editorial: Christine Hurney
Director of Production: Timothy W. Larson
Production Editor: Lori Michelle Ryan
Assistant Production Editor: Katherine Lee
Cover Designer: Leslie Anderson and Valerie King
Design & Production Specialist: Sara Schmidt Boldon

Care has been taken to verify the accuracy of information presented in this book. However, the authors, editors, and publisher cannot accept responsibility for Web, email, newsgroup, or chat room subject matter or content, or for consequences from application of the information in this book, and make no warranty, expressed or implied, with respect to its content.

Trademarks: Some of the product names and company names included in this book have been used for identification purposes only and may be trademarks or registered trade names of their respective manufacturers and sellers. The authors, editors, and publisher disclaim any affiliation, association, or connection with, or sponsorship or endorsement by, such owners.

We have made every effort to trace the ownership of all copyrighted material and to secure permission from copyright holders. In the event of any question arising as to the use of any material, we will be pleased to make the necessary corrections in future printings. Thanks are due to the aforementioned authors, publishers, and agents for permission to use the materials indicated.

ISBN 978-0-76385-454-6 (Text + Disc)
ISBN 978-0-76385-383-9 (Text)

© Paradigm Publishing, Inc.
875 Montreal Way
St. Paul, MN 55102
Email: educate@emcp.com
Website: www.emcp.com

Printed in the United States of America

22 21 20 19 18 17 16 15 14 13   1 2 3 4 5 6 7 8 9 10

Contents

Note: Lesson Blueprints providing detailed lesson plans for a 16-week course are provided on the Instructor disc and on the Internet Resource Center.

Note: Project Model Answers are provided in the student textbook at the beginning of each chapter.

Planning the Course

Most educators would agree that the key to teaching a successful course is careful, thorough planning. And, as noted in Exceptional Teaching: Ideas in Action, published by Paradigm Publishing, "Instructors assess, plan, implement, and evaluate…repeatedly. They do this based on many of the factors that make teaching learner-centered and on several other variables. Before students even think about entering or logging into the classroom, instructors make decisions about the course. These begin with identifying the heart of the course. That is, what, exactly, are the most important outcomes that students should achieve? And what plan of action can the instructor devise that will help ensure those outcomes?" Thinking through a course action plan typically includes four phases:

1. Developing course outcomes
2. Determining the course delivery mode and structure (dividing the course into parts, each with outcomes)
3. Selecting the instructional approach, resources, and activities of the course
4. Developing an assessment strategy

Developing Course Outcomes

In developing course outcomes, some of the key issues to consider are the following:
- When this course is complete, in what ways will the learner be permanently changed? Should instruction result in
  - building knowledge?
  - developing higher-order thinking?
  - developing independent learning skills?
  - developing technical literacy?
- What problems are encountered that are related to course content?
  - What must be communicated?
  - How will the learner find out whether the work is satisfactory?
  - How will the learner receive feedback?

Considering these questions, a set of end-of-course outcomes for a one-semester course on Microsoft Access 2013 could include the following items, stated as performance objectives.

At course conclusion, the student will be able to:
- Create database tables to organize business or personal records
- Modify and manage tables to ensure that data is accurate and up to date
- Perform queries to assist with decision making
- Plan, research, create, revise and publish database information to meet specific communication needs
- Given a workplace scenario requiring the reporting and analysis of data , assess the information requirements and then prepare the materials that achieve the goal efficiently and effectively

Determining the Course Delivery Mode and Structure

Frequently, the course structure has been determined in advance by your department. However, if you are in a position to develop a plan or modify an existing structure, consider these questions:

- What topics in each subject area are essential for demonstrating the course outcomes?
- Is this the only course that will address this subject and skill set?
- What do students already know about each subject? What can they learn on their own without your direct instruction?
- Where in each subject will the instruction begin and end?

Your answers to these questions will help you divide the course content into parts and identify the associated learning outcomes (also called performance objectives). Note that course outcomes are marked by higher and more challenging skill sets and typically require the integration of many skills, while unit or part outcomes are more narrowly defined and focused.

Course Delivery: Traditional Classroom, Online (Distance Learning), or Hybrid?

While the core considerations are the same whether you are planning a traditional on-campus course, an online course (also called a distance learning course), or a hybrid of the two, the instructional delivery differences create distinct needs you must address in the planning stage.

A critical challenge in teaching online courses is the issue of interacting with students. How will you communicate with them? How will they submit assignments and tests? How will you deliver feedback? How will you get to know your students? Here are some additional questions to consider when planning an online or hybrid course:

- What course management system will you use: Blackboard or some other platform?
- Will students work independently offline? How will they use the course management system to review course outcomes, the syllabus, and assignment due dates? How will they communicate with you, take online quizzes, transmit completed work, and participate in chat sessions?
- Will you be able to offer an on-campus orientation meeting for students at the beginning of the course? If so, how will you prepare to answer the questions students will likely have?
- Will students come to the campus or school to take exams? If not, will students be directed to offsite locations where exams can be administered to verify that the person taking the exam is indeed the person getting credit for the course?
- What hardware configuration and/or software requirements must a student have to participate in your course?

Both the student and instructor resources offered with Benchmark Series Microsoft Access 2013, Levels 1 & 2 can be adapted for use in an online learning environment or a hybrid of traditional and online learning contexts. The SNAP Training and Assessment product, in particular, is well suited for these course delivery modes, and these online files are also designed for distance-learning situations.

The Syllabus

A comprehensive syllabus will help you and your students prepare for each part of the course. A well-planned syllabus is useful for traditional, on-campus courses as well as for courses that are delivered online. A syllabus normally includes:

1. Course-identifying data
2. Prerequisites
3. Instructor contact information
4. Course outcomes
5. Required course resources
6. Major assignments
7. Grade composition
8. Class structure
9. Course schedule
10. College/school requirements

Figure 1 shows a traditional, on-campus course syllabus for a 16-week course that meets three times a week and uses Benchmark Access 2013, Levels 1 & 2 as the core courseware. Lesson plans are referenced in the sample syllabus and are available on the Instructor Resources disc as well as on the password-protected part of the Internet Resource Center (IRC) for Benchmark Access 2013 at www.paradigmcollege.net/BenchmarkAccess13.

FIGURE 1   Traditional 16-Week Semester Syllabus Example Using Benchmark Access 2013 Levels 1 & 2

Course Description

This course prepares students to work with Microsoft Access 2013 in a career setting or for personal use. Using courseware that incorporates a step-by-step, project-based approach, students develop a mastery-level competency in Access 2013 and explore the essential features of Windows 8 and Internet Explorer 10. Students also develop an understanding of fundamental computer hardware and software concepts.

Prerequisites: None

Instructor Contact Information

Name:	**Office Location:**
Office Phone:	**Office Hours:**
Office Email:	

Required Course Resources

Benchmark Series Microsoft Access 2013, Levels 1 & 2
by Rutkosky, Seguin, Davidson, Roggenkamp, and Rutkosky, © Paradigm Publishing, Inc.
Student Resources CD (provided with textbook)
Internet Resource Center, www.paradigmcollege.net/BenchmarkAccess13
SNAP Training and Assessment account, snap2013.emcp.com
USB flash drive or other storage medium

Computer Time

Approximately six to eight hours per week of computer time outside of class is recommended for successful completion of course requirements.

Grading

Final grades will be calculated as an average of all of the following assignments:

- Concepts Check   5%
- Skills Check (SNAP Grade It)   10%
- Visual Benchmark   15%
- Case Study   15%
- Unit Performance Assessment   15%
- SNAP Performance Evaluations   20%
- Exams   20%

College and Course Policy Information

- This college conforms to the provisions of the Americans with Disabilities Act. You are invited to report any special needs to your instructor.
- Your attendance is expected at all class sessions.
- We subscribe to the college policy on academic honesty found in the school catalog.

Course Schedule—Benchmark Access 2013
16-week semester, three 1-hour classes per week

Week	Class	Chapter	Lesson Plan File	Description
1	Class 1	Getting Started/ Windows 8	BM-Access2013-L1-Session01	Intro to course, Getting Started, Using Windows 8
	Class 2	Windows 8/ Internet Explorer	BM-Access2013-L1-Session02	Finish Windows 8, Internet Explorer
	Class 3	Level 1, Ch 1	BM-Access2013-L1-Session03	Creating Database Table
2	Class 4	Level 1, Ch 1	BM-Access2013-L1-Session04	Creating Database Table
	Class 5	Level 1, Ch 2	BM-Access2013-L1-Session05	Creating Relationships Between Tables
	Class 6	Level 1, Ch 3	BM-Access2013-L1-Session06	Performing Queries
3	Class 7	Level 1, Ch 3	BM-Access2013-L1-Session07	Performing Queries
	Class 8	Level 1, Ch 4	BM-Access2013-L1-Session08	Modifying and Managing Tables
	Class 9	Level 1, Ch 4	BM-Access2013-L1-Session09	Modifying and Managing Tables
4	Class 10	Level 1, U1	BM-Access2013-L1-Session10	Level 1, U1 Performance Assessments
	Class 11	TEST	BM-Access2013-L1-Session11	Level 1, Unit 1 Test
	Class 12	Level 1, Ch 5	BM-Access2013-L1-Session12	Creating Forms
5	Class 13	Level 1, Ch 5	BM-Access2013-L1-Session13	Creating Forms
	Class 14	Level 1, Ch 6	BM-Access2013-L1-Session14	Creating Reports and Mailing Labels
	Class 15	Level 1, Ch 6	BM-Access2013-L1-Session15	Creating Reports and Mailing Labels

Week	Class	Chapter	Lesson Plan File	Description
6	Class 16	Level 1, Ch 7	BM-Access2013-L1-Session16	Modifying, Filtering and Viewing Data
	Class 17	Level 1, Ch 7	BM-Access2013-L1-Session17	Modifying, Filtering and Viewing Data
	Class 18	Level 1, Ch 8	BM-Access2013-L1-Session18	Importing and Exporting Data
7	Class 19	Level 1, Ch 8	BM-Access2013-L1-Session19	Importing and Exporting Data
	Class 20	Level 1, U2	BM-Access2013-L1-Session20	Level 1, U2 Performance Assessments
	Class 21	Level 1, U2	BM-Access2013-L1-Session21	Level 1, U2 Performance Assessments
8	Class 22	TEST	BM-Access2013-L1-Session21	Level 1, Unit 2 Test
	Class 23	Level 2, Ch 1	BM-Access2013-L2-Session23	Designing the Structure of Tables
	Class 24	Level 2, Ch 1	BM-Access2013-L2-Session24	Designing the Structure of Table
9	Class 25	Level 2, Ch 2	BM-Access2013-L2-Session25	Designing and Building Relationships and Lookup Fields
	Class 26	Level 2, Ch 2	BM-Access2013-L2-Session26	Designing and Building Relationships and Lookup Fields
	Class 27	Level 2, Ch 3	BM-Access2013-L2-Session27	Advanced Query Techniques
10	Class 28	Level 2, Ch 3	BM-Access2013-L2-Session28	Advanced Query Techniques
	Class 29	Level 2, Ch 3	BM-Access2013-L2-Session29	Advanced Query Techniques
	Class 30	Level 2, Ch 4	BM-Access2013-L2-Session30	Creating and Using Custom Forms
11	Class 31	Level 2, Ch 4	BM-Access2013-L2-Session31	Creating and Using Custom Forms
	Class 32	Level 2, Ch 4	BM-Access2013-L2-Session32	Creating and Using Custom Forms
	Class 33	Level 2, U1	BM-Access2013-L2-Session33	Level 2, U1 Performance Assessments
12	Class 34	TEST	BM-Access2013-L2-Session34	Level 2, Unit 1 Test
	Class 35	Level 2, Ch 5	BM-Access2013-L2-Session35	Creating and Using Custom Reports
	Class 36	Level 2, Ch 5	BM-Access2013-L2-Session36	Creating and Using Custom Reports
13	Class 37	Level 2, Ch 5	BM-Access2013-L2-Session37	Creating and Using Custom Reports
	Class 38	Level 2, Ch 6	BM-Access2013-L2-Session38	Using Access Tools and Managing Objects
	Class 39	Level 2, Ch 6	BM-Access2013-L2-Session39	Using Access Tools and Managing Objects
14	Class 40	Level 2, Ch 7	BM-Access2013-L2-Session40	Automating, Customizing and Securing Access
	Class 41	Level 2, Ch 7	BM-Access2013-L2-Session41	Automating, Customizing and Securing Access
	Class 42	Level 2, Ch 8	BM-Access2013-L2-Session42	Integrating Access Data

Week	Class	Chapter	Lesson Plan File	Description
15	Class 43	Level 2, Ch 8	BM-Access2013-L2-Session43	Integrating Access Data
	Class 44	Level 2, U2	BM-Access2013-L2-Session44-45	Level 2, U2 Performance Assessments
	Class 45	Level 2, U2	BM-Access2013-L2-Session44-45	Level 2, U2 Performance Assessments
16	Class 46	TEST	BM-Access2013-L2-Session46	Level 2, Unit 2 Test

Selecting the Instructional Approach, Resources, and Activities

After the course outcomes and structure are determined, it is important to plan the main content of the course. This includes selecting courseware, identifying resources for English language learners, considering instructional support materials, and reviewing other resources.

Student Courseware

Selecting high-quality student courseware is an important step in the planning process. Learning materials should be engaging and accessible. The Benchmark Series offers several valuable learning tools to support course performance objectives.

- Benchmark Access 2013, Levels 1 & 2 textbook with Student Resources CD
- eBook
- Student Internet Resource Center at www.paradigmcollege.net/BenchmarkAccess13
- SNAP Training and Assessment software
- SNAP Tutorials CD
- Blackboard cartridge

Textbook Structure and Features

Benchmark Series Access 2013 prepares students to work with Microsoft Access 2013 in business and academic settings, and also for personal use. Incorporating a project-based approach that organizes instruction and guided exercises around related program features, this text builds student competency in the 2013 version of Access and the essential features of Windows 8 and Internet Explorer 10.

The Access 2013 Levels 1 & 2 text is just one book in the Benchmark Series. The Benchmark Series contains the following eleven textbooks:

- Benchmark Series Microsoft Office 2013
  - Getting Started (essential computer hardware and software concepts)
  - Windows 8
  - Internet Explorer 10
  - Word 2013 (8 chapters)
  - Excel 2013 (8 chapters)
  - Access 2013 (8 chapters)
  - PowerPoint 2013 (8 chapters)
  - Integrating Office 2013 Programs

- Benchmark Series Microsoft Word 2013 Levels 1 and 2
  - Getting Started
  - Windows 8
  - Internet Explorer 10
  - Word 2013 Level 1 (8 chapters)
  - Word 2013 Level 2 (8 chapters)
- Benchmark Series Microsoft Word 2013 Level 1
  - Getting Started
  - Windows 8
  - Internet Explorer 10
  - Word 2013 Level 1 (8 chapters)
- Benchmark Series Microsoft Word 2013 Level 2
  - Word 2013 Level 2 (8 chapters)
- Benchmark Series Microsoft Excel 2013 Levels 1 and 2
  - Getting Started
  - Windows 8
  - Internet Explorer 10
  - Excel 2013 Level 1 (8 chapters)
  - Excel 2013 Level 2 (8 chapters)
- Benchmark Series Microsoft Excel 2013 Level 1
  - Getting Started
  - Windows 8
  - Internet Explorer 10
  - Excel 2013 Level 1 (8 chapters)
- Benchmark Series Microsoft Excel 2013 Level 2
  - Excel 2013 Level 2 (8 chapters)
- Benchmark Series Microsoft Access 2013 Levels 1 and 2
  - Getting Started
  - Windows 8
  - Internet Explorer 10
  - Access 2013 Level 1 (8 chapters)
  - Access 2013 Level 2 (8 chapters)
- Benchmark Series Microsoft Access 2013 Level 1
  - Getting Started
  - Windows 8
  - Internet Explorer 10
  - Access 2013 Level 1 (8 chapters)
- Benchmark Series Microsoft Access 2013 Level 2
  - Access 2013 Level 2 (8 chapters)
- Benchmark Series Microsoft PowerPoint 2013
  - Getting Started
  - Windows 8
  - Internet Explorer 10
  - PowerPoint 2013 (8 chapters)

The main Microsoft application sections of each book in the Benchmark Series contain eight chapters, split into two units. The opening page of a unit lists the four chapter titles included in the unit. Each chapter opener presents the chapter's Performance Objectives, an overview of the skills taught in the chapter, a listing of the SNAP tutorials that support the chapter content, and a CD icon and text identifying a folder of data files to be copied to the student's storage medium. These files are used to complete chapter projects and end-of-chapter activities. Following the opening page, the chapter begins with model answers of the chapter projects that students can reference to confirm they have completed the chapter projects correctly.

Skills instruction in the text is organized around projects that require using a group of related features to complete a document or build a file. A project overview, which lists the project number and title, identifies tasks to accomplish and the features to use in completing the work. The project overview also identifies the number of parts that make up the project. Following each project part (identified with the project number and letter), the text presents instruction on the features and skills necessary to accomplish the next section of the project. Typically, a file remains open throughout all parts of the project. Students save their work incrementally and usually print only at the end of the entire project. Instructors have access to the live project model answer files for the completed project as well as the project parts on the Instructor Resources disc and on the password-protected Instructor section of www.paradigmcollege.net/BenchmarkAccess13.

Page margins include the following elements:
- Quick Steps—brief feature summaries for reference and review
- Hint boxes—trouble-shooting ideas and additional useful information
- Button graphics

Each chapter ends with the following review elements and exercises:
- Chapter Summary—A bulleted list captures the purpose and execution of key features.
- Commands Review—Commands taught in the chapter are listed with button, ribbon tab, and keyboard actions.
- Concepts Check—Short-answer questions allow students to test their comprehension and recall of program features, terminology, and functions. Printouts of the Concepts Check answer keys are provided in the print Instructors Guide and electronic files are available on the Instructor Resources disc and on the password-protected Instructor section of www.paradigmcollege.net/BenchmarkAccess13.
- Skills Check—Semi-guided exercises ask students to demonstrate their mastery of the major features and program skills taught in the chapter. The Instructor's Guide includes printed versions of the Skills Check model answers along with rubrics to assess student work. In addition, rubric Word documents, PDF files of the model answers, and live application model answers are available for instructors on the Instructor Resources disc and on the password-protected Instructor section of www.paradigmcollege.net/BenchmarkAccess13. Items marked with a SNAP Grade It icon have corresponding SNAP activities available online.

- Visual Benchmark—With limited guidance, students are challenged to use their problem-solving skills and mastery of program features to build a file that matches a shown sample file. Grading rubrics, PDF files, and live application model answers are available to instructors to support these activities.
- Case Study—Framed in a workplace project perspective, these less-guided assessments evaluate students' abilities to apply chapter skills and concepts in solving realistic problems. Case Study activities require demonstrating program skills as well as decision-making skills and include Help and Internet-based activities. Grading rubrics, PDF files, and live application model answers are available to instructors to support these activities.

Unit Performance Assessments follow each set of four chapters and offer opportunities for cross-disciplinary, comprehensive evaluation. There are four types of Unit Performance Assessments. Assessing Proficiency is a group of gently guided exercises. Writing Activities involve applying program skills in a communication context. An Internet Research project reinforces research, writing, and program skills. A Job Study activity in the Unit 2 Performance Assessment presents a capstone assessment requiring critical thinking and problem solving. Annotated printouts of the model answers and rubrics for evaluating student work are included in the Instructor's Guide. The Instructor Resources disc and the password-protected Instructor section of www.paradigmcollege.net/BenchmarkAccess13 include live file model answers and rubric Word document files for these assessments.

Student Resources CD

Files that serve as a starting point for completing many of the project and end-of-chapter exercises are included on the CD that accompanies the student text. Typically, students are directed to open one of these files, save the file with a new name, and then edit and print the file. Some chapter work requires the students to start an activity from a blank file. As students begin a chapter, they should copy the folder of files for the chapter exercises to the storage medium of their choice. This folder name is displayed next to a CD icon on the first page of the chapter.

eBook

For student who prefer studying with an eBook, the texts in the Benchmark Series are available in an electronic form. The web-based, password-protected eBooks feature dynamic navigation tools, including bookmarking, a linked table of contents, and the ability to jump to a specific page. The eBook format also supports helpful study tools, such as highlighting and note taking.

Benchmark Access 2013 Internet Resource Center

The Benchmark Access 2013 Resource Center at www.paradigmcollege.net/BenchmarkAccess13 offers valuable information for both instructors and students. For students, the Internet Resource Center includes quick access to the student data files, informational Web links, study aids such as online quizzes, and more. All instructor resources posted on the website are password protected and are not accessible by students.

SNAP Training and Assessment

SNAP is a web-based training and assessment program designed to optimize skill-based learning for Access with Windows and Internet Explorer. SNAP creates a virtual classroom on the Web, allowing instructors to employ an electronic grade book and schedule tutorials, skill and concept exams, Grade It end-of-chapter Skills Check activities, and comprehensive performance evaluations.

SNAP contains:

- a bank of 163 interactive, gradable, multimedia tutorials, aligned to textbook chapters, that can be used for direct instruction or remediation (See Table 1 for a listing of the SNAP tutorials for that are available for Benchmark Access 2013.)
- a bank of 270 performance skill items in which students perform tasks in Microsoft Access 2013 that are reported in the learning management system; instructors can assign pre-defined skills exams or create their own
- a bank of 48 Grade It Skills Check assessment activities, which correspond to end-of-chapter activities
- comprehensive Performance Evaluation activities, one per chapter and one per unit, for comprehensive evaluation of skills mastery
- a bank of 875 concept items that can be used to monitor student understanding of computer literacy and technical knowledge; instructors can assign pre-defined concepts exams or create their own

TABLE 1   Benchmark SNAP Tutorials Correlation

Benchmark Windows 8 SNAP Tutorials

Tutorial	Tutorial Title
1	Exploring the Windows 8 Start Screen
2	Exploring the Windows 8 Desktop
3	Opening and Using Windows
4	Exploring the Taskbar and the Charm Bar
5	Browsing Devices and Files
6	Selecting, Copying, and Moving Folders and Files
7	Changing Folder and View Options
8	Creating a Folder and Renaming a Folder or File
9	Using the Recycle Bin
10	Customizing the Desktop
11	Exploring the Control Panel
12	Getting Help in Windows 8
13	Using Windows Search Tools

Benchmark Internet Explorer SNAP Tutorials

Tutorial	Tutorial Title
1	Navigating the Internet Using Web Addresses
2	Finding Information Using Search Tools
3	Researching Information Using Advanced Search Tools
4	Downloading Content from a Web Page

Benchmark Access Level 1 SNAP Tutorials

Chapter	Tutorial	Tutorial Title
1	1.1	Opening and Closing an Access Database and Table
1	1.2	Using the Recent List
1	1.3	Navigating in Objects
1	1.4	Adding Records in a Table
1	1.5	Deleting Records in a Table
1	1.6	Adjusting Column Width
1	1.7	Previewing and Printing a Table
1	1.8	Creating a New Database; Crating a Table in Datasheet View
1	1.9	Creating a Table Using Quick Starts Fields
1	1.10	Modifying Field Size, Caption, and Default Value Properties
2	2.1	Defining a Primary Key
2	2.2	Deleting a Relationship; Printing a Relationships Report
2	2.3	Creating a Relationship between Two Tables in a Database
2	2.4	Creating a One-to-One Relationship between Tables
2	2.5	Editing a Relationship; Enforcing Referential Integrity; Viewing a Subdatasheet
3	3.1	Creating Queries in Design View
3	3.2	Extracting Records Using Criteria Statements
3	3.3	Creating a Query in Design View Using Multiple Tables
3	3.4	Extracting Records Using AND Criteria; Sorting Query Results
3	3.5	Renaming and Deleting Objects
3	3.6	Extracting Records Using OR Criteria
3	3.7	Creating Queries Using the Simple Query Wizard
3	3.8	Performing Calculations in a Query
3	3.9	Using Aggregate Functions
3	3.10	Creating a Crosstab Query
3	3.11	Creating a Find Duplicates Query
3	3.12	Creating a Find Unmatched Query
4	4.1	Creating a Table in Design View
4	4.2	Creating an Input Mask and Formatting a Field
4	4.3	Validating Field Entries
4	4.4	Creating a Lookup Field
4	4.5	Modifying Table Structure in Design View; Inserting a *Total* Row
4	4.6	Sorting Records in a Table
4	4.7	Formatting Table Data and Printing Specific Records
4	4.8	Completing a Spelling Check
4	4.9	Finding and Replacing Data in Records
4	4.10	Using Help
5	5.1	Creating a Form Using the Form Button
5	5.2	Navigating in a Form
5	5.3	Adding Records in a Form
5	5.4	Creating a Form with a Related Table
5	5.5	Managing Control Objects
5	5.6	Adding Control Objects
5	5.7	Formatting a Form
5	5.8	Applying Conditional Formatting to a Form
5	5.9	Adding Fields to a Form from Another Table
5	5.10	Creating a Split Form and Multiple Items Form

Benchmark Access Level 1 SNAP Tutorials

Benchmark Access Level 2 SNAP Tutorials

Benchmark Access Level 2 SNAP Tutorials

Chapter	Tutorial	Tutorial Title
4	4.2	Binding a Table to a Form and Adding Fields
4	4.3	Moving, Resizing, and Formatting Control Objects
4	4.4	Changing the Tab Order of Fields
4	4.5	Adding a Tab Control and a Subform
4	4.6	Adding Subforms and a New Page to the Tab Control
4	4.7	Adding Calculations to a Form in Design View
4	4.8	Grouping, Aligning, and Spacing Controls
4	4.9	Creating a Datasheet Form and Modifying Form Properties
4	4.10	Sorting and Finding Records in a Form
5	5.1	Creating Custom Reports Using Design View
5	5.2	Connecting a Table or Query to a Report and Adding Fields
5	5.3	Moving Control Objects to Another Section
5	5.4	Inserting a Subreport
5	5.5	Formatting Controls in a Report
5	5.6	Grouping Records in a Report
5	5.7	Creating a Report with a Grouping Level Using the Report Wizard
5	5.8	Adding and Formatting a Calculated Field
5	5.9	Adding Functions to a Group; Keeping a Group Together
5	5.10	Modifying Section Properties; Inserting a Chart
5	5.11	Creating a Report Using the Blank Report Tool
6	6.1	Creating a Database Using a Template
6	6.2	Creating a Table Using a Table Template
6	6.3	Copying a Table Structure to a New Table
6	6.4	Modifying a Table Using the Table Analyzer Wizard
6	6.5	Optimizing Performance Using the Performance Analyzer
6	6.6	Splitting a Database
6	6.7	Documenting a Database
6	6.8	Renaming and Deleting Objects
7	7.1	Creating and Editing a Macro
7	7.2	Creating a Command Button to Run a Macro
7	7.3	Creating a Navigation Form
7	7.4	Adding a Command Button to a Navigation Form
7	7.5	Limiting Ribbon Tabs and Menus in a Database
7	7.6	Customizing the Navigation Pane
7	7.7	Configuring Error Checking Options
7	7.8	Importing and Exporting Customizations
7	7.9	Customizing the Ribbon
8	8.1	Creating and Restoring a Backup Database File
8	8.2	Creating an ACCDE Database File
8	8.3	Viewing Trust Center Settings
8	8.4	Importing Data from Another Access Database
8	8.5	Linking to a Table in Another Access Database
8	8.6	Importing Data to Access from a Text File
8	8.7	Saving and Repeating a Saved Import Process
8	8.8	Exporting Access Data to a Text File
8	8.9	Saving and Repeating Saved Export Specifications
8	8.10	Publishing Database Objects as PDF or XPS Files

SNAP Tutorials CD

A CD of tutorials teaching Access, Windows, and Internet Explorer skills is also available if instructors wish to assign SNAP tutorial work without using the web-based SNAP program.

Blackboard Cartridge

This set of files allows instructors to create a personalized website for their course and provides course content, tests, and the mechanisms for establishing communication via e-discussions and online group conferences. Available content includes a syllabus, test banks, PowerPoint presentations with lecture notes, and supplementary course materials. Upon request, the files can be available within 24–48 hours. Hosting the site is the responsibility of the educational institution.

Resources for English Language Learners[1]

One of the fastest growing groups of students in higher education is comprised of students whose first language is not English and whose English is not yet equivalent to that of native English speakers in lexicon and syntax. The wide differences in fluency among limited English speakers makes planning for meeting their needs somewhat more complex—and very important.

Many instructors find that they must meet the needs of students who are learning English and who need additional help. Because your goal is to help all the students in your course meet the intended outcomes, plan how you're going to assist students with limited English skills.

Begin by assessing the language abilities of your students:

1. One method is a "one-minute preview." Provide sheets of paper and ask students two questions. Give them one minute or so to write their answers. The questions could be about their language skills, but it might be better to ask about something else. That way you get a short writing sample plus information about something, such as why they are taking the course, what they would like to learn, the types of activities they enjoy, or what they are most worried about in the course. You will be able to see which students will need additional help.
2. If your class is small, conduct a discussion early in the course. Make sure you hear each student answer a question or ask one.
3. If you are conducting a pretest for the course, include some questions that ask students if they need to improve their English or writing skills.
4. Tell students to email you if they think they will need language help or extra exam time for reading assignments or tests.

In addition to the suggestions above, consider preparing a list of terms for each session that might be difficult for English language learners. You can suggest that students arrange for tutors to assist them with completing the unguided assessments. You may also want to dedicate a session (or part of one) to instruction on how to prepare the work you expect.

---

[1] Excerpted from *Exceptional Teaching: Ideas in Action*, published by Paradigm Publishing, Inc.

Instructor Resources

Along with the Instructor's Guide, instructional materials available with Benchmark Access 2013, Levels 1 & 2 include:

- Instructor Resources disc with electronic files for all resources included in the Instructor's Guide. The disc also offers the model answer files for end-of-chapter work in live program format and annotated PDF format, PowerPoint presentations with lecture notes, and detailed lesson plans, which include lecture/demonstration notes, discussion topics, tips for students, and possible work for advanced students.
- Instructor resources available at the Internet Resource Center at www. paradigmcollege.net/BenchmarkAccess13, which includes all of the materials in the print Instructor's Guide and on the Instructor Resources disc.
- ExamView® Assessment Suite and test banks with approximately 875 multiple-choice items to create customized web-based or print tests.

Information about Microsoft Office 2013

Microsoft Office 2013 operates on the Windows 8 operating system, as well as on Vista and Windows XP.

Video on the What's New in Office 2013

Microsoft Corporation offers its own downloadable video presentation on the new features in Office 2013 at this address: http://office.microsoft.com/en-us/support/video-whats-new-in-office-2013-VA103147615.aspx?CTT=1http

Quick Start Guides

Microsoft provides a series of Quick Start Guides for the applications in Office 2013 at http://office.microsoft.com/en-us/support/office-2013-quick-start-guides-HA103673669. aspx?CTT=1

Certification: Microsoft Office Specialist

With the release of Office 2013, Microsoft has developed a new set of certification objectives, which are available at http://www.microsoft.com/learning/en/us/mos-certification.aspx. The following books in the Benchmark Series have been validated and approved by ProCert Labs (www.procert.com) as courseware covering the Core-level objectives in the Microsoft Office Specialist Certification exam.

- *Benchmark Series Microsoft Word 2013 Levels 1 & 2*
- *Benchmark Series Microsoft Excel 2013 Levels 1 & 2*
- *Benchmark Series Microsoft Access 2013 Levels 1 & 2*
- *Benchmark Series Microsoft PowerPoint 2013*

Table 2 correlates the *Benchmark Access 2013 Levels 1 & 2* text with the certification exam objectives.

TABLE 2 Benchmark Access Levels 1 & 2 and Microsoft Office Specialist Certification Exam Correlation

Certification Exam Objective	Text Reference
1.0 Create and Manage a Database	
1.1 Create a New Database	
1.1.1 create new databases	L1C1, pg. 5; L1C2, pg.74; L2C1, pgs. 5-10; L2C6 pgs. 257-259
1.1.2 create databases use templates	L2C6, pgs. 227-231
1.1.3 create databases in older formats	L2C8, pgs. 337
1.1.4 create databases use wizards	L2C6, pgs. 257-259
1.2 Manage Relationships and Keys	
1.2.1 edit references between tables	L1C2, pgs. 56, 58; L2C2, pgs. 40- 42; L2C3, pgs. 75-82
1.2.2 create and modify relationships	L1C2, pgs. 45-64; L2C2, pgs. 37-45
1.2.3 set primary key fields	L1C2, pgs. 46-49; L2C1, pgs.6, 9-10; L2C3, pg. 46
1.2.4 enforce referential integrity	L1C2, pgs. 50-55; L2C2, pgs.40-44
1.2.5 set foreign keys	L1C2, pgs. 46, 48, 52; L2C2, pgs. 37-42
1.2.6 view relationships	L1C2, pgs. 53-55; L2C2, pgs. 43-45
1.3 Navigate through a Database	
1.3.1 navigate to specific records	L1C1, pg.11; L1C5, pgs. 187-188; L2C7, pgs. 270-274
1.3.2 set a form as the startup option	L2C7, pgs.289-291
1.3.3 use navigation forms	L2C7, pgs. 285-289
1.3.4 set navigation options	L2C7, pgs. 289-293
1.3.5 change views	L1C5, pgs. 186, 188; L2C1, pgs. 11-12; L2C7, pgs. 289-293
1.4 Protect and Maintain a Database	
1.4.1 compact databases	L1C7, pgs. 276-278
1.4.2 repair databases	L1C7, pgs. 276-278
1.4.3 backup databases	L1C7, pgs. 282-283; L2C8, pgs. 311-313
1.4.4 split databases	L2C6, pgs. 251-253
1.4.5 encrypt databases with a password	L1C7, pgs. 277-278
1.4.6 merge databases	L2C8, pgs. 317-320, L2C3, pgs. 94-95
1.4.7 recover data from a backups	L2C8, pgs. 311-313
1.5 Print and Export a Database	
1.5.1 print reports	L1C6, pgs. 236-240; L2C5, pgs. 188-190
1.5.2 print records	L1C1, pgs. 17-21; L1C4, pgs. 147, 149-152; L2C1, pg. 14
1.5.3 maintain backward compatibility	L1C7 pgs. 281-283; L2C8 pg. 337
1.5.4 save databases as templates	L2C6, pgs. 231-233
1.5.5 save databases to external locations	L1C1, pgs. 3, 6; L2C6, pgs. 258-259
1.5.6 export to alternate formats	L1C8, pg. 304; L2C8, pgs. 330-336

Certification Exam Objective	Text Reference
2.0 Build Tables	
2.1 Create a Table	
2.1.1 create new tables	L1C1, pgs. 22-32; L1C4, pgs. 132-147; L2C1, pgs. 9-10
2.1.2 import external data into tables	L1C8, pgs. 309-310; L2C8, pgs. 324-329
2.1.3 create linked tables from external sources	L1C8, pgs. 305-308; L2C8, pgs. 320-324
2.1.4 import tables from others database	L2C8, pgs. 317-320
2.1.5 create tables from templates and application parts	L2C6, pgs. 234-240
2.2 Format a Table	
2.2.1 hide fields in tables	L1C1, pgs. 15-17; L2C3, pgs. 70-71
2.2.2 change data formats	L1C4, pgs. 148-152; L2C1, pgs. 13-18
2.2.3 add total rows	L1C4, pgs. 143, 147
2.2.4 add table descriptions	L1C4, pgs. 132-135, 138-140
2.2.5 rename tables	L1C1, pgs. 17, 21; L2C6 pgs. 255-257
2.3 Manage Records	
2.3.1 update records	L2C1, pgs. 14, 22-24
2.3.2 add new records	L1C1, pgs. 11-13; L2C1, pgs. 11-12, 20-21
2.3.3 delete records	L1C1, pgs. 11, 13; L2C3, pg. 93
2.3.4 append records from external data	L2C3, pgs. 94-95, L2C8 pg. 342
2.3.5 find and replace data	L1C4, pgs. 154-157
2.3.6 sort records	L1C4, pgs. 147, 149
2.3.7 filter records	L1C7, pgs. 265-273; L2C3, pgs. 70-71
2.3.8 group records	L1C3, pgs.109-112, L1C6, pgs.224-247; L2C5, pgs. 190-193
2.4 Create and Modify Fields	
2.4.1 add fields to tables	L1C1, pgs. 13-14; L2C1, pgs. 9-10, 25-26
2.4.2 add a validation rules to fields	L1C4, pgs. 141, 143-147
2.4.3 change field captions	L1C1, pgs. 27-28; L2C1, pgs. 10-12, L2C3, pgs. 81-85, 87
2.4.4 change field sizes	L1C1, pgs. 29-32; L1C4, pgs. 135, 138-139; L2C1, Pgs. 8-10, L2C8 pgs. 310-313
2.4.5 change field data types	L1C4, pgs. 132-136; L2C1, pgs. 8-10, L2C2, pgs. 47-52; L2C6, pgs. 258-259
2.4.6 configure fields to auto-increment	L2C8, pgs. 326-329; L2C1, pg. 8
2.4.7 set default values	L1C1, pgs. 29-32; L1C4, pgs. 136-140
2.4.8 use input masks	L1C4, pgs. 137-140; L2C1 pgs. 18-21
2.4.9 delete fields	L1C4, pgs. 142-147

Certification Exam Objective	Text Reference
3.0 Create Queries	
3.1 Create a Query	
3.1.1 run queries	L1C3, pgs. 82-119; L2C3, pgs. 72- 74, 77-82, 83-85
3.1.2 create crosstab queries	L1C3, pgs. 112-115
3.1.3 create parameter queries	L2C3, pgs. 72-74
3.1.4 create action queries	L2C3, pgs. 90-96
3.1.5 create multi-table queries	L1C3, pgs. 88-91; L2C3, pgs. 72-73, 77-80
3.1.6 save queries	L1C3, pgs. 82-119; L2C3, pgs. 70-74, 77-84
3.1.7 delete queries	L1C3, pgs. 95-96; L2C3, pg. 90, 93
3.2 Modify a Query	
3.2.1 rename queries	L1C3, pgs. 95-96
3.2.2 add new fields	L1C3, pgs. 92, 94; L2C3, 79-80; L2C5, 192-193
3.2.3 remove fields	L1C3, pgs. 92, 94; L2C3 pgs. 79-80, 89
3.2.4 hide fields	L1C3, pgs. 92-95; L2C3, pgs. 70-71
3.2.5 sort data within queries	L1C3, pgs. 92-95
3.2.6 format fields within queries	L2C3, pgs. 83-84, 86-87
3.3 Utilize Calculated Fields and Grouping within a Query	
3.3.1 add calculated fields	L1C3, pgs. 107-108; L2C3, pgs. 83-85
3.3.2 add conditional logic	L2C3, pgs. 86-87
3.3.3 group and summarize data	L1C3, pgs. 109-112
3.3.4 use comparison operators	L1C3, pgs. 84, 87-91; L2C3, pgs. 83-84
3.3.5 use basic operators	L1C3, pgs. 107-108; L2C3, pgs. 83-85
4.0 Create Forms	
4.1 Create a Form	
4.1.1 create new forms	L1C5, pgs. 186-188, 190-192, 210-217; L2C4, pgs. 107-118, 126-128, 137-138; L2C6, pgs. 243-244
4.1.2 create forms with application parts	L2C6, pgs. 234-240
4.1.3 save forms	L1C5, pgs. 188; L2C4, pgs. 107-118, 126-128, 137-138; L2C6, pgs.238-240
4.1.4 delete forms	L1C5, pgs. 187-188
4.2 Set Form Controls	
4.2.1 move form controls	L15, pgs. 197-201; L2C4, pgs. 114-115, 129-131; L2C6, pgs. 238-240, 243-244; L2C7, pgs. 281-282
4.2.2 add form controls	L1C5, pgs. 194-196; L2C4, pgs. 120-128,138-143; L2C6, pgs. 241-242; L2C7, pgs. 276-280
4.2.3 modify data sources	L2C4, pgs. 110-112, L2C6, pgs. 230-231
4.2.4 remove form controls	L2C4, pgs. 121-125; L2C6, pgs. 232-233, 238-240, 243-244
4.2.5 set form control properties	L2C4, pgs. 110-112, 136-138 L2C6, pgs. 240-242; L2C7, pgs. 281-282
4.2.6 manage labels	L1C5, pgs. 193-194, 196-197; L2C4, pgs. 129-131, 139-143; L2C6, pgs. 240-242

Certification Exam Objective	Text Reference
4.3 Format a Form	
4.3.1 modify Tab order in forms	L2C4, pgs.117-118
4.3.2 format print layouts	L1C5, pgs. 186-188, 192, L2C4 pgs. 137-138
4.3.3 sort records	L1C5, pgs. 189-190; L2C4, pgs.143-146
4.3.4 apply themes	L1C5, pgs. 193-195; L2C4, pgs. 113, 126-128
4.3.5 change margins	L1C5, pgs. 198, 200; L2C4, pgs. 132-134
4.3.6 insert backgrounds	L1C5, pgs. 201-203
4.3.7 auto-order forms	L2C4 pgs. 117-118
4.3.8 insert headers and footers	L2C4, pgs. 107-110
4.3.9 insert images	L1C5, pgs. 193-195, 199; L2C4, pgs. 131-134
4.3.10 modify existing forms	L2C4, pgs. 131-134; L2C6 pgs. 238-240, 242-244
5.0 Create Reports	
5.1 Create a Report	
5.1.1 create new reports	L1C6, pgs. 233-235, 248-252; L2C5, pgs. 174-180, 192-193, 203-205, 210-213
5.1.2 create reports with application parts	L2C6, pgs. 234-237
5.1.3 delete reports	L2C6, pgs. 255-257
5.2 Set Report Controls	
5.2.1 group data by fields	L1C6, pgs. 244-247; L2C5, pgs. 190-193
5.2.2 sort data	L1C6, pgs. 236-237; L2C5, pgs. 190-193
5.2.3 add sub-forms	L2C5, pgs. 209-213
5.2.4 modify data sources	L2C5, pgs. 176-177, 206-208
5.2.5 add report controls	L1C6, pgs. 240-241; L2C5, pgs. 174-179, 208-213
5.2.6 manage labels	L1C6, pgs. 235-237; L2C5, pgs. 178-179, 185-189
5.3 Format a Report	
5.3.1 format reports into multiple columns	L2C5, pgs.203-205
5.3.2 add calculated fields	L2C5, pgs. 198-199
5.3.3 set margins	L1C6, pgs. 236, 239-242, 244
5.3.4 add backgrounds	L1C6, pgs. 240-241, 244
5.3.5 change report orientation	L1C6, pgs. 236, 245, 249, 252
5.3.6 change sort order	L1C6, pgs. 236-237
5.3.7 insert headers and footers	L2C5, pgs. 174-176
5.3.8 insert images	L2C5, pgs. 188-190
5.3.9 insert page numbers	L2C5, pgs. 184-188
5.3.10 apply themes	L1C6, pgs. 240-241; L2C5, pgs. 179-180
5.3.11 modify existing reports	L2C5, pgs. 185-190, 195-197

Microsoft Office 2013 Product Editions

Microsoft Office 2013 is available in the following editions:

- Microsoft Office Starter
- Office Home and Student
- Office Home and Business
- Office Professional
- Microsoft Office Professional Plus
- Microsoft Office Standard
- Microsoft Office Professional Academic

The programs included in each edition at http://office.microsoft.com/ en-us/products/ FX101635841033.aspx.

Microsoft Office 2013 System Requirements

This interactive text is designed for the student to complete chapter work on a computer running a standard installation of Microsoft Office 2013, Office Professional Edition, and the Microsoft Windows 8 operating system. To effectively run the Microsoft Office 2013 suite and operating system, your computer should be outfitted with the following:

- 1 gigahertz (GHz) processor or higher; 1 gigabyte (GB) of RAM
- 3 GB of available hard-disk space
- .NET version 3.5, 4.0, or 4.5
- DirectX 10 graphics card
- Minimum 1024 × 576 monitor resolution (or 1366 × 768 to use the Windows Snap feature)
- Computer mouse, multi-touch device, or compatible pointing device

Office 2013 will also operate on computers running the Windows XP Service Pack 3 or the Windows Vista operating system.

Screen captures for the books in the Benchmark Series were created using a screen resolution display setting of 1600 × 900. Refer to the Customizing Settings section of Getting Started in Office 2013, which follows the textbook's preface for instructions on changing a monitor's resolution. Figure G.10 on page 10 of the textbook illustrates the Microsoft Office Word ribbon at three resolutions for comparison purposes. Choose the resolution that best matches your computer; however, be aware that using a resolution other than 1600 × 900 means that your screens may not match the illustrations in this book.

Developing an Assessment Strategy

The final major phase of planning a course is to develop an assessment strategy based on the purpose of evaluation and on your philosophy of what constitutes high-quality assessments. The obvious purpose of assessing students' learning is to determine whether students have achieved the goals of the course and, if they have, to what degree, resulting in a grade for credits earned. Other functions of evaluation include motivating students, determining the overall effectiveness of your teaching, and meeting accreditation requirements.

In developing your philosophy of assessment, consider these suggestions from Paradigm Publishing's *Exceptional Teaching*.

Assessments should:

- contribute to students' learning by asking them to apply their skills in out-of-school or workplace situations.
- be planned as an integral part of the course design in terms of timing, content, and form.
- have a clear purpose.
- be appropriate for the purpose in terms of content and format.
- be scored as consistently and objectively as possible.
- provide students with feedback on their learning.
- emphasize intellectual traits of value—analytical reading, thinking, decision making, and research skills along with individual creativity and intelligence.
- be conducted at specific, planned checkpoints.
- be conducted in a positive learning environment, with every effort made to lower students' test anxieties.
- allow students to demonstrate their accomplishment of outcomes in various ways, including ways that fit their individual learning styles.

Determining the Number, Level, and Type of Assessments

Formulate your evaluation and grading strategy by answering these course-level questions. Consider if you should include:

- a course pre-assessment?
- a course comprehensive assessment that will determine students' mastery of the major intended outcomes for the entire course?
- pre-assessments for each section?
- comprehensive assessments for each section that assess students' mastery of the major intended outcomes for that section?
- interim or checkpoint assessments that assess students' mastery of intended outcomes of learning within units? How many? How often?

Also ask yourself: once my system is in place, will my students know that I value how and how well they think?

These questions will help you establish approximately how many assessments you wish to include and their place in the course.

The next decisions concern which types of assessment to use: traditional cognitive (objective) tests and/or performance-based assessments. Each of these two major categories of tests has its merits. Traditional cognitive tests such as multiple-choice exams usually work best for testing information recall, comprehension, and analysis. They also are reliable and efficient, and relatively easy to score. On the down side, objective-type tests are criticized for not representing how students will use their new skills in an unfamiliar setting or in the real world of work. On the other hand, performance-based testing requires students to demonstrate what they have learned and to apply it in a realistic context that closely approximates an on-the-job situation. These tests measure how well students can do what the course intended to teach them. As emphasized in

Exceptional Teaching, "Authentic, performance-based assessments ask students to integrate what they have learned and apply it to resolve an issue, solve a problem, create something new, work collaboratively, or use their written and oral communication skills. Authentic assessments stress the process of learning as well as the outcomes of learning."

Creating a Grading Plan

By choosing the types of assessments that will measure students' achievement of course and program outcomes, you will already have established a schema of the major grading components. The next step is to weight the scores before entering them into a grade calculation system, such as, an Excel spreadsheet.

Will you include other factors such as effort and attendance in students' grades? If so, consider how to measure those elements. While it is simple to track attendance, it is not as easy to objectively evaluate effort and attitude. Some experts recommend that teachers provide regular verbal and written feedback on these factors, but confine grades to academic achievement.

The following grading plan, which is part of the sample syllabus presented earlier in this section, offers a starting point as you develop your comprehensive grading strategy:

- Concepts Check assignments   5%
- Skills Check (Grade It) assignments   10%
- Visual Benchmark assignments   15%
- Case Study assignments   15%
- Unit Performance Assessments   15%
- SNAP Performance Evaluations   20%
- Exams   20%

For More Information

Much of the content of this "Planning the Course" article is based on information found in Exceptional Teaching: Ideas in Action. To order a copy of this resource, please visit www.ParadigmCollege.com or contact Customer Care at 800-535-6865, or educate@emcp.com.

Chapter Overviews
Using Windows 8

Performance Objectives

- Use the Start screen to launch programs
- Use desktop icons and the Taskbar to launch programs and open files or folders
- Organize and manage data, including copying moving, creating, and deleting files and folders; and create a shortcut
- Explore the Control Panel and personalize the desktop
- Use the Windows Help and Support features
- Use search tools
- Customize monitor settings

Projects

Project 1	Opening Programs, Switching between Programs, and Manipulating Windows
Project 2	Changing Taskbar Properties
Project 3	Copying a File and Folder and Deleting a File
Project 4	Copying and Deleting Files
Project 5	Creating a New Folder
Project 6	Deleting Files to and Restoring Files from the Recycle Bin
Project 7	Emptying the Recycle Bin
Project 8	Creating a Shortcut
Project 9	Changing the Desktop Theme
Project 10	Customizing the Mouse
Project 11	Customizing with a Shortcut Command
Project12	Getting Help
Project 13	Searching for Programs and Files

Overview

Browsing the Internet Using Internet Explorer 10

Performance Objectives
- Navigate the Internet using URLs and hyperlinks
- Use search engines to locate information
- Download web pages and images

Projects

Overview

Access 2013 Level 1, Chapter 1
Managing and Creating Tables

Performance Objectives
- Open and close objects in a database
- Insert, delete, and move rows and columns in a table
- Hide, unhide, freeze, and unfreeze columns
- Adjust table column width
- Preview and print a table
- Design and create a table
- Rename column headings
- Insert a column name, caption, and description
- Insert Quick Start fields
- Assign a default value and field size

Projects

Project 1		Explore an Access Database
	1	Opening and Closing a Database and Objects in a Database
Project 2		Manage Tables in a Database
	2a	Inserting and Deleting Records in a Table
	2b	Inserting, Moving, and Deleting Fields
	2c	Hiding, Unhiding, Freezing, and Unfreezing Columns and Changing Column Widths
	2d	Previewing, Changing Page Layout, Renaming, Deleting, and Printing Tables
	2e	Creating a Table and Entering Data
	2f	Inserting a Name, Caption, and Description
	2g	Creating a Customers Table

Overview

Access 2013 Level 1, Chapter 2
Creating Relationships between Tables

Performance Objectives
- Define a primary key in a table
- Create a one-to-many relationship
- Specify referential integrity
- Print, edit, and delete relationships
- Create a one-to-one relationship
- View and edit a subdatasheet

Projects
Project 1   Establish Relationships between Tables
    1a   Defining a Primary Key Field
    1b   Creating Relationships between Tables
    1c   Creating a Table and Creating and Editing Relationships
    1d   Editing and Updating Records
Project 2   Create Relationships and Display Subdatasheets in a Database
    2a   Creating One-to-Many and One-to-One Relationships
    2b   Viewing and Editing a Subdatasheet

Overview

Access 2013 Level 1, Chapter 3
Performing Queries

Performance Objectives

- Design query to extract specific data from tables
- Modify queries
- Design queries with *Or* and *And* criteria
- Use the Simple Query Wizard to create queries
- Create a calculated field
- Use aggregate functions in queries
- Create crosstab, duplicate, and unmatched queries

Projects

Project 1   Design Queries
- 1a   Performing Queries on Tables
- 1b   Performing Queries on Related Tables
- 1c   Performing Queries on Related Tables and Sorting in Field Values
- 1d   Modifying Queries
- 1e   Designing Queries with *Or* and *And* Criteria
- 1f   Performing Queries with the Simple Query Wizard
- 1g   Performing and Modifying Queries with the Simple Query Wizard
- 1h   Creating a Calculated Field in a Query

Project 2   Create Aggregate Functions, Crosstab, Find Duplicates, and Find Unmatched Queries
- 2a   Using Aggregate Functions in Queries
- 2b   Using Aggregate Functions and Grouping Records
- 2c   Creating Crosstab Queries
- 2d   Creating a Find Duplicates Query
- 2e   Finding Duplicate Orders
- 2f   Creating a Find Unmatched Query

Overview

Access 2013 Level 1, Chapter 4
Creating and Modifying Tables in Design View

Performance Objectives

- Create a table in Design view
- Assign a default value
- Use the Input Mask Wizard and the Lookup Wizard
- Validate field entries
- Insert, move, and delete fields in Design view
- Insert a Total row
- Sort records in a table
- Print selected records in a table
- Complete a spelling check
- Find specific records in a table
- Find and replace data in records in a table
- Apply text formatting
- Use the Help feature

Projects

Project 1   Create and Modify Tables in a Property Management Database
- 1a   Creating a Table in Design View
- 1b   Creating an Employees Table
- 1c   Validating Field Entries; Using the Lookup Wizard; and Inserting, Moving, and Deleting a Field
- 1d   Sorting, Printing, and Formatting Records and Fields in Tables
- 1e   Checking Spelling in a Table
- 1f   Finding and Replacing Data, Creating Relationships, and Performing Queries
- 1g   Using the Help Feature
- 1h   Getting Help in a Dialog Box and Backstage View

Overview

Access 2013 Level 1, Chapter 5
Creating Forms

Performance Objectives

- Create a form using the Form button
- Change views in a form
- Print and navigate in a form
- Add records to and delete records from a form
- Create a form with a related table
- Customize a form
- Create a split form and multiple items form
- Create a form using the Form Wizard

Projects

Project 1	Create Forms with the Form Button
1a	Creating a Form with the Sales Table and Deleting a Form
1b	Adding and Deleting Records in a Form
1c	Creating a Form with a Related Table
1d	Customizing a Form and Customizing the Design of a Form
1e	Arranging Objects in a Form
1f	Formatting a Form
1g	Applying Conditional Formatting to Fields in Forms
Project 2	Add Fields, Create a Split Form and Multiple Items Form, and Use the Form Wizard
2a	Adding Existing Fields to a Form
2b	Creating a Split Form
2c	Creating a Multiple Items Form
2d	Creating a Form Using the Form Wizard
2e	Creating a Form with Related Tables

Overview

Access 2013 Level 1, Chapter 6
Creating Reports and Mailing Labels

Performance Objectives

- Create a report using the Report button
- Display a report in Print Preview
- Create a report with a query
- Format and customize a report
- Group and sort records in a report
- Create a report using the Report Wizard
- Create mailing labels using the Label Wizard

Projects

Project 1   Create and Customize Reports Using Tables and Queries
      1a   Creating a Report with the Report Button
      1b   Adjusting Control Objects, Renaming Labels, Finding and Sorting Data, Displaying a Report in Print Preview, and Deleting a Report
      1c   Applying Formatting to a Report
      1d   Grouping and Sorting Data

Project 2   Use Wizards to Create Reports and Labels
      2a   Using the Report Wizard to Prepare a Report
      2b   Creating a Report with Fields from Multiple Tables
      2c   Preparing Mailing Labels

Overview

Access 2013 Level 1, Chapter 7
Modifying, Filtering, and Viewing Data

Performance Objectives
- Filter data by selection and form
- Remove a filter
- View object dependencies
- Compact and repair a database
- Encrypt a database with a password
- View and customize document properties
- Customize the Recent tab Backstage view
- Save a database in an earlier version of Access
- Save a database object in PDF file format

Projects

Project 1   Filter Records
- 1a   Filtering Records in a Table, Form, and Report
- 1b   Filtering Records in a Query and Report
- 1c   Filtering Records by Selection
- 1d   Using the *Filter by Form* Option to Display Specific Records

Project 2   View Object Dependencies and Manage a Database, and Save a Database in a Different File Format
- 2a   Viewing Object Dependencies
- 2b   Compact and Repair and Encrypt a Database
- 2c   Viewing and Customizing Database Properties
- 2d   Saving a Database in a Previous Version, Saving an Object in PDF Format, and Backing Up a Database

Overview

Access 2013 Level 1, Chapter 8
Exporting and Importing Data

Performance Objectives
- Export Access data to Excel
- Export Access data to Word
- Merge Access data with a Word document
- Exporting an Access object to a PDF or XPS file
- Import data to a new table
- Link data to a new table
- Use the Office Clipboard

Projects
Project 1   Export Data to Excel and Export and Merge Data to Word
    1a   Exporting a Table and Query to Excel
    1b   Exporting a Table and Report to Word
    1c   Merging Access Data with a Word Document
    1d   Performing a Query and Then Merging with a Word Document
    1e   Exporting an Access Object to a PDF File
Project 2   Import and Link Excel Worksheets with an Access Table
    2a   Importing an Excel Worksheet into an Access Table
    2b   Linking an Excel Worksheet to an Access Table
Project 3   Collect Data in Word and Paste it into an Access Table
    3   Collecting Data in Word and Pasting It in an Access Table

Overview

Access 2013 Level 2, Chapter 1
Designing the Structure of Tables

Performance Objectives

- Design the structure of a table to optimize efficiency and accuracy of data
- Select the appropriate field data type based on analysis of the source data
- Disallow blank field values
- Allow or disallow zero-length strings in a field
- Create a custom format for ShortText, numeric, and Date/Time data type fields
- Create a custom input mask
- Define a rich text formatting for a Long Text data type field
- Store the history of changes to a Long Text data type field
- Define and use an Attachment data type field with multiple attachments

Projects

Project 1   Create Tables by Analyzing Sample Data and Applying Database Design Techniques

    1a   Creating Tables in Design View

    1b   Modifying Field Properties to Add caption and Disallow Blank Values in a Field

    1c   Formatting Short Text Data Type Fields Using a Custom Format

    1d   Formatting Numeric Data Type Fields Using a Custom Format and a Predefined Format

    1e   Formatting a Date/Time Data Type Field Using a Custom Date Format

    1f   Creating Custom Input Masks

    2g   Creating a Customers Table

Project 2   Work with Long Text and Attachment Data Type Fields

    2a   Enabling Rich Text Formatting and Maintaining a History of Changes in a Long Text Data Type Field

    2b   Creating an Attachment Data Type Field, Attaching Files to a Record, and Viewing the Contents of Attached Files

Overview

Access 2013 Level 2, Chapter 2
Building Relationships and Lookup Fields

Performance Objectives
- Create and edit relationships between tables, including one-to-many, one-to-one, and many-to-many relationships
- Define a table with a multiple-field primary key
- Create and modify a lookup field to populate records with data from another table
- Create a lookup field that allows having multiple values in records
- Create single-field and multiple-field indexes
- Define the term *normalization*
- Determine if a table is in first, second, or third normal form

Projects
Project 1   Create and Edit Relationships
     1a   Creating a One-to-many Relationship
     1b   Creating a Second One-to-Many Relationship
     1c   Editing Relationships
     1d   Creating a One-to-One Relationship
Project 2   Create a Table with a Multiple-Field Primary Key and Lookup Fields
     2a   Creating a New Table with a Multiple-Field Primary Key
     2b   Creating a Field to Look Up Data in Another Table
     2c   Modifying Lookup List Properties and Using a Lookup List Field in a Record
     2d   Creating a Table with Lookup Fields, Including a Multiple-Value Field
     2e   Assigning Multiple Values in a Lookup List
Project 3   Create an Index
     3   Creating Indexes

Overview

Access 2013 Level 2, Chapter 3
Advanced Query Techniques

Performance Objectives
- Save a filter as a query
- Create and run a parameter query to prompt for criteria
- Add tables to and remove tables from a query
- Create an inner join, left join, and right join to modify query results
- Create a self-join to match two fields in the same table
- Create a query that incudes a subquery
- Create a query that uses conditional logic
- Assign an alias to a table name and a field name
- Select records using a multiple-value field in a query
- Create a new table using a make-table query
- Remove records from a table using a delete query
- Add records to the end of an existing table using an append query
- Modify records using an update query

Projects

Overview

Access 2013 Level 2, Chapter 4
Creating and Using Custom Forms

Performance Objectives

- Create a custom form in Design view using all three form sections
- Add fields individually and as a group
- Move, size, and format control objects
- Change the tab order of fields
- Create tabbed pages in a form and insert a subform on each page
- Add and format a calculation to a custom form
- Group and ungroup multiple controls
- Adjust the alignment and spacing of controls
- Add graphics to a form
- Anchor a control to a position in a form
- Create a datasheet form
- Modify form properties to restrict actions allowed in records
- Create a blank form
- Add list boxes to a form
- Sort records in a form and locate a record using a wildcard character

Projects

Project 1		Design and Create a Custom Form
	1a	Starting a New Form Using Design View and Adding a Title and Label Object
	1b	Connecting a Table to a Form and Adding Fields
	1c	Moving and Resizing Controls
	1d	Formatting Multiple Controls
	1e	Changing the Tab Order of Fields
	1f	Adding a Tab Control and Subform
	1g	Adding More Subforms and Adding a New Page to the Tab Control
Project 2		Create a New Form with Calculations and Graphics
	2a	Adding and Formatting Calculated Control Objects
	2b	Sizing, Aligning, and Spacing Multiple Controls
	2c	Adding Graphics to a Form
	2d	Anchoring an Image to a Position within a Section
Project 3		Create a Restricted-Use Form
	3	Creating a Datasheet Form and Preventing Record Deletions
Project 4		Create a Blank Form with Lists
	4	Creating a Blank Form with List Boxes
Project 5		Sort and Find Records within a Form
	5	Sorting and Finding Records in a Form

Overview

Access 2013 Level 2, Chapter 5
Creating and Using Custom Reports

Performance Objectives
- Create a custom report in Design view using all five report sections
- Move, size, format, and align control objects
- Insert a subreport into a report
- Add page numbers and date and time controls
- Add graphics to a report
- Group records including adding functions and totals
- Add and format a calculated field to a custom report
- Modify section or group properties to control print options
- Create and modify charts in a report
- Create a blank report
- Add hyperlinks and list boxes to a report
- Change the shape of a tab control
- Change the tab order of fields
- Insert a subform into a report

Projects

Project 1	Design and Create a Custom Report
1a	Starting a New Report Using Design View and Adding a Title and Label Object
1b	Connecting a Table to a Report and Adding Fields
1c	Moving Controls to Another Section
1d	Moving Controls, Resizing Controls, and Applying a Theme
1e	Inserting a Subreport
Project 2	Add Features and Enhance a Report
2a	Adding Page Numbers and the Date and Time to a Report
2b	Adding Graphics and Formatting Controls
Project 3	Group Records and Add Functions to Count and Sum
3a	Creating a Report with a Grouping Level Using the Report Wizard
3b	Adding Functions to a Report
3c	Adding a Calculated Field to a Report
Project 4	Modify Section and Group Properties
4	Modifying Section Properties and Keeping a Group Together
Project 5	Create and Format a Chart
5a	Creating a Report and Inserting a Chart
5b	Changing the Chart Type and Chart Options and Formatting the Chart
Project 6	Create a Blank Report with Hyperlinks, a List, and a Subform
6	Creating a Blank Report with Hyperlinks, a List, and a Subform

Overview

Access 2013 Level 2, Chapter 6
Using Access Tools and Managing Objects

Performance Objectives

- Create a new database using a template
- Add a group of objects to a database using an Application Parts template
- Save a database as a template
- Create a new form using an Application Parts Blank Form
- Create a form to be used as a template in a database
- Create a table by copying the structure of another table
- Evaluate a table using the Table Analyzer Wizard
- Evaluate a database using the Performance Analyzer
- Split a database
- Print documentation about a database using the Database Documenter
- Rename and delete objects
- Create a database using templates, Application Parts, Quick Start, and wizards

Projects

Project 1	Create a New Database Using a Template
1a	Creating a New Contacts Database Using a Template
1b	Entering and Viewing Date in the Contacts Database
1c	Saving a Database as a Template
Project 2	Create Objects Using a Template
2a	Creating a Contacts Table, a Query, Forms, and Reports Using a Template
2b	Creating a New Form Using an Application Parts Blank Form
2c	Creating and Using a User-Defined Form Template
Project 3	Copy Table Structure
3	Copying a Table Structure to Create a New Table
Project 4	Use Access Tools to Optimize and Document a Database
4a	Splitting the Table Using the Table Analyzer Window
4b	Analyzing a Database to Improve Performance
4c	Splitting a Database
4d	Generating a Table Definition Documentation Report
4e	Renaming and Deleting Database Objects
Project 5	Create a Database Using Templates, Application Parts, Quick Start and Wizards

Overview

Access 2013 Level 2, Chapter 7
Automating, Customizing, and Securing Access

Performance Objectives

- Create, run, edit, and delete a macro
- Assign a macro to a command button on a form
- View macro code created for a command button in a form's Property Sheet task pane
- Convert a macro to Visual Basic
- Create and edit a Navigation form
- Change database startup options
- Show and hide the Navigation pane
- Customize the Navigation pane by hiding objects
- Define error-checking options
- Import and export customizations
- Customize the ribbon

Projects

Project 1		Create Macros and Assign Macros to Command Buttons
	1a	Creating a Macro to Open a Form and Find a Record
	1b	Creating a Macro by Dragging and Dropping an Object
	1c	Creating a Macro Using the Action Catalog Task Pane
	1d	Editing and Deleting a Macro
	1e	Creating a Button and Assigning a Macro to a Button in a Form
	1f	Creating Two Command Buttons and Assigning Macros to the Buttons
	1g	Viewing Macro Actions Created by the Command Button Wizard
	1h	Converting a Macro to Visual Basic for Applications
Project 2		Create a Navigation Form
	2a	Creating a Navigation Form
	2b	Adding a Command Button to a Navigation Form and Editing the Form
Project 3		Configure Database Options
	3a	Specifying a Startup Form and Application Title
	3b	Customizing the Navigation Pane
	3c	Customizing Error-Checking Options
	3d	Exporting Customizations
	3e	Customizing the Ribbon
	3f	Restoring the Ribbon

Overview

Access 2013 Level 2, Chapter 8
Integrating Access Data

Performance Objectives

- Create and restore a backup database file
- Create an ACCDE database file
- View Trust Center settings
- Import data from another Access database
- Link to a table in another Access database
- Determine when to import from versus link to external sources
- Reset or refresh links using Linked Table Manager
- Import data from a text file
- Save import specifications
- Export data in an Access table or query as a text file
- Save and run export specifications
- Export an object as an XPS document
- Create a database in an older format

Projects

Project 1		Maintain and Secure a Database
	1a	Creating and Restoring a Backup File
	1b	Making an ACCDE Database File
	1c	Exploring Trust Center Settings
Project 2		Import and Merge Data from External Sources
	2a	Importing a Form and Table from Another Access Database
	2b	Linking to Tables in Another Access Database
	2c	Refreshing a Link
	2d	Importing Data from a Comma Separated Text File and Saving Import Specifications
Project 3		Export Access Data to a Text File
	3a	Exporting a Query as a Text File
	3b	Exporting a Query as a Text File and Saving Export Steps
	3c	Exploring Trust Center Settings
Project 4		Export a Database Object as an XPS Document
	4	Exporting a Report as an XPS Document
Project 5		Create a Database in an Older Format
	5	Creating a Database in an Older Format

Overview of Assessment Venues

The grading sheet on the following pages can be used as a resource to create your grading plan. An electronic copy of this table is provided on the Instructor Resources disc, and you can alter this file to meet your specific course needs. Several venues of different types are available for assessing student achievement in your course.

Comprehension-Based Assessments

- Concepts Check questions appear at the end of each chapter. These short-answer questions test student comprehension and recall of program features, terminology, and functions. Answer keys are included in the *Instructor's Guide*, on the Instructor Resources disc, and on the password-protected Instructor section of the Internet Resource Center. Matching activities based on the Concepts Check questions are available in SNAP.
- ExamView® test generating software and test banks includes multiple-choice items for each chapter of the text. Use ExamView to create web-based or print tests.
- SNAP web-based assessments include multiple-choice items for each chapter of the text (prepared from the ExamView test banks). Instructors can assign pre-designed concepts exams or create their own.
- Quizzes of multiple-choice items for each chapter of the text (different from the items in the ExamView test banks) are available on the Internet Resource Center. Students can take quizzes in either practice mode with immediate feedback or in scores-reported mode with results emailed to the instructor.

Performance-Based Assessments

- End-of-chapter assessments are provided to assess student understanding of major features and program skills taught in the chapter. Instructor support for these assessments is included in the *Instructor's Guide*, on the Instructor Resources disc and, on the password-protected Instructor section of the Internet Resource Center.
  - Skills Check assessments provide additional hands-on computer exercises to reinforce learning. These exercises include some guidance, but less than the chapter projects. Items marked with a SNAP Grade It icon have a corresponding activity available in SNAP, which will automatically score student work. Grading rubrics, annotated PDF files, and live application files are available to instructors to support these activities.
  - Visual Benchmark activities provide limited guidance and challenge students to use their problem-solving skills and mastery of program features to build a file that matches a file displayed with the exercise. Grading rubrics, PDF files, and live application files are available to instructors to support these activities.
  - Case Studies offer realistic scenarios that require taking initiative and determining solutions using skills developed throughout the chapter. Students search the Internet or the program's Help feature to find the additional information they need to create final documents and files. Student work will vary, but grading rubrics, PDF files, and live application files are available to instructors to support these activities.

- Unit Performance Assessments are separate sections at the end of each group of four chapters that include a range of activities to evaluate student achievement. Grading rubrics are provided to instructors to support these activities.
  - Assessing Proficiency exercises involve using program features to create a variety of documents, all with little or no assistance. Annotated PDF files and live application files are available to instructors to support these activities.
  - Writing Activities stress the vital cross-disciplinary skill of writing clearly during the course of preparing specific documents.
  - Internet Research is a scenario-based activity requiring Internet navigation and searching plus information analysis and presentation.
  - Job Study is a culminating case study exercise that simulates workplace tasks and challenges. This Performance Assessment type is found in Unit 2 Performance Assessments.
- SNAP is a web-based training and assessment program designed to optimize skill-based learning. SNAP includes a learning management system that creates a virtual classroom on the Web, allowing the instructor to schedule tutorials, exams, and textbook assignments and to employ an electronic grade book. SNAP support for the *Benchmark Series* includes the following:
  - A bank of 163 interactive, gradable, multimedia tutorials, aligned to support activities found in textbook sections, that can be used for direct instruction or remediation.
  - A bank of 270 performance skill items in which students perform tasks in Microsoft Access 2013 that are evaluated and reported in the learning management system. Instructors can assign pre-defined skill exams or create their own exams from the item bank.
  - A bank of 48 Grade It Skills Check assessment activities, with immediate, automatic scoring with individualized feedback of student work, align with select Skills Check activities in the textbook.
  - Comprehensive Performance Evaluation activities, one per chapter and one per unit, for comprehensive evaluation of skills mastery.
  - Over 875 concept items that can be used to monitor student understanding computer literacy and technical knowledge as well as a concept item generator that will allow instructors to create up to ten kinds of new concept items
- Supplemental activities are provided for use in evaluating student comprehension of program skills. Resources for these assessments are included in the *Instructor's Guide*, on the Instructor Resources disc, and on the Instructor section of the Internet Resource Center.
  - Supplemental Assessments are similar in format to the end-of-chapter Skills Check or Visual Benchmark assessments, and are supported with data files, model answer files, and rubrics. There is one Supplemental Assessment for each unit, or two for each level.
  - Supplemental Case Studies are similar in format to the end-of-chapter Case Studies, and are supported with, data files, model answer files, and rubrics. There is one Supplemental Case Study for each application level.

Grading Sheet

Benchmark Series Microsoft Access 2013 Level 1

Assignment	Title	Start from Scratch	SNAP Grade It	Date Due	Grade
Unit 1: Creating Table and Queries					
Chapter 1 Managing and Creating Tables					
Concepts Check			✓		
Skills Check Assessment 1	Inserting and Deleting Rows and Columns		✓		
Skills Check Assessment 2	Create a Departments Table		✓		
Skills Check Assessment 3	Create a Benefits Table		✓		
Skills Check Assessment 4	Sort Data				
Visual Benchmark	Create an Absences Table				
Case Study Part 1	Elite Limousines: Limousines Table	✓			
Case Study Part 2	Elite Limousines: Drivers Table	✓			
Case Study Part 3	Elite Limousines: Customers Table	✓			
Case Study Part 4	Elite Limousines: Bookings Table	✓			
SNAP Tutorial 1.1	Opening Access, Navigating and Printing a Table				
SNAP Tutorial 1.2	Adding Records in Datasheet View				
SNAP Tutorial 1.3	Creating a New Database				
SNAP Tutorial 1.4	Creating a Table Using Quick Start Fields				
IRC Quiz	Study Quiz				
SNAP Concepts	Quiz				
SNAP Skill Items	Quiz				
SNAP PE	Comprehensive Performance Evaluation				
Chapter 2 Creating Relationships between Tables					
Concepts Check			✓		
Skills Check Assessment 1	Create Relationships in an Insurance Company Database		✓		
Skills Check Assessment 2	Create a New Table and Relate the Table		✓		

Assignment	Title	Start from Scratch	SNAP Grade It	Date Due	Grade
Skills Check Assessment 3	Delete and Edit Records in Tables		✓		
Skills Check Assessment 4	Display and Edit Records in a Subdatasheet		✓		
Visual Benchmark	Create an Agents Table				
Case Study Part 1	Gold Star Cleaning Services: Billing Table	✓			
Case Study Part 2	Gold Star Cleaning Services: Connect Tables with One-to-Many Relationships	✓			
Case Study Part 3	Gold Star Cleaning Services	✓			
SNAP Tutorial 2.1	Creating a Relationship between Two Tables in a Database				
SNAP Tutorial 2.2	Deleting a Relationship; Printing a Relationships Report				
IRC Quiz	Study Quiz				
SNAP Concepts	Quiz				
SNAP Skill Items	Quiz				
SNAP PE	Comprehensive Performance Evaluation				

Chapter 3 Performing Queries

Assignment	Title	Start from Scratch	SNAP Grade It	Date Due	Grade
Concepts Check			✓		
Skills Check Assessment 1	Design Queries in a Legal Services Database		✓		
Skills Check Assessment 2	Use the Simple Query Wizard and Design Queries		✓		
Skills Check Assessment 3	Create a Crosstab Query and Use the Find Duplicates and Find Unmatched Query Wizards		✓		
Skills Check Assessment 4	Design and Hide Fields in a Query				
Visual Benchmark	Creating Relationships and Designing a Query				
Case Study Part 1	Skyline Restaurant: Create Relationships				
Case Study Part 2	Skyline Restaurant: Create Queries				
Case Study Part 3	Skyline Restaurant: Query Wizards				
Case Study Part 4	Skyline Restaurant: Design Queries	✓			
SNAP Tutorial 3.1	Creating Queries in Design View				
SNAP Tutorial 3.2	Using Criteria Statements in Queries				
SNAP Tutorial 3.3	Using And/Or Criteria in Queries				

Assignment	Title	Start from Scratch	SNAP Grade It	Date Due	Grade
SNAP Tutorial 3.4	Creating Queries Using the Simple Query Wizard				
SNAP Tutorial 3.5	Performing Calculations in a Query				
SNAP Tutorial 3.6	Using Aggregate Functions				
SNAP Tutorial 3.7	Using Advanced Queries				
SNAP Tutorial 3.8	Creating Duplicate and Unmatched Queries				
IRC Quiz	Study Quiz				
SNAP Concepts	Quiz				
SNAP Skill Items	Quiz				
SNAP PE	Comprehensive Performance Evaluation				

Chapter 4 Creating and Modifying Tables in Design View

Assignment	Title	Start from Scratch	SNAP Grade It	Date Due	Grade
Concepts Check			✓		
Skills Check Assessment 1	Create an Employees Table with the Input Mask and Lookup Wizards	✓	✓		
Skills Check Assessment 2	Create a Projects Table	✓	✓		
Skills Check Assessment 3	Create an Expenses Table with a Validation Rule and Input Mask	✓	✓		
Skills Check Assessment 4	Edit the Employees Table	✓			
Visual Benchmark	Edit the Expenses Table	✓			
Case Study Part 1	Blue Ridge Enterprises: Representatives Table	✓			
Case Study Part 2	Blue Ridge Enterprises: Clients Table	✓			
Case Study Part 3	Blue Ridge Enterprises: Relationships	✓			
Case Study Part 4	Blue Ridge Enterprises: Queries	✓			
SNAP Tutorial 4.1	Creating a Table and Setting a Primary Key				
SNAP Tutorial 4.2	Modifying Field Properties				
SNAP Tutorial 4.3	Using the Input Mask Wizard and the Lookup Wizard				
SNAP Tutorial 4.4	Validating Data in a Table				
SNAP Tutorial 4.5	Modifying Table Fields				
SNAP Tutorial 4.6	Deleting and Sorting Records				
SNAP Tutorial 4.7	Completing a Spelling Check and Printing Specific Records				

Assignment	Title	Start from Scratch	SNAP Grade It	Date Due	Grade
SNAP Tutorial 4.8	Finding and Replacing Specific Data in Records				
SNAP Tutorial 4.9	Formatting a Datasheet				
SNAP Tutorial 4.10	Using Help				
IRC Quiz	Study Quiz				
SNAP Concepts	Quiz				
SNAP Skill Items	Quiz				
SNAP PE	Comprehensive Performance Evaluation				

Unit 1 Performance Assessments

Assignment	Title	Start from Scratch	SNAP Grade It	Date Due	Grade
Assessment 1	Create Tables in a Cornerstone Catering Database	✓			
Assessment 2	Create Relationships between Tables	✓			
Assessment 3	Modify Tables	✓			
Assessment 4	Design Queries	✓			
Assessment 5	Design a Query with a Calculated Field Entry	✓			
Assessment 6	Design a Query with Aggregate Functions	✓			
Assessment 7	Design a Query Using Fields from Tables and a Query	✓			
Assessment 8	Use the Find Duplicates Query Wizard	✓			
Assessment 9	Use the Find Unmatched Query Wizard	✓			
Writing Activity 1	Create a Payroll Table and Word Report	✓			
Internet Research	Vehicle Search	✓			
Supplemental Assessment 1	Meridian Sales: Use a Database to Track Inventory	✓			
SNAP PE	Comprehensive Performance Evaluation				

Unit 2: Creating Forms and Reports

Chapter 5 Creating Forms

Assignment	Title	Start from Scratch	SNAP Grade It	Date Due	Grade
Concepts Check			✓		
Skills Check Assessment 1	Create and Customize a Sales Form		✓		

Assignment	Title	Start from Scratch	SNAP Grade It	Date Due	Grade
Skills Check Assessment 2	Create and Customize an Orders Form and a Products Form		✓		
Skills Check Assessment 3	Create a Split Form with the Products Table		✓		
Skills Check Assessment 4	Create and Customize an Employees Form		✓		
Skills Check Assessment 5	Create and Customize a Benefits Form				
Visual Benchmark	Create and Format a Properties Form				
Case Study Part 1	Lewis Vision Care Center: Create Relationships				
Case Study Part 2	Lewis Vision Care Center: Create Forms for Tables and Apply Theme				
Case Study Part 3	Lewis Vision Care Center: Apply Form Conditions				
Case Study Part 4	Lewis Vision Care Center: Procedures Manual	✓			
SNAP Tutorial 5.1	Create a Form Using the Form Button				
SNAP Tutorial 5.2	Adding Records and Navigating in a Form				
SNAP Tutorial 5.3	Adding and Modifying Objects				
SNAP Tutorial 5.4	Modifying a Form				
SNAP Tutorial 5.5	Modifying Forms Using Labels and Calculated Controls				
SNAP Tutorial 5.6	Creating a Split Form and Multiple Items Form				
SNAP Tutorial 5.7	Creating a Form				
IRC Quiz	Study Quiz				
SNAP Concepts	Quiz				
SNAP Skill Items	Quiz				
SNAP PE	Comprehensive Performance Evaluation				

Chapter 6 Creating Reports and Mailing Labels

Assignment	Title	Start from Scratch	SNAP Grade It	Date Due	Grade
Concepts Check			✓		
Skills Check Assessment 1	Create and Format Reports in the Hilltop Database		✓		
Skills Check Assessment 2	Create Reports Using the Report Wizard		✓		
Skills Check Assessment 3	Create Mailings Labels		✓		

Assignment	Title	Start from Scratch	SNAP Grade It	Date Due	Grade
Skills Check Assessment 4	Add a Field to a Report				
Visual Benchmark	Design a Query and Create a Report with the Query				
Case Study Part 1	Millstone Legal Services: Enter Data				
Case Study Part 2	Millstone Legal Services: Create and Print Queries, Reports, and Labels				
Case Study Part 3	Millstone Legal Services: Apply Conditions to Fields				
Case Study Part 4	Millstone Legal Services: Procedures Manual	✓			
SNAP Tutorial 6.1	Creating a Report				
SNAP Tutorial 6.2	Modifying a Report				
SNAP Tutorial 6.3	Modifying Reports Using Calculated Columns and Conditional Formatting				
SNAP Tutorial 6.4	Creating a Report Using the Report Wizard				
SNAP Tutorial 6.5	Creating Mailing Labels				
IRC Quiz	Study Quiz				
SNAP Concepts	Quiz				
SNAP Skill Items	Quiz				
SNAP PE	Comprehensive Performance Evaluation				

Chapter 7 Modifying, Filtering, and Viewing Data

Assignment	Title	Start from Scratch	SNAP Grade It	Date Due	Grade
Concepts Check			✓		
Skills Check Assessment 1	Filter Records in Tables		✓		
Skills Check Assessment 2	Save a Table and Database in Different File Formats				
Skills Check Assessment 3	Delete and Rename Objects				
Visual Benchmark	Design a Query and Filter the Query				
Case Study Part 1	Summit View Medical Services: Add Database Information				
Case Study Part 2	Summit View Medical Services: Create Filters and Queries				
Case Study Part 3	Summit View Medical Services: Save a Table as a PDF				
Case Study Part 4	Summit View Medical Services: Procedures Manual	✓			

Assignment	Title	Start from Scratch	SNAP Grade It	Date Due	Grade
SNAP Tutorial 7.1	Filtering Records				
SNAP Tutorial 7.2	Compacting, Repairing, and Backing Up a Database				
SNAP Tutorial 7.3	Encrypting a Database with a Password and Modifying Document Properties				
SNAP Tutorial 7.4	Customizing the Recent tab in Backstage view				
SNAP Tutorial 7.5	Saving Databases and Database Objects in Different Formats				
IRC Quiz	Study Quiz				
SNAP Concepts	Quiz				
SNAP Skill Items	Quiz				
SNAP PE	Comprehensive Performance Evaluation				

Chapter 8 Importing and Exporting Data

Assignment	Title	Start from Scratch	SNAP Grade It	Date Due	Grade
Concepts Check			✓		
Skills Check Assessment 1	Export a Form to Excel and a Report to Word				
Skills Check Assessment 2	Merge Table and Query Data with a Word Document				
Skills Check Assessment 3	Link an Excel Workbook				
Visual Benchmark	Create a Report and Export the Report to Word				
Case Study Part 1	Woodland Dermatology Center: Update a Database				
Case Study Part 2	Woodland Dermatology Center: Merge Database Information Into a Letter				
Case Study Part 3	Woodland Dermatology Center: Save a Database Object as a PDF				
Case Study Part 4	Woodland Dermatology Center: Procedures Manual	✓			
SNAP Tutorial 8.1	Exporting Access Data to Excel and Word				
SNAP Tutorial 8.2	Merging Access Data with a Word Document				
SNAP Tutorial 8.3	Importing and Link Data to a New Table				
SNAP Tutorial 8.4	Using the Office Clipboard				

Assignment	Title	Start from Scratch	SNAP Grade It	Date Due	Grade
IRC Quiz	Study Quiz				
SNAP Concepts	Quiz				
SNAP Skill Items	Quiz				
SNAP PE	Comprehensive Performance Evaluation				

Unit 2 Performance Assessments

Assignment	Title	Start from Scratch	SNAP Grade It	Date Due	Grade
Assessment 1	Create Tables in a Clinic Database				
Assessment 2	Relate Tables and Create Forms in a Clinic Database				
Assessment 3	Create Forms Using the Form Wizard				
Assessment 4	Create Labels with the Label Wizard				
Assessment 5	Filter Records in Tables				
Assessment 6	Export a Table to Excel				
Assessment 7	Merge Records to Create Letters in Word				
Assessment 8	Import and Link Excel Data to an Access Table				
Writing Activity 1	Add a Table to the Clinic Database				
Writing Activity 2	Merge Records to Create Letters to Insurance Companies				
Internet Research	Health Information research	✓			
Job Study	City Improvement Projects	✓			
Supplemental Assessment	Extreme Ski Rentals				
Final Case Study	CellOne Phones				
SNAP PE	Comprehensive Performance Evaluation				

Grading Sheet

Benchmark Office Microsoft Access 2013 Level 2

Assignment	Title	Start from Scratch	SNAP Grade It	Date Due	Grade
Unit 1: Advanced Tables, Relationships, Queries, and Forms					
Chapter 1 Designing the Structure of Tables					
Concepts Check		✓	✓		
Skills Check Assessment 1	Create a New Database	✓	✓		
Skills Check Assessment 2	Add Captions and Disallow Blank Values		✓		
Skills Check Assessment 3	Create Custom Formats and Input Masks		✓		
Skills Check Assessment 4	Add Records		✓		
Visual Benchmark	Create a New Database	✓	✓		
Case Study Part 1	Bestar Plumbing Service: Invoice	✓			
Case Study Part 2	Bestar Plumbing Service: Database	✓			
Case Study Part 3	Bestar Plumbing Service: Field Properties				
SNAP Tutorial 1.1	Diagramming a Database				
SNAP Tutorial 1.2	Creating Tables in Design View				
SNAP Tutorial 1.3	Restricting Data Entry and Data				
SNAP Tutorial 1.4	Creating a Custom Format for Text, Numeric, and Date/Time Fields				
SNAP Tutorial 1.5	Restricting Data Entry Using Input Masks				
SNAP Tutorial 1.6	Working with Long Text Fields				
SNAP Tutorial 1.7	Creating an Attachment Data Type Field				
SNAP Tutorial 1.8	Attaching Files to Records				
IRC Quiz	Study Quiz				
SNAP Concepts	Quiz				
SNAP Skill Items	Quiz				
SNAP PE	Comprehensive Performance Evaluation				

Assignment	Title	Start from Scratch	SNAP Grade It	Date Due	Grade
Chapter 2 Building Relationships and Lookup Fields					
Concepts Check		✓	✓		
Skills Check Assessment 1	Create a Lookup list		✓		
Skills Check Assessment 2	Create a Table with a Multiple-Field Primary Key and Lookup Lists		✓		
Skills Check Assessment 3	Edit Relationships		✓		
Skills Check Assessment 4	Create a Table with a One-to-One Relationship		✓		
Visual Benchmark	Create Lookup Lists and Edit Relationships				
Case Study Part 1	Hillsdale Realty: Database				
Case Study Part 2	Hillsdale Realty: Lookup Lists				
Case Study Part 3	Hillsdale Realty: Preferences Table				
SNAP Tutorial 2.1	Creating a One-to-Many Relationship				
SNAP Tutorial 2.2	Creating a Second One-to-Many Relationship				
SNAP Tutorial 2.3	Editing Relationship Options				
SNAP Tutorial 2.4	Establishing a Many-to-Many Relationship				
SNAP Tutorial 2.5	Defining a Multiple-Field Primary Key				
SNAP Tutorial 2.6	Creating a Field to Look Up Values in Another Table				
SNAP Tutorial 2.7	Creating a Field that Allows Multiple Values				
SNAP Tutorial 2.8	Creating Indexes				
SNAP Tutorial 2.9	Normalizing a Database				
IRC Quiz	Study Quiz				
SNAP Concepts	Quiz				
SNAP Skill Items	Quiz				
SNAP PE	Comprehensive Performance Evaluation				
Chapter 3 Advanced Query Techniques					
Concepts Check		✓	✓		
Skills Check Assessment 1	Extract Records using a Filter and Prompted Queries		✓		
Skills Check Assessment 2	Modify Join Properties		✓		

Assignment	Title	Start from Scratch	SNAP Grade It	Date Due	Grade
Skills Check Assessment 3	Add a Table to a Query and Create and Use a Subquery to Perform Calculations		✓		
Skills Check Assessment 4	Use Action Queries to Archive Records and Update Selling Prices		✓		
Visual Benchmark	Calculate Days Boarded and Amount Due Using Nested Queries				
Case Study Part 1	Hillsdale Realty: Database printouts				
Case Study Part 2	Hillsdale Realty: Highest Sale Prices (Help)				
Case Study Part 3	Hillsdale Realty: Client Preferences				
SNAP Tutorial 3.1	Saving a Filter as a Query				
SNAP Tutorial 3.2	Prompting for Criteria Using a Parameter Query				
SNAP Tutorial 3.3	Creating a Query with Right Outer Join				
SNAP Tutorial 3.4	Creating a Self-Join Query				
SNAP Tutorial 3.5	Creating and Using Subqueries				
SNAP Tutorial 3.6	Assigning Aliases and Using a Multivalued Field in a Query				
SNAP Tutorial 3.7	Performing Operations Using Action Queries				
SNAP Tutorial 3.8	Creating a New Table Using a Query				
SNAP Tutorial 3.9	Adding and Deleting Records to a Table Using a Query				
SNAP Tutorial 3.10	Modifying Records Using an Update Query				
IRC Quiz	Study Quiz				
SNAP Concepts	Quiz				
SNAP Skill Items	Quiz				
SNAP PE	Comprehensive Performance Evaluation				

Chapter 4 Creating and Using Custom Forms

Assignment	Title	Start from Scratch	SNAP Grade It	Date Due	Grade
Concepts Check		✓	✓		
Skills Check Assessment 1	Create a Custom Form Using Design View		✓		
Skills Check Assessment 2	Create a Form Using the Form Wizard; Add a Calculation and Graphics		✓		
Skills Check Assessment 3	Create a Restricted-Use Form		✓		
Skills Check Assessment 4	Create a Custom Form Using the Blank Form Tool and Add a List box		✓		

Assignment	Title	Start from Scratch	SNAP Grade It	Date Due	Grade
Visual Benchmark	Create a Custom Reservations Form				
Case Study Part 1	Hillsdale Realty: Data Entry Form				
Case Study Part 2	Hillsdale Realty: Agents and Clients Form				
Case Study Part 3	Hillsdale Realty: Remove Record Navigation Bar				
SNAP Tutorial 4.1	Creating Custom Forms Using Design View				
SNAP Tutorial 4.2	Binding a Table to a Form and Adding Fields				
SNAP Tutorial 4.3	Moving, Resizing, and Formatting Control Objects				
SNAP Tutorial 4.4	Changing the Tab Order of Fields				
SNAP Tutorial 4.5	Adding a Tab Control and a Subform				
SNAP Tutorial 4.6	Adding Subforms and a New Page to the Tab Control				
SNAP Tutorial 4.7	Adding Calculations to a Form in Design View				
SNAP Tutorial 4.8	Grouping, Aligning, and Spacing Controls				
SNAP Tutorial 4.9	Creating a Datasheet Form and Modifying Form Properties				
SNAP Tutorial 4.10	Sorting and Finding Records in a Form				
IRC Quiz	Study Quiz				
SNAP Concepts	Quiz				
SNAP Skill Items	Quiz				
SNAP PE	Comprehensive Performance Evaluation				

Unit 1 Performance Assessments

Assignment	Title	Start from Scratch	SNAP Grade It	Date Due	Grade
Assessment 1	Create Tables for a Property Management Database	✓			
Assessment 2	Add Captions and Modify Field Properties				
Assessment 3	Add Records				
Assessment 4	Create Lookup Lists and Edit Relationships				
Assessment 5	Create Select Queries				
Assessment 6	Calculate in a Query and Use an Update Query to Increase Rents				
Assessment 7	Design and Create Forms				

Assignment	Title	Start from Scratch	SNAP Grade It	Date Due	Grade
Writing Activity 1	Design Tables for Parking Information in the Property Management Database				
Writing Activity 2	Design Tables for a Soccer League Database	✓			
Internet Research	Plan Your Volunteer Work	✓			
Supplemental Assessment 1	Family Eye Care				
Supplemental Assessment 2	South County Premium Spas and Pools				
SNAP PE	Comprehensive Performance Evaluation				

Unit 2: Advanced Reports, Access Tools, and Customizing Access

Chapter 5 Creating and Using Custom Reports

Assignment	Title	Start from Scratch	SNAP Grade It	Date Due	Grade
Concepts Check		✓	✓		
Skills Check Assessment 1	Create a Custom Report Using Design View		✓		
Skills Check Assessment 2	Enhance the Report		✓		
Skills Check Assessment 3	Create a New Report with Grouping and Totals		✓		
Skills Check Assessment 4	Create and Format a New Report with a Chart		✓		
Skills Check Assessment 5	Create a Custom Report Using the Blank Report Tool		✓		
Visual Benchmark	Create Custom Reservations Report with Totals				
Case Study Part 1	Hillsdale Realty: Reports				
Case Study Part 2	Hillsdale Realty: Client Preferences	✓	·		
Case Study Part 3	Hillsdale Realty: Days on the Market	✓			
Case Study Part 4	Hillsdale Realty: Summary Report (Help)				
SNAP Tutorial 5.1	Creating Custom Reports Using Design View				
SNAP Tutorial 5.2	Connecting a Table or Query to a Report and Adding Fields				
SNAP Tutorial 5.3	Moving Control Objects to Another Section				
SNAP Tutorial 5.4	Inserting a Subreport				
SNAP Tutorial 5.5	Formatting Controls in a Report				
SNAP Tutorial 5.6	Grouping Records in a Report				

Assignment	Title	Start from Scratch	SNAP Grade It	Date Due	Grade
SNAP Tutorial 5.7	Creating a Report with a Grouping Level Using the Report Wizard				
SNAP Tutorial 5.8	Adding and Formatting a Calculated Field				
SNAP Tutorial 5.9	Adding Functions to a Group; Keeping a Group Together				
SNAP Tutorial 5.10	Modifying Section Properties; Inserting a Chart				
SNAP Tutorial 5.11	Creating a Report Using the Blank Report Tool				
IRC Quiz	Study Quiz				
SNAP Concepts	Quiz				
SNAP Skill Items	Quiz				
SNAP PE	Comprehensive Performance Evaluation				

Chapter 6 Using Access Tools and Managing Objects

Assignment	Title	Start from Scratch	SNAP Grade It	Date Due	Grade
Concepts Check		✓	✓		
Skills Check Assessment 1	Create a New Database Using a Template	✓			
Skills Check Assessment 2	Create a Table Using an Applications Parts Template		✓		
Skills Check Assessment 3	Use Access Tools to Improve Design and Performance		✓		
Visual Benchmark 1	Create a Table to Store Groomers' Information				
Visual Benchmark 2	Create a Form Template				
Case Study Part 1	Hillsdale Realty: Home Shows and Conferences				
Case Study Part 2	Hillsdale Realty: Design Improvements				
Case Study Part 3	Hillsdale Realty: Performance Analyzer (Help)				
SNAP Tutorial 6.1	Creating a Database Using a Template				
SNAP Tutorial 6.2	Creating a Table Using a Table Template				
SNAP Tutorial 6.3	Copying a Table Structure to a New Table				
SNAP Tutorial 6.4	Modifying a Table Using the Table Analyzer Wizard				
SNAP Tutorial 6.5	Optimizing Performance Using the Performance Analyzer				

Assignment	Title	Start from Scratch	SNAP Grade It	Date Due	Grade
SNAP Tutorial 6.6	Splitting a Database				
SNAP Tutorial 6.7	Documenting a Database				
SNAP Tutorial 6.8	Renaming and Deleting Objects				
IRC Quiz	Study Quiz				
SNAP Concepts	Quiz				
SNAP Skill Items	Quiz				
SNAP PE	Comprehensive Performance Evaluation				

Chapter 7 Automating, Customizing, and Securing Access

Assignment	Title	Start from Scratch	SNAP Grade It	Date Due	Grade
Concepts Check		✓	✓		
Skills Check Assessment 1	Create and Run Macros				
Skills Check Assessment 2	Edit a Macro and Assign Macros to Command Buttons				
Skills Check Assessment 3	Create a Navigation Form and Configure Database Options		✓		
Skills Check Assessment 4	Customize the Ribbon				
Visual Benchmark	Automate and Customize a Reservation Database				
Case Study Part 1	Hillsdale Realty: Automate the Database				
Case Study Part 2	Hillsdale Realty: Navigation Form	✓			
Case Study Part 3	Hillsdale Realty: Security (Help)	✓			
SNAP Tutorial 7.1	Creating and Editing a Macro				
SNAP Tutorial 7.2	Creating a Command Button to Run a Macro				
SNAP Tutorial 7.3	Creating a Navigation Form				
SNAP Tutorial 7.4	Adding a Command Button to a Navigation Form				
SNAP Tutorial 7.5	Limiting Ribbon Tabs and Menus in a Database				
SNAP Tutorial 7.6	Customizing the Navigation Pane				
SNAP Tutorial 7.7	Configuring Error Checking Options				
SNAP Tutorial 7.8	Importing and Exporting Customizations				
SNAP Tutorial 7.9	Customizing the Ribbon				
IRC Quiz	Study Quiz				
SNAP Concepts	Quiz				
SNAP Skill Items	Quiz				
SNAP PE	Comprehensive Performance Evaluation				

Assignment	Title	Start from Scratch	SNAP Grade It	Date Due	Grade
Chapter 8 Integrating Access Data					
Concepts Check		✓	✓		
Skills Check Assessment 1	Import and Link Objects from Another Access Database		✓		
Skills Check Assessment 2	Import a Text File		✓		
Skills Check Assessment 3	Export and Publish Access Data				
Skills Check Assessment 4	Secure the Database				
Visual Benchmark	Analyze Reservation Database				
Case Study Part 1	Hillsdale Realty: Summarizing Data				
Case Study Part 2	Hillsdale Realty: Data and Report Export				
Case Study Part 3	Hillsdale Realty: Integrate Access and Outlook (Help)	✓			
SNAP Tutorial 8.1	Creating and Restoring a Backup Database File				
SNAP Tutorial 8.2	Creating an ACCDE Database File				
SNAP Tutorial 8.3	Viewing Trust Center Settings				
SNAP Tutorial 8.4	Importing Data from Another Access Database				
SNAP Tutorial 8.5	Linking to a Table in Another Access Database				
SNAP Tutorial 8.6	Importing Data to Access from a Text File				
SNAP Tutorial 8.7	Saving and Repeating a Saved Import Process				
SNAP Tutorial 8.8	Exporting Access Data to a Text File				
SNAP Tutorial 8.9	Saving and Repeating Saved Export Specifications				
SNAP Tutorial 8.10	Publishing Database Objects as PDF or XPS Files				
IRC Quiz	Study Quiz				
SNAP Concepts	Quiz				
SNAP Skill Items	Quiz				
SNAP PE	Comprehensive Performance Evaluation				

Assignment	Title	Start from Scratch	SNAP Grade It	Date Due	Grade
Unit 2 Performance Assessments					
Assessment 1	Import Data from Text Files and Create Reports for a Property Management Database				
Assessment 2	Use Access Tools to Improve the Property Management Database Design				
Assessment 3	Automate the Property Management Database with Macros and Command Buttons				
Assessment 4	Create a Navigation Form and Configure Startup Options for the Property Management Database				
Assessment 5	Configure Security for the Property Management Database				
Assessment 6	Export and Publish Data from the Property Management Database				
Writing Activity 1	Create a New Database for Renovation Contracts by Importing Data	✓			
Writing Activity 2	Design and Publish a Report for a Painting Franchise	✓			
Internet Research	Buying a Home	✓			
Job Study	Meals on Wheels Database	✓			
Supplemental Assessment 1	Family Eye Care				
Supplemental Assessment 2	South County Premium Spas and Pools				
Final Case Study	Global Wholesale Enterprises				
SNAP PE	Comprehensive Performance Evaluation				

Concepts Check Answer Key
Benchmark Access 2013 Level 1, Chapter 1

1.	Click this template at the Access 2013 opening screen to create a new database	Blank desktop database	page 5
2.	This toolbar contains buttons for commonly used commands.	Quick Access	page 7 (Table 1.1)
3.	This displays the names of objects within a database grouped by categories.	Navigation pane	page 7 (Table 1.1)
4.	When you open a table, it displays in this view.	Datasheet	page 11
5.	Use buttons on this bar to navigate in a table.	Record Navigation	page 11
6.	To add a new record, click the New button in this group on the HOME tab.	Records	page 11
7.	At the Print backstage area, click this button to send the table directly to the printer.	Quick Print	page 17
8.	The Landscape button is located in this group on the PRINT PREVIEW tab.	Page Layout	page 19
9.	All fields for one unit, such as an employee or customer, are considered to be this.	record	page 23
10.	Assign this data type to values that involve money.	Currency	page 24 (Table 1.3)
11.	Click this button in the Properties group on the TABLE TOOLS FIELDS tab to display the Enter Field Properties dialog box.	Name & Caption	page 27
12.	With options in this category in the More Fields button drop-down list, you can define a data type and also assign a field name.	*Quick Start*	page 29
13.	If you want to assign the same field value to a column, click this button to display the Expression Builder dialog box and then type the desired value.	Default Value	page 29

Concepts Check Answer Key
Benchmark Access 2013 Level 1, Chapter 2

1.	In Access, one table can be related to another, which is generally referred to as performing this.	a join	page 46
2.	A database table can contain a foreign key field and this type of key field.	primary	page 46
3.	Open a table, click the View button on the HOME tab, and the table displays in this view.	Design	page 47
4.	In a one-to-many relationship, the table containing the "one" is referred to as this.	primary	page 50
5.	In a one-to-many relationship, the table containing the "many" is referred to as this.	related	page 50
6.	In a one-to-many relationship, Access follows a set of rules that enforces consistency between related tables and is referred to as this.	referential integrity	page 50
7.	In related tables, this symbol displays near the black line next to field list box of the related table.	infinity	page 51
8.	The black line that connects the field list boxes of related tables is referred to as this.	join line	page 51
9.	Establish this type of relationship between tables in which each record in the first table matches only one record in the second table and only one record in the second table matches each record in the first table.	one-to-one	page 61
10.	The plus symbol that displays at the beginning of a record in a related table is referred to as this.	expand indicator	page 64
11.	The minus symbol that displays at the beginning of a record in a related table with a subdatasheet displayed is referred to as this.	collapse indicator	page 65
12.	Display subdatasheets for all records by clicking the More button, pointing to *Subdatasheet*, and then clicking this option.	*Expand All*	page 65

Concepts Check Answer Key
Benchmark Access 2013 Level 1, Chapter 3

1.	The Query Design button is located in the Queries group on this tab.	CREATE	page 82
2.	Click the Query Design button and the query window displays with this dialog box open.	Show Table	page 82
3.	To establish a criterion for a query, click in this row in the column containing the desired field name and then type the criterion.	*Criteria*	page 83
4.	This is the term used for the results of the query.	return	page 84
5.	This is the symbol Access automatically inserts before and after a date when writing a criterion for the query.	# (pound symbol)	page 84
6.	Use this symbol to indicate a wildcard character when writing a query criterion.	* (asterisk)	page 84
7.	This is the criterion you would type to return field values greater than $500.	>500	page 85 (Table 3.1)
8.	This is the criterion you would type to return field values that begin with the letter *L*.	L*	page 85 (Table 3.1)
9.	This is the criterion you would type to return field values that are not in Oregon.	not "Oregon"	page 85 (Table 3.1)
10.	You can sort a field in a query in ascending order or in this order.	descending	page 92
11.	Multiple criteria entered in the *Criteria* row in the query design grid become this type of statement.	*Or*	page 96
12.	This wizard guides you through the steps for preparing a query.	Simple Query Wizard	page 100
13.	This type of query calculates aggregate functions, in which field values are grouped by two fields.	crosstab	page 112
14.	Use this type of query to compare two tables and produce a list of the records in one table that have no matching records in the other table.	find duplicates	page 115

Concepts Check Answer Key
Benchmark Access 2013 Level 1, Chapter 4

1.	The lower half of the work area in Design view that displays the properties for the active field is referred to as this.	*Field Properties* section	page 132
2.	When you create a new table in Design view, Access automatically assigns the first field the name *ID* and assigns this data type.	AutoNumber	page 133
3.	The description you type in the *Description* field displays in this location when the field is active in the table in Datasheet view.	Status bar	page 133
4.	Use this field property to set a pattern for how data is entered in a field.	*Input Mask*	page 137
5.	Use this property box in Design view to enter a statement containing a conditional test that is checked each time data is entered into a field.	*Validation Rule*	page 141
6.	Use this wizard to confine the data entered in a field to a specific list of items.	Lookup Wizard	page 141
7.	To insert a new field in a table in Design view, click this button.	Insert Rows	page 142
8.	To insert a *Total* row in a table, click the Totals button in this group on the HOME tab.	Records	page 143
9.	The Ascending and Descending sort buttons are located in this group on the HOME tab.	Sort & Filter	page 147
10.	Click this button to change the text size of data in a table.	Font Size	page 148 (Table 4.2)
11.	Click this button to align all text in the active column in the center of the fields.	Center	page 148 (Table 4.2)
12.	Click this button to specify a color for alternating rows in a table.	Alternate Row Color	page 148 (Table 4.2)
13.	Use options at the Find and Replace dialog box with this tab selected to search for specific data and replace it with other data.	Replace	page 154
14.	This is the keyboard shortcut to display the Access Help window.	F1	page 157

Concepts Check Answer Key
Benchmark Access 2013 Level 1, Chapter 5

1.	The simplest method for creating a form is to click this tab and then click the Form button.	CREATE	page 186
2.	When you click the Form button to create a form, the form displays in this view.	Layout	page 186
3.	To print the current record in a form, click this option at the Print dialog box and then click OK.	*Selected Record(s)*	page 187
4.	Navigate in a form using buttons in this bar.	Record Navigation	page 187
5.	Click this button to add a new record to a form.	New (blank) record	page 189
6.	The FORM LAYOUT TOOLS DESIGN tab is active when a form displays in this view.	Layout	page 192
7.	The Themes group on the FORM LAYOUT TOOLS DESIGN tab contains three buttons: the Themes button, the Colors button, and this button.	Fonts	page 193
8.	Click the Logo button on the FORM LAYOUT TOOLS DESIGN tab and this dialog box displays.	Insert Picture	page 193
9.	To select nonadjacent objects or cells, hold down this key on the keyboard while clicking the desired objects or cells.	Ctrl	page 198
10.	This group on the FORM LAYOUT TOOLS ARRANGE tab contains buttons for selecting and inserting rows and columns in a form.	Rows & Columns	page 198
11.	With this button in the Control Formatting group on the FORM LAYOUT TOOLS FORMAT tab, you can apply formatting to data that meets a specific criterion.	Conditional Formatting	page 203
12.	Click the Add Existing Fields button in the Tools group on the FORM LAYOUT TOOLS DESIGN tab and this task pane displays.	Field List	page 207
13.	Create a split form or multiple items form with options at this button's drop-down list.	More Forms	page 210
14.	When you create a form with the *Split Form* option, the form displays in this view in the top half of the work area.	Layout	page 210

Concepts Check Answer Key

Benchmark Access 2013 Level 1, Chapter 6

1.	The Report button is located in the Reports group on this tab.	CREATE	page 233
2.	Press these keys on the keyboard to select all control objects in a report in Layout view.	Ctrl + A	page 235
3.	The Ascending button is located in this group on the HOME tab.	Sort & Filter	page 236
4.	Four views are available in a report, including Layout View, Report view, Design view, and this view.	Print Preview	page 236
5.	With options on this tab, you can insert controls, insert header or footer data, and add existing fields.	REPORT LAYOUT TOOLS DESIGN	page 240
6.	Click this button in the Grouping & Totals group on the REPORT LAYOUT TOOLS DESING tab to perform functions such as finding the sum, average, maximum, and minimum of the numbers in a column.	Totals	page 240
7.	The Group & Sort button is located in this group on the REPORT LAYOUT TOOLS DESIGN tab.	Grouping & Totals	page 244
8.	Click the Group & Sort button and this pane displays.	Group, Sort, and Total	page 244
9.	Use this to guide you through the steps for creating a report.	Report Wizard	page 248
10.	To create mailing labels, click the desired table, click the CREATE tab, and then click the Labels button in this group.	Reports	page 252

Concepts Check Answer Key
Benchmark Access 2013 Level 1, Chapter 7

1.	The Filter button is located in this group on the HOME tab.	Sort & Filter	page 265
2.	When you filter data, you can switch between the filtered and unfiltered data by clicking this button.	Toggle Filter	page 266
3.	Remove all filtering from an object by using the Filter button or clicking this button and then clicking *Clear All Filters*.	Advanced	page 266
4.	In the Filter by Form window, these two tabs display toward the bottom of the form.	Look for and Or	page 272
5.	Display the structure of a database at this task pane.	Object Dependencies	page 274
6.	Optimize database performance by doing this to the database.	compacting and repairing	page 276
7.	Before encrypting a database with a password, you must open the database in this mode.	Exclusive	page 277
8.	Display the Set Database Password dialog box by clicking this button in the Info backstage area.	Encrypt with Password	page 277
9.	Data in this dialog box provides details about a database, such as its title, author name, and subject.	Properties	page 278
12.	Save a database object in PDF file format with the *PDF or XPS* option in this backstage area.	Save As	page 281

Concepts Check Answer Key
Benchmark Access 2013 Level 1, Chapter 8

1.	Click this tab to display the Export group.	EXTERNAL DATA	page 295
2.	Click this button in the Export group to display the Export - Excel Spreadsheet wizard dialog box.	Excel	page 295
3.	At the first Export - Excel Spreadsheet wizard dialog box, click this option if you want Excel to open with the exported data.	*Open the destination file after the export operation is complete*	page 296
4.	To export Access data to Word, click this button in the Export group on the EXTERNAL DATA tab and then click *Word* at the drop-down list.	More	page 298
5.	When you export Access data to Word, the document is saved in this file format.	RTF (rich-text format)	page 298
6.	When merging data, the data in the Access table is considered this.	data source	page 300
7.	To merge data, click this button in the Export group on the EXTERNAL DATA tab.	Word Merge	page 300
8.	Import an Excel worksheet into an Access database with the Excel button in this group on the EXTERNAL DATA tab.	Import & Link	page 305
9.	If you want imported data connected to the original program, do this to the data.	link	page 307
10.	Use this task pane to collect and paste multiple items.	Clipboard	page 308

Concepts Check Answer Key
Benchmark Access 2013 Level 2, Chapter 1

1.	Use this data type to store alphanumeric text longer than 255 characters.	Long Text	page 8 (Table 1.1)
2.	Use this data type for a field that will hold numeric data that is not a monetary value.	Number	page 8 (Table 1.1)
3.	This data type is restricted to field values used to test conditional logic that can be one of only two conditions.	Yes/No	page 8 (Table 1.1)
4.	The properties that display for a field in the *Field Properties* section in Design view are dependent on this option.	data type	page 10
5.	This property is used to display a more descriptive title for the field in the datasheet.	Caption	page 10
6.	To ensure a field is never left empty, set this property to *Yes*.	Required	page 10
7.	Typing two double quotation marks with no space between them assigns this field value.	zero-length string	page 11
8.	Use this format code to convert all text in the field to uppercase.	>	page 13 (Table 1.2)
9.	This placeholder in a custom numeric format instructs Access to display a 0 if the position is not used.	0 (zero)	page 15 (Table 1.3)
10.	Type this entry in the *Format* property box of a Date/Time field to display dates beginning with the day of the week abbreviated, followed by the month as two digits, the day of the month as two digits, and the year as two digits, with all sections separated with hyphen characters.	ddd-mm-dd-yy	page 17 (Table 1.4)
11.	Type this entry in the *Input Mask* property box to require a three-digit identification number to be entered with the pound symbol (#) used as the placeholder.	000;;#	page 19 (Table 1.5)
12.	Rich text formatting is enabled for a Long Text data type field by changing this property option to *Rich Text*.	Text Format	page 22
13.	For a Long Text data type field with the Append Only property active, right-click in a record and then click this option at the shortcut menu to display a dialog box with the history of the text changes made to the field.	*Show column history*	page 23
14.	Create a field with this data type to store a file with the record.	Attachment	page 24
15.	Add a file to the record by double-clicking this object in the record in Datasheet view.	paper clip	page 24

Concepts Check Answer Key
Benchmark Access 2013 Level 2, Chapter 2

1.	This is the term for a field added to a related table for the purpose of creating a relationship that is the primary key in the other table.	foreign key	page 37
2.	The Relationships button is found on this tab on the ribbon.	DATABASE TOOLS	page 40
3.	Add a table to the Relationships window using this dialog box.	Show Table	page 43
4.	At the Edit Relationships dialog box, the two cascade options do not become active until this option is activated.	*Enforce Referential Integrity*	page 40
5.	This symbol appears on the join line next to the "many" side of a relationship when referential integrity is activated.	infinity symbol	page 42
6.	To open the Edit Relationships dialog box for an existing relationship, perform this action with the mouse while pointing at the black join line in the Relationships window.	double-click	page 42
7.	This type of relationship exists if only one matching record exists in both tables in the relationship.	one-to-one	page 43
8.	A many-to-many relationship is created by establishing two one-to-many relationships using a third table referred to by this term.	junction table	page 45
9.	A primary key that is made up of two or more fields is referred to by this term.	composite key	page 46
10.	A lookup field can be restricted to items within the list by setting this property to Yes.	Limit To List	page 50
11.	Specify a field as a multiple-value field by clicking this check box at the final Lookup Wizard dialog box.	*Allow Multiple Values*	page 51
12.	Set the Indexed property to this option for an index field that is likely to contain more than one record with the same field value, such as a zip code.	*Yes (Duplicates OK)*	page 54
13.	Open this window to create an index that uses two or more fields.	Indexes	page 54
14.	These are the three normalization states that are tested.	first normal form, second normal form, third normal form	page 56
15.	If a field exists in a table for which the field value is not dependent on the primary key, the table is not in this normalization state.	third normal form	page 56

Concepts Check Answer Key
Benchmark Access 2013 Level 2, Chapter 3

1.	Click this button at a Filter By Form datasheet to save the filter's criteria as a query.	Advanced Filter Options	page 70
2.	This is the name for a query that prompts the user to type the criteria in a dialog box when the query is run.	parameter	page 72
3.	Double-clicking the black join line between tables in a query window opens this dialog box.	Join Properties	page 75
4.	This join type displays all of the records from the related table and empty fields if no matching record exists in the primary table.	right outer	page 76
5.	Click this button in the Query Setup group on the QUERY TOOLS DESIGN tab to add a table to an existing query.	Show Table	page 78
6.	This is the term for a query in which two copies of the same table are added to the query window and joined by two fields in the same table that contain matching field values.	self-join	page 80
7.	This is the term used to describe another name with which to reference a table in a query.	alias	page 81
8.	This is the term for a query in which two tables are used in the query window with no join established to connect one table to the other.	cross product or Cartesian product	page 82
9.	This term describes a query nested inside another query.	subquery	page 83
10.	Add this to the end of a multiple-value field name in the *Field* box in the query design grid to display each field value in a separate row.	.Value	page 88
11.	Queries that perform operations on selected records are referred to by this term.	action queries	page 90
12.	Create this type of query to create a new table from existing records in the active database or an archive database.	make-table	page 91
13.	This type of query removes a group of records that meet specified criteria.	delete	page 93
14.	This query adds a group of records to the end of an existing table in the active database or another database.	append	page 94
15.	Create this type of query to increase the prices in all records by 10%.	update	page 95

Concepts Check Answer Key
Benchmark Access 2013 Level 2, Chapter 4

1.	A new form created in Design view initially displays only this section.	*Detail* section	page 107
2.	These three types of control objects are found in a form.	Bound, Unbound, and Calculated	page 108
3.	Before you can add fields to a table, you must first connect the table to the form in this property box in the form's Property Sheet task pane.	Record Source	page 110
4.	The large, dark gray square at the top left of a selected control is referred to by this name.	*Move handle*	page 113
5.	Hold down this key while clicking controls to select multiple control objects to be formatted.	Shift	page 114
6.	Open this dialog box to change the order in which fields are selected when the Tab key is pressed in Form view.	Tab Order	page 117
7.	Add this object to the bottom of a form to display subforms as individual pages.	tab control	page 118
8.	Make sure this feature is active in the Controls group before clicking the Subform/Subreport button so that the Subform Wizard is available.	Use Control Wizards button	page 120
9.	Click this button in the Controls group to add a calculation to a form.	Text Box	page 126
10.	The *Equal Vertical* option is located at the drop-down list for this button on the FORM DESIGN TOOLS ARRANGE tab.	Size/Space	page 131
11.	For a control object containing a clip art image, change this property to *Zoom* to proportionately adjust the image to the height and width of the resized object.	*Size Mode*	page 132
12.	The *Datasheet* form is available at the drop-down list for this button in the Forms group on the CREATE tab.	More Forms	page 136
13.	Click this tab in a form's Property Sheet task pane to locate the *Allow Deletions* property box.	Data	page 136
14.	This form tool opens as a blank, white page in Layout view.	Setting the Data Entry	page 136
15.	These two controls are used to add list boxes to a form.	List Box Wizard and Combo Box Wizard	page 138
16.	Type this entry in the *Find What* text box to search for all of the records in the active field that begin with the zip code 48221 and have any four-character extension.	48221*	page 144 (Table 4.1)

Concepts Check Answer Key
Benchmark Access 2013 Level 2, Chapter 5

1.	Add controls in this section to print grand totals at the end of a report.	*Report Footer*	page 175 (Table 5.1)
2.	Double-click this button to open the Property Sheet task pane for a report.	Report Selector	page 176
3.	The Subform/Subreport button is found in this group within the REPORT DESIGN TOOLS DESIGN tab.	Controls	page 180
4.	The Page Numbers button is located in this group in the REPORT DESIGN TOOLS DESIGN tab.	Header/Footer	page 184
5.	If the date and time are added to a report using the Date and Time dialog box, Access creates the control objects in this report section.	*Report Header*	page 185
6.	At the Report Wizard dialog box, Access displays a grouped field in this color in the preview section.	blue	page 191
7.	Grouping can be added to an existing report by opening this pane	Group, Sort, and Total	page 192
8.	Click this button to expand the group options for a grouped field to add a Sum function to each group.	More Options	page 194
9.	Modify this section property to instruct Access to insert a page break after the section is finished printing.	Force New Page	page 200
10.	Double-click this element in report Design view to open the Property Sheet for a section.	gray section bar	page 199
11.	Use the button in the expanded Controls group to insert a bar chart into a report.	Insert Chart	page 202
12.	Launch the Microsoft Graph application to edit a chart by doing this action with the mouse.	double-click the chart	page 206
13.	When finished editing a chart, exit Microsoft Graph by doing this action with the mouse.	click outside the chart object	page 206
14.	This report tool opens as a blank, white page in Layout view.	Blank Report	page 208
15.	Click this button to create a control object within a report that will display a web page when clicked.	Hyperlink	page 209
16.	This button in the Control Formatting group on the REPORT LAYOUT TOOLS FORMAT tab can be used to change the shape of a selected control.	Change Shape	page 209

Concepts Check Answer Key
Benchmark Access 2013 Level 2, Chapter 6

1.	To create a new database using a template, click on one of the available templates in either of these backstage areas.	Open backstage area and New backstage area	page 227
2.	A predefined table with related objects to store information about Contacts can be imported into the current database using this button in the Templates group on the CREATE tab.	Application Parts	page 234
3.	Access provides 10 prebuilt forms, each with a defined layout and most including titles and command buttons, in this section of the Application Parts button drop-down list.	*Blank Forms*	page 234
4.	Give a form this name to use it as a template for all new forms.	Normal	page 241
5.	Clicking the Paste button after copying a table in the Navigation pane causes this dialog box to open.	Paste Table As	page 242
6.	This wizard analyzes a table for repeated information and proposes a solution in which the table can be split into smaller, related tables.	Table Analyzer Wizard	page 245
7.	Optimize a database using this button in the Analyze group on the DATABASE TOOLS tab.	Analyze Performance	page 248
8.	List the three types of results provided by the Performance Analyzer to optimize selected objects.	recommendation, suggestion, and idea	page 249
9.	Click an item in the *Analysis Results* list and read a description of the optimization method in this section of the Performance Analyzer dialog box.	*Analysis Notes*	page 249
10.	A database can be split into a front-end database file and a back-end database file using this button in the Move Data group on the DATABASE TOOLS tab.	Access Database	page 251
11.	When a database has been split, the back-end database file contains these objects.	tables	page 251
12.	When a database has been split, the front-end database file contains links to these objects.	source tables in back-end database file	page 251
13.	Open this dialog box to print a report with a table's definition and field properties.	Database Documenter	page 253
14.	Rename a database object in the Navigation pane by performing this action.	right-click object name and click *Rename* at shortcut menu.	page 255
15.	Remove a selected object from the database by pressing this key.	Delete	page 255

Concepts Check Answer Key
Benchmark Access 2013 Level 2, Chapter 7

1.	This is the name of the window in which you create actions with associated action arguments for a macro.	Macro Builder	page 271
2.	Add a macro action at the *Add New Action* option box or in this pane.	Action Catalog	page 271
3.	To make Access display the Find dialog box in a macro, choose this action in the *Add New Action* option box.	RunMenuCommand	page 272
4.	Drag a form name from the Navigation pane to the *Add New Action* option box to insert this macro action.	OpenForm	page 274
5.	Edit a macro by right-clicking the macro name in the Navigation pane and selecting this option at the shortcut menu.	*Design View*	page 276
6.	At the first Command Button Wizard dialog box, click this option in the *Categories* list box to locate the *Run Macro* action.	*Miscellaneous*	page 278
7.	This type of macro is not shown as a macro object within the Navigation pane.	embedded macro	page 282
8.	When a macro has been converted to Visual Basic for Applications (VBA), Access opens this window.	Microsoft Visual Basic	page 284
9.	This type of form is used to create a menu to allow end users to select forms and reports by clicking tabs.	Navigation	page 285
10.	Open this dialog box to specify a display form to open whenever the database is opened.	Access Options	page 289
11.	Hide the Tables group in the Navigation pane by opening this dialog box.	Navigation Options	page 291
12.	Click this option in the left pane at the Access Options dialog box to change an error-checking option.	*Object Designers*	page 294
13.	Click this option in the left pane at the Access Options dialog box to create a custom ribbon tab.	*Customize Ribbon*	page 295
14.	Click this button in the *Customize Ribbon* section in the Access Options dialog box to save the current ribbon settings.	Import/Export	page 297

Concepts Check Answer Key
Benchmark Access 2013 Level 2, Chapter 8

1.	Do this on a regular basis to minimize the risk of data loss due to system failures or design mistakes	back up	page 311
2.	Save a database as this type of file to disallow Design view and Layout view for the database objects.	ACCDE or .accde	page 313
3.	View and/or change the macro security setting at this dialog box.	Trust Center	page 315
4.	Click this button at the Import Objects dialog box to choose whether or not relationships between tables will be imported.	Options	page 319
5.	Click this option at the Get External Data - Access Database dialog box to create a table in which changes to data are automatically updated in the source or destination database.	*Link to the data source by creating a linked table*	page 321
6.	Data that will not likely be changed should be brought into the active database from another database using this method.	importing	page 323
7.	Data that will be updated frequently should be brought into the active database from another database using this method.	linking	page 323
8.	If the location of a source database has moved, refresh the link to the source table by opening this dialog box.	Linked Table Manager	page 323
9.	This type of file format is used to exchange data between programs for which an application-specific file format converter is not available.	text	pages 324 and 330
10.	A file in which fields are separated by commas has this file extension.	.csv	page 325
11.	Click this check box at the last Get External Data dialog box to store the steps used in the import process for use of the routine at a future date.	*Save import steps*	page 325
12.	The Export Text Wizard is launched from this button in the Export group in the EXTERNAL DATA tab.	Export to text file	page 330
13.	XPS is a file format that stands for this type of document specification.	XML paper specification	page 335

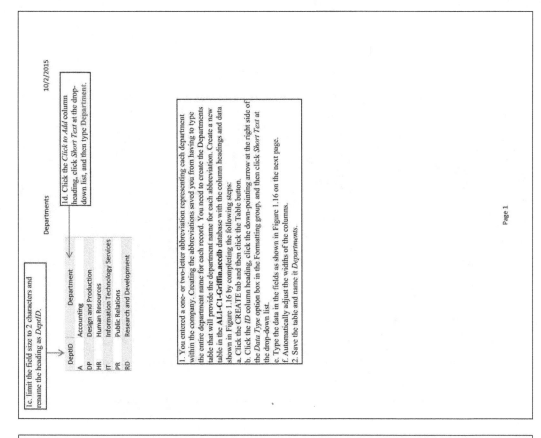

Departments   10/2/2015

1c. limit the field size to 2 characters and rename the heading as *DeptID*.

1d. Click the *Click to Add* column heading, click *Short Text* at the drop-down list, and then type Department.

DeptID	Department
A	Accounting
DP	Design and Production
HR	Human Resources
IT	Information Technology Services
PR	Public Relations
RD	Research and Development

Page 1

1. You entered a one- or two-letter abbreviation representing each department within the company. Creating the abbreviations saved you from having to type the entire department name for each record. You need to create the Departments table that will provide the department name for each abbreviation. Create a new table in the **AL1-C1-Griffin.accdb** database with the column headings and data shown in Figure 1.16 by completing the following steps:
a. Click the CREATE tab and then click the Table button.
b. Click the *ID* column heading, click the down-pointing arrow at the right side of the *Data Type* option box in the Formatting group, and then click *Short Text* at the drop-down list.
e. Type the data in the fields as shown in Figure 1.16 on the next page.
f. Automatically adjust the widths of the columns.
2. Save the table and name it *Departments*.

AL1-C1-A1-Griffen_DepartmentsTable(A2).accdb

---

5. Insert the following records: empID: 1010 empID: 1052 lastName: Harrington lastName: Reeves FirstName: Tyler FirstName: Carrie birthdate: 9/7/1976 birthdate: 12/4/1978 AnnualSalary: $53,350 AnnualSalary: $38,550 HireDate: 10/1/2010 HireDate: 10/1/2012

Employees   10/2/2015

EmpID	LastName	FirstName	BirthDate	DeptID	AnnualSalary	HireDate
1001	Navarro	Kate	1/4/1962	HR	$74,500.00	6/1/2008
1002	Sorenson	Lorraine	12/13/1974	RD	$67,700.00	2/1/2009
1003	Zamora	Deanna	7/23/1979	IT	$51,350.00	6/1/2009
1005	Sargent	Trevor	11/28/1978	DP	$46,510.00	7/15/2009
1010	Harrington	Tyler	9/7/1976	DP	$53,350.00	10/1/2010
1013	Frye	Stacy	10/17/1978	RD	$48,800.00	10/1/2009
1015	Brummel	Janelle	2/26/1979	HR	$51,000.00	2/15/2010
1020	Alvarado	Melissa	6/22/1981	A	$58,575.00	4/1/2010
1023	Chovanak	Peter	9/23/1982	IT	$40,150.00	5/15/2010
1030	Marshall	Charlene	4/7/1980	PR	$42,450.00	7/15/2010
1033	Rowe	Edward	9/12/1978	A	$55,730.00	10/15/2010
1040	Spencer	Christina	5/5/1982	DP	$42,500.00	2/1/2011
1043	Sadler	Daniel	4/20/1974	HR	$68,525.00	10/1/2011
1045	Tanner	Helen	7/23/1984	RD	$38,500.00	4/1/2012
1050	Weatherhill	Kevin	1/4/1983	IT	$39,750.00	9/1/2012
1052	Reeves	Carrie	12/4/1978	PR	$38,550.00	10/1/2012
1053	Yoshimoto	David	10/8/1985	HR	$38,425.00	11/15/2012
1063	Wakefield	Patricia	6/23/1986	DP	$32,600.00	4/1/2013
1065	Quinones	Santos	7/20/1982	DP	$38,750.00	11/15/2013
1080	Vignola	John	8/3/1975	IT	$65,250.00	7/1/2013
1083	Lincoln	William	1/5/1978	HR	$59,750.00	10/15/2014
1085	Hollinger	Eleanor	5/13/1968	PR	$58,000.00	11/15/2014
1090	Koenig	Wesley	9/19/1965	RD	$57,525.00	2/1/2015
1093	McLeod	Yolanda	8/4/1986	A	$61,500.00	6/15/2015
1095	Weyland	Richard	3/8/1980	RD	$45,250.00	7/1/2015

7. Looking at the database diagram in Figure 1.15, you realize that the employees table includes a *DeptID* field. Open the employees table, insert the new field in the employees table, and name it *DeptID*. Change the field size to 2 characters (since department abbreviations are only one or two letters in length). At the message telling you that some data may be lost, click the Yes button. Type the department identification for each record as shown below (the records are listed from left to right): 1001: HR 1002: RD 1003: IT 1005: DP 1010: DP 1013: RD 1015: HR 1020: A 1023: IT 1030: PR 1033: A 1040: DP 1043: HR 1045: RD 1050: IT 1052: PR 1053: HR 1063: DP 1065: DP 1080: IT 1083: HR 1085: PR 1090: RD 1093: A 1095: RD

1. In Access, open **AL1-C1-Griffin.accdb** from the AI1C1 folder on your storage medium and enable the contents.
2. Double-click *Employees* in the Tables group in the Navigation pane.
3. Delete the record for Scott Jorgensen (employee number 1025).
4. Delete the record for Leanne Taylor (employee number 1060).
6. Close the employees table.
8. Move the *DeptID* column so it is positioned between the *BirthDate* column and the *AnnualSalary* column.
9. Automatically adjust the widths of the columns.
10. Save the table.
11. Display the table in Print Preview, change the top margin to 1.5 inches, change the left margin to 1.25 inches, and then print the table.

AL1-C1-A1-Griffen_EmployeesTable(A1).accdb

Benefits

AL1-C1-A1-Griffen_BenefitsTable(A4).accdb

EmployeeID	Health Plan	Dental Plan	Life Insurance	Vacation
130			$200,000.00	3 weeks
105			$200,000.00	3 weeks
153			$200,000.00	2 weeks
109			$200,000.00	3 weeks
112			$200,000.00	4 weeks
120			$200,000.00	3 weeks
128			$200,000.00	3 weeks
170			$185,000.00	1 week
110			$185,000.00	4 weeks
143			$175,000.00	3 weeks
165			$150,000.00	1 week
106			$150,000.00	3 weeks
155			$150,000.00	1 week
152			$125,000.00	3 weeks
125			$125,000.00	2 weeks
138			$125,000.00	1 week
173			$125,000.00	1 week
163			$100,000.00	4 weeks
103			$100,000.00	3 weeks
117			$100,000.00	2 weeks
149			$100,000.00	2 weeks
141			$85,000.00	3 weeks
122			$75,000.00	1 week
159			$75,000.00	1 week
132			$50,000.00	2 weeks

5. Open the Benefits table and then sort the records in descending order by life insurance amounts.

6. Save, print, and then close the Benefits table.

Page 1

Benefits

AL1-C1-A1-Griffen_BenefitsTable(A3).accdb

2. Display the table in Print Preview, change the top and left margins to 1.5 inches, and then print the table.

EmployeeID	Health Plan	Dental Plan	Life Insurance	Vacation
103			$100,000.00	4 weeks
105			$200,000.00	3 weeks
106			$150,000.00	3 weeks
109			$200,000.00	3 weeks
110			$185,000.00	4 weeks
112			$200,000.00	3 weeks
117			$100,000.00	2 weeks
120			$200,000.00	4 weeks
122			$75,000.00	1 week
125			$125,000.00	2 weeks
128			$200,000.00	3 weeks
130			$200,000.00	3 weeks
132			$50,000.00	2 weeks
138			$125,000.00	2 weeks
141			$85,000.00	3 weeks
143			$175,000.00	3 weeks
149			$100,000.00	2 weeks
152			$150,000.00	2 weeks
153			$200,000.00	2 weeks
155			$150,000.00	1 week
159			$75,000.00	1 week
163			$125,000.00	1 week
165			$185,000.00	1 week
170			$150,000.00	1 week
173			$125,000.00	1 week

1. Create a new table in **AL1-C1-Griffin.accdb** with the data shown in Figure 1.17 and with the following specifications:

a. Name the fields as shown in the benefits table in the diagram in Figure 1.15 and create the caption names for the fields as shown in Figure 1.17. (For example, name the life insurance field *LifeIns* and create the caption *Life Insurance*.)

b. For the first column (empID), click the *ID* column heading, click the down-pointing arrow at the right side of the *Data Type* option box in the Formatting group, and then click *Short Text* at the drop-down list. limit the field size to 4 characters and rename the field as *EmpID*.

c. Apply the Yes/No data type to the second column, make the default value a check mark (by typing *Yes* at the expression builder dialog box), and provide the description *A check mark indicates the employee has signed up for the health plan.*

d. Apply the Yes/No data type to the third column, make the default value a check mark (by typing *Yes* at the Expression Builder dialog box), and provide the description *A check mark indicates the employee has signed up for the dental plan.*

e. Apply the Currency data type to the fourth column.

f. Apply the Short Text data type to the fifth column and limit the field size to 8 characters.

g. Type the data in each record as shown in Figure 1.17.

h. Automatically adjust the column widths.

i. Save the table and name it *Benefits*.

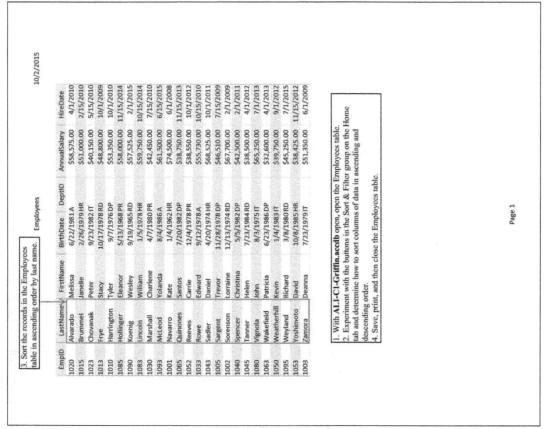

Absences   10/2/2015

AbsenceID	EmpID	Absent Date	Absent Reason
1	141	1/2/2015	Sick Day
2	141	1/5/2015	Sick Day
3	105	1/6/2015	Sick Day
4	163	1/9/2015	Sick Day
5	125	1/9/2015	Bereavement
6	125	1/12/2015	Bereavement
7	125	1/12/2015	Bereavement
8	117	1/13/2015	Sick Day
9	170	1/14/2015	Personal Day
10	153	1/16/2015	Sick Day
11	153	1/19/2015	Sick Day
12	103	1/19/2015	Personal Day
13	109	1/20/2015	Sick Day
14	109	1/22/2015	Sick Day
15	167	1/23/2015	Personal Day
16	138	1/29/2015	Sick Day
17	159	1/30/2015	Sick Day

Page 1

AL1-C1-VB-Griffen_AbsencesTable(VB).accdb

---

3. Sort the records in the Employees table in ascending order by last name.

Employees   10/2/2015

EmpID	LastName	FirstName	BirthDate	DeptID	AnnualSalary	HireDate
1020	Alvarado	Melissa	6/22/1981	A	$58,575.00	4/1/2010
1015	Brummel	Janelle	2/26/1979	HR	$51,000.00	2/15/2010
1023	Chovanak	Peter	9/23/1982	IT	$40,150.00	5/15/2010
1013	Frye	Stacy	10/17/1978	RD	$48,800.00	10/1/2009
1010	Harrington	Tyler	9/7/1976	DP	$53,350.00	10/1/2010
1085	Hollinger	Eleanor	5/13/1968	PR	$58,000.00	11/15/2014
1090	Koenig	Wesley	9/19/1965	RD	$57,525.00	2/1/2015
1083	Lincoln	William	1/5/1978	HR	$59,750.00	10/15/2014
1030	Marshall	Charlene	4/7/1980	PR	$42,450.00	7/15/2010
1093	McLeod	Yolanda	8/4/1986	A	$61,500.00	6/15/2015
1001	Navarro	Kate	1/4/1962	HR	$74,500.00	6/1/2008
1065	Quinones	Santos	7/20/1982	DP	$38,750.00	11/15/2013
1052	Reeves	Carrie	12/4/1978	PR	$38,550.00	10/1/2012
1033	Rowe	Edward	9/12/1978	A	$55,730.00	10/15/2010
1043	Sadler	Daniel	4/20/1974	HR	$68,525.00	10/1/2011
1005	Sargent	Trevor	11/28/1978	DP	$46,510.00	7/15/2009
1002	Sorenson	Lorraine	12/13/1974	RD	$67,700.00	2/1/2009
1040	Spencer	Christina	5/5/1982	DP	$42,500.00	2/1/2011
1045	Tanner	Helen	7/23/1984	RD	$38,500.00	4/1/2012
1080	Vignola	John	8/3/1975	IT	$65,250.00	7/1/2013
1063	Wakefield	Patricia	6/23/1986	DP	$32,600.00	4/1/2013
1050	Weatherhill	Kevin	1/4/1983	IT	$39,750.00	9/1/2012
1095	Weyland	Richard	3/8/1980	RD	$45,250.00	7/1/2015
1053	Yoshimoto	David	10/8/1985	HR	$38,425.00	11/15/2012
1003	Zamora	Deanna	7/23/1979	IT	$51,350.00	6/1/2009

1. With **AL1-C1-Griffin.accdb** open, open the Employees table.
2. Experiment with the buttons in the Sort & Filter group on the Home tab and determine how to sort columns of data in ascending and descending order.
4. Save, print, and then close the Employees table.

Page 1

AL1-C1-A4-Griffin_EmployeesTable(A4).accdb

Benchmark Access 2013 Level 1   Model Answers   79

Driver ID	Last Name	First Name	Address	City	State	ZIP Postal	Telephone	Cellphone
101	Brennan	Andrea	4438 Gowan Rd.	Las Vegas	NV	89115	(702) 555-3481	(702) 555-1322
114	Gould	Randall	330 Aura Ave.	Las Vegas	NV	89052	(702) 555-1239	(702) 555-7474
120	Martinelli	Albert	107 Cameo Dr.	Las Vegas	NV	89138	(702) 555-0349	(702) 555-6649
125	Nunez	Frank	4832 Helena St.	Las Vegas	NV	89129	(702) 555-3748	(702) 555-2210

AL1-C1-C1-CS-Elite_DriversTable(CS).accdb

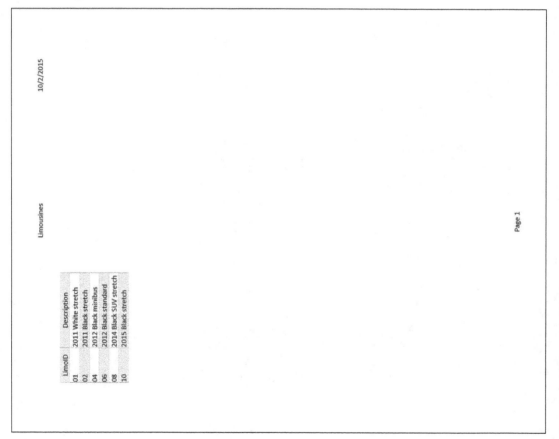

Limousines

10/2/2015

LimoID	Description
01	2011 White stretch
02	2011 Black stretch
04	2012 Black minibus
06	2012 Black standard
08	2014 Black SUV stretch
10	2015 Black stretch

Page 1

AL1-C1-CS-Elite_LimousinesTable(CS).accdb

Customers

10/2/2015

Customer ID	Last Name	First Name	Telephone	Cellphone
1001	Spencer	Maureen	(513) 555-3943	(513) 555-4884
1002	Tsang	Lee	(702) 555-4775	(702) 555-4211
1010	Chavez	Blake	(206) 555-3774	(206) 555-3006
1028	Gabriel	Nicholas	(612) 555-7885	(612) 555-7230
1031	Marshall	Patricia	(702) 555-6410	(702) 555-0137
1044	Vanderhage	Vernon	(213) 555-8846	(213) 555-4635

Page 1

AL1-C1-CS-Elite_CustomersTable(CS).accdb

Bookings

10/2/2015

Booking ID	Customer ID	Limo ID	Driver ID	Booking Date	Hours
1	1044	02	114	7/1/2015	6
2	1001	10	120	7/1/2015	8
3	1002	04	101	7/6/2015	8
4	1028	02	125	7/6/2015	4
5	1010	06	125	7/3/2015	3
6	1031	08	120	7/7/2015	5

Page 1

AL1-C1-CS-Elite_BookingsTable(CS).accdb

Access Level 1, Chapter 2 Model Answers

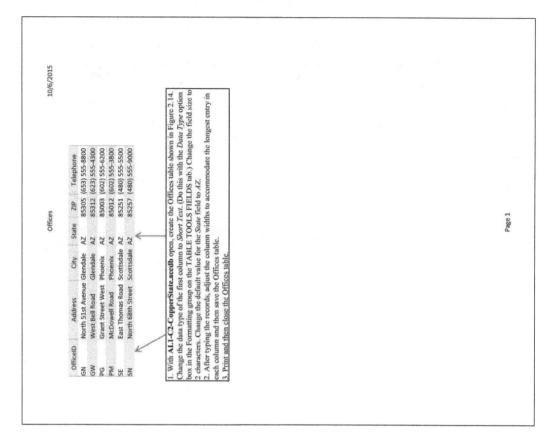

Offices

10/6/2015

OfficeID	Address	City	State	ZIP	Telephone
GN	North 51st Avenue	Glendale	AZ	85305	(653) 555-8800
GW	West Bell Road	Glendale	AZ	85312	(623) 555-4300
PG	Grant Street West	Phoenix	AZ	85003	(602) 555-6200
PM	McDowell Road	Phoenix	AZ	85012	(602) 555-3800
SE	East Thomas Road	Scottsdale	AZ	85251	(480) 555-5500
SN	North 68th Street	Scottsdale	AZ	85257	(480) 555-9000

1. With **AL1-C2-CopperState.accdb** open, create the Offices table shown in Figure 2.14. Change the data type of the first column to *Short Text*. (Do this with the *Data Type* option box in the Formatting group on the TABLE TOOLS FIELDS tab.) Change the field size to 2 characters. Change the default value for the *State* field to *AZ*.
2. After typing the records, adjust the column widths to accommodate the longest entry in each column and then save the Offices table.
3. Print and then close the Offices table.

Page 1

AL1-C2-A2-CopperState_OfficesTable(A2).accdb

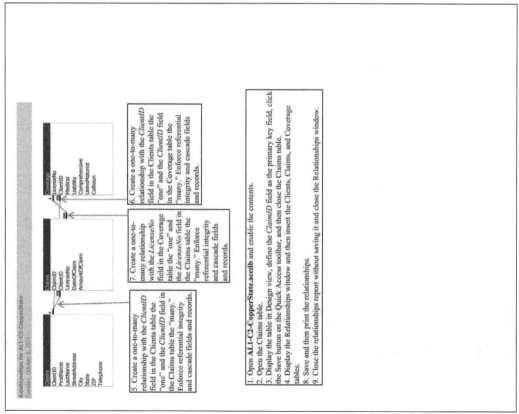

Relationships for AL1-C2-CopperState
Tuesday, October 6, 2015

5. Create a one-to-many relationship with the *ClientID* field in the Clients table the "one" and the *ClientID* field in the Claims table the "many." Enforce referential integrity and cascade fields and records.

7. Create a one-to-many relationship with the *LicenseNo* field in the Coverage table the "one" and the *LicenseNo* field in the Claims table the "many." Enforce referential integrity and cascade fields and records.

6. Create a one-to-many relationship with the *ClientID* field in the Clients table the "one" and the *ClientID* field in the Coverage table the "many." Enforce referential integrity and cascade fields and records.

1. Open **AL1-C2-CopperState.accdb** and enable the contents.
2. Open the Claims table.
3. Display the table in Design view, define the *ClaimID* field as the primary key field, click the Save button on the Quick Access toolbar, and then close the Claims table.
4. Display the Relationships window and then insert the Clients, Claims, and Coverage tables.
8. Save and then print the relationships.
9. Close the relationships report without saving it and close the Relationships window.

AL1-C2-A1-CopperState_Relationships(A1).accdb

82   *Benchmark Access 2013 Level 1* Model Answers

Clients   10/6/2015

ClientID	FirstName	LastName	StreetAddress	City	State	ZIP	Telephone
0214	Alice	Ryckman	84126 East Aldridge Drive	Phoenix	AZ	85009	(602) 555-788
1331	Erin	Hagedorn	4818 Oakes Boulevard	Phoenix	AZ	85018	(602) 555-489
1379	Claire	Azevedo	621 Pacific Avenue	Scottsdale	AZ	85260	(480) 555-215
1574	Joanne	Donnelly	13669 Panorama Drive	Glendale	AZ	85301	(623) 555-123
2768	Marcus	LeVigne	15676 North 32nd	Phoenix	AZ	85009	(602) 555-748
3120	Spenser	Winters	12304 132nd Street	Glendale	AZ	85310	(632) 555-456
3156	Brenda	Lazzuri	2014 North Highlands Road	Scottsdale	AZ	85266	(480) 555-466
3164	Bret	Mardock	193 Queens Way	Glendale	AZ	85310	(623) 555-319
3976	Joely	Lindhal	8809 South 142nd Street	Scottsdale	AZ	85260	(480) 555-791
2560	Paul	Vuong	3451 South Varner	Glendale	AZ	85308	(623) 555-467
4567	Bonnie	Metzger	7883 North Westridge	Scottsdale	AZ	85254	(480) 555-159
4786	Lenora	Chisham	22158 18th Avenue	Phoenix	AZ	85018	(602) 555-789
4852	Phillip	Cole	1456 Brookdale Drive	Glendale	AZ	85301	(623) 555-124
4868	Eric	Zadinski	1301 North Meridian	Phoenix	AZ	85031	(602) 555-648
4875	Michael	Nicolo	393 Lawrence Street	Scottsdale	AZ	85266	(480) 555-288
5231	Helena	Myerson	9032 45th Street East	Phoenix	AZ	85009	(602) 555-998
5645	Eileen	Hanley	9117 87th Street	Glendale	AZ	85310	(623) 555-741
5665	Suzanne	Lundberg	121 Hill Terrace Drive	Scottsdale	AZ	85254	(480) 555-317
5982	Alan	Couturier	78857 Gravelly Road	Scottsdale	AZ	85266	(480) 555-258
6478	Parma	Moreno	610 Sheridan Avenue	Phoenix	AZ	85031	(602) 555-458
7139	Donald	Rutledge	1878 Del Monte Avenue	Glendale	AZ	85301	(623) 555-311
7521	Fredrick	Guthrie	4905 Broadview Drive	Glendale	AZ	85301	(623) 555-486
8223	Cecilia	Ortiz	3730 Rodesco Road	Glendale	AZ	85308	(623) 555-166
8854	Edward	Bakalarski	184 Vandermark Lane	Scottsdale	AZ	85254	(480) 555-488
9383	Elaine	Hueneka	9088 Graham Road	Scottsdale	AZ	85260	(480) 555-789
9746	Carlos	Alvarez	48994 East Chestnut Road	Glendale	AZ	85308	(623) 555-247
9775	Carla	Waterman	3979 19th Avenue	Phoenix	AZ	85031	(602) 555-321
9872	Sun	Cheong	783 Marshall Circle	Scottsdale	AZ	85266	(480) 555-136
9897	Rachel	Kaelin	40778 Myers Road	Phoenix	AZ	85018	(602) 555-913

Page 1

AL1-C2-A3-CopperState_ClientsTable(A3).accdb

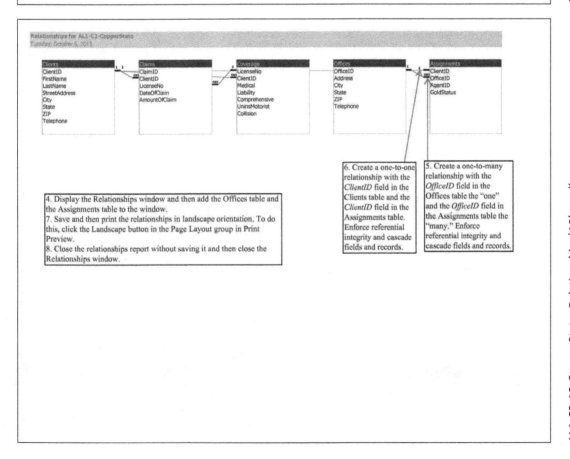

AL1-C2-A2-CopperState_Relationships(A2).accdb

2. Click the expand indicator (plus symbol) that displays at the left side of the record for Erin Hagedorn. At the Insert Subdatasheet dialog box, click *Claims* in the list box and then click OK.

3. Change the amount of the claim from *$1,450.00* to *$1,797.00*, change Erin's street address from *4818 Oakes Boulevard* to *763 51st Avenue*, and change her zip code from *85018* to *85014*.

4. Click the collapse indicator (minus symbol) that displays at the left side of the record for Erin Hagedorn.

9. Change the telephone number for Claire Azevedo (client number 1379) from *480-555-2154* to *480-555-2143* and insert check marks in the *Medical* field and the *UninsMotorist* field.

10. Change the last name of Joanne Donnelly (client number 1574) to *Marquez* and remove the check mark from the *Collision* field.

ClientID	FirstName	LastName	StreetAddress	City	State	ZIP	Telephone
0214	Alice	Ryckman	84126 East Aldridge Drive	Phoenix	AZ	85009	(602) 555-7887
1331	Erin	Hagedorn	763 51st Avenue	Phoenix	AZ	85014	(602) 555-4894
1379	Claire	Azevedo	621 Pacific Avenue	Scottsdale	AZ	85260	(480) 555-2143
1574	Joanne	Marquez	13669 Panorama Drive	Glendale	AZ	85301	(623) 555-1234
2560	Paul	Vuong	3451 South Varner	Glendale	AZ	85308	(623) 555-4674
2768	Marcus	LeVigne	15676 North 32nd	Phoenix	AZ	85009	(602) 555-7487
3120	Spenser	Winters	12304 132nd Street	Glendale	AZ	85310	(632) 555-4568
3156	Brenda	Lazzuri	2014 North Highlands Road	Scottsdale	AZ	85266	(480) 555-4668
3164	Bret	Mardock	193 Queens Way	Glendale	AZ	85310	(623) 555-3197
3976	Joely	Lindhal	8809 South 142nd Street	Scottsdale	AZ	85260	(480) 555-7918
4567	Bonnie	Metzger	7883 North Westridge	Scottsdale	AZ	85254	(480) 555-1596
4786	Lenora	Chisham	22158 18th Avenue	Phoenix	AZ	85018	(602) 555-7895
4852	Phillip	Cole	1456 Brookdale Drive	Glendale	AZ	85301	(623) 555-1247
4868	Eric	Zadinski	1301 North Meridian	Phoenix	AZ	85031	(602) 555-6485
4875	Michael	Nicolo	393 Lawrence Street	Scottsdale	AZ	85266	(480) 555-2885
5231	Helena	Myerson	9032 45th Street East	Phoenix	AZ	85009	(602) 555-9987
5645	Eileen	Hanley	9117 87th Street	Glendale	AZ	85310	(623) 555-7412
5665	Suzanne	Lundberg	121 Hill Terrace Drive	Scottsdale	AZ	85254	(480) 555-3179
5982	Alan	Couturier	78857 Gravelly Road	Scottsdale	AZ	85266	(480) 555-2582
6478	Parma	Moreno	610 Sheridan Avenue	Phoenix	AZ	85031	(602) 555-4582
7139	Donald	Rutledge	1878 Del Monte Avenue	Glendale	AZ	85301	(623) 555-3114
7521	Fredrick	Guthrie	4905 Broadview Drive	Glendale	AZ	85301	(623) 555-4862
8223	Cecilia	Ortiz	3730 Rodesco Road	Glendale	AZ	85308	(623) 555-1668
8854	Edward	Bakalarski	184 Vandermark Lane	Scottsdale	AZ	85254	(480) 555-4885
9383	Elaine	Hueneka	9088 Graham Road	Scottsdale	AZ	85260	(480) 555-7895
9746	Carlos	Alvarez	48994 East Chestnut Road	Glendale	AZ	85308	(623) 555-2471
9775	Carla	Waterman	3979 19th Avenue	Phoenix	AZ	85031	(602) 555-3215
9872	Sun	Cheong	783 Marshall Circle	Scottsdale	AZ	85266	(480) 555-1364
9897	Rachel	Kaelin	40778 Myers Road	Phoenix	AZ	85018	(602) 555-9137

1. With **AL1-C2-CopperState.accdb** open, open the Clients table.

5. Remove the connection between the Clients and Claims tables by clicking the more button in the Records group on the HOME tab, pointing to *Subdatasheet*, and then clicking *Remove*.

6. Click the more button in the Records group, point to *Subdatasheet*, and then click *Subdatasheet*.

7. At the Insert Subdatasheet dialog box, click *Coverage* in the list box and then click OK.

8. Expand all records by clicking the more button, pointing to *Subdatasheet*, and then clicking *Expand All*.

12. Click in any field heading and then collapse all records.

13. Remove the connection between the Clients and Coverage tables.

14. Save, print, and then close the Clients table. (make sure the table displays in landscape orientation.)

Page 1

10/6/2015

Claims

ClaimID	ClientID	LicenseNo	DateOfClaim	AmountOfClaim
102394	9383	776 ERU	1/9/2012	$1,235.00
121039	2560	877 BNN	2/3/2012	$5,230.00
136695	4567	937 PQX	2/27/2012	$1,840.00
147851	5982	823 IUN	2/1/2012	$3,250.50
147858	4875	734 APL	1/23/2012	$875.00
153001	9383	776 ERU	2/10/2012	$535.00
158954	1574	014 BZW	1/12/2012	$1,050.75
158962	8223	019 TMW	1/9/2012	$2,830.50
174223	8854	958 HGN	2/6/2012	$950.50
178545	2560	877 BNN	1/16/2012	$4,858.30
198745	1331	852 YRN	1/25/2012	$1,797.00
200147	6478	717 TUQ	1/25/2012	$925.75
210369	4868	154 EDC	1/12/2012	$2,675.00
211458	1574	014 BZW	2/27/2012	$1,645.50
241485	9775	362 PAZ	2/21/2012	$4,500.00
248210	8854	958 HGN	2/1/2012	$2,150.00

6. Open the Claims table, print the table, and then close the table. (The Claims table initially contained two entries for client number 9879 and one entry for 7335. These entries were deleted automatically when you deleted the records in the Clients table.)

Page 1

---

84   *Benchmark Access 2013 Level 1* Model Answers

Agents

AgentID	FirstName	LastName	OfficePhone	CellPhone	Office
103	Finn	Karamek	415-555-0078	415-555-3841	San Francisco
104	Marion	Bhayana	213-555-0906	323-555-3948	Los Angeles
107	Jenna	Parr	213-555-0939	562-555-3495	Los Angeles
108	Ryan	O'Donovan	905-555-4387	647-555-2847	Toronto
109	Wanda	Fournier	213-555-0911	415-555-8831	Toronto
110	William	Ashby	213-555-0905	562-555-1028	Los Angeles
112	Laurie	Redick	415-555-0054	323-555-3840	Los Angeles
114	Sylvia	El-Kerdi	415-555-0071	510-555-3185	San Francisco
115	Wayne	Postovic	213-555-0937	510-555-3921	San Francisco
123	Willow	Postovic	415-555-0052	310-555-3487	Los Angeles
125	Luanne	Redick	213-555-0922	415-555-9341	San Francisco
129	Seth	Mennill	905-555-4321	562-555-8738	Los Angeles
131	Rene	Forbrege	213-555-0931	647-555-4389	Toronto
134	Deanna	Lopez	905-555-4377	310-555-0349	Los Angeles
140	Vince	Doxtator	213-555-0932	647-555-1127	Los Angeles
142	Quin	De Papp	905-555-4352	323-555-4728	Los Angeles
144	Gloria	Sanderson		905-555-1834	Toronto

AL1-C2-VB-CarefreeTravel_AgentsTable(VB).accdb

> 10. Change the last name of Joanne Donnelly (client number 1574) to *Marquez* and remove the check mark from the *Collision* field.

> 11. At the record for Brenda Lazzuri (client number 3156), insert check marks in the *UninsMotorist* field and *Collision* field for both vehicles.

> 9. Change the telephone number for Claire Azevedo (client number 1379) from *480-555-2154* to *480-555-2143* and insert check marks in the *Medical* field and the *UninsMotorist* field.

LicenseNo	ClientID	Medical	Liability	Comprehensive	UninsMotorist	Collision
014 BZW	1574	✔		✔	✔	✔
019 TMW	8223	✔	✔		✔	✔
027 BWP	7139	✔	✔	✔	✔	✔
106 WRT	4786	✔	✔	✔	✔	✔
154 EDC	4868	✔	✔	✔	✔	✔
207 ZAR	9872	✔	✔	✔	✔	✔
273 BNE	9746		✔	✔	✔	✔
297 QES	7521	✔	✔	✔	✔	✔
310 YTV	3120	✔	✔	✔	✔	✔
328 BZS	3156	✔	✔	✔	✔	✔
341 BNV	8223			✔	✔	
341 VIT	3120	✔	✔	✔	✔	✔
349 IPN	4852	✔	✔	✔	✔	✔
362 PAZ	9775	✔	✔		✔	✔
387 GOE	2768	✔	✔	✔	✔	✔
439 PQC	1379		✔	✔	✔	✔
452 XOS	0214	✔	✔		✔	✔
458 IRD	5231	✔	✔	✔	✔	✔
473 GHM	3156	✔	✔	✔	✔	✔
489 WIF	9897		✔	✔	✔	✔
587 ERI	3976	✔	✔	✔	✔	✔
717 TUQ	6478	✔	✔	✔	✔	✔
734 APL	4875	✔	✔	✔	✔	✔
758 BQI	5645	✔	✔	✔	✔	✔
763 ARM	4852	✔	✔	✔	✔	✔
776 ERU	9383	✔	✔	✔	✔	✔
823 IUN	5982	✔	✔		✔	✔
852 YRN	1331	✔	✔	✔	✔	✔
877 BNN	2560	✔	✔	✔	✔	✔
923 HSC	5665	✔	✔		✔	✔
937 PQX	4567	✔	✔	✔	✔	✔
948 NLQ	3164	✔	✔		✔	✔
958 HGN	8854	✔	✔	✔	✔	✔
958 RMD	5645	✔	✔	✔	✔	✔

AL1-C2-A4-CopperState_CoverageTable(A4).accdb

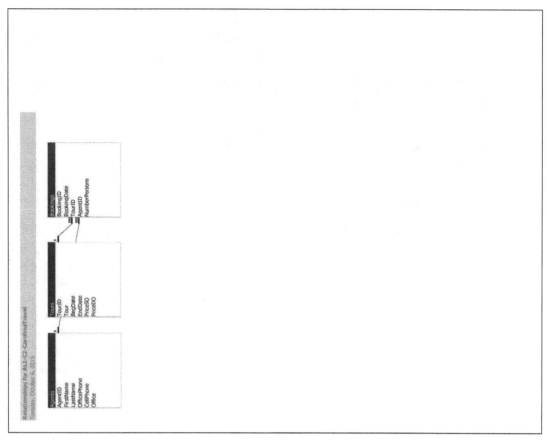

AL1-C2-VB-CarefreeTravel_Relationships(VB).accdb

Bookings

Booking Number	Booking Date	Tour ID	Agent ID	Number of People
1	6/1/2015	AF02	114	8
2	6/1/2015	HC01	109	2
3	6/3/2015	CR02	103	2
4	6/4/2015	AK01	137	4
5	6/5/2015	HC01	109	2
6	6/6/2015	AT02	109	4
7	6/8/2015	HS02	104	2
8	6/10/2015	HC01	125	2
9	6/11/2015	AK01	142	4
10	6/13/2015	AT01	112	2
11	6/15/2015	HC03	129	2

10/6/2015

AL1-C2-VB-CarefreeTravel_BookingsTable(VB,Step2).accdb

Client ID	Company Name	Address	City	State	ZIP	Company Contact	Telephone	Service ID	Rate ID
101	Smithson Realty	492 Papin Street	St Louis	MO	63108	Danielle Snowden	(314) 555-3588	GS-1	B
102	Air-Flow Systems	1058 Pine Street	St Louis	MO	63186	Nick Cline	(314) 555-9452	GS-3	A
107	Mainstreet Mortgage	North 22nd Street	St Louis	MO	63134	Ted Farrell	(314) 555-7744	GS-1	D
110	Firstline Finances	104 Scott Avenue	St Louis	MO	63126	Robert Styer	(314) 555-8343	GS-2	A
112	GB Construction	988 Lucas Avenue	St Louis	MO	63175	Joy Ewing	(314) 555-0036	GS-1	C
115	Simko Equipment	1200 Market Street	St Louis	MO	63140	Dale Aldrich	(314) 555-3315	GS-3	C

AL1-C2-Goldstar_ClientsTable(CS1).accdb

Client ID	Company Name	Address	City	State	ZIP	Company Contact	Telephone	Service ID	Rate ID
101	Smithson Realty	492 Papin Street	St Louis	MO	63108	Danielle Snowden	(314) 555-3588	GS-1	B
102	Air-Flow Systems	1058 Pine Street	St Louis	MO	63186	Nick Cline	(314) 555-9452	GS-3	A
107	Mainstreet Mortgage	North 22nd Street	St Louis	MO	63134	Ted Farrell	(314) 555-7744	GS-1	D
110	Firstline Finances	104 Scott Avenue	St Louis	MO	63126	Robert Styer	(314) 555-8343	GS-2	A
112	GB Construction	988 Lucas Avenue	St Louis	MO	63175	Joy Ewing	(314) 555-0036	GS-1	C
115	Simko Equipment	1200 Market Street	St Louis	MO	63140	Dale Aldrich	(314) 555-3315	GS-3	C

AL1-C2-VB-CarefreeTravel_BookingsTable(VB,Step10).accdb

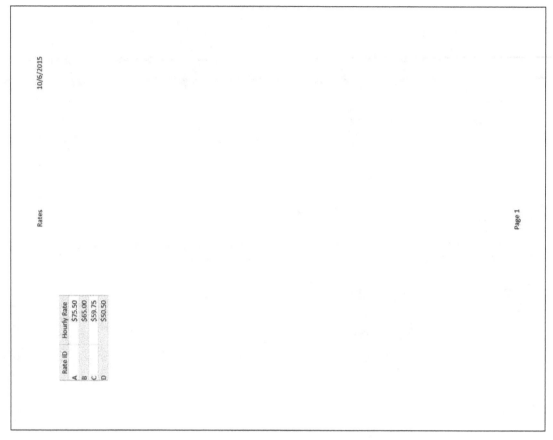

Rates

10/6/2015

Rate ID	Hourly Rate
A	$75.50
B	$65.00
C	$59.75
D	$50.50

Page 1

AL1-C2-Goldstar_RatesTable(CS1).accdb

Services

10/6/2015

Service ID	Service
GS-1	Deep cleaning all rooms and surfaces, garbage removal, recycling, carpet cleaning, disinfecting
GS-2	Deep cleaning all rooms and surfaces, garbage removal, disinfecting
GS-3	Deep cleaning all rooms and surfaces, disinfecting

Page 1

AL1-C2-Goldstar_ServicesTable(CS1).accdb

Clients
ClientID
CoName
Address
City
State
ZIP
Contact
Telephone
ServiceID
RateID

Services
ServiceID
Service

Rates
RateID
HrlyRate

Billing
BillingID
ClientID
BillingDate
RateID
TotalHours
Amount

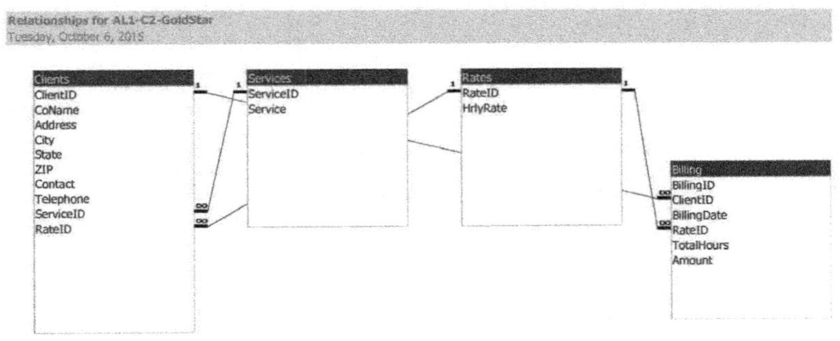

AL1-C2-Goldstar_Relationships(CS2).accdb

Billing
10/6/2015

BillingID	ClientID	BillingDate	RateID	TotalHours	Amount
40	101	4/1/2015	B	26	$1,690.00
41	102	4/1/2015	A	32	$2,416.00
42	107	4/1/2015	D	15	$747.50
43	110	4/1/2015	A	30	$2,265.00
44	112	4/1/2015	C	20	$1,195.00
45	115	4/1/2015	C	22	$1,314.50

AL1-C2-Goldstar_BillingTable(CS1).accdb

10/6/2015

Client ID	Company Name	Address	City	State	ZIP	Company Contact	Telephone	Service ID
101	Smithson Realty	492 Papin Street	St Louis	MO	63108	Danielle Snowden	(314) 555-3588	GS-A
102	Air-Flow Systems	1058 Pine Street	St Louis	MO	63186	Nick Cline	(314) 555-9452	GS-C
107	Mainstreet Mortgage	North 22nd Street	St Louis	MO	63134	Ted Farrell	(314) 555-7744	GS-A
110	Firstline Finances	104 Scott Avenue	St Louis	MO	63126	Robert Styer	(314) 555-8343	GS-B
115	Simko Equipment	1200 Market Street	St Louis	MO	63140	Dale Aldrich	(314) 555-3315	GS-C
108	Cedar Ridge Products	6400 Olive Street	St Louis	MO	63114	Penny Childers	(314) 555-7660	GS-B

Page 1

AL1-C2-Goldstar_ClientsTable(CS3).accdb (1 of 2)

10/6/2015

Service ID	Service
GS-A	Deep cleaning all rooms and surfaces, garbage removal, recycling, carpet cleaning, disinfecting
GS-B	Deep cleaning all rooms and surfaces, garbage removal, disinfecting
GS-C	Deep cleaning all rooms and surfaces, disinfecting

Page 1

AL1-C2-Goldstar_ServicesTable(CS3).accdb

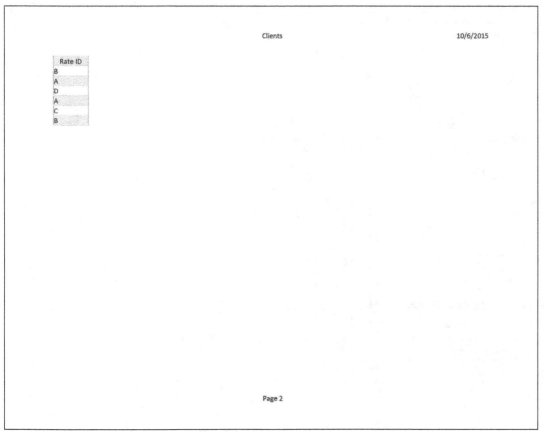

Billing   10/6/2015

BillingID	ClientID	BillingDate	RateID	TotalHours	Amount
40	101	4/1/2015	B	26	$1,690.00
41	102	4/1/2015	A	32	$2,416.00
42	107	4/1/2015	D	15	$747.50
43	110	4/1/2015	A	30	$2,265.00
45	115	4/1/2015	C	22	$1,314.50

Page 1

AL1-C2-Goldstar_BillingTable(CS3).accdb

Clients   10/6/2015

Rate ID
B
A
D
A
C
B

Page 2

AL1-C2-Goldstar_ClientsTable(CS3).accdb (2 of 2)

Access Level 1, Chapter 3 Model Answers

SECategoryBillingQuery   10/8/2015

BillingID	ClientID	CategoryID
2225		SE
5138		SE
10138		SE
12110		SE
14138		SE
19110		SE
21144		SE
24110		SE
29275		SE
37287		SE
40311		SE
43275		SE

1. Display the Open dialog box with the AL1C3 folder on your storage medium the active folder.
2. Open **AL1-C3-WarrenLegal.accdb** and enable the contents.
3. Design a query that extracts information from the Billing table with the following specifications: a. Include the fields *BillingID, ClientID,* and *CategoryID* in the query.
b. extract those records with the *SE* category. (Type "SE" in the *Criteria* row field in the *CategoryID* column. You need to type the quotation marks to tell Access that *Se* is a criterion and not a built-in Access function.)
c. Save the query and name it *SECategoryBillingQuery*. d. Print and then close the query.

Page 1

AL1-C3-A1-WarrenLegal_SECategoryBillingQuery(A1).accdb

June8-15BillingQuery   10/8/2015

BillingID	ClientID	Date
25	225	6/8/2015
26	187	6/8/2015
27	130	6/8/2015
29	275	6/9/2015
30	321	6/9/2015
31	205	6/9/2015
32	263	6/9/2015
33	143	6/9/2015
34	130	6/10/2015
35	129	6/10/2015
36	241	6/10/2015
37	287	6/10/2015
38	225	6/11/2015
39	303	6/11/2015
40	311	6/11/2015
41	116	6/11/2015
42	164	6/11/2015
43	275	6/12/2015
44	298	6/12/2015
45	255	6/12/2015
46	141	6/12/2015
47	321	6/12/2015
48	263	6/12/2015
49	217	6/15/2015
50	129	6/15/2015
51	157	6/15/2015
52	241	6/15/2015
53	129	6/15/2015

4. Design a query that extracts information from the Billing table with the following specifications:
a. Include the fields *BillingID, ClientID,* and *Date.*
b. extract those records in the *Date* field with dates between 6/8/2015 and 6/15/2015.
c. Save the query and name it *June8-15BillingQuery.*
d. Print and then close the query.

Page 1

AL1-C3-A1-WarrenLegal_June8-15BillingQuery(A1).accdb

92   *Benchmark Access 2013 Level 1*   Model Answers

BillingID	ClientID	Date	RateID	Rate
1	164	6/1/2015	3	$300.00
6	164	6/2/2015	3	$300.00
7	263	6/2/2015	3	$300.00
11	205	6/2/2015	3	$300.00
13	130	6/3/2015	3	$300.00
15	164	6/3/2015	3	$300.00
31	205	6/9/2015	3	$300.00
32	263	6/9/2015	3	$300.00
34	130	6/10/2015	3	$300.00
44	298	6/12/2015	3	$300.00
48	263	6/12/2015	3	$300.00
51	157	6/15/2015	3	$300.00
3	321	6/1/2015	4	$325.00
8	187	6/2/2015	4	$325.00
9	164	6/2/2015	4	$325.00
20	125	6/4/2015	4	$325.00
22	321	6/5/2015	4	$325.00
23	164	6/5/2015	4	$325.00
30	321	6/9/2015	4	$325.00
41	116	6/11/2015	4	$325.00
42	164	6/11/2015	4	$325.00

6. Design a query that extracts information from two tables with the following specifications:
a. Include the fields *BillingID, ClientID, Date,* and *RateID* from the Billing table.
b. Include the field *Rate* from the rates table.
c. extract those records with rate IDs greater than 2.
d. Save the query and name it *RateIDGreaterThan2Query*.
e. Print and then close the query.

AL1-C3-A1-WarrenLegal_RateIDGreaterThan2Query(A1).accdb

---

5. Design a query that extracts information from the Clients table with the following specifications:
a. Include the fields *FirstName, LastName,* and *City.*
b. extract those records with cities other than Kent in the *City* field.
c. Save the query and name it *ClientsNotInKentQuery*.
d. Print and then close the query.

FirstName	LastName	City
Margaret	Kasper	Auburn
Haley	Brown	Auburn
Doris	Sturtevant	Auburn
Maddie	Singh	Renton
Abigail	Jefferson	Auburn
Mira	Valencia	Renton
Matthew	Waide	Renton
Carlina	McFadden	Auburn
Arthur	Jefferson	Renton
Chris	Cervantez	Renton
Karl	Cordes	Renton
Jennifer	Czubek	Renton
Ewan	Aragato	Auburn
Charles	Hobart	Renton
Tricia	O'Connor	Auburn
Taylor	Reyes	Renton
Eric	Rosenthal	Auburn

AL1-C3-WarrenLegal_ClientsNotInKentQuery(A1).accdb

AttorneyID	First Name	Last Name	Category	RateID	Rate	Date	Hours
17	Kathleen	Jordan	Paternity	4	$325.00	6/2/2015	0.75
17	Kathleen	Jordan	Child Custody	4	$325.00	6/11/2015	1.50

8. Design a query that extracts information from four tables with the following specifications:
a. Include the fields *AttorneyID*, *FName*, and *LName* from the Attorneys table.
b. Include the field *Category* from the Categories table.
c. Include the fields *RateID* and *Rate* from the rates table.
d. Include the fields *Date* and *Hours* from the Billing table.
e. extract those records with an attorney ID of *17* and a rate ID of *4*.
f. Save the query and name it *Attorney17RateID4Query*.
g. Print the query in landscape orientation and then close the query.

AttorneyID	First Name	Last Name	FirstName	LastName	Date	Hours
12	Thomas	Zieger	Jennifer	Czubek	6/1/2015	1.75
12	Thomas	Zieger	Mira	Valencia	6/1/2015	0.50
12	Thomas	Zieger	Mira	Valencia	6/2/2015	0.75
12	Thomas	Zieger	Jennifer	Czubek	6/3/2015	2.00
12	Thomas	Zieger	Ewan	Aragato	6/4/2015	1.50
12	Thomas	Zieger	Carlina	McFadden	6/4/2015	1.00
12	Thomas	Zieger	Jennifer	Czubek	6/5/2015	0.50
12	Thomas	Zieger	James	Weyland	6/8/2015	1.50
12	Thomas	Zieger	Ewan	Aragato	6/10/2015	0.25
12	Thomas	Zieger	Jennifer	Czubek	6/11/2015	0.25
12	Thomas	Zieger	Consuelo	Day	6/12/2015	1.00
12	Thomas	Zieger	James	Weyland	6/15/2015	0.50
12	Thomas	Zieger	Ewan	Aragato	6/15/2015	0.25
12	Thomas	Zieger	James	Weyland	6/15/2015	0.50

7. Design a query that extracts information from three tables with the following specifications:
a. Include the fields *AttorneyID*, *FName*, and *LName* from the Attorneys table.
b. Include the fields *FirstName* and *LastName* from the Clients table.
c. Include the fields *Date* and *Hours* from the Billing table.
d. extract those records with an attorney ID of *12*.
e. Save the query and name it *Attorney12Query*.
f. Print and then close the query.

10/8/2015

Attorneys Query

AttorneyID	First Name	Last Name	Category	Hours
14	Marjorie	Shaw	Guardianship	1.00
14	Marjorie	Shaw	Guardianship	1.75
14	Marjorie	Shaw	Incorporation	0.75
14	Marjorie	Shaw	Guardianship	1.50
14	Marjorie	Shaw	Support Enforcement	2.00
14	Marjorie	Shaw	Incorporation	1.00
14	Marjorie	Shaw	Guardianship	1.50
14	Marjorie	Shaw	Support Enforcement	1.00
14	Marjorie	Shaw	Guardianship	1.25
14	Marjorie	Shaw	Support Enforcement	1.50
14	Marjorie	Shaw	Divorce	1.00
14	Marjorie	Shaw	Divorce	1.50
14	Marjorie	Shaw	Incorporation	1.00
14	Marjorie	Shaw	Incorporation	0.50
14	Marjorie	Shaw	Guardianship	1.00
14	Marjorie	Shaw	Incorporation	1.00
14	Marjorie	Shaw	Divorce	0.25
14	Marjorie	Shaw	Incorporation	0.25
14	Marjorie	Shaw	Divorce	1.50

1. With **AL1-C3-WarrenLegal.accdb** open, use the Simple Query Wizard to extract specific information from three tables with the following specifications:
a. At the first Simple Query Wizard dialog box, include the following fields: From Attorneys table: *AttorneyID, FName,* and *LName* From Categories table: *Category* From Billing table: *Hours*
b. At the second Simple Query Wizard dialog box, click Next.
c. At the third Simple Query Wizard dialog box, click the *Modify the query design* option and then click the Finish button.
d. At the query window, insert *14* in the *Criteria* row field in the *AttorneyID* column.
e. run the query.
f. Save the query with the default name.
g. Print and then close the query.

Page 1

Attorney17&19RateID4Query

10/8/2015

AttorneyID	First Name	Last Name	Category	RateID	Rate	Date	Hours
17	Kathleen	Jordan	Paternity	4	$325.00	6/2/2015	0.75
17	Kathleen	Jordan	Child Custody	4	$325.00	6/11/2015	1.50
19	Daniel	McKay	Child Custody	4	$325.00	6/1/2015	1.50
19	Daniel	McKay	Child Custody	4	$325.00	6/4/2015	1.50
19	Daniel	McKay	Child Custody	4	$325.00	6/5/2015	1.00
19	Daniel	McKay	Child Custody	4	$325.00	6/9/2015	1.50

9. Open the Attorney17rateID4Query query, click the View button on the HOME tab to display the query in Design view, and then modify the query so it displays records with a rate ID of *4* and attorney IDs of *17* and *19* by making the following changes:
a. Click below the field value *"17 "* in the *AttorneyID* column and then type 19.
b. Click below the field value *"4"* in the *RateID* column, type 4, and then press enter.
c. run the query.
d. Save the query with the new name *Attorney17&19RateID4Query. **Hint: Do this at the Save As dialog box. Display this dialog box by clicking the FILE tab, clicking the Save As option, clicking the Save Object As option, and then clicking the Save As button.***
e. Print the query in landscape orientation and then close the query.

Page 1

AttorneyHoursQuery

First Name	Last Name	AttorneyID	SumOfHours
Daniel	McKay	19	12
Kathleen	Jordan	17	12
Marjorie	Shaw	14	21.25
Thomas	Zieger	12	12.5

3. Create a query in Design view with the following specifications:
a. Add the Attorneys table and Billing table to the query window.
b. Insert the *FName* field from the *Attorneys* field list box to the first *Field* row field.
c. Insert the *LName* field from the *Attorneys* field list box to the second *Field* row field.
d. Insert the *AttorneyID* field from the *Billing* field list box to the third *Field* row field. (You will need to scroll down the *Billing* field list box to display the *AttorneyID* field.)
e. Insert the *Hours* field from the *Billing* field list box to the fourth *Field* row field.
f. Click the Totals button in the Show/Hide group.
g. Insert *Sum* in the fourth *Total* row field in the *Hours* column.
h. run the query.
i. Save the query and name it *AttorneyHoursQuery*.
j. Print and then close the query.

HoursAmountQuery

SumOfHours	MinOfHours	MaxOfHours	CountOfHours
57.75	0.25	2.25	53

2. Create a query in Design view with the Billing table with the following specifications: a. Insert the *Hours* field from the *Billing* field list box to the first, second, third, and fourth *Field* row fields.
b. Click the Totals button in the Show/Hide group.
c. Insert *Sum* in the first *Total* row field.
d. Insert *Min* in the second *Total* row field.
e. Insert *Max* in the third *Total* row field.
f. Insert *Count* in the fourth *Total* row field.
g. run the query.
h. Automatically adjust the widths of the columns.
i. Save the query and name it *HoursAmountQuery*.
j. Print and then close the query.

AttorneyClientHours   10/8/2015

AttorneyID	ClientID	Category	Hours
14	164	Guardianship	1.00
12	225	Support Enforcement	1.75
19	321	Child Custody	1.50
17	187	Paternity	2.00
12	138	Support Enforcement	0.50
14	164	Guardianship	1.75
14	263	Incorporation	0.75
17	187	Paternity	0.75
14	164	Guardianship	1.50
12	138	Support Enforcement	0.75
19	205	Paternity	1.00
14	110	Support Enforcement	2.00
14	130	Incorporation	1.00
12	138	Support Enforcement	2.00
14	164	Guardianship	1.50
19	321	Child Visitation	0.75
12	225	Child Visitation	1.50
12	241	Guardianship	1.00
14	110	Support Enforcement	1.00
19	125	Child Custody	1.50
12	144	Support Enforcement	0.25
19	321	Child Custody	1.00
14	164	Guardianship	1.25
14	110	Support Enforcement	1.50
12	225	Child Visitation	0.50
17	187	Paternity	2.00
14	130	Divorce	1.50
14	255	Divorce	2.25
17	275	Support Enforcement	1.50
19	321	Child Custody	1.00
19	205	Paternity	1.00
14	263	Incorporation	1.00
17	143	Adoption	0.50
14	130	Incorporation	1.50
12	129	Divorce	0.25
12	241	Guardianship	1.00
17	287	Support Enforcement	0.25
12	225	Child Visitation	1.50
19	303	Divorce	1.00
17	311	Support Enforcement	1.50
14	116	Guardianship	1.00
17	275	Support Enforcement	0.50

4. Create a query in Design view with the following specifications:

a. Add the Attorneys, Clients, Categories, and Billing tables to the query window.
b. Insert the *AttorneyID* field from the *Attorneys* field list box to the first *Field* row field. c. Insert the *ClientID* field from the *Clients* field list box to the second *Field* row field.
d. Insert the *Category* field from the *Categories* field list box to the third *Field* row field. e. Insert the *Hours* field from the *Billing* field list box to the fourth *Field* row field.
f. run the query.
g. Save the query and name it *AttorneyClientHours*.
h. Print and then close the query.

AttorneyClientHours   10/8/2015

AttorneyID	ClientID	Category	Hours
14	298	Incorporation	1.00
14	255	Divorce	0.25
12	141	Guardianship	1.00
19	321	Child Custody	1.25
14	263	Incorporation	0.25
19	217	Child Visitation	1.00
12	129	Divorce	0.50
14	157	Divorce	1.50
12	241	Guardianship	0.25
12	129	Divorce	0.50

LastName	ClientID	FirstName	StreetAddress	City	State	ZipCode	Telephone
Day	321	Jeffrey	317 Meridian Street	Kent	WA	98033	(253) 555-3129
Day	141	Consuelo	13321 North Lake Drive	Kent	WA	98036	(253) 555-0998
Jefferson	157	Arthur	23110 North 33rd Street	Renton	WA	98230	(253) 555-4889
Jefferson	130	Abigail	1204 Meridian Road	Auburn	WA	98001	(253) 555-5665

2. Use the Find Duplicates Query Wizard to find those clients with the same last name with the following specifications:
a. At the first wizard dialog box, click *Table: Clients* in the list box.
b. At the second wizard dialog box, click *LastName* in the *Available fields* list box and then click the One Field button.
c. At the third wizard dialog box, click the All Fields button.
d. At the fourth wizard dialog box, name the query *DuplicateLastNamesQuery*.
e. Print the query in landscape orientation and then close the query.

AL1-C3-A3-Warren_Legal_DuplicateLastNamesQuery(A3).accdb

AttorneyID	Total Of Hours	Adoption	Child Custody	Child Visitation	Divorce	Guardianship	Incorporation	Paternity	Support Enforce
12	12.5			2.25	2.5	2.5			5.25
14	21.25				4.25	8	4.5		4.5
17	12	1	1.5					4.75	4.75
19	12		6.75	1.75	1.5			2	

1. With **AL1-C3-WarrenLegal.acedb** open, create a crosstab query that summarizes the hours by attorney by category with the following specifications:
a. At the first Crosstab Query Wizard dialog box, click the *Queries* option in the *View* section and then click *Query: AttorneyClientHours* in the list box.
b. At the second Crosstab Query Wizard dialog box with *AttorneyID* selected in the *Available Fields* list box, click the One Field button.
c. At the third Crosstab Query Wizard dialog box, click *Category* in the list box.
d. At the fourth Crosstab Query Wizard dialog box, click *Hours* in the *Fields* list box and click *Sum* in the *Functions* list box.
e. At the fifth Crosstab Query Wizard dialog box, select the current name in the *What do you want to name your query?* text box and then type HoursByAttorneyByCategory.
f. Display the query in Print Preview, change to landscape orientation, change the left and right margins to 0.5 inch, and then print the query.
g. Close the query.

AL1-C3-A3-Warren_Legal_HoursByAttorneyByCategory(A3).accdb

ClientBillingQuery   10/8/2015

1c. Insert in the fifth *Field* row field the calculated field *Total:[Hours]*[Rate]*.

1. You can use the check boxes in the query design grid *Show* row to show or hide fields in the query. Experiment with these check boxes and then with **AL1-C3-WarrenLegal.accdb** open design the following query:
a. At the Show Table dialog box, add the Clients table, the Billing table, and the Rates table.
b. At the query window, insert the following fields in *Field* row fields: Clients table: *FirstName LastName* Billing table: *Hours* Rates table: *Rate* fields.
d. Hide the *Hours* and *Rate* fields.
e. Run the query.
f. Save the query and name it *ClientBillingQuery*.

FirstName	LastName	Total
Jean	Briggs	300
Jennifer	Czubek	350
Jeffrey	Day	487.5
Chris	Cervantez	500
Mira	Valencia	100
Jean	Briggs	525
Charles	Hobart	225
Chris	Cervantez	243.75
Jean	Briggs	487.5
Mira	Valencia	187.5
Karl	Cordes	300
Margaret	Kasper	400
Abigail	Jefferson	300
Mira	Valencia	400
Jean	Briggs	450
Jeffrey	Day	150
Jennifer	Czubek	300
Ewan	Aragato	250
Margaret	Kasper	200
Maddie	Singh	487.5
Carlina	McFadden	50
Jeffrey	Day	325
Jean	Briggs	406.25
Margaret	Kasper	300
Jennifer	Czubek	100
Chris	Cervantez	500
Abigail	Jefferson	250
Janice	Saunders	375
Tricia	O'Connor	450
Jeffrey	Day	487.5
Karl	Cordes	300
Charles	Hobart	300
Matthew	Waide	250
Abigail	Jefferson	150
James	Weyland	375
Ewan	Aragato	62.5
Taylor	Reyes	200
Jennifer	Czubek	50
Eric	Rosenthal	375
Carol	Kendall	200
Kevin	Stein	487.5
Jean	Briggs	325
Tricia	O'Connor	100

Page 1

Clients Without Matching Billing   10/8/2015

ClientID	FirstName	LastName	StreetAddress	City	State	ZipCode	Telephone
112	Haley	Brown	3219 North 33rd Street	Auburn	WA	98001	(253) 555-3948
121	Doris	Sturtevant	3713 Nelton Road	Auburn	WA	98001	(253) 555-3120
230	Christina	Miles	13043 South 25th Avenue	Kent	WA	98036	(253) 555-9904

3. Use the Find Unmatched Query Wizard to find all clients who do not have any billing hours with the following specifications:
a. At the first wizard dialog box, click *Table: Clients* in the list box.
b. At the second wizard dialog box, click *Table: Billing* in the list box.
c. At the third wizard dialog box, make sure *ClientID* is selected in both the *Fields in 'Clients'* list box and in the *Fields in 'Billing'* list box.
d. At the fourth wizard dialog box, click the All Fields button to move all fields from the *Available fields* list box to the *Selected fields* list box.
e. At the fifth wizard dialog box, click the Finish button. (Let the wizard determine the query name: *Clients Without Matching Billing*.)
4. Print the query in landscape orientation and then close the query.

Page 1

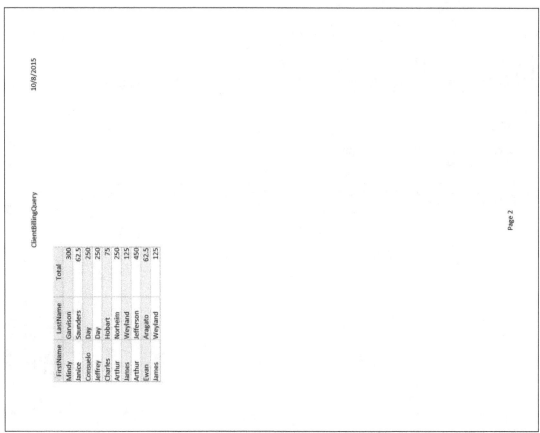

Relationships for AL1-C3-MRInvestments
Thursday, October 8, 2015

Absences
AbsenceID
EmpID
AbsenceDate
AbsenceReason

Benefits
EmpID
HealthPlan
DentalPlan
LifeInsce
Vacation

Employees
EmpID
LastName
FirstName
BirthDate
AnnualSalary
HireDate
DeptID

Departments
DeptID
Department

AL1-C3-VB-MRInvestments_Relationships(VB).accdb

ClientBillingQuery   10/8/2015

FirstName	LastName	Total
Mindy	Garvison	300
Janice	Saunders	62.5
Consuelo	Day	250
Jeffrey	Day	250
Charles	Hobart	75
Arthur	Norheim	250
James	Weyland	125
Arthur	Jefferson	450
Ewan	Aragato	62.5
James	Weyland	125

Page 2

AL1-C3-A4-Warren_Legal_ClientBillingQuery(A4).accdb (2 of 2)

Benchmark Access 2013 Level 1 Model Answers

Relationships for AL1-C3-Skyline
Thursday, October 8, 2015

Employees
EmployeeID
FName
LName
StreetAddress
City
State
ZipCode
Telephone
HireDate

Events
EventID
Event

Banquets
ReservationID
EmployeeID
ResDate
FirstName
LastName
Telephone
EventID
AmountTotal
AmountPaid

Inventory
ItemID
Item
SupplierID
Unit

Orders
OrderID
ItemID
UnitsOrdered
UnitPrice
OrderDate
SupplierID

Suppliers
SupplierID
SupplierName
ContactName
StreetAddress
City
State
ZipCode
Telephone

AL1-C3-CS-Skyline_Relationships(CS1).accdb

10/8/2015

EmployeeSalaryOver$50000InPR&RDQuery

FirstName	LastName	AnnualSalary	Department
Mary	Vanderhoff	$59,750.00	Public Relations
Blaine	Kaiser	$64,500.00	Public Relations
Sally	Farrell	$58,000.00	Public Relations
Glenn	Ishimoto	$68,525.00	Research and Development
Brett	Dupree	$58,550.00	Research and Development

Page 1

AL1-C3-VB-MRInvestments_EmployeeSalaryOver$50000InPR&RDQuery(VB).accdb

SuppliersInFortMyersQuery   10/8/2015

SupplierID	SupplierName	City	Telephone
2	Coral Produce	Fort Myers	(239) 555-3455
3	Meridian Bakery	Fort Myers	(239) 555-1220
5	Sunshine Dairy	Fort Myers	(239) 555-4400

Page 1

AL1-C3-CS-Skyline_SuppliersInFortMyersQuery(CS2).accdb

SuppliersNotInFortMyersQuery   10/8/2015

SupplierID	SupplierName	City	Telephone
1	Frannie's Fish Market	Cape Coral	(239) 555-3743
4	Grocery Wholesalers	Sarasota	(941) 555-7722
6	Moreland Products	Sarasota	(941) 555-3411
7	Myers Meat Wholesalers	Sarasota	(941) 555-8394

Page 1

AL1-C3-CS-Skyline_SuppliersNotInMyersQuery(CS2).accdb

Benchmark Access 2013 Level 1 Model Answers

EmployeesHiredIn2012Query

10/8/2015

EmployeeID	FName	LName	HireDate
05	Michelle	Zachary	2/10/2012
07	Donald	Sellars	6/6/2012
10	Marilyn	Sundstrom	11/1/2012

Page 1

EmployeesWithHealthInsuranceQuery

10/8/2015

FName	LName	HealthIns
Heather	Montgomery	✔
Vadim	Sayenko	✔
Tamara	Overfield	✔
Donald	Sellars	✔
Elizabeth	Mohr	✔
Marilyn	Sundstrom	✔
Dennis	Adkins	✔

Page 1

BanqResBetweenJune14-30Query 10/8/2015

ReservationID	ResDate	FirstName	LastName	Telephone	FName	LName
12	6/14/2015	Aaron	Williams	(239) 555-3821	Vadim	Sayenko
13	6/14/2015	Willow	Earhart	(239) 555-0034	Vadim	Sayenko
14	6/16/2015	Jason	Haley	(239) 555-6641	Tamara	Overfield
15	6/17/2015	Lillian	Krakosky	(239) 555-8890	Owen	Pasqual
16	6/18/2015	Mallory	Satter	(239) 555-8512	Vadim	Sayenko
17	6/18/2015	Heidi	Thompson	(941) 555-3215	Heather	Montgomery
18	6/19/2015	Anthony	Wiegand	(239) 555-7853	Nicole	Bateman
19	6/19/2015	Julio	Rivas	(239) 555-9977	Michelle	Zachary
20	6/20/2015	Robin	Gehring	(239) 555-0126	Tamara	Overfield
21	6/20/2015	David	Fitzgerald	(941) 555-3792	Heather	Montgomery
22	6/27/2015	Shane	Rozier	(239) 555-1033	Dennis	Adkins
23	6/27/2015	Kirsten	Simpson	(941) 555-4425	Wayne	Weber

Page 1

AL1-C3-CS-Skyline_BanqResBetweenJune14-30Query(CS2).accdb

WeddingReceptionsBookedQuery 10/8/2015

ReservationID	ResDate	EventID	FirstName	LastName	Telephone
2	6/5/2015	WR	Andrea	Wyatt	(239) 555-4282
10	6/13/2015	WR	Janis	Semala	(239) 555-0476
16	6/18/2015	WR	Mallory	Satter	(239) 555-8512
19	6/19/2015	WR	Julio	Rivas	(239) 555-9977

Page 1

AL1-C3-CS-Skyline_WeddingReceptionsBookedQuery(CS2).accdb

WieReservationQuery   10/8/2015

FName	LName	FirstName	LastName	Telephone
Nicole	Bateman	Anthony	Wiegand	(239) 555-7853

Page 1

AL1-C3-CS-Skyline_WieReservationQuery(CS2).accdb

UnconfirmedReservationsQuery   10/8/2015

ReservationID	ResDate	Confirmed	FirstName	LastName	FName	LName
3	6/6/2015	☐	Luis	Castillo	Nicole	Bateman
5	6/7/2015	☐	Bridget	Kohn	Wayne	Weber
7	6/12/2015	☐	Tim	Drysdale	Wayne	Weber
9	6/12/2015	☐	Cliff	Osborne	Dennis	Adkins
11	6/13/2015	☐	Tristan	Strauss	Owen	Pasqual
14	6/16/2015	☐	Jason	Haley	Tamara	Overfield
15	6/17/2015	☐	Lillian	Krakosky	Owen	Pasqual
18	6/19/2015	☐	Anthony	Wiegand	Nicole	Bateman
21	6/20/2015	☐	David	Fitzgerald	Heather	Montgomery
23	6/27/2015	☐	Kirsten	Simpson	Wayne	Weber

Page 1

AL1-C3-CS-Skyline_UnconfirmedReservationsQuery(CS2).accdb

UnitsOrderedFromSupplier2Query   10/8/2015

OrderID	SupplierID	UnitsOrdered	UnitPrice	Item	Total
06-001	2	3	$10.50	Potatoes	$31.50
06-010	2	2	$10.95	Onions	$21.90
06-005	2	2	$15.75	Green beans	$31.50
06-031	2	2	$15.75	Green beans	$31.50
06-003	2	1	$24.00	Iceberg lettuce	$24.00
06-029	2	2	$39.40	Iceberg lettuce	$78.80
06-022	2	1	$31.00	Cantaloupes	$31.00
06-028	2	2	$11.25	Relish	$22.50

Page 1

AL1-C3-CS-Skyline_UnitsOrderedFromSupplier2Query(CS2).accdb

DuplicateItemsOrderedQuery   10/8/2015

ItemID	OrderID	UnitsOrdered	UnitPrice	OrderDate	SupplierID
014	06-031	2	$15.75	6/29/2015	2
014	06-005	2	$15.75	6/4/2015	2
016	06-029	2	$39.40	6/25/2015	2
016	06-003	1	$24.00	6/4/2015	2
020	06-032	2	$18.75	6/29/2015	4
020	06-004	2	$18.75	6/4/2015	4
033	06-033	1	$33.50	6/29/2015	1
033	06-002	1	$73.50	6/1/2015	1
035	06-030	1	$17.00	6/29/2015	4
035	06-011	1	$17.00	6/11/2015	4

Page 1

AL1-C3-CS-Skyline_DuplicateItemsOrderedQuery(CS3).accdb

OrderAmountsBySupplierQuery   10/8/2015

SupplierID	Total Of UnitPri	002	003	004	012	013	014	016	018
1	$208.50								
2	$158.60	$10.50		$10.95			$31.50	$63.40	
3	$89.90								
4	$271.25				$30.25	$14.00			$45.00
6	$64.00		$7.25						
7	$490.00								

Page 1

EmployeesWithoutBanqResQuery   10/8/2015

EmployeeID	FName	LName	StreetAddress	City	State	ZipCode	Telephone	HireDate	HealthIns
07	Donald	Sellars	23103 Summer Highway	Fort Myers	FL	33919	(239) 555-4348	6/6/2012	✔
08	Christopher	Tappan	704 Tenth Street	Lehigh Acres	FL	33970	(239) 555-1022	10/8/2010	☐
09	Elizabeth	Mohr	1818 Brookdale Road	Fort Myers	FL	33902	(239) 555-0430	5/1/2011	✔
10	Marilyn	Sundstrom	3482 68th Avenue	Cape Coral	FL	33914	(239) 555-8155	11/1/2012	✔

Page 1

OrderAmountsBySupplierQuery   10/8/2015

033	034	035	036	037	039	040	041	044	053
$107.00									
				$11.25					
					$3.50	$4.95			$52.00
	$13.75	$34.00	$17.00						
							$6.50	$50.25	

Page 3

OrderAmountsBySupplierQuery   10/8/2015

020	021	022	023	025	026	027	028	030	032
									$101.50
	$31.00								
		$16.50	$12.95						
$37.50				$28.50	$29.25	$22.00			
							$315.00	$175.00	

Page 2

Benchmark Access 2013 Level 1 Model Answers

Access Level 1, Chapter 4 Model Answers

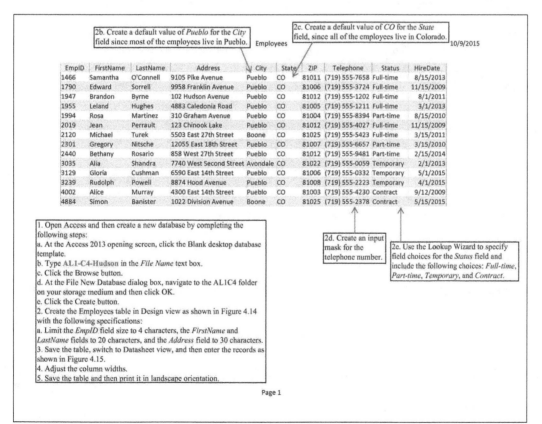

6. Switch to Design view and then add a row immediately above the *FirstName* row. Type Title in the *Field Name* field, limit the field size to 20 characters, and type the description Enter employee job title.

Employees   10/9/2015

EmpID	Status	Title	FirstName	LastName	Address	City	State	ZIP	Telephone
1466	Full-time	Design Director	Samantha	O'Connell	9105 Pike Avenue	Pueblo	CO	81011	(719) 555-7658
1790	Full-time	Assistant	Edward	Sorrell	9958 Franklin Avenue	Pueblo	CO	81006	(719) 555-3724
1947	Full-time	Resources Director	Brandon	Byrne	102 Hudson Avenue	Pueblo	CO	81012	(719) 555-1202
1955	Full-time	Accountant	Leland	Hughes	4883 Caledonia Road	Pueblo	CO	81005	(719) 555-1211
1994	Part-time	Assistant	Rosa	Martinez	310 Graham Avenue	Pueblo	CO	81004	(719) 555-8394
2019	Full-time	Production Director	Jean	Perrault	123 Chinook Lake	Pueblo	CO	81012	(719) 555-4027
2120	Full-time	Assistant	Michael	Turek	5503 East 27th Street	Boone	CO	81025	(719) 555-5423
2301	Part-time	Assistant	Gregory	Nitsche	12055 East 18th Street	Pueblo	CO	81007	(719) 555-6657
2440	Part-time	Assistant	Bethany	Rosario	858 West 27th Street	Pueblo	CO	81012	(719) 555-9481
3035	Temporary	Clerk	Alia	Shandra	7740 West Second Street	Avondale	CO	81022	(719) 555-0059
3129	Temporary	Clerk	Gloria	Cushman	6590 East 14th Street	Pueblo	CO	81006	(719) 555-0332
3239	Temporary	Assistant	Rudolph	Powell	8874 Hood Avenue	Pueblo	CO	81008	(719) 555-2223
4002	Contract	Contractor	Alice	Murray	4300 East 14th Street	Pueblo	CO	81003	(719) 555-4230
4884	Contract	Contractor	Simon	Banister	1022 Division Avenue	Boone	CO	81025	(719) 555-2378

11c. Apply the Aqua Blue 2 alternating row color (ninth column, third row in the *Standard Colors* section) to the table.

8. Move the *Status* field so it is positioned between the *EmpID* row and the *Title* row.

11b. Center the data in the *EmpID* field column and the *State* field column.

7. Delete the *HireDate* field.
9. Save the table and then switch to Datasheet view.
10. Enter the following information in the *Title* field:

EmpID Title	EmpID Title
1466 Design Director	2301 Assistant
1790 Assistant	2440 Assistant
1947 Resources Director	3035 Clerk
1955 Accountant	3129 Clerk
1994 Assistant	3239 Assistant
2019 Production Director	4002 Contractor
2120 Assistant	4884 Contractor

11. Apply the following text formatting to the table:
a. Change the font to Arial and the font size to 10 points.
12. Adjust the column widths.
13. Save the table and then print it in landscape orientation with left and right margins of 0.5 inch.

AL1-C4-A1-Hudson_EmployeesTable(A1,Step13).accdb

2b. Create a default value of *Pueblo* for the *City* field since most of the employees live in Pueblo.

2c. Create a default value of *CO* for the *State* field, since all of the employees live in Colorado.

Employees   10/9/2015

EmpID	FirstName	LastName	Address	City	State	ZIP	Telephone	Status	HireDate
1466	Samantha	O'Connell	9105 Pike Avenue	Pueblo	CO	81011	(719) 555-7658	Full-time	8/15/2013
1790	Edward	Sorrell	9958 Franklin Avenue	Pueblo	CO	81006	(719) 555-3724	Full-time	11/15/2009
1947	Brandon	Byrne	102 Hudson Avenue	Pueblo	CO	81012	(719) 555-1202	Full-time	8/1/2011
1955	Leland	Hughes	4883 Caledonia Road	Pueblo	CO	81005	(719) 555-1211	Full-time	3/1/2013
1994	Rosa	Martinez	310 Graham Avenue	Pueblo	CO	81004	(719) 555-8394	Part-time	8/15/2010
2019	Jean	Perrault	123 Chinook Lake	Pueblo	CO	81012	(719) 555-4027	Full-time	11/15/2009
2120	Michael	Turek	5503 East 27th Street	Boone	CO	81025	(719) 555-5423	Full-time	3/15/2011
2301	Gregory	Nitsche	12055 East 18th Street	Pueblo	CO	81007	(719) 555-6657	Part-time	3/15/2010
2440	Bethany	Rosario	858 West 27th Street	Pueblo	CO	81012	(719) 555-9481	Part-time	2/15/2014
3035	Alia	Shandra	7740 West Second Street	Avondale	CO	81022	(719) 555-0059	Temporary	2/1/2014
3129	Gloria	Cushman	6590 East 14th Street	Pueblo	CO	81006	(719) 555-0332	Temporary	5/1/2015
3239	Rudolph	Powell	8874 Hood Avenue	Pueblo	CO	81008	(719) 555-2223	Temporary	4/1/2015
4002	Alice	Murray	4300 East 14th Street	Pueblo	CO	81003	(719) 555-4230	Contract	9/12/2009
4884	Simon	Banister	1022 Division Avenue	Boone	CO	81025	(719) 555-2378	Contract	5/15/2015

2d. Create an input mask for the telephone number.

2e. Use the Lookup Wizard to specify field choices for the *Status* field and include the following choices: *Full-time, Part-time, Temporary,* and *Contract.*

1. Open Access and then create a new database by completing the following steps:
a. At the Access 2013 opening screen, click the Blank desktop database template.
b. Type AL1-C4-Hudson in the *File Name* text box.
c. Click the Browse button.
d. At the File New Database dialog box, navigate to the AL1C4 folder on your storage medium and then click OK.
e. Click the Create button.
2. Create the Employees table in Design view as shown in Figure 4.14 with the following specifications:
a. Limit the *EmpID* field size to 4 characters, the *FirstName* and *LastName* fields to 20 characters, and the *Address* field to 30 characters.
3. Save the table, switch to Datasheet view, and then enter the records as shown in Figure 4.15.
4. Adjust the column widths.
5. Save the table and then print it in landscape orientation.

Page 1

AL1-C4-A1-Hudson_EmployeesTable(A1,Step5).accdb

10/9/2015

Projects

ProjID	EmpID	BegDate	EndDate	EstCosts
08-A	2019	8/1/2015	10/31/2015	$5,250.00
08-B	1466	8/15/2015	12/15/2015	$2,000.00
10-A	1947	10/1/2015	1/15/2016	$10,000.00
10-B	2019	10/1/2015	12/15/2015	$35,000.00
11-A	1466	11/1/2015	2/1/2016	$8,000.00
11-B	1947	11/1/2015	3/31/2016	$12,000.00

1. With **AL1-C4-Hudson.accdb** open, create a Projects table in Design view. Include the following fields (making sure the *ProjID* field is identified as the primary key) and create an appropriate description for each field:

Field Name Data Type
ProjID Short Text (field size = 4 characters)
EmpID Short Text (field size = 4 characters)
BegDate Date/Time
EndDate Date/Time
EstCosts Currency

2. Save the table, switch to Datasheet view, and then type the following data in the specified field:

ProjID 08-A *ProjID* 08-B
EmpID 2019 *EmpID* 1466
BegDate 8/1/2015 *BegDate* 8/15/2015
EndDate 10/31/2015 *EndDate* 12/15/2015
EstCosts $5,250.00 *EstCosts* $2,000.00
ProjID 10-A *ProjID* 10-B
EmpID 1947 *EmpID* 2019
BegDate 10/1/2015 *BegDate* 10/1/2015
EndDate 1/15/2016 *EndDate* 12/15/2015
EstCosts $10,000.00 *EstCosts* $35,500.00
ProjID 11-A *ProjID* 11-B
EmpID 1466 *EmpID* 1947
BegDate 11/1/2015 *BegDate* 11/1/2015
EndDate 2/1/2016 *EndDate* 3/31/2016
EstCosts $8,000.00 *EstCosts* $12,000.00

3. Adjust the column widths.
4. Save, print, and then close the Projects table.

Page 1

AL1-C4-A2-Hudson_ProjectsTable(A2).accdb

---

14. Find all occurrences of *Director* and replace them with *Manager*.
Hint: Position the insertion point in the first entry in the Title column and then display the Find and Replace dialog box. At the dialog box, change the Match option to Any Part of Field.

Employees

10/9/2015

EmpID	Status	Title	FirstName	LastName	Address	City	State	ZIP	Telephone
1466	Full-time	Design Manager	Samantha	O'Connell	9105 Pike Avenue	Pueblo	CO	81011	(719) 555-7658
1790	Full-time	Associate	Edward	Sorrell	9958 Franklin Avenue	Pueblo	CO	81006	(719) 555-3724
1947	Full-time	Resources Manager	Brandon	Byrne	102 Hudson Avenue	Pueblo	CO	81012	(719) 555-1202
1955	Full-time	Accountant	Leland	Hughes	4883 Caledonia Road	Pueblo	CO	81005	(719) 555-1211
1994	Part-time	Associate	Rosa	Martinez	310 Graham Avenue	Pueblo	CO	81004	(719) 555-8394
2019	Full-time	Production Manager	Jean	Perrault	123 Chinook Lake	Pueblo	CO	81012	(719) 555-4027
2120	Full-time	Associate	Michael	Turek	5503 East 27th Street	Boone	CO	81025	(719) 555-5423
2301	Part-time	Associate	Gregory	Nitsche	12055 East 18th Street	Pueblo	CO	81007	(719) 555-6657
2440	Part-time	Associate	Bethany	Rosario	858 West 27th Street	Pueblo	CO	81012	(719) 555-9481
3035	Temporary	Clerk	Alia	Shandra	7740 West Second Street	Avondale	CO	81022	(719) 555-0059
3129	Temporary	Clerk	Gloria	Cushman	6590 East 14th Street	Pueblo	CO	81006	(719) 555-0332
3239	Temporary	Associate	Rudolph	Powell	8874 Hood Avenue	Pueblo	CO	81008	(719) 555-2223
4002	Contract	Contractor	Alice	Murray	4300 East 14th Street	Pueblo	CO	81003	(719) 555-4230
4684	Contract	Contractor	Simon	Banister	1022 Division Avenue	Boone	CO	81025	(719) 555-2378

15. Find all occurrences of *Assistant* and replace them with *Associate*.

16. Save the table, print it in landscape orientation with left and right margins of 0.5 inch, and then close it.

Page 1

AL1-C4-A1-Hudson_EmployeesTable(A1,Step16).accdb

Benchmark Access 2013 Level 1 Model Answers

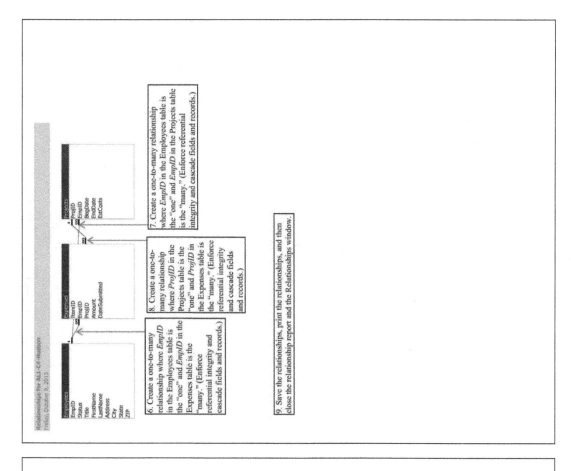

Relationships for AL1-C4-Hudson
Friday, October 9, 2015

Employees
EmpID
Status
Title
FirstName
LastName
Address
City
State
ZIP

Expenses
ItemID
EmpID
ProjID
Amount
DateSubmitted

Projects
ProjID
EmpID
BegDate
EndDate
EstCosts

6. Create a one-to-many relationship where *EmpID* in the Employees table is the "one" and *EmpID* in the Expenses table is the "many." (Enforce referential integrity and cascade fields and records.)

7. Create a one-to-many relationship where *EmpID* in the Employees table is the "one" and *EmpID* in the Projects table is the "many." (Enforce referential integrity and cascade fields and records.)

8. Create a one-to-many relationship where *ProjID* in the Projects table is the "one" and *ProjID* in the Expenses table is the "many." (Enforce referential integrity and cascade fields and records.)

9. Save the relationships, print the relationships, and then close the relationship report and the Relationships window.

AL1-C4-A3-Hudson_Relationships(A3).accdb

10/9/2015

Expenses

ItemID	EmpID	ProjID	Amount	DateSubmitted
1	1466	08-B	$245.79	9/4/2015
2	2019	08-A	$500.00	9/10/2015
3	4002	08-B	$150.00	9/18/2015
4	1947	10-A	$500.00	10/3/2015
5	2019	10-B	$487.25	10/22/2015
6	1947	10-A	$85.75	10/24/2015
7	1466	08-B	$175.00	10/29/2015
8	1790	08-A	$110.50	10/30/2015
9	2120	10-A	$75.00	11/5/2015
10	1466	08-B	$300.00	11/7/2015
11	1466	11-A	$75.00	11/14/2015
12	2019	10-B	$300.00	11/19/2915
Total			**$3,004.29**	

4. Insert a *Total* row with the following specifications:
a. Click the Totals button in the *Records* group on the Home tab.
b. Click in the blank field in the *Amount* column in the *Total* row.
c. Click the down-pointing arrow at the left side of the field and then click *Sum* at the drop-down list.
d. Click in any other field.

1. With **AL1-C4-Hudson.accdb** open, create an Expenses table in Design view. Include the following fields (making sure the *ItemID* field is identified as the primary key) and include an appropriate description for each field: **Field Name Data Type** *ItemID* AutoNumber *EmpID* Short Text (field size = 4 characters) *ProjID* Short Text (field size = 4 characters) *Amount* Currency (Type a condition in the *Validation Rule* property box that states the entry must be $500 or less. Type an appropriate error message in the *Validation Text* property box.) *DateSubmitted* Date/Time (Use the Input Mask to control the date so it is entered as a short date.)
2. Save the table, switch to Datasheet view, and then type the following data in the fields (recall that Access automatically fills in the *ItemID* field): EmpID 1466 EmpID 2019 ProjID 2019 ProjID 08-B ProjID 08-A Amount $245.79 Amount $500.00 DateSubmitted 09/04/2015 DateSubmitted 09/10/2015 EmpID 4002 EmpID 1947 ProjID 08-B ProjID 10-A Amount $150.00 Amount $500.00 DateSubmitted 09/18/2015 DateSubmitted 10/03/2015 EmpID 2019 EmpID 1947 ProjID 10-A Amount $487.25 Amount $85.75 DateSubmitted 10/22/2015 DateSubmitted 10/24/2015 EmpID 1466 EmpID 1790 ProjID 08-B ProjID 08-A Amount $175.00 Amount $110.50 DateSubmitted 10/29/2015 DateSubmitted 10/30/2015 EmpID 2120 EmpID 1466 ProjID 10-A ProjID 08-B Amount $75.00 Amount $300.00 DateSubmitted 11/05/2015 DateSubmitted 11/07/2015 EmpID 1466 EmpID 2019 ProjID 11-A ProjID 10-B Amount $75.00 Amount $300.00 DateSubmitted 11/14/2015 DateSubmitted 11/19/20153.
Adjust the column widths.
5. Save, print, and then close the Expenses table.

Page 1

AL1-C4-A3-Hudson_ExpensesTable(A3).accdb

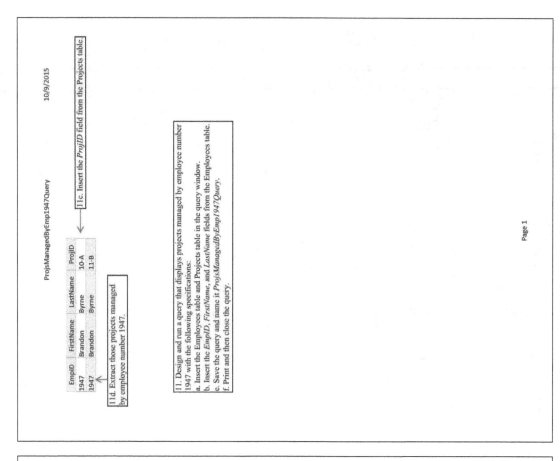

ProjsManagedByEmp1947Query   10/9/2015

11c. Insert the *ProjID* field from the Projects table.

EmpID	FirstName	LastName	ProjID
1947	Brandon	Byrne	10-A
1947	Brandon	Byrne	11-B

11d. Extract those projects managed by employee number 1947.

11. Design and run a query that displays projects managed by employee number 1947 with the following specifications:
a. Insert the Employees table and Projects table in the query window.
b. Insert the *EmpID*, *FirstName*, and *LastName* fields from the Employees table.
c. Save the query and name it *ProjsManagedByEmp1947Query*.
f. Print and then close the query.

Page 1

Hudson_ProjsManagedByEmp1947Query(A3).accdb

FTEmpsQuery   10/9/2015

FirstName	LastName	Status
Samantha	O'Connell	Full-time
Edward	Sorrell	Full-time
Brandon	Byrne	Full-time
Leland	Hughes	Full-time
Jean	Perrault	Full-time
Michael	Turek	Full-time

10. Design and run a query that displays all full-time employees with the following specifications:
a. Insert the Employees table in the query window.
b. Insert the *EmpID*, *FirstName*, *LastName*, and *Status* fields.
c. Click in the check box in the *Show* row field in the *EmpID* column to remove the check mark. (This hides the EmpID numbers in the query results.)
d. Extract full-time employees.
e. Save the query and name it *FTEmpsQuery*.
f. Print and then close the query.

Page 1

AL1-C4-A3-Hudson_FTEmpsQuery(A3).accdb

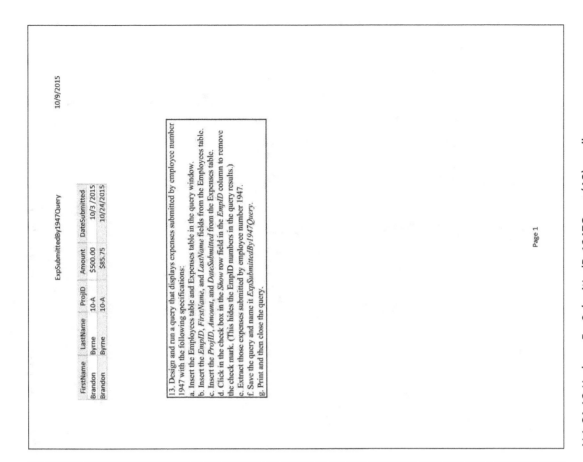

ExpSubmittedBy1947Query   10/9/2015

FirstName	LastName	ProjID	Amount	DateSubmitted
Brandon	Byrne	10-A	$500.00	10/3/2015
Brandon	Byrne	10-A	$85.75	10/24/2015

13. Design and run a query that displays expenses submitted by employee number 1947 with the following specifications:
  a. Insert the Employees table and Expenses table in the query window.
  b. Insert the *EmpID*, *FirstName*, and *LastName* fields from the Employees table.
  c. Insert the *ProjID*, *Amount*, and *DateSubmitted* from the Expenses table.
  d. Click in the check box in the *Show* row field in the *EmpID* column to remove the check mark. (This hides the EmpID numbers in the query results.)
  e. Extract those expenses submitted by employee number 1947.
  f. Save the query and name it *ExpSubmittedBy1947Query*.
  g. Print and then close the query.

Page 1

AL1-C4-A3-Hudson_ExpSubmittedBy1947Query(A3).accdb

ExpensesOver$250Query   10/9/2015

Amount	DateSubmitted	FirstName	LastName
$500.00	9 /10/2015	Jean	Perrault
$500.00	10/3 /2015	Brandon	Byrne
$487.25	10/22/2015	Jean	Perrault
$300.00	11/7 /2015	Samantha	O'Connell
$300.00	11/19/2915	Jean	Perrault

12e. Extract those expense amounts over $250.

12. Design and run a query that displays expense amounts over $250 and the employees submitting the expenses with the following specifications:
  a. Insert the Expenses table and Employees table in the query window.
  b. Insert the *ItemID*, *Amount*, and *DateSubmitted* fields from the Expenses table.
  c. Insert the *FirstName* and *LastName* fields from the Employees table.
  d. Hide the *ItemID* field in the query results by clicking in the check box in the *Show* row field in the *ItemID* column to remove the check mark.
  f. Save the query and name it *ExpensesOver$250Query*.
  g. Print and then close the query.

Page 1

AL1-C4-A3-ExpensesOver$250Query(A3).accdb

OrderDate	SupplierName	ProductID	UnitsOrdered	UnitPrice	Total
5/4/2015	Manning, Inc.	101-S2R	15	$129.95	1949.25
5/4/2015	Manning, Inc.	101-S3B	15	$119.95	1799.25
5/4/2015	Freedom Corporation	209-L	25	$6.95	173.75
5/4/2015	Freedom Corporation	209-XL	25	$7.20	180
5/4/2015	Freedom Corporation	209-XXL	20	$7.29	145.8
5/4/2015	Freedom Corporation	210-M	15	$6.49	97.35
5/4/2015	Freedom Corporation	210-L	25	$6.49	162.25
5/18/2015	Sound Supplies	299-M2	10	$88.79	887.9
5/18/2015	Sound Supplies	299-M3	10	$88.79	887.9
5/18/2015	Sound Supplies	299-M5	10	$88.79	887.9
5/18/2015	Sound Supplies	299-W1	8	$75.29	602.32
5/18/2015	Sound Supplies	299-W3	10	$75.29	752.9
5/18/2015	Sound Supplies	299-W4	10	$75.29	752.9
5/18/2015	Sound Supplies	299-W5	10	$75.29	752.9
5/18/2015	Emerald City Products	602-XR	5	$429.00	2145
Total				**$1,280.85**	**12177.37**

Page 1

AL1-C4-VB-AlpineServices_OrderTotal(VB).accdb

EmpID	Status	Title	FirstName	LastName	Address	City	State	ZIP	Telephone
1466	Full-time	Design Manager	Samantha	O'Connell	9105 Pike Avenue	Pueblo	CO	81011-	(719) 555-7658
1790	Full-time	Associate	Edward	Sorrell	9958 Franklin Avenue	Pueblo	CO	81006-	(719) 555-3724
1947	Full-time	Resources Manager	Brandon	Byrne	102 Hudson Avenue	Pueblo	CO	81012-	(719) 555-1202
1955	Full-time	Accountant	Leland	Hughes	4883 Caledonia Road	Pueblo	CO	81005-	(719) 555-1211
1994	Part-time	Associate	Rosa	Martinez	310 Graham Avenue	Pueblo	CO	81004-	(719) 555-8394
2019	Full-time	Production Manager	Jean	Perrault	123 Chinook Lake	Pueblo	CO	81012-	(719) 555-4027
2120	Full-time	Associate	Michael	Turek	5503 East 27th Street	Boone	CO	81025-	(719) 555-5423
2301	Part-time	Associate	Gregory	Nitsche	12055 East 18th Street	Pueblo	CO	81007-	(719) 555-6657
2440	Part-time	Associate	Bethany	Rosario	858 West 27th Street	Pueblo	CO	81012-	(719) 555-9481
3035	Temporary	Clerk	Alia	Shandra	7740 West Second Street	Avondale	CO	81022-	(719) 555-0059
3129	Temporary	Clerk	Gloria	Cushman	6590 East 14th Street	Pueblo	CO	81006-	(719) 555-0332
3239	Temporary	Associate	Rudolph	Powell	8874 Hood Avenue	Pueblo	CO	81008-	(719) 555-2223
4002	Contract	Contractor	Alice	Murray	4300 East 14th Street	Pueblo	CO	81003-	(719) 555-4230
4884	Contract	Contractor	Simon	Banister	1022 Division Avenue	Boone	CO	81025-	(719) 555-2378
2286	Full-time	Associate	Erica	Bonari	4850 55th Street	Pueblo	CO	81005-5002	(719) 555-1293
2970	Full-time	Associate	Daniel	Ortiz	12021 Cedar Lane	Pueblo	CO	81011-1255	(719) 555-0790

6. Insert the following new records: EmpID 2286 EmpID 2970 Status Full-time Status Full-time Title Associate Title Associate FirstName Erica FirstName Daniel LastName Bonari LastName Ortiz Address 4850 55th Street Address 12021 Cedar Lane City (Pueblo automatically inserted) City (Pueblo automatically inserted) State (CO automatically inserted) State (CO automatically inserted) ZIP 81005-5002 ZIP 81011-1255 Telephone (719) 555-1293 Telephone (719) 555-0790
7. Adjust the width of the ZIP column. (Only the two new records will contain the nine-digit zip code.)

1. With **AL1-C4-Hudson.accdb** open, open the Employees table.
2. Display the table in Design view, click in the ZIP field row in the *Data Type* column, and then click in the *Input Mask* property box in the *Field Properties* section.
3. Use the Input Mask Wizard to create a nine-digit zip code input mask.
4. Save the table and then switch to Datasheet view.
5. Delete the records for employee number 3035 (Alia Shandra), employee number 3129 (Gloria Cushman), and employee number 4884 (Simon Banister).
8. Save the Employees table.
9. Display the table in Print Preview, change to landscape orientation, and then change the left and right margins to 0.5 inch.

Page 1

AL1-C4-A4-Hudson_EmployeesTable(A4).accdb

ClientID	RepID	CompanyName	Address	City	State	Zip	Telephone	BusinessType
AS	401	Aspen Source	400 Elliott Avenue	Seattle	WA	98168	(206) 555-6691	Retailer
SS	404	Simple Solvers Inc	6300 Aurora Avenue	Seattle	WA	98167	(206) 555-6188	Wholesaler
VW	405	Value Wholesalers	5550 45th Avenue South	Seattle	WA	98166	(206) 555-1833	Wholesaler
PP	406	Product People	55674 Pine Street	Seattle	WA	98198	(206) 555-2420	Wholesaler
UW	406	Uptown Wholesaler Inc	808 University Place	Seattle	WA	98198	(206) 555-8355	Wholesaler
GB	408	Brother Giants	2058 16th Street SW	Seattle	WA	98168	(206) 555-3819	Wholesaler
TV	409	True Ventures	2002 Fourth Avenue	Seattle	WA	98166	(206) 555-3281	Wholesaler
MS	409	McLewis and Sons	300 Stewart Drive	Seattle	WA	98168	(206) 555-0050	Wholesaler

Page 1

AL1-C4-BlueRidge_Clients(CS2).accdb

RepID	RepFirstName	RepLastName	Telephone	InsPlan	YrlyBonus
401	John	Marks	(206) 555-5663	Premium	$7,500.00
404	Marianne	Rodriguez	(206) 555-2213	Standard	$5,000.00
405	Joseph	Jackson	(206) 555-1175	None	$2,000.00
406	Lucie	LaFranc	(206) 555-8573	Platinum	$10,000.00
408	Finn	McConnor	(206) 555-3373	Standard	$4,500.00
409	Marcus	Tate	(206) 555-7510	Platinum	$9,500.00
Total					$38,500.00

Page 1

AL1-C4-BlueRidge_Representatives(CS1).accdb

Relationships for AL1-C4-BlueRidge
Friday, October 9, 2015

RepresentativesBonusOver$5000Query

10/9/2015

RepID	RepFirstName	RepLastName	YrlyBonus
401	John	Marks	$7,500.00
404	Marianne	Rodriguez	$5,000.00
406	Lucie	LaFranc	$10,000.00
409	Marcus	Tate	$9,500.00

Page 1

AL1-C4-BlueRidge_RepresentativesBonusOver$5000Query(CS4).accdb

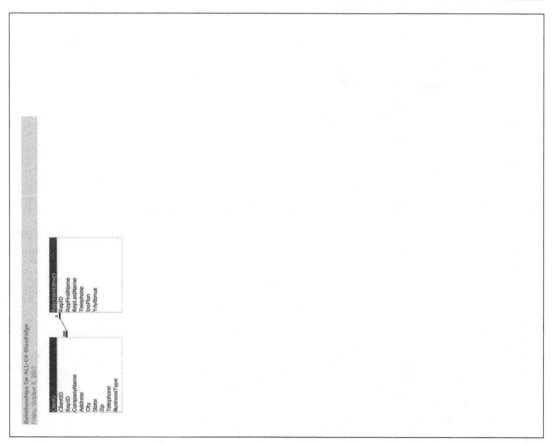

Clients
ClientID
RepID
CompanyName
Address
City
State
Zip
Telephone
BusinessType

Representatives
RepID
RepFirstName
RepLastName
Telephone
InsPlan
YrlyBonus

AL1-C4-BlueRidge_Relationship(CS3).accdb

Benchmark Access 2013 Level 1 Model Answers

RepresentativesWithPlatinumInsQuery

10/9/2015

RepID	RepFirstName	RepLastName	InsPlan
406	Lucie	LaFranc	Platinum
409	Marcus	Tate	Platinum

Page 1

AL1-C4-BlueRidge_RepresentativesWithPlatinumInsQuery(CS4).accdb

WholesalerClientsQuery

10/9/2015

ClientID	CompanyName	BusinessType
GB	Brother Giants	Wholesaler
MS	McLewis and Sons	Wholesaler
PP	Product People	Wholesaler
SS	Simple Solvers Inc	Wholesaler
TV	True Ventures	Wholesaler
UW	Uptown Wholesaler Inc	Wholesaler
VW	Value Wholesalers	Wholesaler

Page 1

AL1-C4-BlueRidge_WholesalerClientsQuery(CS4).accdb

Rep406ClientsQuery

10/9/2015

ClientID	CompanyName	RepID	RepFirstName	RepLastName
PP	Product People	406	Lucie	LaFranc
UW	Uptown Wholesaler Inc	406	Lucie	LaFranc

Page 1

AL1-C4-BlueRidge_Rep406ClientsQuery(CS4).accdb

Access Performance Assessment Unit 1 Model Answers

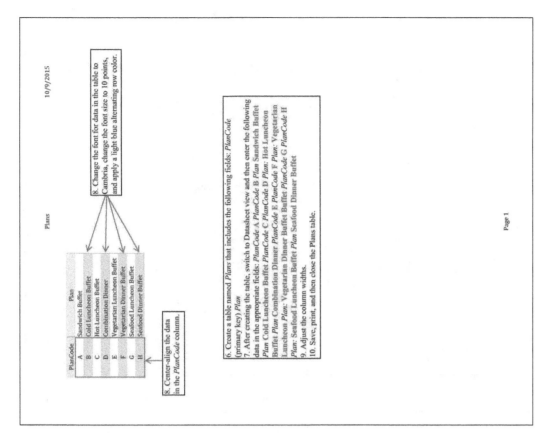

Plans   10/9/2015

PlanCode	Plan
A	Sandwich Buffet
B	Cold Luncheon Buffet
C	Hot Luncheon Buffet
D	Combination Dinner
E	Vegetarian Luncheon Buffet
F	Vegetarian Dinner Buffet
G	Seafood Luncheon Buffet
H	Seafood Dinner Buffet

8. Change the font for data in the table to Cambria, change the font size to 10 points, and apply a light blue alternating row color.

8. Center-align the data in the *PlanCode* column.

6. Create a table named *Plans* that includes the following fields: *PlanCode* (primary key) *Plan*
7. After creating the table, switch to Datasheet view and then enter the following data in the appropriate fields: *PlanCode* A *PlanCode* B *Plan* Sandwich Buffet *Plan* Cold Luncheon Buffet *PlanCode* C *PlanCode* D *Plan*: Hot Luncheon Buffet *Plan* Combination Dinner *PlanCode* E *PlanCode* F *Plan*: Vegetarian Luncheon *Plan*: Vegetarian Dinner Buffet *Plan* Buffet *PlanCode* G *PlanCode* H *Plan*: Seafood Luncheon Buffet *Plan* Seafood Dinner Buffet
9. Adjust the column widths.
10. Save, print, and then close the Plans table.

Page 1

AL1-U1-A1-Cornerstone_PlansTable(A1).accdb

Employees   10/9/2015

EmployeeID	FirstName	LastName	CellPhone
10	Erin	Jergens	(505) 555-3193
14	Mikio	Ogami	(505) 555-1087
19	Martin	Vaughn	(505) 555-4461
21	Isabelle	Baptista	(505) 555-4425
24	Shawn	Kettering	(505) 555-3885
26	Madison	Harris	(505) 555-2256
28	Victoria	Lamesa	(505) 555-6650
30	Isaac	Hobart	(505) 555-7430
32	Lester	Franklin	(505) 555-0440
35	Manuela	Harte	(505) 555-1221

3. Change the font for data in the table to Cambria, change the font size to 10 points, and apply a light blue alternating row color.

3. Center-align the data in the *EmployeeID* column.

1. Use Access to create tables for Cornerstone Catering. Name the database **AL1-U1-A1-Cornerstone**. Create a table named *Employees* that includes the following fields. If no data type is specified for a field, use the Short Text data type. You determine the field size and specify the same field size for a field that is contained in different tables. For example, if you specify a field size of 2 characters for the *EmployeeID* field in the Employees table, specify a field size of 2 characters for the *EmployeeID* field in the Events table. Provide a description for each field. *EmployeeID* (primary key) *FirstName LastName CellPhone* (Use the Input Mask Wizard for this field.)
2. After creating the table, switch to Datasheet view and then enter the following data in the appropriate fields: *EmployeeID* 10 *EmployeeID* 14 *FirstName* Erin *FirstName* Mikio *LastName* Jergens *LastName* Ogami *CellPhone* (505) 555-3193 *CellPhone* (505) 555-1087 *EmployeeID* 19 *EmployeeID* 21 *FirstName* Martin *FirstName* Isabelle *LastName* Vaughn *LastName* Baptista *CellPhone* (505) 555-4461 *CellPhone* (505) 555-4425 *EmployeeID* 24 *EmployeeID* 26 *FirstName* Shawn *FirstName* Madison *LastName* Kettering *LastName* Harris *CellPhone* (505) 555-3885 *CellPhone* (505) 555-2256 *EmployeeID* 28 *EmployeeID* 30 *FirstName* Victoria *FirstName* Isaac *LastName* Lamesa *LastName* Hobart *CellPhone* (505) 555-6650 *CellPhone* (505) 555-7430 *EmployeeID* 32 *EmployeeID* 35 *FirstName* Lester *FirstName* Manuela *LastName* Franklin *LastName* Harte *CellPhone* (505) 555-0440 *CellPhone* (505) 555-1221
4. Adjust the column widths.
5. Save, print, and then close the Employees table.

Page 1

AL1-U1-A1-Cornerstone_EmployeesTable(A1).accdb

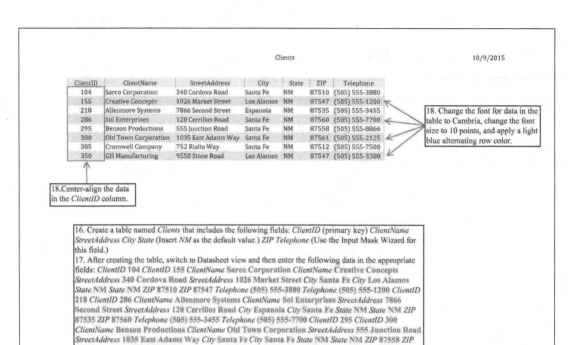

Clients   10/9/2015

ClientID	ClientName	StreetAddress	City	State	ZIP	Telephone
104	Sarco Corporation	340 Cordova Road	Santa Fe	NM	87510	(505) 555-3880
155	Creative Concepts	1026 Market Street	Los Alamos	NM	87547	(505) 555-1200
218	Allenmore Systems	7866 Second Street	Espanola	NM	87535	(505) 555-3455
286	Sol Enterprises	120 Cerrillos Road	Santa Fe	NM	87560	(505) 555-7700
295	Benson Productions	555 Junction Road	Santa Fe	NM	87558	(505) 555-8866
300	Old Town Corporation	1035 East Adams Way	Santa Fe	NM	87561	(505) 555-2125
305	Cromwell Company	752 Rialto Way	Santa Fe	NM	87512	(505) 555-7500
350	GH Manufacturing	9550 Stone Road	Los Alamos	NM	87547	(505) 555-3388

18. Change the font for data in the table to Cambria, change the font size to 10 points, and apply a light blue alternating row color.

18. Center-align the data in the *ClientID* column.

16. Create a table named *Clients* that includes the following fields: *ClientID* (primary key) *ClientName* *StreetAddress* *City* *State* (Insert *NM* as the default value.) *ZIP* *Telephone* (Use the Input Mask Wizard for this field.)

17. After creating the table, switch to Datasheet view and then enter the following data in the appropriate fields: *ClientID* 104 *ClientID* 155 *ClientName* Sarco Corporation *ClientName* Creative Concepts *StreetAddress* 340 Cordova Road *StreetAddress* 1026 Market Street *City* Santa Fe *City* Los Alamos *State* NM *State* NM *ZIP* 87510 *ZIP* 87547 *Telephone* (505) 555-3880 *Telephone* (505) 555-1200 *ClientID* 218 *ClientID* 286 *ClientName* Allenmore Systems *ClientName* Sol Enterprises *StreetAddress* 7866 Second Street *StreetAddress* 120 Cerrillos Road *City* Espanola *City* Santa Fe *State* NM *State* NM *ZIP* 87535 *ZIP* 87560 *Telephone* (505) 555-3455 *Telephone* (505) 555-7700 *ClientID* 295 *ClientID* 300 *ClientName* Benson Productions *ClientName* Old Town Corporation *StreetAddress* 555 Junction Road *StreetAddress* 1035 East Adams Way *City* Santa Fe *City* Santa Fe *State* NM *State* NM *ZIP* 87558 *ZIP* 87561 *Telephone* (505) 555-8866 *Telephone* (505) 555-2125 *ClientID* 305 *ClientID* 350 *ClientName* Cromwell Company *ClientName* GH Manufacturing *StreetAddress* 752 Rialto Way *StreetAddress* 9550 Stone Road *City* Santa Fe *City* Los Alamos *State* NM *State* NM *ZIP* 87512 *ZIP* 87547 *Telephone* (505) 555-7500 *Telephone* (505) 555-3388

19. Adjust the column widths.
20. Save the table and then print it in landscape orientation.
21. Close the Clients table.

Page 1

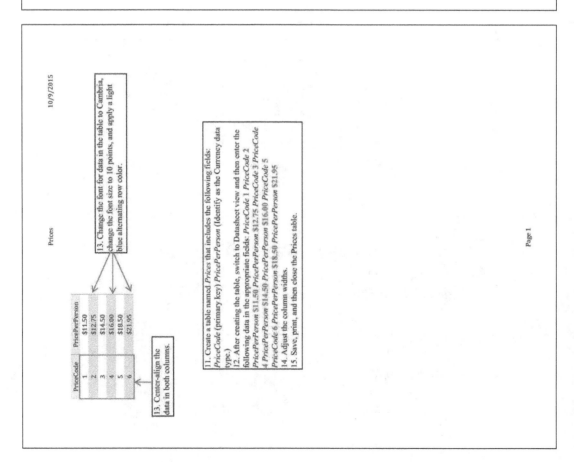

Prices   10/9/2015

13. Change the font for data in the table to Cambria, change the font size to 10 points, and apply a light blue alternating row color.

PriceCode	PricePerPerson
1	$11.50
2	$12.75
3	$14.50
4	$16.00
5	$18.50
6	$21.95

13. Center-align the data in both columns.

11. Create a table named *Prices* that includes the following fields: *PriceCode* (primary key) *PricePerPerson* (Identify as the Currency data type.)
12. After creating the table, switch to Datasheet view and then enter the following data in the appropriate fields: *PriceCode* 1 *PriceCode* 2 *PriceCode* 3 *PriceCode* 4 *PriceCode* 5 *PriceCode* 6 *PricePerPerson* $11.50 *PricePerPerson* $12.75 *PricePerPerson* $14.50 *PricePerPerson* $16.00 *PricePerPerson* $18.50 *PricePerPerson* $21.95
14. Adjust the column widths.
15. Save, print, and then close the Prices table.

Page 1

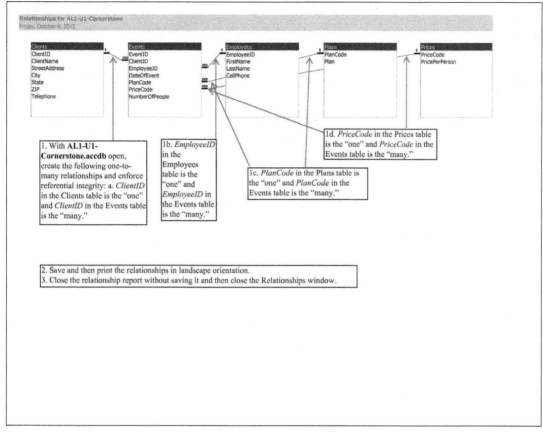

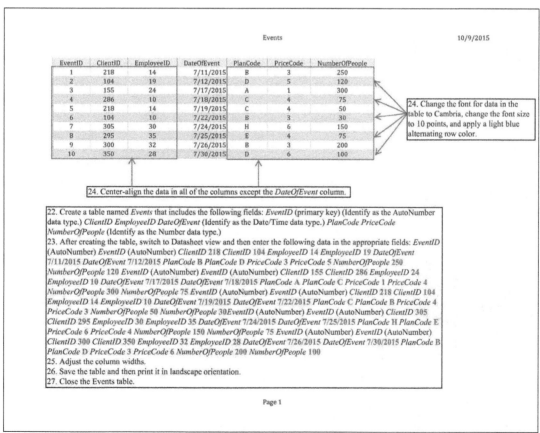

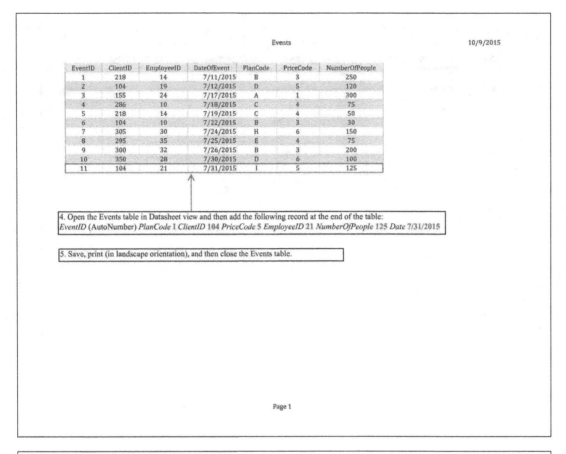

Events   10/9/2015

EventID	ClientID	EmployeeID	DateOfEvent	PlanCode	PriceCode	NumberOfPeople
1	218	14	7/11/2015	B	3	250
2	104	19	7/12/2015	D	5	120
3	155	24	7/17/2015	A	1	300
4	286	10	7/18/2015	C	4	75
5	218	14	7/19/2015	C	4	50
6	104	10	7/22/2015	B	3	30
7	305	30	7/24/2015	H	6	150
8	295	35	7/25/2015	E	4	75
9	300	32	7/26/2015	B	3	200
10	350	28	7/30/2015	D	6	100
11	104	21	7/31/2015	I	5	125

4. Open the Events table in Datasheet view and then add the following record at the end of the table:
EventID (AutoNumber) *PlanCode* I *ClientID* 104 *PriceCode* 5 *EmployeeID* 21 *NumberOfPeople* 125 *Date* 7/31/2015

5. Save, print (in landscape orientation), and then close the Events table.

Page 1

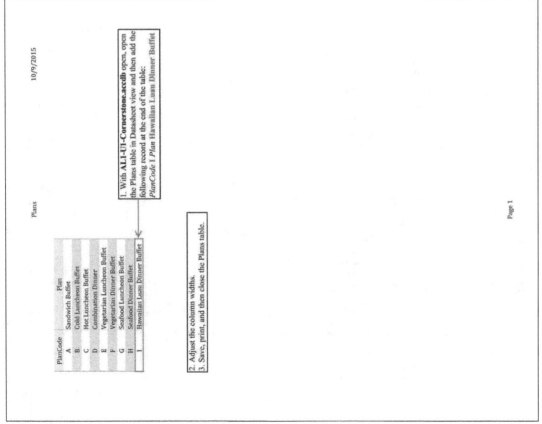

10/9/2015

Plans

PlanCode	Plan
A	Sandwich Buffet
B	Cold Luncheon Buffet
C	Hot Luncheon Buffet
D	Combination Dinner
E	Vegetarian Luncheon Buffet
F	Vegetarian Dinner Buffet
G	Seafood Luncheon Buffet
H	Seafood Dinner Buffet
I	Hawaiian Luau Dinner Buffet

1. With **AL1-U1-Cornerstone.accdb** open, open the Plans table in Datasheet view and then add the following record at the end of the table:
PlanCode I *Plan* Hawaiian Luau Dinner Buffet

2. Adjust the column widths.

3. Save, print, and then close the Plans table.

Page 1

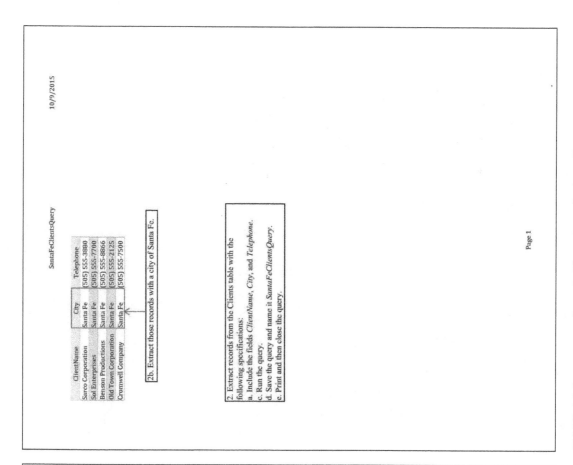

SantaFeClientsQuery   10/9/2015

ClientName	City	Telephone
Sarco Corporation	Santa Fe	(505) 555-3880
Sol Enterprises	Santa Fe	(505) 555-7700
Benson Productions	Santa Fe	(505) 555-8866
Old Town Corporation	Santa Fe	(505) 555-2125
Cromwell Company	Santa Fe	(505) 555-7500

2b. Extract those records with a city of Santa Fe.

2. Extract records from the Clients table with the following specifications:
a. Include the fields *ClientName*, *City*, and *Telephone*.
c. Run the query.
d. Save the query and name it *SantaFeClientsQuery*.
e. Print and then close the query.

Page 1

AL1-U1-A4-Cornerstone_SantaFeClientsQuery(A4).accdb

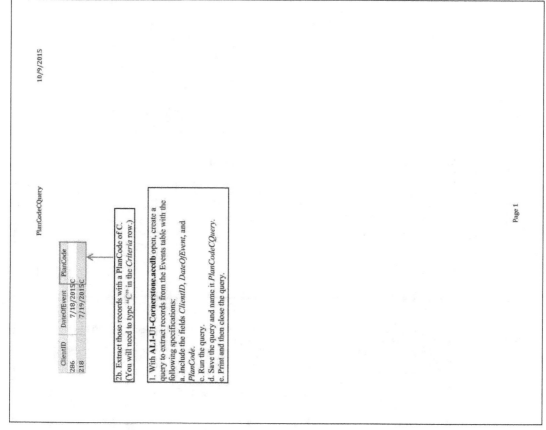

PlanCodeCQuery   10/9/2015

ClientID	DateOfEvent	PlanCode
286	7/18/2015	C
218	7/19/2015	C

2b. Extract those records with a PlanCode of C. (You will need to type "C" in the *Criteria* row.)

1. With AL1-U1-Cornerstone.accdb open, create a query to extract records from the Events table with the following specifications:
a. Include the fields *ClientID*, *DateOfEvent*, and *PlanCode*.
c. Run the query.
d. Save the query and name it *PlanCodeCQuery*.
e. Print and then close the query.

Page 1

AL1-U1-A4-Cornerstone_PlanCodeCQuery(A4).accdb

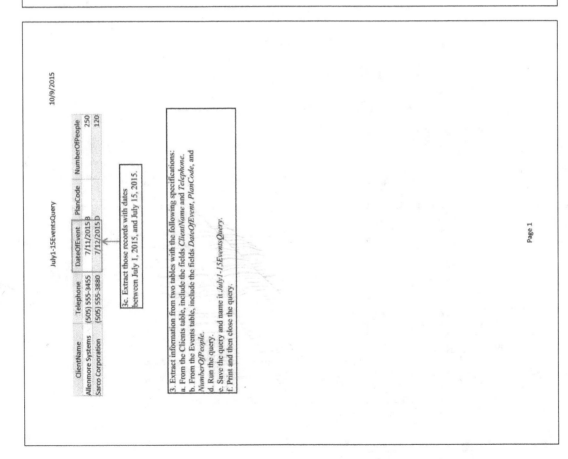

EventAmountsQuery — 10/9/2015

EventID	DateOfEvent	NumberOfPeople	PricePerPerson	Amount
3	7/17/2015	300	$11.50	$3,450.00
1	7/11/2015	250	$14.50	$3,625.00
6	7/22/2015	30	$14.50	$435.00
9	7/26/2015	200	$14.50	$2,900.00
4	7/18/2015	75	$16.00	$1,200.00
5	7/19/2015	50	$16.00	$800.00
8	7/25/2015	75	$16.00	$1,200.00
2	7/12/2015	120	$18.50	$2,220.00
11	7/31/2015	125	$18.50	$2,312.50
7	7/24/2015	150	$21.95	$3,292.50
10	7/30/2015	100	$21.95	$2,195.00

2. Insert the following calculated field entry in the fifth *Field* row field: *Amount: [NumberOfPeople]*[PricePerPerson]*.

1. With **AL1-U1-Cornerstone.accdb** open, create a query in Design view with the Events table and Prices table and insert the following fields in the specified locations:
a. Insert *EventID* from the Events table to the first *Field* row field.
b. Insert *DateOfEvent* from the Events table to the second *Field* row field.
c. Insert *NumberOfPeople* from the Events table to the third *Field* row field. d. Insert *PricePerPerson* from the Prices table to the fourth *Field* row field. 3. Run the query.
4. Save the query and name it *EventAmountsQuery*.

Page 1

AL1-U1-A5-Cornerstone_EventAmountsQuery(A5).accdb

July1-15EventsQuery — 10/9/2015

ClientName	Telephone	DateOfEvent	PlanCode	NumberOfPeople
Allenmore Systems	(505) 555-3455	7/11/2015	B	250
Sarco Corporation	(505) 555-3880	7/12/2015	D	120

3c. Extract those records with dates between July 1, 2015, and July 15, 2015.

3. Extract information from two tables with the following specifications:
a. From the Clients table, include the fields *ClientName* and *Telephone*.
b. From the Events table, include the fields *DateOfEvent*, *PlanCode*, and *NumberOfPeople*.
d. Run the query.
e. Save the query and name it *July1-15EventsQuery*.
f. Print and then close the query.

Page 1

AL1-U1-A4-Cornerstone_July1-15EventsQuery(A4).accdb

5b. At the second Crosstab Query Wizard dialog box, click *LastName* in the *Available Fields* list box and then click the One Field button.

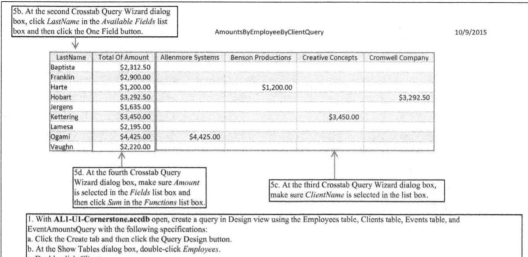

AmountsByEmployeeByClientQuery   10/9/2015

LastName	Total Of Amount	Allenmore Systems	Benson Productions	Creative Concepts	Cromwell Company
Baptista	$2,312.50				
Franklin	$2,900.00				
Harte	$1,200.00		$1,200.00		
Hobart	$3,292.50				$3,292.50
Jergens	$1,635.00				
Kettering	$3,450.00			$3,450.00	
Lamesa	$2,195.00				
Ogami	$4,425.00	$4,425.00			
Vaughn	$2,220.00				

5d. At the fourth Crosstab Query Wizard dialog box, make sure *Amount* is selected in the *Fields* list box and then click *Sum* in the *Functions* list box.

5c. At the third Crosstab Query Wizard dialog box, make sure *ClientName* is selected in the list box.

1. With **AL1-U1-Cornerstone.accdb** open, create a query in Design view using the Employees table, Clients table, Events table, and EventAmountsQuery with the following specifications:
a. Click the Create tab and then click the Query Design button.
b. At the Show Tables dialog box, double-click *Employees*.
c. Double-click *Clients*.
d. Double-click *Events*.
e. Click the Queries tab, double-click *EventAmountsQuery* in the list box, and then click the Close button.
f. Insert the *LastName* field from the *Employees* field list box to the first *Field* row field.
g. Insert the *ClientName* field from the *Clients* field list box to the second *Field* row field.
h. Insert the *Amount* field from *EventAmountsQuery* field list box to the third *Field* row field.
i. Insert the *DateOfEvent* field from the *Events* field list box to the fourth *Field* row field.
2. Run the query.
3. Save the query and name it *EmployeeEventsQuery*.
4. Close the query.
5. Using the Crosstab Query Wizard, create a query that summarizes the total event amounts by employee by client using the following specifications:
a. At the first Crosstab Query Wizard dialog box, click the *Queries* option in the *View* section and then click *Query: EmployeeEventsQuery* in the list box.
e. At the fifth Crosstab Query Wizard dialog box, type AmountsByEmployeeByClientQuery in the *What do you want to name your query?* text box.
6. Automatically adjust the column widths.
7. Print the query in landscape orientation and then close the query.

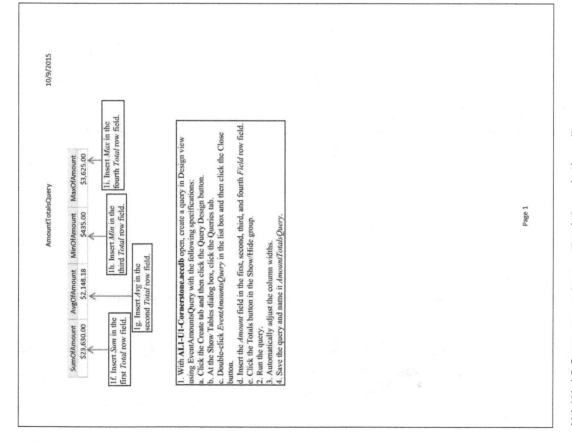

10/9/2015

AmountTotalsQuery

SumOfAmount	AvgOfAmount	MinOfAmount	MaxOfAmount
$23,630.00	$2,148.18	$435.00	$3,625.00

1f. Insert *Sum* in the first *Total* row field.

1g. Insert *Avg* in the second *Total* row field.

1h. Insert *Min* in the third *Total* row field.

1i. Insert *Max* in the fourth *Total* row field.

1. With **AL1-U1-Cornerstone.accdb** open, create a query in Design view using EventAmountsQuery with the following specifications:
a. Click the Create tab and then click the Query Design button.
b. At the Show Tables dialog box, click the Queries tab.
c. Double-click *EventAmountsQuery* in the list box and then click the Close button.
d. Insert the *Amount* field in the first, second, third, and fourth *Field* row field.
e. Click the Totals button in the Show/Hide group.
2. Run the query.
3. Automatically adjust the column widths.
4. Save the query and name it *AmountTotalsQuery*.

Page 1

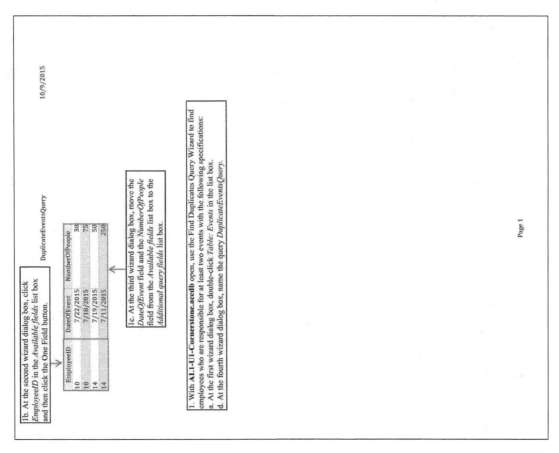

10/9/2015

DuplicateEventsQuery

1b. At the second wizard dialog box, click *EmployeeID* in the *Available fields* list box and then click the One Field button.

EmployeeID	DateOfEvent	NumberOfPeople
10	7/22/2015	30
10	7/18/2015	75
14	7/19/2015	50
14	7/11/2015	250

1c. At the third wizard dialog box, move the *DateOfEvent* field and the *NumberOfPeople* field from the *Available fields* list box to the *Additional query fields* list box.

1. With **AL1-U1-Cornerstone.accdb** open, use the Find Duplicates Query Wizard to find employees who are responsible for at least two events with the following specifications:
a. At the first wizard dialog box, double-click *Table: Events* in the list box.
d. At the fourth wizard dialog box, name the query *DuplicateEventsQuery*.

Page 1

AL1-U1-A8-Cornerstone_DuplicateEventsQuery(A8).accdb

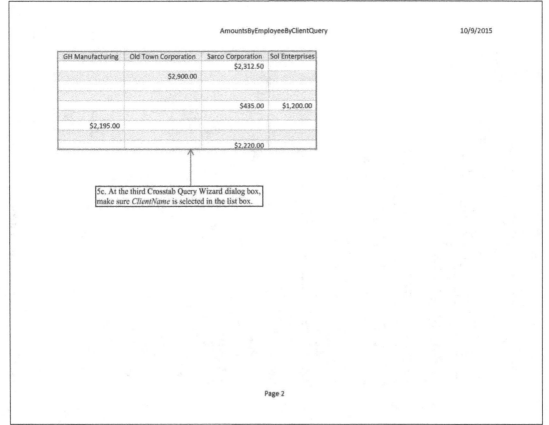

AmountsByEmployeeByClientQuery   10/9/2015

GH Manufacturing	Old Town Corporation	Sarco Corporation	Sol Enterprises
		$2,312.50	
	$2,900.00		
		$435.00	$1,200.00
$2,195.00			
		$2,220.00	

5c. At the third Crosstab Query Wizard dialog box, make sure *ClientName* is selected in the list box.

Page 2

AL1-U1-A7-Cornerstone_AmountsByEmployeeByClientQuery(A7).accdb (2 of 2)

Employees Without Matching Events   10/9/2015

EmployeeID	FirstName	LastName	CellPhone
26	Madison	Harris	(505) 555-2256

1. With **AL1-U1-Cornerstone.accdb** open, use the Find Unmatched
Query Wizard to find employees who do not have upcoming events
scheduled with the following specifications:
a. At the first wizard dialog box, click *Table: Employees* in the list box.
b. At the second wizard dialog box, click *Table: Events* in the list box.
c. At the third wizard dialog box, make sure *EmployeeID* is selected in the
Fields in 'Employees' list box and in the *Fields in 'Events'* list box.
d. At the fourth wizard dialog box, click the All Fields button to move all
fields from the *Available fields* list box to the *Selected fields* list box.
e. At the fifth wizard dialog box, click the Finish button. (Let the wizard
determine the query name: *Employees Without Matching Events*.)
2. Print and then close the *Employees Without Matching Events* query.

Page 1

AL1-U1-A9-Cornerstone_Employees Without Matching Events(A9).accdb

Access Level 1, Chapter 5 Model Answers

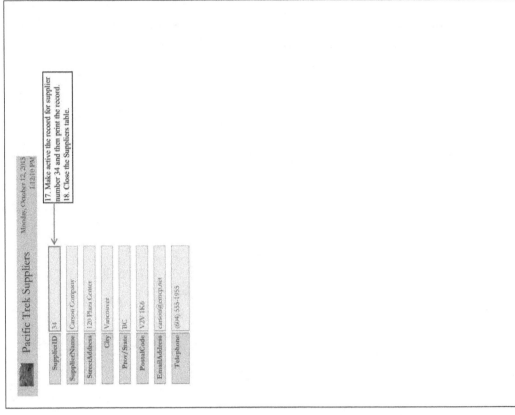

Pacific Trek Suppliers

Monday, October 12, 2015
1:12:10 PM

SupplierID	34
SupplierName	Carson Company
StreetAddress	120 Plaza Center
City	Vancouver
Prov/State	BC
PostalCode	V2V 1K6
EmailAddress	carson@emcp.net
Telephone	(604) 555-1955

17. Make active the record for supplier number 34 and then print the record.
18. Close the Suppliers table.

AL1-C5-A1-PacTrek_SuppliersForm(A1,SupplierID34).accdb

Pacific Trek Suppliers

Monday, October 12, 2015
1:11:11 PM

SupplierID	12
SupplierName	Seaside Suppliers
StreetAddress	4120 Shoreline Drive
City	Vancouver
Prov/State	BC
PostalCode	V2V 8K4
EmailAddress	seaside@emcp.net
Telephone	(604) 555-7945

7. Select and delete the logo object in the *Form Header* section and then click the Logo button in the Header/Footer group. At the Insert Picture dialog box, navigate to the AL1C5 folder on your storage medium and then double-click *River.jpg*.

8. Create the title *Pacific Trek Suppliers* for the form. Click in any field outside the title and then click in the title (which selects the header control object). Drag the right border of the title control object to the left until the border displays near the title.

9. Insert the date and time in the *Form Header* section.

10. Select the date and time control objects, drag in the left border until the border displays near the date and time, and then drag the objects so they are positioned near the title.

11. Click the text box control object containing the supplier number and then drag the right border to the left until *Lines: 1 Characters: 30* displays at the left side of the Status bar.

12. Select the fields in the first column (*SupplierID* through *Telephone*) and then apply the following formatting:
a. Apply bold formatting.
b. Apply the Dark Blue font color (ninth column, bottom row in the *Standard Colors* section).
c. Apply the Align right alignment.
d. Apply the Light Blue 2 shape fill (fifth column, third row in the *Standard Colors* section).
e. Apply the Dark Blue shape outline color (ninth column, bottom row in the *Standard Colors* section).

13. Select the second column and then apply the following formatting:
a. Apply the Light Blue 1 shape fill (fifth column, second row in the *Standard Colors* section).
b. Apply the Dark Blue shape outline color (ninth column, bottom row in the *Standard Colors* section).

16. Make active the record for supplier number 12 (one of the new records you entered) and then print the record. (Make sure you print only the record for supplier number 12.)

1. Display the Open dialog box with the AL1C5 folder on your storage medium as the active folder.
2. Open **AL1-C5-PacTrek.accdb** and enable the contents.
3. Use the Form button in the Forms group on the CREATE tab to create a form with the Suppliers table.
4. Switch to Form view and then add the following records to the Suppliers form:
SupplierID 12 SupplierName Seaside Suppliers StreetAddress 4120 Shoreline Drive City Vancouver Prov/State BC PostalCode V2V 8K4 EmailAddress seaside@emcp.net Telephone 6045557945 SupplierID 34 SupplierName Carson Company StreetAddress 120 Plaza Center City Vancouver Prov/State BC PostalCode V2V 1K6 EmailAddress carson@emcp.net Telephone 6045551955
5. Delete the record containing information on Manning, Inc.
6. Switch to Layout view and then apply the Organic theme to the form.
14. Switch to Form view.
15. Save the form with the name *Suppliers*.

AL1-C5-A1-PacTrek_SuppliersForm(A1,SupplierID12).accdb

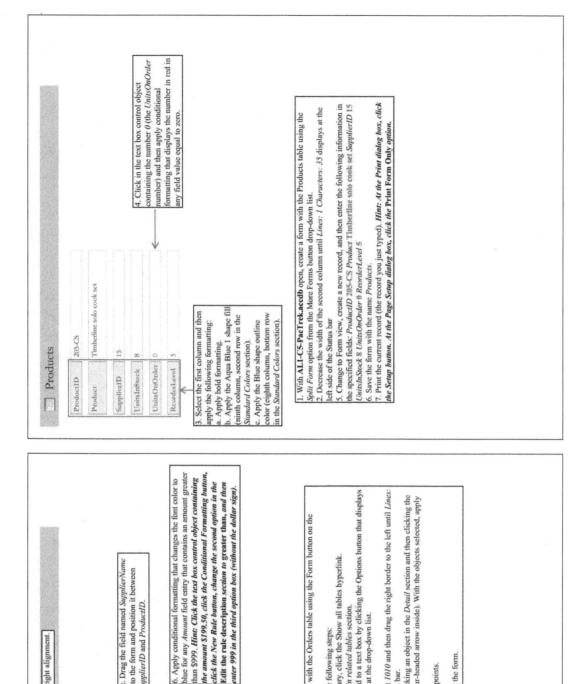

Products

ProductID	205-CS
Product	Timberline solo cook set
SupplierID	15
UnitsInStock	8
UnitsOnOrder	0
ReorderLevel	5

4. Click in the text box control object containing the number *0* (the *UnitsOnOrder* number) and then apply conditional formatting that displays the number in red in any field value equal to zero.

3. Select the first column and then apply the following formatting:
a. Apply bold formatting.
b. Apply the Aqua Blue 1 shape fill (ninth column, second row in the *Standard Colors* section).
c. Apply the Blue shape outline color (eighth column, bottom row in the *Standard Colors* section).

1. With **AL1-C5-PacTrek.accdb** open, create a form with the Products table using the *Split Form* option from the More Forms button drop-down list.
2. Decrease the width of the second column until *Lines: 1 Characters: 35* displays at the left side of the Status bar
3. Change to Form view, create a new record, and then enter the following information in the specified fields: *ProductID* 205-CS *Product* Timberline solo cook set *SupplierID* 15 *UnitsInStock* 8 *UnitsOnOrder* 0 *ReorderLevel* 5
6. Save the form with the name *Products*.
7. Print the current record (the record you just typed). ***Hint: At the Print dialog box, click the Setup button. At the Page Setup dialog box, click the Print Form Only option.***

AL1-C5-A3-PacTrek_ProductsForm(A3).accdb

Orders

4b. Apply the Align right alignment.

OrderID	1032
OrderDate	2/16/2015
SupplierID	35
SupplierName	Emerald City Products
ProductID	602-XR
UnitsOrdered	5
Amount	$2,145.00

2c. Drag the field named *SupplierName* into the form and position it between *SupplierID* and *ProductID*.

6. Apply conditional formatting that changes the font color to blue for any *Amount* field entry that contains an amount greater than $999. ***Hint: Click the text box control object containing the amount $199.50, click the Conditional Formatting button, click the New Rule button, change the second option in the Edit the rule description section to greater than, and then enter 999 in the third option box (without the dollar sign).***

5. Select the first column and then apply the following formatting:
a. Apply the green 2 shape fill (seventh column, third row in the *Standard Colors* section).
b. Apply bold formatting.

1. With **AL1-C5-PacTrek.accdb** open, create a form with the Orders table using the Form button on the CREATE tab.
2. Insert a field from a related table by completing the following steps:
a. Display the Field List task pane and then, if necessary, click the Show all tables hyperlink.
b. Expand the Suppliers table in the *Fields available in related tables* section.
c. Change the *SupplierName* field from a Lookup field to a text box by clicking the Options button that displays below the field and then clicking *Change to Text Box* at the drop-down list.
e. Close the Field List task pane.
3. Click the text box control object containing the text *1010* and then drag the right border to the left until *Lines: 1 Characters: 30* displays at the left side of the Status bar.
4. Select all of the objects in the *Detail* section by clicking an object in the *Detail* section and then clicking the table move handle (the small, square button with a four-headed arrow inside). With the objects selected, apply the following formatting:
a. Change the font to Cambria and the font size to 12 points.
7. Save the form with the name *Orders*.
8. Print the fifteenth record in the form and then close the form.

AL1-C5-A2-PacTrek_OrdersForm(A2).accdb

Sun Properties

Monday, October 12, 2015
1:56:31 PM

PropID	1001
CatID	C
MoRent	$1,500.00
Address	4102 Tenth Street
City	Citrus Heights
State	CA
ZIP	95611

AL1-C5-VB-SunProperties_PropertiesForm(VB).accdb

Employees

EmpID	1099
LastName	Williamson
FirstName	Carrie
BirthDate	6/24/1986
HireDate	8/1/2014
DeptID	RD

1. Open **AL1-C5-Griffin.accdb** from the AL1C5 folder on your storage medium and enable the contents.
2. Suppose you want to create a form for entering employee information but you do not want to include the employees' salaries, since that is confidential information and accessible only to the account manager. Use the Form Wizard to create an Employees form that includes all fields *except* the *AnnualSalary* field and name the form *Employees*.
3. Type a new record with the following information in the specified fields: *EmpID* 1099 *LastName* Williamson *FirstName* Carrie *BirthDate* 6/24/1986 *HireDate* 8/1/2014 *DeptID* RD
4. Switch to layout view, apply the Slice theme, change the theme colors to *Blue Warm*, and change the theme fonts to *Franklin Gothic*.
5. Print the new record you typed.

AL1-C5-A4-Griffin_EmployeesForm(A4).accdb

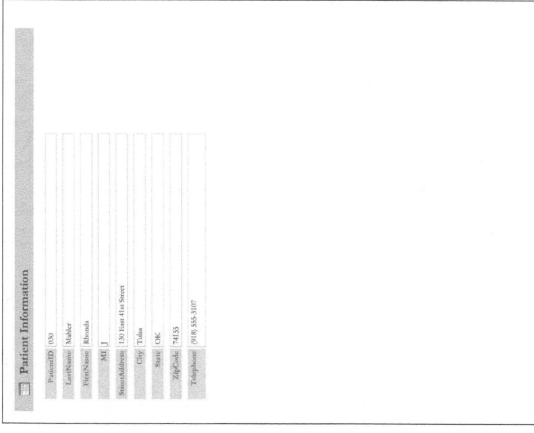

AL1-C5-CS-LewisCenter_PatientsForm(CS2).accdb

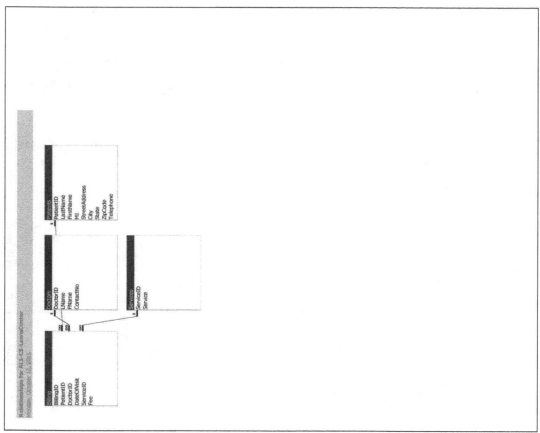

AL1-C5-CS-LewisCenter_Relationships(CS1).accdb

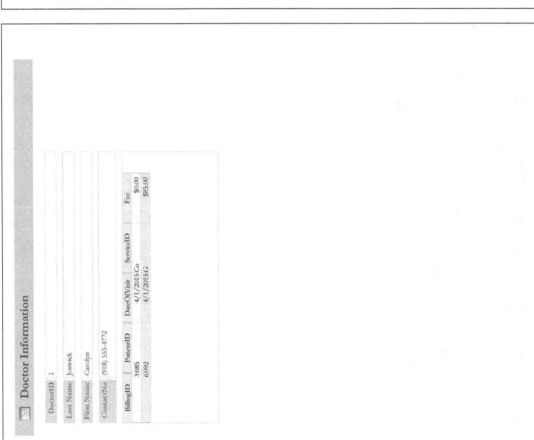

Patient Services

ServiceID: Co

Service: Consultation

BillingID	PatientID	DoctorID	DateOfVisit	Fee
	3085	1	4/1/2015	$0.00

AL1-C5-CS-LewisCenter_ServicesForm(CS2).accdb

Doctor Information

DoctorID: 1

Last Name: Joswick

First Name: Carolyn

ContactNo: (918) 555-4772

BillingID	PatientID	DateOfVisit	ServiceID	Fee
	3085	4/1/2015	Co	$0.00
	6092	4/1/2015	G	$85.00

AL1-C5-CS-LewisCenter_DoctorsForm(CS2).accdb

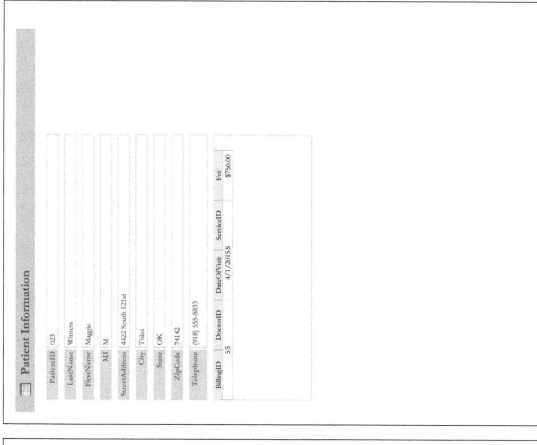

Patient Information

PatientID	023
LastName	Winters
FirstName	Maggie
MI	M
StreetAddress	4422 South 121st
City	Tulsa
State	OK
ZipCode	74142
Telephone	(918) 555-8833

BillingID	DoctorID	DateOfVisit	ServiceID	Fee
55		4/1/2015 S		$750.00

AL1-C5-CS-LewisCenter_PatientsForm(CS3).accdb

Billing

BillingID	1
PatientID	076
DoctorID	2
DateOfVisit	4/1/2015
ServiceID	C
Fee	$85.00

AL1-C5-CS-LewisCenter_BillingForm(CS2).accdb

FORM FORMATTING

To enhance the visual appearance of Lewis Vision Care Center's database, the *Organic* theme and a blue theme color was applied to all forms in the database. A light blue shading was also applied to the first column of control objects, along with blue font color. The text in the first column was also aligned to the right.

CONDITIONAL FORMATTING

Frequently it can be helpful to have fields that meet certain conditions "stand out." For the Lewis Center database, we have defined two such conditions.

1. It is important to know if patients are from Tulsa or Broken Arrow. In tracking patients this makes a difference of which clinic the patient visit. As a result in the *Patients* form, if a patient's home city is Tulsa the city name will be red and if the patient's home city it Broken Arrow it will display in blue

2. In addition, billing is an important part of any business. It is important to track any procedures that cost more than $99. Therefore, in the *Billing* form those procedures will be green.

AL1-C5-CS-CS-Manual(CS4).docx

Billing

BillingID	2
PatientID	076
DoctorID	3
DateOfVisit	4/1/2015
ServiceID	V
Fee	$150.00

AL1-C5-CS-LewisCenter_BillingForm(CS3).accdb

Access Level 1, Chapter 6 Model Answers

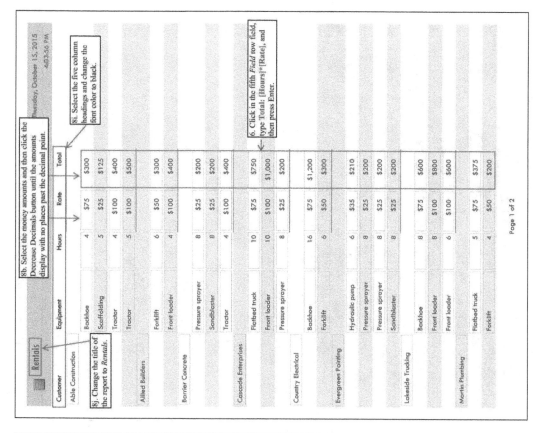

AL1-C6-A1-Hilltop_RentalReport(A1).accdb (1 of 2)

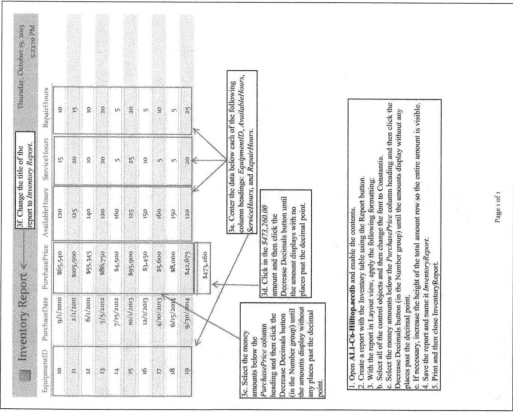

AL1-C6-A1-Hilltop_InventoryReport(A1).accdb

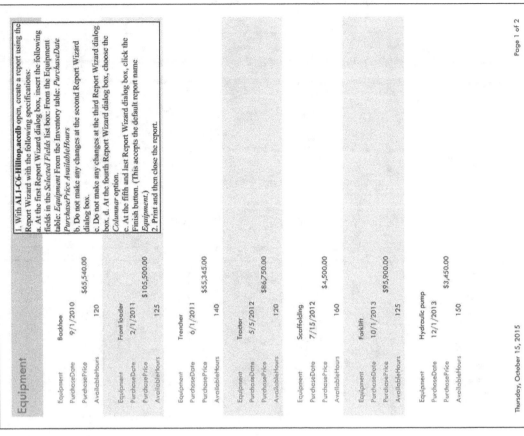

Equipment

Equipment	Backhoe	
PurchaseDate	9/1/2010	
PurchasePrice		$65,540.00
AvailableHours	120	

Equipment	Front loader	
PurchaseDate	2/1/2011	
PurchasePrice		$105,500.00
AvailableHours	125	

Equipment	Trencher	
PurchaseDate	6/1/2011	
PurchasePrice		$55,345.00
AvailableHours	140	

Equipment	Tractor	
PurchaseDate	5/5/2012	
PurchasePrice		$86,750.00
AvailableHours	120	

Equipment	Scaffolding	
PurchaseDate	7/15/2012	
PurchasePrice		$4,500.00
AvailableHours	160	

Equipment	Forklift	
PurchaseDate	10/1/2013	
PurchasePrice		$95,900.00
AvailableHours	125	

Equipment	Hydraulic pump	
PurchaseDate	12/1/2013	
PurchasePrice		$3,450.00
AvailableHours	150	

Thursday, October 15, 2015

AL1-C6-A2-Hilltop_Equipment(A2).accdb (1 of 2)

1. With **AL1-C6-Hilltop.accdb** open, create a report using the Report Wizard with the following specifications:
a. At the first Report Wizard dialog box, insert the following fields in the *Selected Fields* list box: From the Equipment table: *Equipment* From the Inventory table: *PurchaseDate PurchasePrice AvailableHours*
b. Do not make any changes at the second Report Wizard dialog box.
c. Do not make any changes at the third Report Wizard dialog box. d. At the fourth Report Wizard dialog box, choose the *Columnar* option.
e. At the fifth and last Report Wizard dialog box, click the Finish button. (This accepts the default report name *Equipment*.)
2. Print and then close the report.

Customer	Equipment	Hours	Rate	Total
	Hydraulic pump	8	$35	$280
	Trencher	4	$50	$200
Miles Contracting				
	Forklift	10	$50	$500
	Hydraulic pump	10	$35	$350
	Sandblaster	8	$25	$200
	Scaffolding	6	$25	$150
	Trencher	4	$50	$200
				$11,540

8g. Display the Group, Sort, and Total pane; group the records by *Customer*; sort by *Equipment*; and then close the pane.

8c. Click in the *Total* column and then total the amounts by clicking the REPORT LAYOUT TOOLS DESIGN tab, clicking the Totals button in the Grouping & Totals group, and then clicking *Sum* at the drop-down list.
d. Click the total amount (located at the bottom of the *Total* column), click the REPORT LAYOUT TOOLS FORMAT tab, and then click the Apply Currency Format button in the Number group.
e. Increase the height of the total amount row so the entire amount is visible.

6. Create a query in Design view with the following specifications:
a. Add the Customers, Equipment, Invoices, and Rates tables to the query window.
b. Insert the *Customer* field from the *Customers* field list box in the first *Field* row field.
c. Insert the *Equipment* field from the *Equipment* field list box in the second *Field* row field.
d. Insert the *Hours* field from the *Invoices* field list box in the third *Field* row field.
e. Insert the *Rate* field from the *Rates* field list box in the fourth *Field* row field.
g. Run the query.
h. Save the query and name it *CustomerRentals* and then close the query.
7. Create a report with the CustomerRentals query using the Report button.
8. With the report in Layout view, apply the following formatting:
a. Decrease the widths of the columns so the right border of each column displays near the right side of the longest entry.
f. Select and then delete the amount that displays at the bottom of the *Rate* column.
h. Apply the Integral theme. (Do this with the Themes button in the Themes group on the REPORT LAYOUT TOOLS DESIGN tab.)

AL1-C6-A1-Hilltop_RentalReport(A1).accdb (2 of 2)

Benchmark Access 2013 Level 1 Model Answers

Rentals

Customer	BillingDate	Hours	Equipment	Rate
Miles Contracting	5/11/2015	4	Trencher	$50.00
	5/13/2015	6	Scaffolding	$25.00
	5/15/2015	8	Sandblaster	$25.00
	5/5/2015	10	Hydraulic pump	$35.00
Barrier Concrete	5/4/2015	10	Forklift	$50.00
	5/6/2015	8	Sandblaster	$25.00
	5/6/2015	8	Pressure sprayer	$25.00
	5/14/2015	4	Tractor	$100.00
Country Electrical	5/4/2015	16	Backhoe	$75.00
	5/12/2015	6	Forklift	$50.00
Cascade Enterprises	5/7/2015	10	Flatbed truck	$75.00
	5/7/2015	10	Front loader	$100.00
	5/13/2015	8	Pressure sprayer	$25.00
Martin Plumbing	5/1/2015	4	Trencher	$50.00
	5/12/2015	5	Flatbed truck	$75.00
	5/15/2015	4	Forklift	$50.00
	5/8/2015	8	Hydraulic pump	$35.00
Evergreen Painting	5/5/2015	8	Pressure sprayer	$25.00
	5/8/2015	8	Sandblaster	$25.00
	5/8/2015	8	Pressure sprayer	$25.00
	5/14/2015	6	Hydraulic pump	$35.00
Able Construction	5/11/2015	4	Tractor	$100.00
	5/4/2015	5	Tractor	$100.00
	5/11/2015	4	Backhoe	$75.00
	5/4/2015	5	Scaffolding	$25.00
Lakeside Trucking	5/12/2015	6	Front loader	$100.00
	5/1/2015	8	Backhoe	$75.00
	5/7/2015	8	Front loader	$100.00
Allied Builders	5/1/2015	6	Forklift	$50.00
	5/15/2015	4	Front loader	$100.00

3. Create a report using the Report Wizard with the following specifications:
a. At the first Report Wizard dialog box, insert the following fields in the *Selected Fields* list box: From the Customers table: *Customer* From the Invoices table: *BillingDate Hours* From the Equipment table: *Equipment* From the Rates table: *Rate*
b. Do not make any changes at the second Report Wizard dialog box.
c. Do not make any changes at the third Report Wizard dialog box.
d. Do not make any changes at the fourth Report Wizard dialog box.
e. At the fifth Report Wizard dialog box, choose the *Block* option.
f. At the sixth and last Report Wizard dialog box, name the report *Rentals*.
4. Print and then close the report.

AL1-C6-A2-Hilltop_Rentals(A2).accdb

Equipment	Pressure sprayer	
PurchaseDate	4/10/2013	
PurchasePrice		$5,600.00
AvailableHours	160	

Equipment	Sandblaster	
PurchaseDate	6/15/2014	
PurchasePrice		$8,000.00
AvailableHours	150	

Equipment	Flatbed truck	
PurchaseDate	9/30/2014	
PurchasePrice		$42,675.00
AvailableHours	120	

AL1-C6-A2-Hilltop_Equipment(A2).accdb (2 of 2)

Able Construction
8800 Evans Avenue
Denver, CO 80128-3488

Allied Builders
550 Alameda Avenue
Denver, CO 80135-7643

Barrier Concrete
220 Colorado Boulevard
Denver, CO 80125-2204

Cascade Enterprises
24300 Quincy Avenue
Englewood, CO 80118-3800

Country Electrical
12032 Sixth Avenue
Aurora, CO 80023-5473

Evergreen Painting
1045 Colfax Avenue
Denver, CO 80130-4337

Lakeside Trucking
566 Jewell Avenue
Denver, CO 80125-1298

Martin Plumbing
1010 Santa Fe Drive
Littleton, CO 80135-4886

Miles Contracting
640 Smith Road
Aurora, CO 80041-6400

1. With **AL1-C6-Hilltop.accdb** open, click *Customers* in the Tables group in the Navigation pane.
2. Use the Label Wizard to create mailing labels (you determine the label type) with customer names and addresses and sort the labels by customer names. Name the mailing label report *CustomerMailingLabels*.
3. Print the mailing labels.

Rentals

Thursday, October 15, 2015
4:25:28 PM

Customer	Equipment	BillingDate	Hours	Rate	Total
Able Construction					
	Backhoe	5/11/2015	4	$75	$300
	Scaffolding	5/4/2015	5	$25	$125
	Tractor	5/11/2015	4	$100	$400
	Tractor	5/4/2015	5	$100	$500
Allied Builders					
	Forklift	5/7/2015	6	$50	$300
	Front loader	5/15/2015	4	$100	$400
Barrier Concrete					
	Pressure sprayer	5/6/2015	8	$25	$200
	Sandblaster	5/6/2015	8	$25	$200
	Tractor	5/14/2015	4	$100	$400
Cascade Enterprises					
	Flatbed truck	5/7/2015	10	$75	$750
	Front loader	5/7/2015	10	$100	$1,000
	Pressure sprayer	5/13/2015	8	$25	$200
Country Electrical					
	Backhoe	5/4/2015	16	$75	$1,200
	Forklift	5/12/2015	6	$50	$300
Evergreen Painting					
	Hydraulic pump	5/14/2015	6	$35	$210
	Pressure sprayer	5/8/2015	8	$25	$200
	Pressure sprayer	5/5/2015	8	$25	$200
	Sandblaster	5/8/2015	8	$25	$200
Lakeside Trucking					
	Backhoe	5/1/2015	8	$75	$600
	Front loader	5/1/2015	8	$100	$800
	Front loader	5/12/2015	6	$100	$600
Martin Plumbing					
	Flatbed truck	5/12/2015	5	$75	$375
	Forklift	5/15/2015	4	$50	$200

Page 1 of 2

Benchmark Access 2013 Level 1 Model Answers

Suppliers 2 and 4 Orders

Thursday, October 15, 2015
5:08:46 PM

SupplierID	SupplierName	ItemID	UnitPrice	UnitsOrdered	Total
2	Coral Produce	002	$10.50	3	$31.50
2	Coral Produce	016	$24.00	1	$24.00
4	Grocery Wholesalers	020	$18.75	2	$37.50
2	Coral Produce	014	$15.75	2	$31.50
4	Grocery Wholesalers	025	$28.50	1	$28.50
4	Grocery Wholesalers	036	$17.00	2	$34.00
4	Grocery Wholesalers	013	$14.00	2	$28.00
2	Coral Produce	004	$10.95	2	$21.90
4	Grocery Wholesalers	035	$17.00	1	$17.00
4	Grocery Wholesalers	027	$22.00	1	$22.00
4	Grocery Wholesalers	026	$29.25	1	$29.25
2	Coral Produce	021	$31.00	1	$31.00
4	Grocery Wholesalers	034	$13.75	2	$27.50
4	Grocery Wholesalers	012	$30.25	1	$30.25
4	Grocery Wholesalers	018	$45.00	1	$45.00
2	Coral Produce	016	$39.40	2	$78.80
4	Grocery Wholesalers	035	$17.00	1	$17.00
2	Coral Produce	014	$15.75	2	$31.50
4	Grocery Wholesalers	020	$18.75	2	$37.50
					$603.70

Page 1 of 1

AL1-C6-Skyline_Suppliers2&4OrdersRpt(VB).accdb

Customer	Equipment	BillingDate	Hours	Rate	Total
Miles Contracting					
	Hydraulic pump	5/8/2015	8	$35	$280
	Trencher	5/1/2015	4	$50	$200
	Forklift	5/4/2015	10	$50	$500
	Hydraulic pump	5/5/2015	10	$35	$350
	Sandblaster	5/15/2015	8	$25	$200
	Scaffolding	5/13/2015	6	$25	$150
	Trencher	5/11/2015	4	$50	$200
					$11,540

1c. Drag the *BillingDate* field from the Invoices table so the field is positioned between the *Equipment* column and *Hours* column.

1. In Chapter 5, you added a field list to an existing form using the Field List task pane. Experiment with adding a field to an existing report and then complete the following:
a. Open the RentalReport report (created in Assessment 1) in Layout view.
b. Display the Field List task pane and display all of the tables.
d. At the message indicating that Access will modify the RecordSource property and asking if you want to continue, click Yes.
e. Close the Field List task pane.

Page 2 of 2

ClientBilling

ClientID	FirstName	LastName	LName	BillingDate	Fee
31	Sabrina	Fairbanks	Parente	3/2/2015	$125.00
25	Nicole	Gallion	Leland	3/2/2015	$75.00
20	Shelley	Gonzales	Sheehan	3/2/2015	$200.00
36	Thomas	Johnson	Ryder	3/3/2015	$150.00
38	Laura	Malone	Leland	3/3/2015	$75.00
29	Daniel	Casey	Parente	3/3/2015	$125.00
37	Nathan	Knudsen	Sheehan	3/4/2015	$250.00
31	Sabrina	Fairbanks	Parente	3/4/2015	$100.00
40	Katrina	Novak	Parente	3/4/2015	$225.00
32	Luanne	Hedges	Leland	3/4/2015	$150.00
22	Darren	Washington	Sheehan	3/5/2015	$225.00
41	Duane	Reece	Parente	3/5/2015	$200.00
36	Thomas	Johnson	Ryder	3/5/2015	$275.00
29	Daniel	Casey	Parente	3/6/2015	$150.00
28	Patricia	Heckard	Parente	3/6/2015	$275.00
37	Nathan	Knudsen	Sheehan	3/6/2015	$100.00
40	Katrina	Novak	Leland	3/9/2015	$250.00
25	Nicole	Gallion	Ryder	3/9/2015	$150.00
28	Patricia	Heckard	Parente	3/9/2015	$125.00
38	Laura	Malone	Leland	3/10/2015	$250.00
41	Duane	Reece	Parente	3/10/2015	$150.00
20	Shelley	Gonzales	Sheehan	3/10/2015	$100.00
32	Luanne	Hedges	Leland	3/11/2015	$300.00
38	Laura	Malone	Leland	3/11/2015	$275.00
36	Thomas	Johnson	Ryder	3/12/2015	$125.00
32	Luanne	Hedges	Leland	3/12/2015	$200.00
21	Roger	Tolman	Ryder	3/12/2015	$125.00
31	Sabrina	Fairbanks	Parente	3/13/2015	$100.00
40	Katrina	Novak	Leland	3/13/2015	$225.00
29	Daniel	Casey	Parente	3/13/2015	$100.00
37	Nathan	Knudsen	Sheehan	3/13/2015	$150.00
28	Patricia	Heckard	Parente	3/13/2015	$200.00
40	Katrina	Novak	Leland	3/13/2015	$150.00
42	Martin	Costanzo	Sheehan	3/15/2015	$150.00
43	Susan	Nordyke	Ryder	3/15/2015	$175.00
44	Monica	Sommers	Leland	3/15/2015	$250.00

AL1-C6-Millstone_ClientBillingQuery(CS2).accdb

Clients

ClientID	FirstName	LastName	StreetAddress	City	State	ZipCode	Telephone
20	Shelley	Gonzales	321 South Poplar	Casper	WY	82605	(307) 555-7283
21	Roger	Tolman	15344 Fairline South	Mills	WY	82644	(307) 555-2341
22	Darren	Washington	341 North 32nd	Casper	WY	82602	(307) 555-4882
25	Nicole	Gallion	21534 148th Street	Casper	WY	82605	(307) 555-7039
28	Patricia	Heckard	806 Hamilton Drive	Mills	WY	82644	(307) 555-0994
29	Daniel	Casey	23119 257th Avenue	Casper	WY	82602	(307) 555-3643
31	Sabrina	Fairbanks	430 Corrin Street	Mills	WY	82644	(307) 555-2322
32	Luanne	Hedges	15121 Tubbs Road	Casper	WY	82604	(307) 555-8547
36	Thomas	Johnson	18032 150th Street East	Casper	WY	82601	(307) 555-3444
37	Nathan	Knudsen	301 Wheaton Road	Mills	WY	82644	(307) 555-8874
38	Laura	Malone	15743 144th Street East	Casper	WY	82602	(307) 555-6462
40	Katrina	Novak	13504 State Street	Mills	WY	82644	(307) 555-9986
41	Duane	Reece	14300 232nd Avenue	Casper	WY	82605	(307) 555-5347
42	Martin	Costanzo	1002 Thomas Drive	Casper	WY	82602	(307) 555-5001
43	Susan	Nordyke	23193 Ridge Circle East	Mills	WY	82644	(307) 555-2719
44	Monica	Sommers	1105 Riddell Avenue	Casper	WY	82609	(307) 555-1188

AL1-C6-Millstone_ClientsReport(CS2).accdb

ClientDirectory

LastName	FirstName	Telephone
Casey	Daniel	(307) 555-3643
Costanzo	Martin	(307) 555-5001
Fairbanks	Sabrina	(307) 555-2322
Gallion	Nicole	(307) 555-7039
Gonzales	Shelley	(307) 555-7283
Heckard	Patricia	(307) 555-0994
Hedges	Luanne	(307) 555-8547
Johnson	Thomas	(307) 555-3444
Knudsen	Nathan	(307) 555-8874
Malone	Laura	(307) 555-6462
Nordyke	Susan	(307) 555-2719
Novak	Katrina	(307) 555-9986
Reece	Duane	(307) 555-5347
Sommers	Monica	(307) 555-1188
Tolman	Roger	(307) 555-2341
Washington	Darren	(307) 555-4882

Thursday, October 15, 2015

Page 1 of 1

AL1-C6-Millstone_ClientDirectory(CS2).accdb

ClientBilling

Thursday, October 15, 2015
5:23:28 PM

LName	ClientID	FirstName	LastName	BillingDate	Fee
Leland					
	25	Nicole	Gallion	3/2/2015	$75.00
	32	Luanne	Hedges	3/4/2015	$150.00
	32	Luanne	Hedges	3/11/2015	$200.00
	32	Luanne	Hedges	3/12/2015	$125.00
	38	Laura	Malone	3/3/2015	$75.00
	38	Laura	Malone	3/10/2015	$200.00
	38	Laura	Malone	3/11/2015	$300.00
	40	Katrina	Novak	3/12/2015	$100.00
	40	Katrina	Novak	3/13/2015	$200.00
	40	Katrina	Novak	3/9/2015	$250.00
	44	Monica	Sommers	3/15/2015	$250.00
Parente					
	29	Daniel	Casey	3/3/2015	$125.00
	29	Daniel	Casey	3/13/2015	$225.00
	29	Daniel	Casey	3/10/2015	$100.00
	29	Daniel	Casey	3/6/2015	$150.00
	31	Sabrina	Fairbanks	3/2/2015	$125.00
	31	Sabrina	Fairbanks	3/4/2015	$100.00
	31	Sabrina	Fairbanks	3/12/2015	$125.00
	28	Patricia	Heckard	3/9/2015	$125.00
	28	Patricia	Heckard	3/13/2015	$150.00
	28	Patricia	Heckard	3/6/2015	$275.00
	40	Katrina	Novak	3/4/2015	$225.00
	41	Duane	Reece	3/10/2015	$250.00
	41	Duane	Reece	3/5/2015	$200.00
Ryder					
	25	Nicole	Gallion	3/9/2015	$150.00
	36	Thomas	Johnson	3/11/2015	$275.00
	36	Thomas	Johnson	3/3/2015	$150.00
	36	Thomas	Johnson	3/5/2015	$275.00

Page

AL1-C6-Millstone_ClientBillingRpt(CS2).accdb

Client Billing 3/10/2015 to 3/13/2015

ClientID	FirstName	LastName	LName	BillingDate	Fee
38	Laura	Malone	Leland	3/10/2015	$200.00
32	Luanne	Hedges	Leland	3/10/2015	$200.00
38	Laura	Malone	Leland	3/11/2015	$300.00
32	Luanne	Hedges	Leland	3/11/2015	$125.00
40	Katrina	Novak	Leland	3/12/2015	$100.00
40	Katrina	Novak	Leland	3/13/2015	$200.00
41	Duane	Reece	Parente	3/10/2015	$250.00
29	Daniel	Casey	Parente	3/10/2015	$100.00
31	Sabrina	Fairbanks	Parente	3/12/2015	$125.00
29	Daniel	Casey	Parente	3/13/2015	$225.00
28	Patricia	Heckard	Parente	3/13/2015	$150.00
36	Thomas	Johnson	Ryder	3/11/2015	$275.00
21	Roger	Tolman	Ryder	3/12/2015	$200.00
20	Shelley	Gonzales	Sheehan	3/10/2015	$150.00
37	Nathan	Knudsen	Sheehan	3/13/2015	$100.00
					$2,700.00

Page

AL1-C6-Millstone_ClientBilling10-13Rpt(CS2).accdb

ClientBilling10-13

10/15/2015

ClientID	FirstName	LastName	LName	BillingDate	Fee
38	Laura	Malone	Leland	3/10/2015	$200.00
41	Duane	Reece	Parente	3/10/2015	$250.00
20	Shelley	Gonzales	Sheehan	3/10/2015	$150.00
29	Daniel	Casey	Parente	3/10/2015	$100.00
32	Luanne	Hedges	Leland	3/11/2015	$200.00
38	Laura	Malone	Leland	3/11/2015	$300.00
36	Thomas	Johnson	Ryder	3/11/2015	$275.00
32	Luanne	Hedges	Leland	3/12/2015	$125.00
21	Roger	Tolman	Ryder	3/12/2015	$200.00
31	Sabrina	Fairbanks	Parente	3/12/2015	$125.00
29	Daniel	Casey	Parente	3/13/2015	$225.00
37	Nathan	Knudsen	Sheehan	3/13/2015	$100.00
28	Patricia	Heckard	Parente	3/13/2015	$150.00
40	Katrina	Novak	Leland	3/13/2015	$200.00

Page 1

AL1-C6-Millstone_ClientBilling10-13Query(CS2).accdb

Clients

ClientID	FirstName	LastName	StreetAddress	City	State	ZipCode	Telephone
20	Shelley	Gonzales	321 South Poplar	Casper	WY	82605	(307) 555-7283
21	Roger	Tolman	15344 Fairline South	Mills	WY	82644	(307) 555-2341
22	Darren	Washington	341 North 32nd	Casper	WY	82602	(307) 555-4882
25	Nicole	Gallion	21534 148th Street	Casper	WY	82605	(307) 555-7039
28	Patricia	Heckard	806 Hamilton Drive	Mills	WY	82644	(307) 555-0994
29	Daniel	Casey	23119 257th Avenue	Casper	WY	82602	(307) 555-3643
31	Sabrina	Fairbanks	430 Corrin Street	Mills	WY	82644	(307) 555-2322
32	Luanne	Hedges	15121 Tubbs Road	Casper	WY	82604	(307) 555-8547
36	Thomas	Johnson	18032 150th Street East	Casper	WY	82601	(307) 555-3444
37	Nathan	Knudsen	301 Wheaton Road	Mills	WY	82644	(307) 555-8874
38	Laura	Malone	15743 144th Street East	Casper	WY	82602	(307) 555-6462
40	Katrina	Novak	13504 State Street	Mills	WY	82644	(307) 555-9986
41	Duane	Reece	14300 232nd Avenue	Casper	WY	82605	(307) 555-5347
42	Martin	Costanzo	1002 Thomas Drive	Casper	WY	82602	(307) 555-5001
43	Susan	Nordyke	23193 Ridge Circle East	Mills	WY	82644	(307) 555-2719
44	Monica	Sommers	1105 Riddell Avenue	Casper	WY	82609	(307) 555-1188

Page

AL1-C6-Millstone_ClientsReport(CS3).accdb

Shelley Gonzales
321 South Poplar
Casper, WY 82605

Roger Tolman
15344 Fairline South
Mills, WY 82644

Darren Washington
341 North 32nd
Casper, WY 82602

Nicole Gallion
21534 148th Street
Casper, WY 82605

Patricia Heckard
806 Hamilton Drive
Mills, WY 82644

Daniel Casey
23119 257th Avenue
Casper, WY 82602

Sabrina Fairbanks
430 Corrin Street
Mills, WY 82644

Luanne Hedges
15121 Tubbs Road
Casper, WY 82604

Thomas Johnson
18032 150th Street East
Casper, WY 82601

Nathan Knudsen
301 Wheaton Road
Mills, WY 82644

Laura Malone
15743 144th Street East
Casper, WY 82602

Katrina Novak
13504 State Street
Mills, WY 82644

Duane Reece
14300 232nd Avenue
Casper, WY 82605

Martin Costanzo
1002 Thomas Drive
Casper, WY 82602

Susan Nordyke
23193 Ridge Circle East
Mills, WY 82644

Monica Sommers
1105 Riddell Avenue
Casper, WY 82609

AL1-C6-Millstone_ClientLabels(CS2).accdb

ClientBilling

Thursday, October 15, 2015
5:27:43 PM

LName	ClientID	FirstName	LastName	BillingDate	Fee
Leland					
	25	Nicole	Gallion	3/2/2015	$75.00
	32	Luanne	Hedges	3/4/2015	$150.00
	32	Luanne	Hedges	3/11/2015	$200.00
	32	Luanne	Hedges	3/12/2015	$125.00
	38	Laura	Malone	3/3/2015	$75.00
	38	Laura	Malone	3/10/2015	$200.00
	38	Laura	Malone	3/11/2015	$300.00
	40	Katrina	Novak	3/12/2015	$100.00
	40	Katrina	Novak	3/13/2015	$200.00
	40	Katrina	Novak	3/9/2015	$250.00
	44	Monica	Sommers	3/15/2015	$250.00
Parente					
	29	Daniel	Casey	3/3/2015	$125.00
	29	Daniel	Casey	3/13/2015	$225.00
	29	Daniel	Casey	3/10/2015	$100.00
	29	Daniel	Casey	3/6/2015	$150.00
	31	Sabrina	Fairbanks	3/2/2015	$125.00
	31	Sabrina	Fairbanks	3/4/2015	$100.00
	31	Sabrina	Fairbanks	3/12/2015	$125.00
	28	Patricia	Heckard	3/9/2015	$125.00
	28	Patricia	Heckard	3/13/2015	$150.00
	28	Patricia	Heckard	3/6/2015	$275.00
	40	Katrina	Novak	3/4/2015	$225.00
	41	Duane	Reece	3/10/2015	$250.00
	41	Duane	Reece	3/5/2015	$200.00
Ryder					
	25	Nicole	Gallion	3/9/2015	$150.00
	36	Thomas	Johnson	3/11/2015	$275.00
	36	Thomas	Johnson	3/3/2015	$150.00
	36	Thomas	Johnson	3/5/2015	$275.00

Page

LName	ClientID	FirstName	LastName	BillingDate	Fee
	43	Susan	Nordyke	3/15/2015	$175.00
	21	Roger	Tolman	3/12/2015	$200.00
Sheehan					
	42	Martin	Costanzo	3/15/2015	$150.00
	20	Shelley	Gonzales	3/2/2015	$200.00
	20	Shelley	Gonzales	3/10/2015	$150.00
	37	Nathan	Knudsen	3/4/2015	$250.00
	37	Nathan	Knudsen	3/6/2015	$100.00
	37	Nathan	Knudsen	3/13/2015	$100.00
	22	Darren	Washington	3/5/2015	$225.00
					$6,500.00

Page

Benchmark Access 2013 Level 1 Model Answers

g. Type a comma (,) and then press the spacebar.
h. With *State* selected in the *Available fields* list box, click the button containing the greater than symbol (>).
i. Press the space bar.
j. With *ZipCode* selected in the *Available fields* list box, click the button containing the greater than symbol (>).
k. Click the Next button.
8. At the fourth Label Wizard dialog box, specify the desired sorting, and then click the Next button.
9. At the fifth Label Wizard dialog box, type the desired name in the *What name would you like for your report?* text box and then click the Finish button.

Steps for Creating a Report with the Report Button
1. Open the desired database and then enable the contents.
2. Click the desired table in the Navigation pane.
3. Click the CREATE tab.
4. Click the Report button in the Reports group.
5. Click the Save button on the Quick Access toolbar.
6. Type the desired name in the *Report Name* text box in the Save As dialog box and then click OK.

Steps for Creating a Report with the Report Wizard
1. Open the desired database and enable the contents.
2. Click the CREATE tab.
3. Click the Report Wizard button in the Reports group.
4. At the first Report Wizard dialog box, choose the desired table and/or query and insert the desired fields in the Selected Fields list box.
5. Click the Next button.
6. At the second Report Wizard dialog box, specify any grouping levels and then click the Next button.
7. At the third Report Wizard dialog box, specify any desired sort order and then click the Next button.
8. At the fourth Report Wizard dialog box, click the desired report layout and orientation and then click the Next button.
9. At the fifth Report Wizard dialog box, click the desired report style in the list box and then click the Next button.
10. At the sixth Report Wizard dialog box, type a title for the report in the *What title do you want for your report?* text box and then click the Finish button.

Steps for Preparing Mailing Labels
1. Open the desired database and enable the contents.
2. Click the desired table in the Navigation pane.
3. Click the CREATE tab.
4. Click the Labels button in the Reports group.
5. At the first Label Wizard dialog box, choose the desired label type and product number and then click the Next button.
6. At the second Label Wizard dialog box, make any desired changes to the font or font color and then click the Next button.
7. At the third Label Wizard dialog box, complete the following steps to insert the fields in the Prototype label:
a. Click *FirstName* in the *Available fields* list box and then click the button containing the greater than symbol (>).
b. Press the space bar, make sure *LastName* is selected in the *Available fields* list box, and then click the button containing the greater than symbol (>).
c. Press the Enter key (this moves the insertion point down to the next line in the Prototype label).
d. With *Street Address* selected in the *Available fields* list box, click the button containing the greater than symbol (>).
e. Press the Enter key.
f. With *City* selected in the *Available fields* list box, click the button containing the greater than symbol (>).

Access Level 1, Chapter 7 Model Answers

Clients   10/16/2015

ClientID	FirstName	LastName	StreetAddress	City	State	ZipCode	Telephone
298	Mindy	Garvison	68 Queens Avenue	Kent	WA	98033	(253) 555-1195
321	Jeffrey	Day	317 Meridian Street	Kent	WA	98033	(253) 555-3129

3b. Display only those records of clients with the zip code of 98033.
When the records of clients with the zip code 98033 display, print the
results in landscape orientation and then remove the filter.
4. Close the Clients table without saving the changes.

Page 1

Clients   10/16/2015

ClientID	FirstName	LastName	StreetAddress	City	State	ZipCode	Telephone
125	Maddie	Singh	450 Mill Avenue	Renton	WA	98228	(253) 555-6673
138	Mira	Valencia	114 Springfield Avenue	Renton	WA	98056	(425) 555-2216
143	Matthew	Waide	18391 North 45th Street	Renton	WA	98055	(425) 555-5599
157	Arthur	Jefferson	23110 North 33rd Street	Renton	WA	98230	(253) 555-4889
187	Chris	Cervantez	8722 Riverside Road	Renton	WA	98228	(425) 555-7263
205	Karl	Cordes	240 Mill Avenue	Renton	WA	98055	(425) 555-2811
225	Jennifer	Czubek	8790 34th Avenue	Renton	WA	98228	(425) 555-3441
263	Charles	Hobart	11038 132nd Street	Renton	WA	98056	(425) 555-1323
287	Taylor	Reyes	201 Northwest Boulevard	Renton	WA	98056	(425) 555-8866

1. Display the open dialog box with the AL1C7 folder on your storage medium the active folder.
2. Open **AL1-C7-WarrenLegal.accdb** and enable the contents.
3. Open the Clients table and then filter the records to display the following records:
a. Display only those records of clients who live in Renton. When the records of clients in Renton display, print the
results in landscape orientation and then remove the filter. ***Hint: Change to landscape orientation in Print Preview.***

Page 1

AL1-C7-A1-WarrenLegal_Billing_Attorney12(A1).accdb

10/16/2015

Billing

BillingID	ClientID	Date	CategoryID	Hours	RateID	AttorneyID
2	225	6/1/2015	SE	1.75	1	12
5	138	6/1/2015	SE	0.50	1	12
10	138	6/2/2015	SE	0.75	2	12
14	138	6/3/2015	SE	2.00	1	12
17	225	6/4/2015	CV	1.50	1	12
18	241	6/4/2015	G	1.00	2	12
21	144	6/5/2015	SE	0.25	1	12
25	225	6/8/2015	CV	0.50	1	12
35	129	6/10/2015	D	1.50	2	12
36	241	6/10/2015	G	0.25	2	12
38	225	6/11/2015	CV	0.25	1	12
46	141	6/12/2015	G	1.00	2	12
50	129	6/15/2015	D	0.50	2	12
52	241	6/15/2015	G	0.25	2	12
53	129	6/15/2015	D	0.50	2	12

5b. Display only those records with an attorney ID of 12. Print the records and then remove the filter.

Page 1

AL1-C7-A1-WarrenLegal_Billing_CategoryCC(A1).accdb

10/16/2015

Billing

BillingID	ClientID	Date	CategoryID	Hours	RateID	AttorneyID
3	321	6/1/2015	CC	1.50	4	19
20	125	6/4/2015	CC	1.50	4	19
22	321	6/5/2015	CC	1.00	4	19
30	321	6/9/2015	CC	1.50	4	19
41	116	6/11/2015	CC	1.50	4	17
47	321	6/12/2015	CC	1.25	1	19

5. Open the billing table and then filter the records by selection to display the following records:
a. Display only those records with a category of CC. Print the records and then remove the filter.

Page 1

ClientID	FirstName	LastName	StreetAddress	City	State	ZipCode	Telephone
110	Margaret	Kasper	40210 42nd Avenue	Auburn	WA	98001	(253) 555-9003
112	Haley	Brown	3219 North 33rd Street	Auburn	WA	98001	(253) 555-3948
121	Doris	Sturtevant	3713 Nelton Road	Auburn	WA	98001	(253) 555-3120
125	Maddie	Singh	450 Mill Avenue	Renton	WA	98228	(253) 555-6673
130	Abigail	Jefferson	1204 Meridian Road	Auburn	WA	98001	(253) 555-5665
138	Mira	Valencia	114 Springfield Avenue	Renton	WA	98056	(425) 555-2216
143	Matthew	Waide	18391 North 45th Street	Renton	WA	98055	(425) 555-5599
144	Carlina	McFadden	7809 52nd Street East	Auburn	WA	98001	(253) 555-2939
157	Arthur	Jefferson	23110 North 33rd Street	Renton	WA	98230	(253) 555-4889
187	Chris	Cervantez	8722 Riverside Road	Renton	WA	98228	(425) 555-7263
205	Karl	Cordes	240 Mill Avenue	Renton	WA	98055	(425) 555-2811
225	Jennifer	Czubek	8790 34th Avenue	Renton	WA	98228	(425) 555-3441
241	Ewan	Aragato	904 Marine View Drive	Auburn	WA	98002	(253) 555-0113
263	Charles	Hobart	11038 132nd Street	Renton	WA	98056	(425) 555-1323
275	Tricia	O'Connor	3824 Sanders Court	Auburn	WA	98002	(253) 555-4493
287	Taylor	Reyes	201 Northwest Boulevard	Renton	WA	98056	(425) 555-8866
303	Eric	Rosenthal	1230 Maplewood Road	Auburn	WA	98071	(253) 555-3375

7. Open the Clients table and then use the *Filter By Form* option to display clients in Auburn or Renton. (Be sure to use the or tab at the bottom of the table.) Print the table in landscape orientation and then remove the filter.
8. Close the Clients table without saving the changes.

Page 1

AL1-C7-A1-WarrenLegal_Clients_Auburn&Renton(A1).accdb

BillingID	ClientID	Date	CategoryID	Hours	RateID	AttorneyID
1	164	6/1/2015	G	1.00	3	14
2	225	6/1/2015	SE	1.75	1	12
3	321	6/1/2015	CC	1.50	4	19
4	187	6/1/2015	P	2.00	2	17
5	138	6/1/2015	SE	0.50	1	12
6	164	6/2/2015	G	1.75	3	14
7	263	6/2/2015	IN	0.75	4	14
8	187	6/2/2015	P	0.75	4	17
9	164	6/2/2015	G	1.50	4	14
10	138	6/2/2015	SE	0.75	2	12
11	205	6/2/2015	P	1.00	3	19
12	110	6/3/2015	SE	2.00	1	14
13	130	6/3/2015	IN	1.00	3	14
14	138	6/3/2015	SE	2.00	1	12
15	164	6/3/2015	G	1.50	3	14
16	321	6/3/2015	CV	0.75	1	19
17	225	6/4/2015	CV	1.50	1	12
18	241	6/4/2015	P	1.00	2	12
19	110	6/4/2015	SE	1.00	1	14
20	125	6/4/2015	CC	1.50	4	19
21	144	6/5/2015	SE	0.25	1	12
22	321	6/5/2015	CC	1.00	4	19
23	164	6/5/2015	G	1.25	4	14
24	110	6/5/2015	CV	1.50	1	12
25	225	6/8/2015	P	0.50	1	17
26	187	6/8/2015	P	2.00	2	14
27	130	6/8/2015	D	1.00	2	17
28	275	6/9/2015	CC	2.25	1	19
29	275	6/9/2015	P	1.50	4	14
30	321	6/9/2015	CC	1.00	3	19
31	205	6/9/2015	P	1.00	2	14
32	263	6/9/2015	A	1.00	2	17
33	143	6/9/2015	IN	1.00	3	14
34	130	6/10/2015	IN	1.00	2	14
35	129	6/10/2015	D	1.50	2	12
36	241	6/10/2015	G	0.25	2	12
37	287	6/10/2015	SE	1.00	1	17

5c. Display only those records with dates between 6/1/2015 and 6/10/2015. Print the records and then remove the filter.
6. Close the billing table without saving the changes.

Page 1

AL1-C7-A1-WarrenLegal_Billing_DateBetween(A1).accdb

A2,Step2_PrintScreen.docx

Billing

10/16/2015

BillingID	ClientID	Date	CategoryID	Hours	RateID	AttorneyID
1	164	6/1/2015	G	1.00	3	14
4	187	6/1/2015	P	2.00	2	17
6	164	6/2/2015	G	1.75	3	14
8	187	6/2/2015	P	0.75	4	17
9	164	6/2/2015	G	1.50	4	14
11	205	6/2/2015	P	1.00	3	19
15	164	6/3/2015	G	1.50	3	14
18	241	6/4/2015	G	1.00	2	12
23	164	6/5/2015	G	1.25	4	14
26	187	6/8/2015	P	2.00	2	17
31	205	6/9/2015	P	1.00	3	19
36	241	6/10/2015	P	0.25	2	12
42	164	6/11/2015	G	1.00	4	14
46	141	6/12/2015	G	1.00	2	12
52	241	6/15/2015	G	0.25	2	12

9. Open the billing table and then use the *Filter By Form* option to display category G or P. Print the table and then remove the filter.
10. Close the billing table without saving the changes.

Page 1

AL1-C7-A1-WarrenLegal_Billing_CategoryG&P(A1).accdb

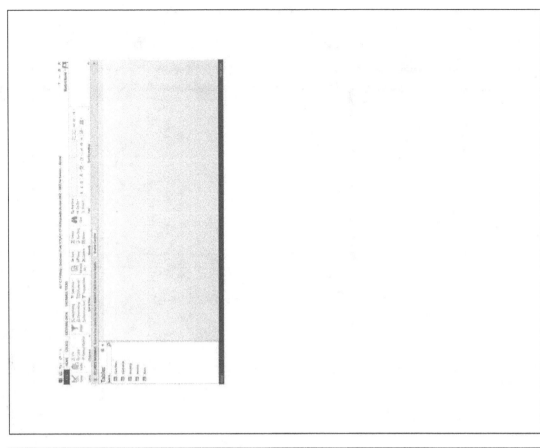

A2,Step12_PrintScreen.docx

Invoices   10/16/2015

InvoiceID	BillingDate	CustomerID	EquipmentID	Hours	RateID
1	5/1/2015	310	10	8	D
2	5/1/2015	310	11	8	E
3	5/1/2015	267	12	4	C
4	5/4/2015	196	10	16	D
5	5/4/2015	305	13	5	E
6	5/4/2015	305	14	5	A
7	5/4/2015	106	15	10	C
8	5/5/2015	106	16	10	B
9	5/5/2015	275	17	8	A
10	5/6/2015	154	18	8	A
11	5/6/2015	154	17	8	A
12	5/7/2015	209	11	10	E
13	5/7/2015	209	19	10	D
14	5/7/2015	316	15	6	C
15	5/8/2015	267	16	8	B
16	5/8/2015	275	18	8	A
17	5/8/2015	275	17	8	A
18	5/11/2015	305	10	4	D
19	5/11/2015	305	13	4	E
20	5/11/2015	196	12	4	C
21	5/12/2015	196	15	6	C
22	5/12/2015	267	19	5	D
23	5/12/2015	310	11	6	E
24	5/13/2015	209	17	8	A
25	5/13/2015	106	14	6	A
26	5/14/2015	275	16	6	B
27	5/14/2015	154	13	4	E
28	5/15/2015	316	11	4	E
29	5/15/2015	267	15	4	C
30	5/15/2015	106	18	8	A

Page 1

Invoices(A2).accdb

ProductsOnOrderQuery   10/16/2015

SupplierName	ProductID	Product	UnitsOnOrder
Hopewell, Inc.	152-H	Lantern hanger	15
Hopewell, Inc.	155-20	Shursite angle-head flashlight	20
Hopewell, Inc.	155-35	Shursite portable camp light	10
Cascade Gear	250-L	Cascade R4 jacket, ML	10
Cascade Gear	250-XL	Cascade R4 jacket, MXL	10
Cascade Gear	255-M	Cascade R4 jacket, WM	5
Cascade Gear	255-XL	Cascade R4 jacket, WXL	5

AL1-C7-PacTrek_ProductsOnOrderQuery(VB).accdb

BillingDate	Equipment	Hours	Rate
5/1/2015	Backhoe	8	$75.00
5/1/2015	Front loader	8	$100.00
5/1/2015	Trencher	4	$50.00
5/4/2015	Backhoe	16	$75.00
5/4/2015	Tractor	5	$100.00
5/4/2015	Scaffolding	5	$25.00
5/4/2015	Forklift	10	$50.00
5/5/2015	Hydraulic pump	10	$35.00
5/5/2015	Pressure sprayer	8	$25.00
5/6/2015	Sandblaster	8	$25.00
5/6/2015	Pressure sprayer	8	$25.00
5/7/2015	Front loader	10	$100.00
5/7/2015	Flatbed truck	10	$75.00
5/7/2015	Forklift	6	$50.00
5/8/2015	Hydraulic pump	8	$35.00
5/8/2015	Sandblaster	8	$25.00
5/8/2015	Pressure sprayer	8	$25.00
5/11/2015	Backhoe	4	$75.00
5/11/2015	Tractor	4	$100.00
5/11/2015	Trencher	4	$50.00
5/12/2015	Forklift	6	$50.00
5/12/2015	Flatbed truck	5	$75.00
5/12/2015	Front loader	6	$100.00
5/13/2015	Pressure sprayer	8	$25.00
5/13/2015	Scaffolding	6	$25.00
5/14/2015	Hydraulic pump	6	$35.00
5/14/2015	Tractor	4	$100.00
5/15/2015	Front loader	4	$100.00
5/15/2015	Forklift	4	$50.00
5/15/2015	Sandblaster	8	$25.00

1. Open **AL1-C7-Hilltop.accdb**. (Make sure you open the AL1-C7-Hilltop database with the .accdb file extension.)

2. Right-click an object in the Navigation pane, experiment with options in the shortcut menu, and then complete these steps using the shortcut menu:

   a. Delete the Inventory form.

   b. Rename the form Equipment as *EquipForm*.

   c. Rename the report InvReport as *InventoryReport*.

   d. Export (using the shortcut menu) the *EquipmentQuery* to a Word RTF file. *Hint: Click the Browse button at the Export - RTF File dialog box and make the folder AL1C7 the active folder.*

   e. Open the *EquipmentQuery.rtf* file in Word, print the file, and then close Word.

AL1-C7-A3-Hilltop-EquipmentQuery(A3).accdb

Billing

BillingID	PatientID	DoctorID	DateOfVisit	ServiceID	Fee
6	110	18	4/2/2015	V	$100.00
7	112	15	4/2/2015	E	$150.00
8	112	15	4/2/2015	F	$50.00
9	120	18	4/2/2015	I	$100.00
10	115	16	4/2/2015	WC	$175.00
11	116	16	4/2/2015	WC	$175.00

Page 1

AL1-C7-CS2-SummitView_Billing_April2(CS2).accdb

Billing

BillingID	PatientID	DoctorID	DateOfVisit	ServiceID	Fee
2	117	18	4/1/2015	P	$125.00
4	106	18	4/1/2015	WC	$175.00
6	110	18	4/2/2015	V	$100.00
9	120	18	4/2/2015	I	$100.00
15	118	18	4/5/2015	WC	$175.00
17	110	18	4/5/2015	I	$100.00
22	106	18	4/6/2015	I	$100.00

Page 1

AL1-C7-CS2-SummitView_Billing_Doctor18(CS2).accdb

Patients

Friday, October 16, 2015
3:05:19 PM

FirstName	LastName	StreetAddress	City	State	ZipCode
Roberta	Poulsen	1005 132nd Street	East Helena	MT	59635
Rosemarie	Dahlquist	19083 Harman Way	East Helena	MT	59635
Mary	Garcia	25403 Ferndale Road	East Helena	MT	59635
Timothy	Piper	342 North Ridge Drive	East Helena	MT	59635
Luke	Oberman	770 Pine Street	East Helena	MT	59635
Ellen	Augustine	12590 148th Street	East Helena	MT	59635

AL1-C7-CS2-SummitView_EastHelenaReport(CS2).accdb

Patients

Friday, October 16, 2015
3:04:44 PM

FirstName	LastName	StreetAddress	City	State	ZipCode
Joel	Trujillo	3210 Eldridge Road	Helena	MT	59604
Autumn	Warner	11290 West Lowell	Helena	MT	59620
Martin	Baldwin	15409 Pioneer Drive	Helena	MT	59624
Jerry	Gaynor	14403 210th Avenue	Helena	MT	59601
Rachel	Kolowski	1120 Tenth Street	Helena	MT	59626
Brian	Mahoney	17034 261st Court East	Helena	MT	59623
Genevieve	Palmer	10032 144th Street	Helena	MT	59624
Gianni	Cordova	5576 South 22nd Street	Helena	MT	59620
Brian	Gould	2887 Nelson Street	Helena	MT	59604
Jeff	Masura	3218 Eldridge Avenue	Helena	MT	59624

AL1-C7-CS2-SummitView_Patients_HelenaReport(CS2).accdb

DoctorBillingFees

DoctorID	LName	PatientID	DateOfVisit	Fee
15	Rowe	109	4/1/2015	$125.00
15	Rowe	112	4/2/2015	$150.00
15	Rowe	112	4/2/2015	$50.00
15	Rowe	105	4/5/2015	$75.00
15	Rowe	123	4/6/2015	$175.00
16	Wallace	115	4/2/2015	$175.00
16	Wallace	116	4/2/2015	$100.00
16	Wallace	116	4/5/2015	$75.00
16	Wallace	121	4/6/2015	$75.00
17	Kennedy	104	4/1/2015	$50.00
17	Kennedy	104	4/5/2015	$75.00
17	Kennedy	114	4/5/2015	$90.00
17	Kennedy	122	4/6/2015	$75.00
17	Kennedy	109	4/6/2015	$125.00
17	Kennedy	114	4/1/2015	$175.00
18	Pena	117	4/1/2015	$100.00
18	Pena	106	4/2/2015	$100.00
18	Pena	110	4/2/2015	$100.00
18	Pena	120	4/5/2015	$175.00
18	Pena	118	4/5/2015	$100.00
18	Pena	110	4/6/2015	$100.00

AL1-C7-CS2-SummitView_DoctorBillingFees(CS2).accdb

DoctorBillingFees

DoctorID	LName	PatientID	DateOfVisit	Fee
17	Kennedy	104	4/1/2015	$75.00
17	Kennedy	106	4/1/2015	$50.00
17	Kennedy	104	4/5/2015	$50.00
17	Kennedy	114	4/5/2015	$75.00
17	Kennedy	122	4/6/2015	$90.00
17	Kennedy	109	4/6/2015	$75.00
17	Kennedy	114	4/1/2015	$125.00
18	Pena	106	4/2/2015	$100.00
18	Pena	110	4/2/2015	$100.00
18	Pena	120	4/5/2015	$175.00
18	Pena	118	4/5/2015	$100.00
18	Pena	110	4/5/2015	$100.00
18	Pena	106	4/6/2015	$100.00

AL1-C7-CS2-SummitView_DcotorsKennedy&Pena(CS2).accdb

Billing 10/16/2015

BillingID	PatientID	DoctorID	DateOfVisit	ServiceID	Fee
1	104	17	4/1/2015	V	$75.00
2	117	18	4/1/2015	P	$125.00
3	106	17	4/1/2015	F	$50.00
4	106	18	4/1/2015	WC	$175.00
5	109	15	4/1/2015	P	$125.00
6	110	18	4/2/2015	V	$100.00
7	112	15	4/2/2015	E	$150.00
8	112	15	4/2/2015	F	$50.00
9	120	18	4/2/2015	I	$100.00
10	115	16	4/2/2015	WC	$175.00
11	116	16	4/2/2015	WC	$175.00
12	116	16	4/5/2015	I	$100.00
13	105	15	4/5/2015	V	$75.00
14	104	17	4/5/2015	F	$50.00
15	118	18	4/5/2015	WC	$175.00
16	114	17	4/5/2015	V	$75.00
17	110	18	4/5/2015	I	$100.00
18	121	16	4/6/2015	V	$75.00
19	122	17	4/6/2015	CS	$90.00
20	123	15	4/6/2015	X	$75.00
21	109	17	4/6/2015	CS	$90.00
22	106	18	4/6/2015	I	$100.00
23	114	17	4/6/2015	X	$75.00

Page 1

AL1-C7-CS3-SummitView_BillingTable(CS3).accdb

DoctorBillingFees 10/16/2015

DoctorID	LName	PatientID	DateOfVisit	Fee
16	Wallace	116	4/5/2015	$100.00
15	Rowe	105	4/5/2015	$75.00
17	Kennedy	104	4/5/2015	$50.00
18	Pena	118	4/5/2015	$175.00
17	Kennedy	114	4/5/2015	$75.00
18	Pena	110	4/5/2015	$100.00
16	Wallace	121	4/6/2015	$75.00
17	Kennedy	122	4/6/2015	$90.00
15	Rowe	123	4/6/2015	$75.00
17	Kennedy	109	4/6/2015	$90.00
18	Pena	106	4/6/2015	$100.00
17	Kennedy	114	4/6/2015	$75.00

Page 1

AL1-C7-CS2-SummitView_DateBetween(CS2).accdb

Access Level 1, Chapter 8 Model Answers

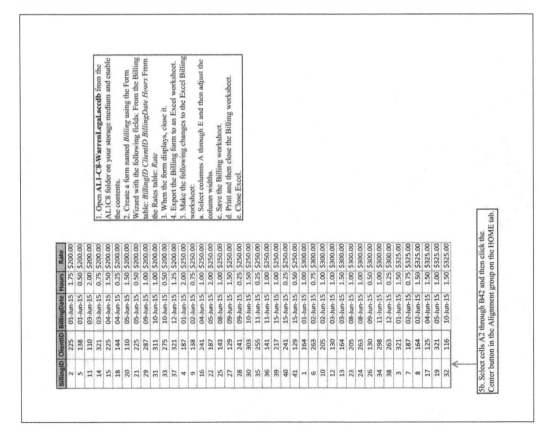

Billing-Excel worksheet

Instructions:

1. Open **AL1-C8-WarrenLegal.accdb** from the AL1C8 folder on your storage medium and enable the contents.
2. Create a form named *Billing* using the Form Wizard with the following fields: From the Billing table: *BillingID ClientID BillingDate Hours* From the Rates table: *Rate*
3. When the form displays, close it.
4. Export the Billing form to an Excel worksheet.
5. Make the following changes to the Excel Billing worksheet:
   a. Select columns A through E and then adjust the column widths.
   c. Save the Billing worksheet.
   d. Print and then close the Billing worksheet.
   e. Close Excel.

5b. Select cells A2 through B42 and then click the Center button in the Alignment group on the HOME tab.

BillingID	ClientID	BillingDate	Hours	Rate
2	225	01-Jun-15	1.75	$200.00
5	138	01-Jun-15	0.50	$200.00
11	110	03-Jun-15	2.00	$200.00
14	321	04-Jun-15	0.75	$200.00
15	225	04-Jun-15	1.50	$200.00
18	144	04-Jun-15	0.25	$200.00
20	110	05-Jun-15	1.50	$200.00
21	225	05-Jun-15	0.50	$200.00
29	287	09-Jun-15	1.00	$200.00
31	311	10-Jun-15	0.50	$200.00
33	275	10-Jun-15	0.50	$200.00
37	321	12-Jun-15	1.25	$200.00
4	187	01-Jun-15	2.00	$250.00
9	138	02-Jun-15	0.75	$250.00
16	241	04-Jun-15	1.00	$250.00
22	187	05-Jun-15	2.00	$250.00
25	143	08-Jun-15	1.00	$250.00
27	129	09-Jun-15	1.50	$250.00
28	241	09-Jun-15	0.25	$250.00
30	303	10-Jun-15	1.50	$250.00
35	255	11-Jun-15	0.25	$250.00
36	141	11-Jun-15	1.00	$250.00
39	217	15-Jun-15	1.00	$250.00
40	241	15-Jun-15	0.25	$250.00
41	129	15-Jun-15	0.50	$250.00
1	164	01-Jun-15	1.00	$300.00
6	263	02-Jun-15	0.75	$300.00
10	205	02-Jun-15	1.00	$300.00
12	130	03-Jun-15	1.00	$300.00
13	164	03-Jun-15	1.50	$300.00
23	205	08-Jun-15	1.00	$300.00
24	263	08-Jun-15	1.00	$300.00
26	130	09-Jun-15	0.50	$300.00
34	298	11-Jun-15	1.00	$300.00
38	263	12-Jun-15	0.25	$300.00
3	321	01-Jun-15	1.50	$325.00
7	187	02-Jun-15	1.50	$325.00
8	164	02-Jun-15	1.50	$325.00
17	125	04-Jun-15	1.50	$325.00
19	321	05-Jun-15	1.00	$325.00
32	116	10-Jun-15	1.50	$325.00

AL1-C8-A1-WarrenLegal_Billing-Excel(A1).accdb

Client Billing of Legal Services report

9b. Insert a space between *Client* and *Billing* in the title.

9c. Position the insertion point immediately right of the word *Billing*, press the spacebar, and then type *of Legal Services*.

Client Billing of Legal Services

6. In Access, close the Export Wizard.
7. Create a report named *ClientBilling* using the Report Wizard (at the fifth wizard dialog box, change the layout to *Block*) with the following fields: From the Clients table: *FirstName LastName* From the Billing table: *BillingDate Hours* From the Rates table: *Rate*

FirstName	LastName	Date	Hours	Rate
Margaret	Kasper	6/5/2015	1.50	$200.00
		6/3/2015	2.00	$200.00
Kevin	Stein	6/10/2015	1.50	$325.00
Maddie	Singh	6/4/2015	1.50	$325.00
James	Weyland	6/9/2015	1.50	$250.00
		6/15/2015	0.50	$250.00
Abigail	Jefferson	6/3/2015	1.00	$300.00
		6/9/2015	0.50	$300.00
Mira	Valencia	6/2/2015	0.75	$250.00
		6/1/2015	0.50	$200.00
Consuelo	Day	6/11/2015	1.00	$250.00
Matthew	Waide	6/8/2015	1.00	$250.00
Carlina	McFadden	6/4/2015	0.25	$200.00
Jean	Briggs	6/1/2015	1.00	$300.00
		6/2/2015	1.50	$325.00
Chris	Cervantez	6/3/2015	2.00	$300.00
		6/1/2015	0.75	$250.00
		6/5/2015	2.00	$250.00
Karl	Cordes	6/8/2015	1.00	$300.00
		6/15/2015	1.00	$250.00
Arthur	Norheim	6/1/2015	1.75	$200.00
Jennifer	Czubek	6/4/2015	1.50	$200.00
		6/5/2015	0.50	$250.00
Ewan	Aragato	6/4/2015	1.00	$250.00
		6/9/2015	0.25	$250.00
Janice	Saunders	6/11/2015	0.25	$250.00
Charles	Hobart	6/2/2015	0.75	$300.00
		6/8/2015	1.00	$300.00
Tricia	O'Connor	6/12/2015	0.25	$300.00
Taylor	Reyes	6/10/2015	0.50	$200.00
Mindy	Garvison	6/11/2015	1.00	$300.00
Eric	Rosenthal	6/10/2015	1.50	$250.00
Carol	Kendall	6/10/2015	1.00	$200.00
Jeffrey	Day	6/12/2015	1.25	$325.00
		6/1/2015	1.50	$200.00
		6/3/2015	0.75	$325.00
		6/5/2015	1.00	$325.00

Monday, October 19, 2015

Page 1 of 1

8. Close the report.
9. Create a Word document with the ClientBilling report and save it to the AL1C8 folder on your storage medium with the default name. In the Word document, make the following changes:
a. Press Ctrl + A to select the entire document, change the font color to Black, and then deselect the text.
10. Save and then print **ClientBilling.rtf**.

AL1-C8-A1-WarrenLegal_ClientBilling-Word(A1).accdb

October 19, 2015

Haley Brown
3219 North 33rd Street
Auburn, WA 98001

Ladies and Gentlemen:

The last time you visited our offices, you may have noticed how crowded we were. To alleviate the overcrowding, we are leasing new offices in the Meridian Building and will be moving in at the beginning of next month.

Stop by and see our new offices at our open house planned for the second Friday of next month. Drop by any time between 2:00 and 5:30 p.m. We look forward to seeing you.

Sincerely,

Marjorie Shaw
Senior Partner

XX
AL1-C8-WLLtrs.docx

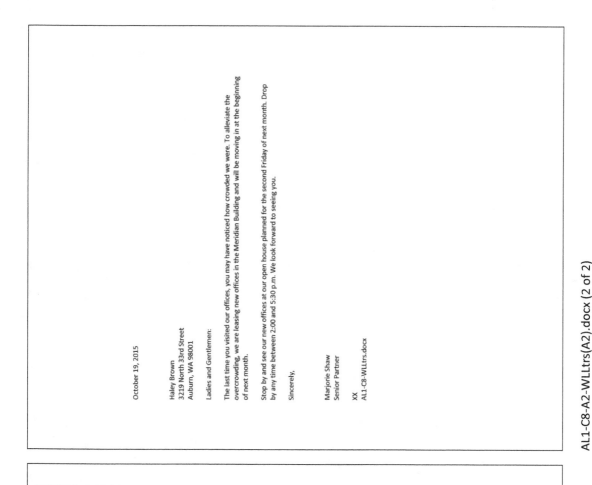

1. With **AL1-C8-WarrenLegal.accdb** open, merge data in the Clients table to a new Word document using the Word Merge button.
2. Maximize the Word document, close the Mail Merge task pane, and then compose a letter with the following elements:
a. Click the Home tab and then click the *No Spacing* style option in the Styles group.
3. Merge to a new document and then save the document with the name **AL1-C8-WLLtrs**.
4. Print only the first two letters in the document and then close **AL1-C8- WLLtrs.docx**.
5. Save the main document and name it **AL1-C8-WLLtrMD1**. Close the document and then close Word.

2b. Press Enter six times, type the current date, and then press Enter four times.

2c. Click the Mailings tab and then insert the «*AddressBlock*» composite field.

2d. Press Enter twice and then type the salutation **Ladies and Gentlemen:**

October 19, 2015

Margaret Kasper
40210 42nd Avenue
Auburn, WA 98001

Ladies and Gentlemen:

The last time you visited our offices, you may have noticed how crowded we were. To alleviate the overcrowding, we are leasing new offices in the Meridian Building and will be moving in at the beginning of next month.

Stop by and see our new offices at our open house planned for the second Friday of next month. Drop by any time between 2:00 and 5:30 p.m. We look forward to seeing you.

Sincerely,

Marjorie Shaw
Senior Partner

XX
AL1-C8-WLLtrs.docx

2e. Press Enter twice and then type the following text (press Enter twice after typing the first paragraph of text): The last time you visited our offices, you may have noticed how crowded we were. To alleviate the overcrowding, we are leasing new offices in the Meridian Building and will be moving in at the beginning of next month. Stop by and see our new offices at our open house planned for the second Friday of next month. Drop by any time between 2:00 and 5:30 p.m. We look forward to seeing you. f. After typing the second paragraph, press Enter twice, type Sincerely, and then press Enter four times. Type Marjorie Shaw, press the Enter key, and then type Senior Partner. Press Enter twice, type your initials, press Enter, and then type AL1-C8-WLLtrs.docx.

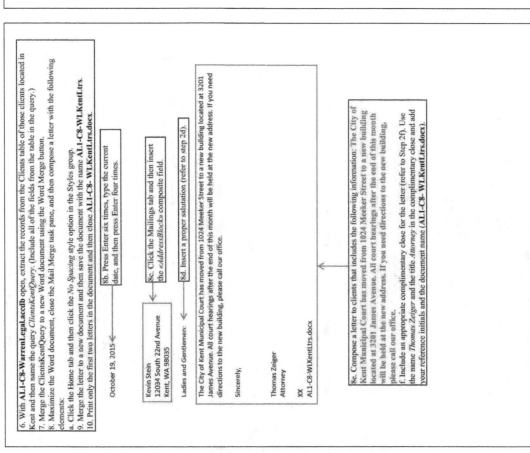

6. With **AL1-C8-WarrenLegal.accdb** open, extract the records from the Clients table of those clients located in Kent and then name the query *ClientsKentQuery*. (Include all of the fields from the table in the query.)
7. Merge the ClientsKentQuery to a new Word document using the Word Merge button.
8. Maximize the Word document, close the Mail Merge task pane, and then compose a letter with the following elements:
a. Click the Home tab and then click the *No Spacing* style option in the Styles group.
9. Merge the letter to a new document and then save the document with the name **AL1-C8-WLKentLtrs**.
10. Print only the first two letters in the document and then close **AL1-C8- WLKentLtrs.docx**.

October 19, 2015

8b. Press Enter six times, type the current date, and then press Enter four times.

Kevin Stein
12034 South 22nd Avenue
Kent, WA 98035

8c. Click the Mailings tab and then insert the *«AddressBlock»* composite field.

Ladies and Gentlemen:

8d. Insert a proper salutation (refer to step 2d).

The City of Kent Municipal Court has moved from 1024 Meeker Street to a new building located at 3201 James Avenue. All court hearings after the end of this month will be held at the new address. If you need directions to the new building, please call our office.

Sincerely,

Thomas Zeiger
Attorney

XX
AL1-C8-WLKentLtrs.docx

8e. Compose a letter to clients that includes the following information: **The City of Kent Municipal Court has moved from 1024 Meeker Street to a new building located at 3201 James Avenue. All court hearings after the end of this month will be held at the new address. If you need directions to the new building, please call our office.**
f. Include an appropriate complimentary close for the letter (refer to Step 2f). Use the name *Thomas Zeiger* and the title *Attorney* in the complimentary close and add your reference initials and the document name (**AL1-C8- WLKentLtrs.docx**).

AL1-C8-A2-WLKentLtrs(A2).docx (1 of 2)

October 19, 2015

James Weyland
2533 145th Street East
Kent, WA 98031

Ladies and Gentlemen:

The City of Kent Municipal Court has moved from 1024 Meeker Street to a new building located at 3201 James Avenue. All court hearings after the end of this month will be held at the new address. If you need directions to the new building, please call our office.

Sincerely,

Thomas Zeiger
Attorney

XX
AL1-C8-WLKentLtrs.docx

AL1-C8-A2-WLKentLtrs(A2).docx (2 of 2)

CaseID	ClientID	TotalBilling
30-D	225	$ 2,145
45-A	164	850
93-B	217	1,125
97-B	110	500
48-A	298	795
50-D	321	3,650
57-D	130	$ 1,100
42-A	144	3,250
29-C	125	$ 900

5. Apply the Accounting formatting with a dollar sign and no decimal places to cells C8, C9, and C10.

4. Open Excel, open the **AL1-C8-Cases.xlsx** workbook and then add the following data in the specified cells:
A8: 57-D B8: 130 C8: 1,100 A9: 42-A B9: 144 C9: 3,250
A10: 29-C B10: 125 C10: 900
6. Save, print, and then close **AL1-C8-Cases.xlsx**.
7. Close Excel.

10/19/2015

Cases

CaseID	ClientID	TotalBilling
30-D	225	$2,145
45-A	164	$850
93-B	217	$1,125
97-B	110	$500
48-A	298	$795
50-D	321	$3,650

1. With **AL1-C8-WarrenLegal.accdb** open, link **AL1-C8-Cases.xlsx** into a new table named *Cases*.
2. Open the Cases table in Datasheet view.
3. Print and then close the Cases table.

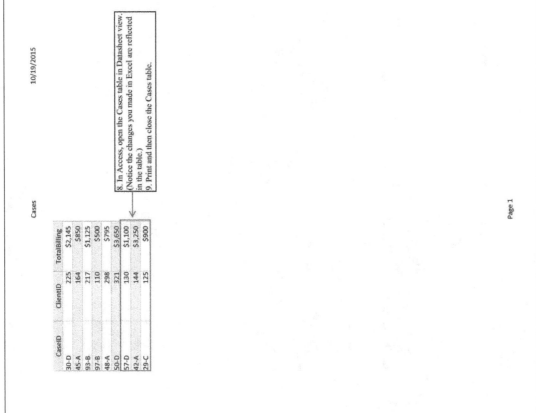

RepQuotas

Quota	RepName	Telephone
$100,000.00	Robin Rehberg	(317) 555-9812
	Andre Kulisek	(317) 555-2264
	Edward Harris	(317) 555-3894
	Cecilia Ortega	(317) 555-4810
$150,000.00	David DeBruler	(317) 555-8779
	Jaren Newman	(317) 555-6790
	Lee Hutchinson	(765) 555-4277
	Craig Johnson	(317) 555-4391
$200,000.00	Isabelle Marshall	(765) 555-8822
	Maureen Pascual	(317) 555-5513
	Linda Foster	(317) 555-2101
	Catherine Singleton	(317) 555-0172
$250,000.00	Kwan Im	(317) 555-8374
	William Ludlow	(317) 555-0991
	Lydia Alvarado	(765) 555-4996
$300,000.00	Gina Tapparo	(317) 555-0044
	Alfred Silva	(317) 555-3211

Monday, October 19, 2015

Page 1 of 1

AL1-C8-VB-Dearborn-RepQuotas-Access(VB).accdb

Cases

10/19/2015

CaseID	ClientID	TotalBilling
30-D	225	$2,145
45-A	164	$850
93-B	217	$1,125
97-B	110	$500
48-A	298	$795
50-D	321	$3,650
57-D	130	$1,100
42-A	144	$3,250
29-C	125	$900

8. In Access, open the Cases table in Datasheet view. (Notice the changes you made in Excel are reflected in the table.)
9. Print and then close the Cases table.

Page 1

AL1-C8-A3-WarrenLegal_Cases-Access(A3,Step9).xlsx

Representatives Quotas

Quota	RepName	Telephone
$100,000.00	Robin Rehberg	(317) 555-9812
	Andre Kulisek	(317) 555-2264
	Edward Harris	(317) 555-3894
	Cecilia Ortega	(317) 555-4810
$150,000.00	David DeBruler	(317) 555-8779
	Jaren Newman	(317) 555-6790
	Lee Hutchinson	(765) 555-4277
	Craig Johnson	(317) 555-4391
$200,000.00	Isabelle Marshall	(765) 555-8822
	Maureen Pascual	(317) 555-5513
	Linda Foster	(317) 555-2101
	Catherine Singleton	(317) 555-0172
$250,000.00	Kwan Im	(317) 555-8374
	William Ludlow	(317) 555-0991
	Lydia Alvarado	(765) 555-4996
$300,000.00	Gina Tapparo	(317) 555-0044
	Alfred Silva	(317) 555-3211

Tuesday, February 5, 2013

Page 1 of 1

AL1-C8-VB-Dearborn-RepQuotas-Word(VB).docx

WeeklyPayroll

10/19/2015

Employee	Hours	Wage	Total
Dale Jorgensen	30	$16.50	$495.00
Edward Moore	40	$25.25	$1,010.00
Holly Nolan	40	$26.20	$1,048.00
Irene Vaughn	25	$15.40	$385.00
Mark Bigelow	40	$19.70	$788.00
Monica Saunde	20	$10.00	$200.00

Page 1

AL1-C8-CS-Woodland-WeeklyPayroll-Access(CS1,BeforeUpdate).accdb

Keith Heaton
3322 Bridge Southeast
Mill Run, PA 15464

Miguel Trinidad
1304 Thompson Road
Altoona, PA 16603

Kimberly Lee
22120 151st Street
Altoona, PA 16601

Summer Grogan
14332 148th Street
Altoona, PA 16601

Lola Woolery
24372 North 52nd Street
Altoona, PA 16602

Grace Reichert
1174 Tenth Street
Mill Run, PA 15464

Rose Colecchi
1889 Granger Road
Altoona, PA 16601

Martin Sogura
332 Aspen Lane
Mill Run, PA 15464

Denise Tressler
20433 45th Avenue
Altoona, PA 16603

Jacob Nunnally
22837 32nd Street
Altoona, PA 16602

Harold Zimmerman
4302 Graham Drive
Altoona, PA 16602

Sheila Jones
203 Rider Road
Mill Run, PA 15464

Scott Darby
13291 South 141st
Mill Run, PA 15464

PatientID	FirstName	LastName	LName	DateOfVisit	Fee
03	Miguel	Trinidad	Young	9/1/2015	$100.00
07	Lola	Woolery	Moyer	9/1/2015	$75.00
13	Denise	Tressler	Moyer	9/1/2015	$100.00
20	Scott	Darby	Tsai	9/1/2015	$150.00
20	Scott	Darby	Tobias	9/2/2015	$75.00
14	Jacob	Nunnally	Tsai	9/2/2015	$100.00
02	Keith	Heaton	Tsai	9/2/2015	$125.00
08	Grace	Reichert	Tobias	9/2/2015	$125.00
05	Summer	Grogan	Tobias	9/2/2015	$75.00
15	Harold	Zimmerman	Tobias	9/3/2015	$75.00
15	Harold	Zimmerman	Tobias	9/3/2015	$100.00
11	Martin	Sogura	Tsai	9/3/2015	$75.00
08	Grace	Reichert	Young	9/4/2015	$125.00
11	Martin	Sogura	Moyer	9/4/2015	$500.00
09	Rose	Colecchi	Tobias	9/4/2015	$125.00
17	Sheila	Jones	Young	9/4/2015	$125.00
13	Denise	Tressler	Tsai	9/7/2015	$125.00
03	Miguel	Trinidad	Young	9/7/2015	$750.00
14	Jacob	Nunnally	Tsai	9/7/2015	$125.00

WeeklyPayroll

Employee	Hours	Wage	Total
Edward Moore	40	$25.25	$1,010.00
Irene Vaughn	30	$15.40	$462.00
Holly Nolan	40	$26.20	$1,048.00
Monica Saunde	20	$10.50	$210.00
Mark Bigelow	40	$19.70	$788.00
Dale Jorgensen	20	$16.50	$330.00

Page 1

AL1-C8-CS-Woodland-WeeklyPayroll-Access(CS1,AfterUpdate).accdb

Employee	Hours	Wage	Total
Edward Moore	40	$ 25.25	$ 1,010.00
Irene Vaughn	30	$ 15.40	$ 462.00
Holly Nolan	40	$ 26.20	$ 1,048.00
Monica Saunders	20	$ 10.50	$ 210.00
Mark Bigelow	40	$ 19.70	$ 788.00
Dale Jorgensen	20	$ 16.50	$ 330.00

AL1-C8-CS-Payroll-Excel(CS1).xlsx

When to back up an Access Database

Backing up a database is helpful to avoid loss of valuable time and information. The backup schedule for a database should be decided based on the intentional use of the file. Reference databases that are rarely altered or accessed do not need to be backed up as frequently as working databases. Those that are used regularly, or have many different users should be backed up on a much more frequent basis in the event that a mistake is make, database components are altered, or something is deleted without cause.

It is always good practice to err on side of caution and back up your work regularly, even if you think you will not need it. Work lost takes much time to recreate and can lead to missing information and/or inadequate recreation. Based on the critical information in the Woodland database, the database should be backed up once a week.

Backing up a database is quick and easy. Use the help file information as shown to back up your file.

Access Help ⁻

🔍 backup

Back up a database

When you back up a database, Access saves and closes objects that are open in Design view and saves a copy of the database file by using a name and location that you specify.

NOTE   Access reopens objects as specified by the value of the object Default View property.

Open the database for which you want to create a backup copy and do the following:

1. Click File, and then click Save As.

2. Under File Types, click Save Database As.

3. Under Advanced, click Back Up Database, and then click Save As.

4. In the Save As dialog box, in the File name box, review the name for your database backup.

You can change the name if you want, but the default name captures both the name of the original database file and the date that you make the backup.

TIP   When you restore data or objects from a backup, you usually want to know which database the backup came from and when the backup was created, so it's good practice to use the default file name.

AL1-C8-CS-Manual(CS3).docx

Access Performance Assessment Unit 2 Model Answers

10/15/2015

Clients

ClientNumber	ClientName	StreetAddress	City	State	ZipCode
1831	George Charoni	3980 Broad Street	Philadelphia	PA	19149
3219	Marian Wilke	12032 South 39th	Jenkintown	PA	19209
2874	Arthur Shroeder	3618 Fourth Avenue	Philadelphia	PA	19176
5831	Roshawn Collins	12110 52nd Court East	Cheltenham	PA	19210
4419	Lorena Hearron	3112 96th Street East	Philadelphia	PA	19132
1103	Raymond Mandato	631 Garden Boulevard	Jenkintown	PA	19209

Page 1

1. Use Access to create a database for clients of a mental health clinic. Name the database **AL1-U2-LancasterClinic**. Create a table named *Clients* that includes the following fields. (You determine the field name, data type, field size, and description.)
ClientNumber (primary key) *ClientName StreetAddress City State ZipCode Telephone DateOfBirth DiagnosisID*
2. After creating the table, switch to Datasheet view and then enter the following data in the appropriate fields: *ClientNumber:* 1831 *ClientNumber:* 3219 George Charoni Marian Wilke 3980 Broad Street 12032 South 39th Philadelphia, PA 19149 Jenkintown, PA 19209 (215) 555-3482 (215) 555-9083 *DateOfBirth:* 4/12/1961 *DateOfBirth:* 10/23/1984 *DiagnosisID:* SC *DiagnosisID:* OCD *ClientNumber:* 2874 *ClientNumber:* 5831 Arthur Shroeder Roshawn Collins 3618 Fourth Avenue 12110 52nd Court East Philadelphia, PA 19176 Cheltenham, PA 19210 (215) 555-8311 (215) 555-4779 *DateOfBirth:* 3/23/1961 *DateOfBirth:* 11/3/1968 *DiagnosisID:* OCD *DiagnosisID:* SC *ClientNumber:* 4419 *ClientNumber:* 1103 Lorena Hearron Raymond Mandato 3112 96th Street East 631 Garden Boulevard Philadelphia, PA 19132 Jenkintown, PA 19209 (215) 555-3281 (215) 555-0957 *DateOfBirth:* 7/2/1987 *DateOfBirth:* 9/20/1982 *DiagnosisID:* AD *DiagnosisID:* MDD
3. Automatically adjust the column widths.
4. Save, print, and then close the Clients table.

AL1-U2-A1-LancasterClinic_Clients(A1).accdb (1 of 2)

10/15/2015

Clients

Telephone	DateOfBirth	DiagnosisID
(215) 555-3482	4/12/1961	SC
(215) 555-9083	10/23/1984	OCD
(215) 555-8311	3/23/1961	OCD
(215) 555-4770	11/3/1968	SC
(215) 555-3281	7/2/1987	AD
(215) 555-0957	9/20/1982	MDD

Page 2

AL1-U2-A1-LancasterClinic_Clients(A1).accdb (2 of 2)

AL1-U2-A1-LancasterClinic_Fees(A1).accdb

Fees   10/15/2015

FeeCode	HourlyFee
A	$75.00
B	$80.00
C	$85.00
D	$90.00
E	$95.00
F	$100.00
G	$105.00
H	$110.00

9. Create a table named *Fees* that includes the following fields. (You determine the field name, data type, field size, and description.) *FeeCode* (primary key) *HourlyFee*
10. After creating the table, switch to Datasheet view and then enter the following data in the appropriate fields: *FeeCode*: A *HourlyFee*: $75.00 *FeeCode*: B *HourlyFee*: $80.00 *FeeCode*: C *HourlyFee*: $85.00 *FeeCode*: D *HourlyFee*: $90.00 *FeeCode*: E *HourlyFee*: $95.00 *FeeCode*: F *HourlyFee*: $100.00 *FeeCode*: G *HourlyFee*: $105.00 *FeeCode*: H *HourlyFee*: $110.00
11. Automatically adjust the column widths.
12. Save, print, and then close the Fees table.

Page 1

AL1-U2-A1-LancasterClinic_Diagnoses(A1).accdb

Diagnoses   10/15/2015

DiagnosisID	Diagnosis
AD	Adjustment Disorder
MDD	Manic-Depressive Disorder
OCD	Obsessive-Compulsive Disorder
SC	Schizophrenia

5. Create a table named *Diagnoses* that includes the following fields: *DiagnosisID* (primary key) *Diagnosis*
6. After creating the table, switch to Datasheet view and then enter the following data in the appropriate fields: *DiagnosisID*: AD *Diagnosis*: Adjustment Disorder *DiagnosisID*: MDD *Diagnosis*: Manic-Depressive Disorder *DiagnosisID*: OCD *Diagnosis*: Obsessive-Compulsive Disorder *DiagnosisID*: SC *Diagnosis*: Schizophrenia
7. Automatically adjust the column widths.
8. Save, print, and then close the Diagnoses table.

Page 1

BillingNumber	ClientNumber	DateOfService	Insurer	ProviderNumber	Hours	FeeCode
1	4419	3/2/2015	Health Plus	15	2	B
2	1831	3/2/2015	Self	33	1	H
3	3219	3/3/2015	Health Plus	15	1	D
4	5831	3/3/2015	Penn-State Health	18	2	C
5	4419	3/4/2015	Health Plus	15	1	A
6	1103	3/4/2015	Penn-State Health	18	0.5	A
7	1831	3/5/2015	Self	33	1	H
8	5831	3/5/2015	Penn-State Health	18	0.5	C

17. Create a table named *Billing* that includes the following fields. (You determine the field name, data type, field size, and description.) *BillingNumber* (primary key; apply the AutoNumber data type) *ClientNumber DateOfService* (apply the Date/Time data type) *Insurer ProviderNumber Hours* (Apply the Number data type, the *Field Size* option in the *Field Properties* section to *Double*, and the *Decimal Places* option in the *Field Properties* section in Design view to *1*. Two of the records will contain a number requiring this format.) *FeeCode*

18. After creating the table, switch to Datasheet view and then enter the following data in the appropriate fields: *ClientNumber:* 4419 *ClientNumber:* 1831 *DateOfService:* 3/2/2015 *DateOfService:* 3/2/2015 *Insurer:* Health Plus *Insurer:* Self *ProviderNumber:* 15 *ProviderNumber:* 33 *Hours:* 2 *Hours:* 1 *FeeCode:* B *FeeCode:* H *ClientNumber:* 3219 *ClientNumber:* 5831 *DateOfService:* 3/3/2015 *DateOfService:* 3/3/2015 *Insurer:* Health Plus *Insurer:* Penn-State Health *ProviderNumber:* 15 *ProviderNumber:* 18 *Hours:* 1 *Hours:* 2 *FeeCode:* D *FeeCode:* C *ClientNumber:* 4419 *ClientNumber:* 1103 *DateOfService:* 3/4/2015 *DateOfService:* 3/4/2015 *Insurer:* Health Plus *Insurer:* Penn-State Health *ProviderNumber:* 15 *ProviderNumber:* 18 *Hours:* 1 *Hours:* 0.5 *FeeCode:* A *FeeCode:* A *ClientNumber:* 1831 *ClientNumber:* 5831 *DateOfService:* 3/5/2015 *DateOfService:* 3/5/2015 *Insurer:* Self *Insurer:* Penn-State Health *ProviderNumber:* 33 *ProviderNumber:* 18 *Hours:* 1 *Hours:* 0.5 *FeeCode:* H *FeeCode:* C

19. Automatically adjust the column widths.

20. Save, print in landscape orientation, and then close the Billing table.

AL1-U2-A1-LancasterClinic_Billing(A1).accdb

ProviderNumber	ProviderName	Title	Extension
29	James Schouten	Psychologies	399
15	Lynn Yee	Child Psychologist	102
33	Janice Grisham	Psychiatrist	11
18	Craig Chilton	Psychologist	20

13. Create a table named *Employees* that includes the following fields. (You determine the field name, data type, field size, and description.) *ProviderNumber* (primary key) *ProviderName Title Extension*

14. After creating the table, switch to Datasheet view and then enter the following data in the appropriate fields: *ProviderNumber:* 29 *ProviderNumber:* 15 *ProviderName:* James Schouten *ProviderName:* Lynn Yee *Title:* Psychologist *Title:* Child Psychologist *Extension:* 399 *Extension:* 102 *ProviderNumber:* 33 *ProviderNumber:* 18 *ProviderName:* Janice Grisham *ProviderName:* Craig Chilton *Title:* Psychiatrist *Title:* Psychologist *Extension:* 11 *Extension:* 20

15. Automatically adjust the column widths.

16. Save, print, and then close the Employees table.

AL1-U2-A1-LancasterClinic_Employees(A1).accdb

State	PA
ZipCode	19149
Telephone	(215) 555-3482
DateOfBirth	4/12/1961
DiagnosisID	SC

BillingNumber	DateOfService	Insurer	ProviderNumber	Hours	FeeCode
2	3/2/2015	Self	33	1	H
7	3/5/2015	Self	33	1	H

ClientNumber	2874
ClientName	Arthur Shroeder
StreetAddress	3618 Fourth Avenue
City	Philadelphia
State	PA
ZipCode	19176
Telephone	(215) 555-8311
DateOfBirth	3/23/1961
DiagnosisID	OCD

Clients

ClientNumber	1103
ClientName	Raymond Mandato
StreetAddress	631 Garden Boulevard
City	Jenkintown
State	PA
ZipCode	19209
Telephone	(215) 555-0957
DateOfBirth	9/20/1982
DiagnosisID	MDD

1. With **AL1-U2-LancasterClinic.accdb** open, create the following one-to-many relationships and enforce referential integrity and cascade fields and records:
a. *ClientNumber* in the Clients table is the "one" and *ClientNumber* in the Billing table is the "many."
b. *DiagnosisID* in the Diagnoses table is the "one" and *DiagnosisID* in the Clients table is the "many."
c. *ProviderNumber* in the Employees table is the "one" and *ProviderNumber* in the Billing table is the "many."
d. *FeeCode* in the Fees table is the "one" and *FeeCode* in the Billing table is the "many."
2. Create a form with the data in the Clients table.
4. Save the form with the default name, print the form in landscape orientation, and then close the form.

BillingNumber	DateOfService	Insurer	ProviderNumber	Hours	FeeCode
6	3/4/2015	Penn-State Health	18	0.5	A

ClientNumber	1831
ClientName	George Charoni
StreetAddress	3980 Broad Street
City	Philadelphia

ClientNumber 4419

ClientName Lorena Hearron

StreetAddress 3112 96th Street East

City Philadelphia

State PA

ZipCode 19132

Telephone (215) 555-3281

DateOfBirth 7/2/1987

DiagnosisID AD

BillingNumber	DateOfService	Insurer	ProviderNumber	Hours	FeeCode
1	3/2/2015	Health Plus	15	2	B
5	3/4/2015	Health Plus	15	1	A

ClientNumber 5831

ClientName Roshawn Collins

StreetAddress 12110 52nd Court East

City Cheltenham

State PA

ClientNumber 3219

ClientName Marian Wilke

StreetAddress 12032 South 39th

City Jenkintown

State PA

ZipCode 19209

Telephone (215) 555-9083

DateOfBirth 10/23/1984

DiagnosisID OCD

BillingNumber	DateOfService	Insurer	ProviderNumber	Hours	FeeCode
3	3/3/2015	Health Plus	15	1	D

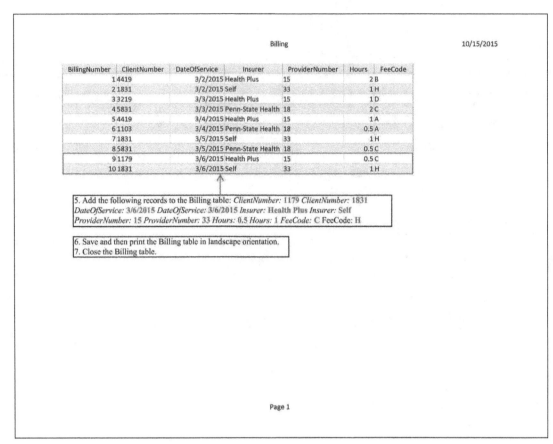

Billing   10/15/2015

BillingNumber	ClientNumber	DateOfService	Insurer	ProviderNumber	Hours	FeeCode
1	4419	3/2/2015	Health Plus	15	2	B
2	1831	3/2/2015	Self	33	1	H
3	3219	3/3/2015	Health Plus	15	1	D
4	5831	3/3/2015	Penn-State Health	18	2	C
5	4419	3/4/2015	Health Plus	15	1	A
6	1103	3/4/2015	Penn-State Health	18	0.5	A
7	1831	3/5/2015	Self	33	1	H
8	5831	3/5/2015	Penn-State Health	18	0.5	C
9	1179	3/6/2015	Health Plus	15	0.5	C
10	1831	3/6/2015	Self	33	1	H

5. Add the following records to the Billing table: *ClientNumber: 1179 ClientNumber: 1831 DateOfService: 3/6/2015 DateOfService: 3/6/2015 Insurer: Health Plus Insurer: Self ProviderNumber: 15 ProviderNumber: 33 Hours: 0.5 Hours: 1 FeeCode: C FeeCode: H*

6. Save and then print the Billing table in landscape orientation.
7. Close the Billing table.

Page 1

AL1-U2-A2-LancasterClinic_Billing(A2).accdb

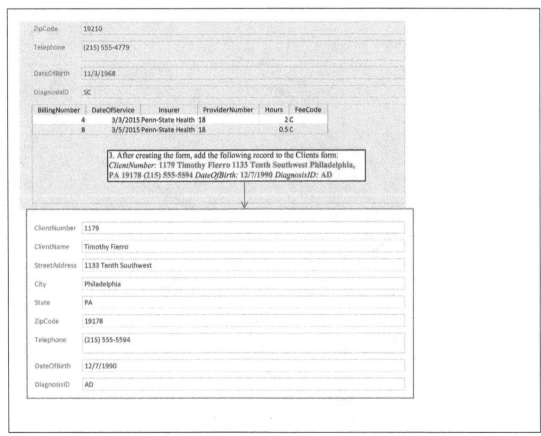

	ZipCode	19210
Telephone	(215) 555-4779
DateOfBirth	11/3/1968
DiagnosisID	SC

BillingNumber	DateOfService	Insurer	ProviderNumber	Hours	FeeCode
4	3/3/2015	Penn-State Health	18	2	C
8	3/5/2015	Penn-State Health	18	0.5	C

3. After creating the form, add the following record to the Clients form: *ClientNumber: 1179 Timothy Fierro 1133 Tenth Southwest Philadelphia, PA 19178 (215) 555-5594 DateOfBirth: 12/7/1990 DiagnosisID: AD*

ClientNumber	1179
ClientName	Timothy Fierro
StreetAddress	1133 Tenth Southwest
City	Philadelphia
State	PA
ZipCode	19178
Telephone	(215) 555-5594
DateOfBirth	12/7/1990
DiagnosisID	AD

AL1-U2-A2-LancasterClinic_ClientsForm(A2).accdb (5 of 5)

ProviderInformation

ClientNumber 1103

DateOfBirth 9/20/1982

DiagnosisID MDD

Billing

Insurer	Provider
Penn-State Health	18

1. With **AL1-U2-LancasterClinic.accdb** open, create a form with fields from related tables using the Form Wizard with the following specifications:
a. At the first Form Wizard dialog box, insert the following fields in the *Selected Fields* list box: From the Clients table: *ClientNumber DateOfBirth DiagnosisID* From the Billing table: *Insurer ProviderNumber*
b. Do not make any changes at the second Form Wizard dialog box.
c. Do not make any changes at the third Form Wizard dialog box.
d. At the fourth Form Wizard dialog box, type the name ProviderInformation in the *Form* text box.
2. When the first record displays, print the first record.

AL1-U2-A3-LancasterClinic_ProviderInformation(A3).accdb

Lorena Hearron
3112 96th Street East
Philadelphia, PA 19132

George Charoni
3980 Broad Street
Philadelphia, PA 19149

Arthur Shroeder
3618 Fourth Avenue
Philadelphia, PA 19176

Timothy Fierro
1133 Tenth Southwest
Philadelphia, PA 19178

Marian Wilke
12032 South 39th
Jenkintown, PA 19209

Raymond Mandato
631 Garden Boulevard
Jenkintown, PA 19209

Roshawn Collins
12110 52nd Court East
Cheltenham, PA 19210

1. With **AL1-U2-LancasterClinic.accdb** open, use the Label Wizard to create mailing labels with the client names and addresses and sort by zip code. Name the mailing label report **ClientMailingLabels**.
2. Print the mailing labels.

AL1-U2-A4-LancasterClinic_ClientMailingLabels(A4).accdb

BillingNumber	ClientNumber	DateOfService	Insurer	ProviderNumber	Hours	FeeCode
1	4419	3/2/2015	Health Plus	15	2	B
5	4419	3/4/2015	Health Plus	15	1	A

1b. Display only those records with a client ID number
of 4419. Print the results and then remove the filter.

AL1-U2-A5-Lancaster_Billing_4419(A5).accdb

BillingNumber	ClientNumber	DateOfService	Insurer	ProviderNumber	Hours	FeeCode
1	4419	3/2/2015	Health Plus	15	2	B
3	3219	3/3/2015	Health Plus	15	1	D
5	4419	3/4/2015	Health Plus	15	1	A
9	1179	3/6/2015	Health Plus	15	0.5	C

1. With **AL1-U2-LancasterClinic.accdb** open, open the Billing
table and then filter the records to display the following records:
a. Display only those records with the Health Plus insurer. Print
the results in landscape orientation and then remove the filter.

AL1-U2-A5-Lancaster_HealthPlus(A5).accdb

Billing   10/15/2015

BillingNumber	ClientNumber	DateOfService	Insurer	ProviderNumber	Hours	FeeCode
1	4419	3/2/2015	Health Plus	15	2	B
3	3219	3/3/2015	Health Plus	15	1	D
5	4419	3/4/2015	Health Plus	15	1	A
9	1179	3/6/2015	Health Plus	15	0.5	C

1. With **AL1-U2-LancasterClinic.accdb** open, open the Billing table and then filter the records to display the following records:
a. Display only those records with the Health Plus insurer. Print the results in landscape orientation and then remove the filter.

AL1-U2-A5-Lancaster_HealthPlus(A5).accdb

Billing   10/15/2015

BillingNumber	ClientNumber	DateOfService	Insurer	ProviderNumber	Hours	FeeCode
4	5831	3/3/2015	Penn-State Health	18	2	C
8	5831	3/5/2015	Penn-State Health	18	0.5	C
9	1179	3/6/2015	Health Plus	15	0.5	C

2. Filter records by selection to display the following records: a. Display only those records with a fee code of C. Print the results and then remove the filter.

AL1-U2-A5-Lancaster_Billing_C(A5).accdb

Clients   10/15/2015

ClientNumber	ClientName	StreetAddress	City	State	ZipCode
1103	Raymond Mandato	631 Garden Boulevard	Jenkintown	PA	19209
3219	Marian Wilke	12032 South 39th	Jenkintown	PA	19209
5831	Roshawn Collins	12110 52nd Court East	Cheltenham	PA	19210

4. Open the Clients table and then use the *Filter By Form* option to display clients in Jenkintown or Cheltenham. Print the results and then remove the filter.

Page 1

Billing   10/15/2015

BillingNumber	ClientNumber	DateOfService	Insurer	ProviderNumber	Hours	FeeCode
1	4419	3/2/2015	Health Plus	15	2	B
2	1831	3/2/2015	Self	33	1	H
3	3219	3/3/2015	Health Plus	15	1	D
4	5831	3/3/2015	Penn-State Health	18	2	C
5	4419	3/4/2015	Health Plus	15	1	A
6	1103	3/4/2015	Penn-State Health	18	0.5	A

2b. Display only those records between the dates of 3/2/2015 and 3/4/2015. Print the results and then remove the filter.

Page 1

BillingNumber	ClientNumber	DateOfService	Insurer	ProviderNumber	Hours	FeeCode
1	4419	02-Mar-15	Health Plus	15	2	B
2	1831	02-Mar-15	Self	33	1	H
3	3219	03-Mar-15	Health Plus	15	1	D
4	5831	03-Mar-15	Penn-State Health	18	2	C
5	4419	04-Mar-15	Health Plus	15	1	A
6	1103	04-Mar-15	Penn-State Health	18	0.5	A
7	1831	05-Mar-15	Self	33	1	H
8	5831	05-Mar-15	Penn-State Health	18	0.5	C
9	1179	06-Mar-15	Health Plus	15	0.5	C
10	1831	06-Mar-15	Self	33	1	H

1. With **AL1-U2-LancasterClinic.accdb** open, export the Billing table to an Excel workbook to your AL1U2 folder.
2. Apply formatting to the cells in the Excel workbook to enhance the appearance of the data. 3. Change the page orientation to landscape.

AL1-U2-A6-Billing-Excel(A6).xlsx

10/15/2015

Clients

Telephone	DateOfBirth	DiagnosisID
(215) 555-0957	9/20/1982	MDD
(215) 555-9083	10/23/1984	OCD
(215) 555-4779	11/3/1968	SC

Page 2

AL1-U2-A5-Lancaster_Billing_JenkintownOrCheltenham(A5).accdb (2 of 2)

March 12, 2015

«ClientName»
«StreetAddress»
«City», «State» «ZipCode»

Ladies and Gentlemen:

The building of a new wing for the Lancaster Clinic will begin April 1, 2015. We are excited about this new addition to our clinic. With the new facilities, we will be able to offer additional community and group services along with enhanced child-play therapy treatment.

During the construction, the main entrance will be moved to the north end of the building. Please use this entrance until the construction of the wing is completed. We apologize in advance for any inconvenience this causes you.

Sincerely,

Marianne Lambert
Clinic Director

XX
AL1-U2-A7-LCLtrs.docx

AL1-U2-A7-ConstLtrMD(A7).docx

March 12, 2015

Raymond Mandato
631 Garden Boulevard
Jenkintown, PA 19209

Ladies and Gentlemen:

The building of a new wing for the Lancaster Clinic will begin April 1, 2015. We are excited about this new addition to our clinic. With the new facilities, we will be able to offer additional community and group services along with enhanced child-play therapy treatment.

During the construction, the main entrance will be moved to the north end of the building. Please use this entrance until the construction of the wing is completed. We apologize in advance for any inconvenience this causes you.

Sincerely,

Marianne Lambert
Clinic Director

XX
AL1-U2-A7-LCLtrs.docx

AL1-U2-A7-LCLtrs(A7).docx (1 of 2)

Name	Hours	Rate	Wage
Glenda Carras	40	$ 23.15	$ 926.00
Niles Davidson	20	$ 19.00	$ 380.00
Tashia Emery	40	$ 18.75	$ 750.00
Manuel Ramirez	24	$ 16.45	$ 394.80
David Heywood	15	$ 11.50	$ 172.50
Chris Ishihara	15	$ 11.50	$ 172.50

AL1-U2-StaffHours(A8).accdb

March 12, 2015

Timothy Fierro
1133 Tenth Southwest
Philadelphia, PA 19178

Ladies and Gentlemen:

The building of a new wing for the Lancaster Clinic will begin April 1, 2015. We are excited about this new addition to our clinic. With the new facilities, we will be able to offer additional community and group services along with enhanced child-play therapy treatment.

During the construction, the main entrance will be moved to the north end of the building. Please use this entrance until the construction of the wing is completed. We apologize in advance for any inconvenience this causes you.

Sincerely,

Marianne Lambert
Clinic Director

XX
AL1-U2-A7-LCLtrs.docx

AL1-U2-A7-LCLtrs(A7).docx (2 of 2)

StaffHours

Name	Hours	Rate	Wage
Glenda Carras	40	$23.15	$926.00
Niles Davidson	20	$19.00	$380.00
Tashia Emery	40	$18.75	$750.00
Manuel Ramire	24	$16.45	$394.80
David Heywoo	15	$11.50	$172.50
Chris Ishihara	15	$11.50	$172.50

5. Insert a formula in cell D2 that multiplies B2 with C2 and then copy the formula down to cells D3 through D7.

4. Open AL1-U2-StaffHours.xlsx in Excel.
6. Save and then close AL1-U2-StaffHours.xlsx.
7. Close Excel.
8. In Access with AL1-U2-LancasterClinic.acedb open, open the StaffHours table.
9. Print and then close the StaffHours table.

AL1-U2-A8-LancasterClinic_StaffHours(A8,Step9).xlsx

StaffHours

Name	Hours	Rate	Wage
Glenda Carras	40	$23.15	
Niles Davidson	20	$19.00	
Tashia Emery	40	$18.75	
Manuel Ramire	24	$16.45	
David Heywoo	15	$11.50	
Chris Ishihara	15	$11.50	

1. With AL1-U2-LancasterClinic.acedb open, import and link AL1-U2- StaffHours.xlsx to a new table named *StaffHours*.
2. Open the StaffHours table in Datasheet view.
3. Print and then close the StaffHours table.

AL1-U2-A8-LancasterClinic_StaffHours(A8,Step3).xlsx

Benchmark Access 2013 Level 1 Model Answers

Creating a Table in Access 2013

Using tables in access is key to information management. Tables will allow you to quickly and easily find the information and details that pertain to your business and database needs. Clean and concise tables will help you to be more efficient in the workplace.

To create a table of organized information, first determine the information you want to include. From here, click the CREATE tab on the Access database you are working within.

Click the Table button to begin. You can tab across your table in the Datasheet View, inputting the desired categories, and continue to tab through the table, inputting your desired information.

To streamline the process, you may wish to create a table in Design View. From this view, you add all the desired table headings and can set the default values, and field sizes, if desired. Once you have created the frame work for you table in this view, switch to the Datasheet view and input the information in the proper fields by tabbing through the table.

Save your table with a name that clearly identifies the information included within.

AL1-U2-Act1-LCRpt.docx

InsuranceComp   10/15/2015

Company	CoAddress	CoCity	CoState	CoZip	RepPhone	Representative
Health Plus	4102 22nd Street	Philadelphia	PA	19166	(212) 555-0990	Byron Tolleson
Penn-State Health	5933 Lehigh Avnue	Philadelhia	PA	19148	(212) 555-3477	Tracey Pavone
Quality Medical	51 Cecil B Moore Avenue	Philadelphia	PA	19168	(212) 555-4600	Lee Stafford
Delaware Health	4418 Front Street	Philadelphia	PA	19132	(212) 555-6770	Melanie Chon

Page 1

AL1-U2-Lancaster_InsuranceCompt(Act1).accdb

October 19, 2015

Melanie Chon
Delaware Health
4418 Front Street
Philadelphia, PA 19132

Dear Melanie Chon:

Lancaster Clinic is progressing into the treatment of mental health services and we are seeking information on services and limitations regarding our patient's insurance as provided by their employers. We are focusing on mental health counseling at this time and are requesting any information or direction that you can provide.

Enclosed is a brochure introducing Lancaster Clinic's practice. If you have any questions, please do not hesitate to contact me directly.

Sincerely,

Marianne Lambert
Clinic Director

XX
AL1-U2-Act2-LCIns.docx

October 19, 2015

Byron Tolleson
Health Plus
4102 22nd Street
Philadelphia, PA 19166

Dear Byron Tolleson:

Lancaster Clinic is progressing into the treatment of mental health services and we are seeking information on services and limitations regarding our patient's insurance as provided by their employers. We are focusing on mental health counseling at this time and are requesting any information or direction that you can provide.

Enclosed is a brochure introducing Lancaster Clinic's practice. If you have any questions, please do not hesitate to contact me directly.

Sincerely,

Marianne Lambert
Clinic Director

XX
AL1-U2-Act2-LCIns.docx

City	State	ZIP	Telephone
Washington	DC	20009	(202) 332-9595
San Francisco	CA	94111	(877) 726-4727
Chicago	IL	60654	(800) 826-3632
Washington	DC	20015	
Rutherford	CA	94573	(707) 963-4197
Seattle	WA	98122	(206) 302-2200
Bloomington	MN	55431	(800) 273-8255
Melbourne	FL	32902	

Organization	Specialty	Website	Address
Active Minds	Stigma	www.activeminds.org	2001 S Street, Suite 450
Bring Change 2 Mind	Stigma	www.bringchange2mind.org	1265 Battery Street, Fifth Floor
Depression and Bipolar Support Alliance	Bipolar & Depression	www.dbsalliance.org	730 N Franklin Street, Suite 501
International Association for Suicide Prevention	Suicide	www.iasp.info	5221 Wisconsin Avenue NW
International Mental Health Research Organizatio	Mental Illnesses	www.imhro.org	PO Box 680
Sound Mental Health	Bipolar & Depression	www.smh.org	1600 East Olive
Suicide Awareness Voices of Education	Suicide	www.save.org	8120 Penn Avenue South, Suite 47
To Write Love on Her Arms	Depression	www.twloha.com	PO Box 2203

Mental Health Organizations

Thursday, October 15, 2015
1:08:22 PM

Organization	Specialty	Website	Address	City	State	ZIP	Telephone
Active Minds	Stigma	www.activeminds.org	2001 S Street, Suite 450	Washington	DC	20009	(202) 332-9595
Bring Change 2 Mind	Stigma	www.bringchange2mind.org	1265 Battery Street, Fifth Floor	San Francisco	CA	94111	(877) 726-4727
Depression and Bipolar Support Alliance	Bipolar & Depression	www.dbsalliance.org	730 N Franklin Street, Suite 501	Chicago	IL	60654	(800) 826-3632
International Association for Suicide Prevention	Suicide	www.iasp.info	5221 Wisconsin Avenue NW	Washington	DC	20015	
International Mental Health Research Organization	Mental Illnesses	www.imhro.org	PO Box 680	Rutherford	CA	94573	(707) 963-4197
Sound Mental Health	Bipolar & Depression	www.smco.org	1600 East Olive	Seattle	WA	98122	(206) 302-2200
Suicide Awareness Voices of Education	Suicide	www.save.org	8120 Penn Avenue South, Suite 470	Bloomington	MN	55431	(800) 273-8255
To Write Love on Her Arms	Depression	www.twloha.com	PO Box 2203	Melbourne	FL	32902	

Page 1 of 1

AL1-U2-IR-HealthInfo_MentalHealthOrg-Report(IR).accdb (1 of 2)

AL1-U2-IR-HealthInfo_MentalHealthOrg-Report(IR).accdb (2 of 2)

January 29, 2013

Active Minds
2001 S Street, Suite 450
Washington, DC 20009

To Whom It May Concern:

I am writing today for further information regarding your mental health organization. As a significant number of Americans are inflicted with mental health issues, I feel it is imperative to learn more and seek out where I can be of assistance in my city, state, and community.

I would sincerely appreciate any information you can provide, including brochures, handouts, flyers, and any event specific information to share with my friends and family. I look forward to the opportunity to get more involved with your organization.

Regards,

Student Name

January 29, 2013

Bring Change 2 Mind
1265 Battery Street, Fifth Floor
San Francisco, CA 94111

To Whom It May Concern:

I am writing today for further information regarding your mental health organization. As a significant number of Americans are inflicted with mental health issues, I feel it is imperative to learn more and seek out where I can be of assistance in my city, state, and community.

I would sincerely appreciate any information you can provide, including brochures, handouts, flyers, and any event specific information to share with my friends and family. I look forward to the opportunity to get more involved with your organization.

Regards,

Student Name

Description	BudgetAllotted	BudgetSpent	TimeAllotted	TimeSpent	BudgetedDollarsSpent	BudgetedTimeSpent
St. Patrick Fountain	$3,500.00	$1,800.00	30	18	51%	60%
McMann's Skate Park	$2,000.00	$850.00	14	6	43%	43%
Cushman's Wading Pool	$1,500.00	$600.00	14	3	40%	21%
Sidewalks - Main Street	$13,000.00	$7,500.00	160	41	58%	26%
Lamp posts - Main Street	$8,000.00	$4,200.00	90	23	53%	26%
Total	$28,000.00	$14,950.00				

AL1-U2-JS-CityImprovement_ProjectCompletionPercentage(JS).accdb

Mental health is a fascinating subject that until recently has been hidden under the cloud of shame and stigma. As more and more Americans are facing the realities of mental health in our communities, there is greater light being shone on the issues and many people are able to step out of the mental darkness and seek help and support.

One of the more fascinating things I learned in my online mental health research is that this is certainly not a new illness with many notable history makers thought to have also battled internally. It is believed that President Abraham Lincoln had severe clinical depression (Shenk, 2005) and his wife may have suffered from depression, post-partum, or schizophrenia as well. While today, Lincoln's mental illness would be viewed as a character issue and possible making him illegible for presidency, he certainly cannot be faulted for it considering the dramatic and powerful role he has played in our countries history.

With more awareness and education, it is possible that the stigma of mental health will dissolve allowing for more to feel comfortable in seeking professional help and diagnosis.

AL-U2-IR-DidYouKnow.docx

Access Level 2, Chapter 1 Model Answers

Cell Phone	Birth Date	Category	Family Member?
(602) 555-3496	May 03 1964	Gold	☑
(480) 555-1699	Oct 15 1977	Silver	☐

Page 2

AL2-01-Members(A4,Step2).accdb

ID Number	First Name	Last Name	Street Address	City	State	ZIP	Home Phone
100	Hilary	Sampson	300 South Saguaro Drive	Apache Junction	AZ	85220-4956	(602) 555-1587
110	Jesse	Reynolds	7229 E University Drive	Mesa	AZ	85207-6501	(480) 555-1385

1. With **AL2-C1-BenchmarkGolf.accdb** open, add the following
records. Type the text in the *State* field as shown to test your format
code. As you type the zip codes, telephone numbers, and dates, be
careful to watch the placeholders and enter data in the required pattern.

Field	Record 1	Record 2
ID Number	100	110
First Name	Hilary	Jesse
Last Name	Sampson	Reynolds
Street Address	300 South Saguaro Drive	7229 E University Drive
City	Apache Junction	Mesa
State	Az	Az
ZIP Code	85220 4956	85207 6501
Home Phone	602 555 1587	480 555 1385
Cell Phone	602 555 3496	480 555 1699
Birth Date	May 03 1964	Oct 15 1977
Category	Gold	Silver
Family Member?	Yes	No

Page 1

AL2-01-Members(A4,Step2).accdb

Category	Annual Fee	Monthly Fee	Restrictions
Gold	$2,500.00	60.00	Unlimited weekdays and weekends; weekend ballot first
Silver	$1,775.00	52.00	Unlimited weekdays; weekend ballot second
Bronze	$1,550.00	35.00	Unlimited weekdays; weekends after 3 P.M.

1. With **AL2-C1-BenchmarkGolf.accdb** open, add the following records. Type the text in the *State* field as shown to test your format code. As you type the zip codes, telephone numbers, and dates, be careful to watch the placeholders and enter data in the required pattern.

Field	Record 1	Record 2	Record 3
Category	Gold	Silver	Bronze
Annual Fee	2500	1775	1550
Monthly Fee	60	52	35
Restrictions	Unlimited weekdays and weekends; weekend ballot first	Unlimited weekdays; weekend ballot second	Unlimited weekdays; weekends after 3 P.M.

Family ID Number	Member ID Number	First Name	Last Name	Birth Date	Social Member?
610	100	Kayla	Sampson	Jul 18 1996	☐
611	100	Roy	Sampson	Mar 16 1994	☐

1. With **AL2-C1-BenchmarkGolf.accdb** open, add the following records. Type the text in the *State* field as shown to test your format code. As you type the zip codes, telephone numbers, and dates, be careful to watch the placeholders and enter data in the required pattern.

Field	Record 1	Record 2
Family ID Number	610	611
Member ID Number	100	100
First Name	Kayla	Roy
Last Name	Sampson	Sampson
Birth Date	Jul 18 1996	Mar 16 1994
Social Member?	No	No

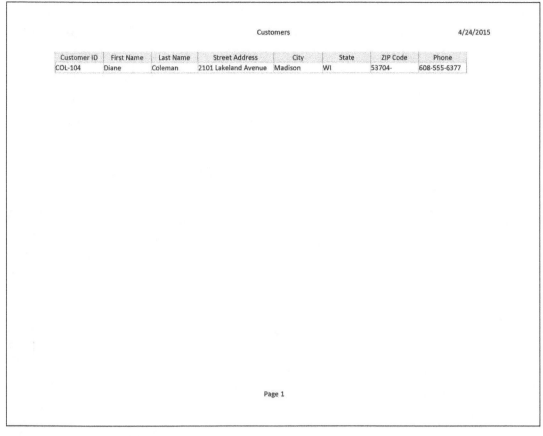

Customers								4/24/2015
Customer ID	First Name	Last Name	Street Address	City	State	ZIP Code	Phone	
COL-104	Diane	Coleman	2101 Lakeland Avenue	Madison	WI	53704-	608-555-6377	

Page 1

AL2-C1-CS-P3-Customers(P3).accdb

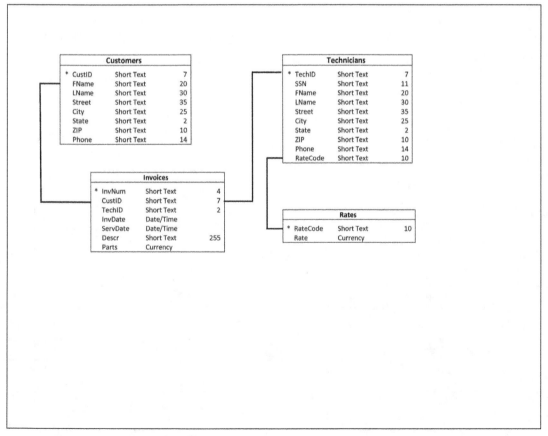

AL2-C1-CS-P1-BestarPlumbing(P1).docx

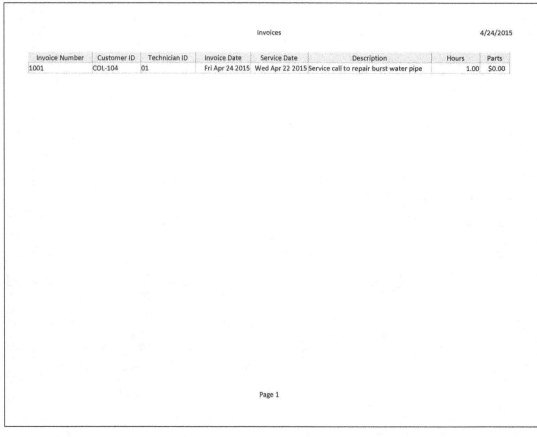

Technicians   4/24/2015

Technician ID	Social Security No	First Name	Last Name	Street Address	City	State	ZIP Code	Phone	Rate Code
01	123-45-6789	Jose	Martinez						SeniorTech

Page 1

AL2-C1-CS-P3-Technicians(P3).accdb

Invoices   4/24/2015

Invoice Number	Customer ID	Technician ID	Invoice Date	Service Date	Description	Hours	Parts
1001	COL-104	01	Fri Apr 24 2015	Wed Apr 22 2015	Service call to repair burst water pipe	1.00	$0.00

Page 1

AL2-C1-CS-P3-Invoices(P3).accdb

Rates

4/24/2015

Rate Code	Rate
Apprentice	28.00
SeniorTech	41.75

Page 1

AL2-C1-CS-P3-Rates(P3).accdb

WebOrders

4/9/2013

Web Order ID	Customer ID	Date Ordered
10001	101	Feb-15-2015
10002	102	Feb-15-2015
10003	103	Feb-16-2015
10004	104	Feb-22-2015
10005	108	Feb-22-2015
10006	110	Feb-23-2015
10007	106	Feb-26-2015

1. Open **AL2-C2-ViewIt.accdb** and enable the content.
2. Open all of the tables in Datasheet view and review the tables' fields and records to familiarize yourself with the database. Close all of the tables when finished.
3. Open the Relationships window and close the Show Table dialog box. Notice that no relationships have been created in the database. Close the Relationships window.
4. The *CustID* field in the WebOrders table can be made easier to use by changing it to a lookup list that presents customer names and numbers from the WebCustomers table. Open the WebOrders table in Design view, make *CustID* the active field, and then create a lookup list to display values from another table using the following information:
a. Display the *CustID*, *FirstName*, and *LastName* fields from the WebCustomers table.
b. Sort the list in ascending order by the *LastName* field.
c. Remove the check box from the *Hide key column* check box.
d. Store the *CustID* value.
e. Accept the default label of *CustID* for the column.
5. Modify the Lookup property for the *CustID* field that will ensure only items within the list can be entered into the field.
6. Save the table, switch to Datasheet view, and then enter the following record to test the lookup list:
Web Order ID 10007
Customer ID Select 106 Gary Gallagher in the lookup list.
Date Ordered Feb 26 2015
7. Print the datasheet.

Page 1

AL2-C2-WebOrders(A1,Step7).accdb

WebOrderDetails

4/9/2013

Web Order ID	Product ID	Quantity
10001	To Kill a Mockingbird	1
10001	Blue Hawaii	1
10002	The Great Escape	2
10003	Cool Hand Luke	1
10003	Doctor Zhivago	1
10003	The Longest Day	1
10004	Dial M for Murder	1

1. With **AL2-C2-ViewIt.accdb** open, create a new table using Design view to track the videos downloaded by a customer using the following information:

Field Name	Data Type	Field Size	Caption
WebOrdID	Short Text	5	Web Order ID
WebProdID	Short Text	7	Product ID
Qty	Number	–	Quantity

2. A customer can choose to buy more than one video on the same order. When this occurs, the same order number is associated with more than one record in the table. Therefore, the primary key cannot be based on the *WebOrdID* field alone. Assign a multiple-field primary key using both the *WebOrdID* and *WebProdID* fields. The combination of the order identification number and product identification number will uniquely describe each record in the table.
3. Save the table and name it *WebOrderDetails*.
4. Create a lookup list for the *WebOrdID* field that connects to the *WebOrdID* field in the WebOrders table. Add all three of the fields in the WebOrders table to the lookup list, do not specify a sort field, remove the check mark from the *Hide key column* check box, store *WebOrdID* in the field, and then accept the default field name. Modify the Lookup property to ensure only items within the list can be entered into the field.
5. Create a lookup list for the *WebProdID* field that connects to the *WebProdID* field in the WebProducts table. Display the *Product* field sorted in ascending order, make sure the column is wide enough to display the entire video title in the list, hide the key column, and then accept the default field name. Modify the Lookup property to ensure only items within the list can be entered into the field.
6. Save the table and switch to Datasheet view. Add the following records to the WebOrderDetails datasheet to test the lookup lists:

Web Order ID	Product ID	Quantity
10001	To Kill a Mockingbird	1
10001	Blue Hawaii	1
10002	The Great Escape	2
10003	Cool Hand Luke	1
10003	Doctor Zhivago	1
10003	The Longest Day	1
10004	Dial M for Murder	1

7. Adjust all of the column widths to best fit and print the datasheet.

Page 1

AL2-C2-WebOrderDetails(A2-Step7).accdb

Customer ID	Credit Card Type	Credit Card Number	Expiry Month	Expiry Year	Email Address
106	Visa	0009100876453152	7	2017	garyg@emcp.net

WebCustPymnt   4/21/2013

1. With **AL2-C2-ViewIt.accdb** open, create a new table using Design view to store a customer's credit card information using the following information:

Field Name	Data Type	Field Size	Caption
CustID	Short Text	3	Customer ID
CCType	Short Text	20	Credit Card Type
CCNumber	Short Text	16	Credit Card Number
CCExpMonth	Number	–	Expiry Month
CCExpYear	Number	–	Expiry Year
EmailAdd	Short Text	30	Email Address

2. Assign the primary key to the *CustID* field.
3. Save the table and name it *WebCustPymnt*.
4. Create a lookup list for the *CustID* field that connects to the *CustID* field in the WebCustomers table. Include the *FirstName*, *LastName*, and *HPhone* fields. Sort the list by *LastName* and then by *FirstName*. Remove the check mark from the *Hide key column* check box. Accept all of the other defaults. Modify the Lookup property to ensure only items within the list can be entered into the field.
5. Save the table, switch to Datasheet view, and enter the following record: *Customer ID* Select *106 Gary Gallagher* in the lookup list
Credit Card Type Visa
Credit Card Number 0009100876453152
Expiry Month 7
Expiry Year 2017
Email Address garyg@emcp.net
6. Adjust all of the column widths to best fit and print the datasheet in landscape orientation.

Page 1

AL2-C2-WebCustPymnt(A4,Step6).accdb

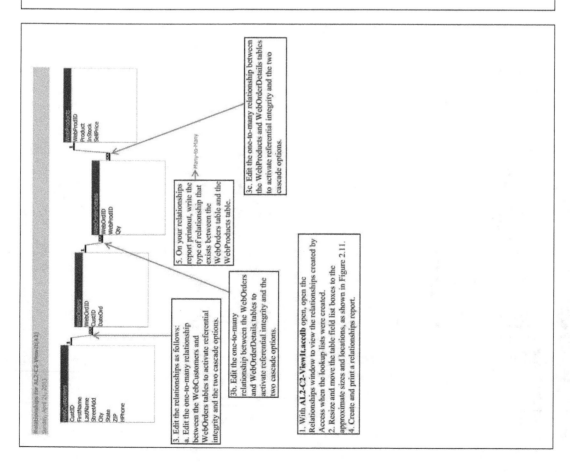

AL2-C2-RelationshipReport(A3,Step4).accdb

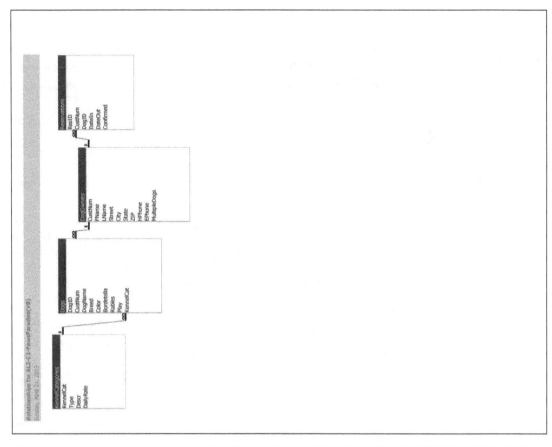

AL2-C2-RelationshipReport(VB,Step6).accdb

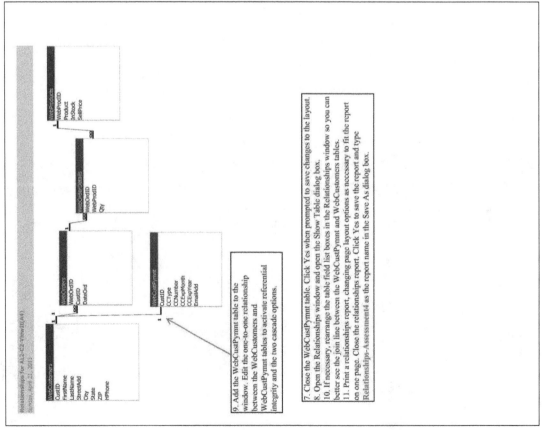

9. Add the WebCustPymnt table to the window. Edit the one-to-one relationship between the WebCustomers and WebCustPymnt tables to activate referential integrity and the two cascade options.

7. Close the WebCustPymnt table. Click Yes when prompted to save changes to the layout.
8. Open the Relationships window and open the Show Table dialog box.
10. If necessary, rearrange the table field list boxes in the Relationships window so you can better see the join line between the WebCustPymnt and WebCustomers tables.
11. Print a relationships report, changing page layout options as necessary to fit the report on one page. Close the relationships report. Click Yes to save the report and type Relationships-Assessment4 as the report name in the Save As dialog box.

AL2-C2-RelationshipReport(A4,Step11).accdb

Agents 4/24/2015

Agent ID	Agent First Name	Agent Last Name	Telephone	Quota Code
10	Kwan	Im	(317) 555-8374	4
11	William	Ludlow	(317) 555-0991	4
12	Catherine	Singleton	(317) 555-0172	3
14	Jaren	Newman	(317) 555-6790	2
15	Lee	Hutchinson	(765) 555-4277	2
16	Cecilia	Ortega	(317) 555-4810	1
17	Robin	Rehberg	(317) 555-9812	1
18	Andre	Kulisek	(317) 555-2264	1
19	Isabelle	Marshall	(765) 555-8822	3
20	Craig	Johnson	(317) 555-4391	2
21	Maureen	Pascual	(317) 555-5513	3

Page 1

AL2-C2-CS-P1-Agents(P1).accdb

Relationships for AL2-C2-HillsdaleRealty(P2)
Friday, April 24, 2015

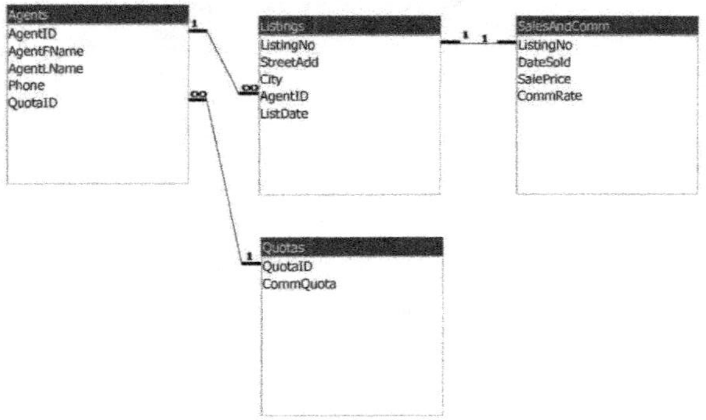

Agents
AgentID
AgentFName
AgentLName
Phone
QuotaID
Listings
ListingNo
StreetAdd
City
AgentID
ListDate
SalesAndComm
ListingNo
DateSold
SalePrice
CommRate
Quotas
QuotaID
CommQuota
1
∞
1
1
∞
1

AL2-C2-CS-P2-RelationshipReport(P2).accdb

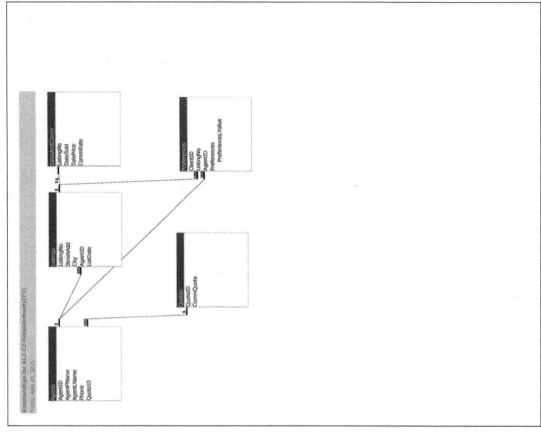

AL2-C2-CS-P3-RelationshipReport.accdb

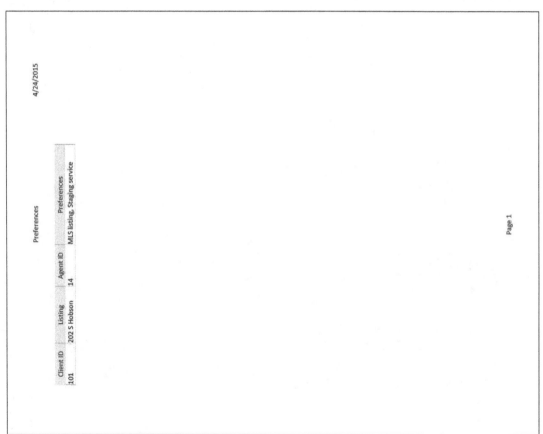

AL2-C2-CS-P3-Preferences(P3).accdb

Access Level 2, Chapter 3 Model Answers

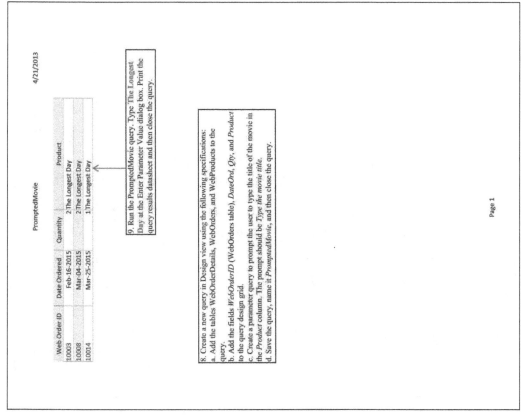

PromptedMovie   4/21/2013

Web Order ID	Date Ordered	Quantity	Product
10003	Feb-16-2015	2	The Longest Day
10008	Mar-04-2015	2	The Longest Day
10014	Mar-25-2015	1	The Longest Day

9. Run the PromptedMovie query. Type The Longest Day at the Enter Parameter Value dialog box. Print the query results datasheet and then close the query.

8. Create a new query in Design view using the following specifications:
a. Add the tables WebOrderDetails, WebOrders, and WebProducts to the query.
b. Add the fields *WebOrderID* (WebOrders table), *DateOrd, Qty,* and *Product* to the query design grid.
c. Create a parameter query to prompt the user to type the title of the movie in the *Product* column. The prompt should be *Type the movie title.*
d. Save the query, name it *PromptedMovie,* and then close the query.

Page 1

AL2-C3-PromptedMovie(A1,Step9).accdb

CustBurlington05401   4/21/2013

Customer ID	First Name	Last Name	Street Address	City	State	ZIP Code	Home Phone
101	Vincent	Gale	350 Manhattan Drive	Burlington	VT	05401-4245	802-555-1635
103	Terri	Lesniak	200 Park Street	Burlington	VT	05401-5175	802-555-4986
104	Franco	Felisatti	93 Hildred Drive	Burlington	VT	05401-3688	802-555-3487
105	Blaine	Yiu	76 Austin Drive	Burlington	VT	05401-5409	802-555-7544
111	Dana	Gorski	12 Henry Street	Burlington	VT	05401-3329	802-555-6122
113	Keenan	Smith	188 Loomis Street	Burlington	VT	05401-3334	802-555-4338
116	Matthew	Siemens	32 Pearl Street	Burlington	VT	05401-5388	802-555-7685
119	Paulina	Mykonos	400 North Avenue	Burlington	VT	05401-2923	802-555-6788
120	Jasmine	Patel	77 Fairmont Place	Burlington	VT	05401-1928	802-555-3414

3. Using the Filter By Form feature, display only those customers who reside in Burlington with zip codes that begin with 05401. *Hint: Type 05401* in the ZIP field to specify only the first five characters in the ZIP code. The asterisk is a wildcard character that allows you to filter by specifying only a portion of the field value.*

1. Open **AL2-C3-ViewIt.accdb** and enable the content.
2. Open the WebCustomers table.
4. Save the filter as a query named *CustBurlington05401.*
5. Close the Filter By Form datasheet and close the table. Click No when prompted to save changes to the table design.
6. Open the CustBurlington05401 query.
7. Print the query results datasheet in landscape orientation and then close the query.

Page 1

AL2-C3-CustBurlington05401(A1,Step7).accdb

CustWebOrders

Customer ID	First Name	Last Name	Web Order ID
101	Vincent	Gale	10001
101	Vincent	Gale	10014
102	Anna	Behr	10002
102	Anna	Behr	10008
102	Anna	Behr	10013
103	Terri	Lesniak	10003
103	Terri	Lesniak	10010
104	Franco	Felisatti	10004
104	Franco	Felisatti	10009
105	Blaine	Yiu	
106	Gary	Gallagher	10007
106	Gary	Gallagher	10015
107	Mel	Baronet	
108	Nanci	Fernando	10005
108	Nanci	Fernando	10012
108	Nanci	Fernando	10016
109	Grant	Kedziora	
110	Bobbie	Vanderwyst	10006
110	Bobbie	Vanderwyst	10011
111	Dana	Gorski	10025
112	Susan	O'Leary	10021
113	Keenan	Smith	10023
114	Pat	Portowski	10018
115	Claude	Dion	10026
116	Matthew	Siemens	10019
117	Liam	Flannigan	10022
118	Stephanie	Vuegas	10020
119	Paulina	Mykonos	10024
120	Jasmine	Patel	10017

Page 1

1. With **AL2-C3-ViewIt.accdb** open, create a new query in Design view using the following specifications:
a. Add the WebCustomers and WebOrders tables to the query.
b. Add the fields *CustID, FirstName, LastName,* and *WebOrderID* to the query design grid. *Note: Add **CustID** from the **WebCustomers** table.*
c. Modify the join type between the WebCustomers table and WebOrders table to a left outer join.
d. Save the query and name it *CustWebOrders*.
2. Run the query. Print the query results datasheet and then close the query.

AL2-C3-CustWebOrders(A2,Step2).accdb

PromptedOrderDates

Web Order ID	Date Ordered	Quantity	Product
10001	Feb-15-2015	1	Blue Hawaii
10001	Feb-15-2015	1	To Kill a Mockingbird
10002	Feb-15-2015	2	The Great Escape
10003	Feb-16-2015	1	Doctor Zhivago
10003	Feb-16-2015	1	Cool Hand Luke
10004	Feb-16-2015	2	The Longest Day
10004	Feb-22-2015	1	Dial M for Murder
10005	Feb-22-2015	1	Gone with the Wind
10005	Feb-22-2015	1	Ben Hur
10006	Feb-23-2015	1	The Wizard of Oz
10007	Feb-26-2015	1	The Maltese Falcon
10007	Feb-26-2015	1	Stormy Weather

11. Run the PromptedOrderDates query. Type February 1, 2015 as the beginning date and February 28, 2015 as the ending date. Print the query results datasheet and then close the query.

10. Open the PromptedMovie query in Design view. Use Save As to name the query *PromptedOrderDates*. Delete the prompt message in the *Product* column. Create a parameter query to prompt the user to type beginning and ending dates to view Web orders in the *DateOrd* column. The prompts should be *Type starting date* and *Type ending date*. Save and then close the query.

Page 1

AL2-C3-PromptedOrderDates(A1,Step11).accdb

1e. Create a calculated field with the column label *TotalSale* that multiplies the quantity ordered times the selling price. Change the caption to *Total Sale.*

WebSalesWithTotal

First Name	Last Name	Web Order ID	Date Ordered	Quantity	Selling Price	Total Sale
Vincent	Gale	10001	Feb-15-2015	1	$10.95	$10.95
Vincent	Gale	10001	Feb-15-2015	1	$11.95	$11.95
Anna	Behr	10002	Feb-15-2015	2	$18.95	$37.90
Terri	Lesniak	10003	Feb-16-2015	1	$22.95	$22.95
Terri	Lesniak	10003	Feb-16-2015	1	$11.95	$11.95
Terri	Lesniak	10003	Feb-16-2015	2	$12.95	$25.90
Franco	Felisatti	10004	Feb-22-2015	1	$9.95	$9.95
Nanci	Fernando	10005	Feb-22-2015	1	$18.95	$18.95
Nanci	Fernando	10005	Feb-22-2015	1	$11.95	$11.95
Bobbie	Vanderwyst	10006	Feb-23-2015	1	$11.95	$11.95
Gary	Gallagher	10007	Feb-26-2015	1	$9.95	$9.95
Gary	Gallagher	10007	Feb-26-2015	1	$12.95	$12.95
Anna	Behr	10008	Mar-04-2015	2	$12.95	$25.90
Franco	Felisatti	10009	Mar-08-2015	1	$11.95	$11.95
Terri	Lesniak	10010	Mar-10-2015	1	$10.95	$10.95
Bobbie	Vanderwyst	10011	Mar-15-2015	1	$18.95	$18.95
Bobbie	Vanderwyst	10011	Mar-15-2015	1	$9.95	$9.95
Nanci	Fernando	10012	Mar-16-2015	1	$12.95	$12.95
Nanci	Fernando	10012	Mar-16-2015	1	$9.95	$9.95
Nanci	Fernando	10012	Mar-16-2015	1	$13.95	$13.95
Anna	Behr	10013	Mar-22-2015	1	$15.95	$15.95
Vincent	Gale	10014	Mar-25-2015	1	$12.95	$12.95
Gary	Gallagher	10015	Mar-27-2015	2	$11.95	$23.90
Nanci	Fernando	10016	Mar-30-2015	1	$11.95	$11.95
Nanci	Fernando	10016	Mar-30-2015	1	$11.95	$11.95
Jasmine	Patel	10017	Apr-01-2015	1	$14.95	$14.95
Jasmine	Patel	10017	Apr-01-2015	1	$11.95	$11.95
Pat	Portowski	10018	Apr-03-2015	1	$11.95	$11.95
Matthew	Siemens	10019	Apr-05-2015	1	$10.95	$10.95
Stephanie	Vuegas	10020	Apr-05-2015	1	$11.95	$11.95
Susan	O'Leary	10021	Apr-08-2015	1	$15.95	$15.95
Liam	Flannigan	10022	Apr-10-2015	1	$9.95	$9.95
Keenan	Smith	10023	Apr-11-2015	1	$10.95	$10.95
Paulina	Mykonos	10024	Apr-12-2015	1	$11.95	$11.95
Dana	Gorski	10025	Apr-12-2015	1	$18.95	$18.95
Claude	Dion	10026	Apr-13-2015	1	$18.95	$18.95
Claude	Dion	10026	Apr-13-2015	1	$11.95	$11.95

1. With AL2-C3-ViewIt.accdb open, open the CustWebOrders query in Design view, use Save As to name the new query *WebSalesWithTotal*, and then modify the query as follows:
a. Modify the join type between the WebCustomers table and WebOrders table to an inner join.
b. Add the WebOrderDetails table and WebProducts table to the query.
c. Add the fields named *DateOrd, Qty, Product,* and *SellPrice* to the query design grid.
d. Delete the *CustID* field from the query.
2. Save and then run the query. Print the query results datasheet with the left and right margins set to 0.5 inch and then close the query.

AL2-C3-WebSalesWithTotal(A3,Step2).accdb

---

3. Create a new query in Design view using the following specifications: a. Add the WebOrderDetails and WebProducts tables to the query. b. Add the fields *WebOrdID, WebProdID,* and *Product* to the query design grid. *Note: Add **WebProdID** from the **WebProducts table.*** c. Modify the join type between the WebProducts table and the WebOrderDetails table to a left outer join. d. Save the query and name it *WebProductOrders.* 4. Run the query. Print the query results datasheet and then close the query.

WebProductOrders

Web Order ID	Product ID	Product
10013	CV-1001	Abbot & Costello Go to Mars
10021	CV-1001	Abbot & Costello Go to Mars
	CV-1002	Miracle on 34th Street
10012	CV-1003	Moby Dick
10004	CV-1004	Dial M for Murder
10012	CV-1004	Dial M for Murder
10016	CV-1005	Breakfast at Tiffany's
10005	CV-1006	Gone with the Wind
10011	CV-1006	Gone with the Wind
10026	CV-1006	Gone with the Wind
10003	CV-1007	Doctor Zhivago
10002	CV-1008	The Great Escape
10025	CV-1008	The Great Escape
10010	CV-1009	The Odd Couple
10023	CV-1009	The Odd Couple
10015	CV-1010	The Sound of Music
10026	CV-1010	The Sound of Music
10011	CV-1011	A Christmas Carol
10003	CV-1012	The Bridge on the River Kwai
10009	CV-1013	Cool Hand Luke
10026	CV-1014	Patton
10001	CV-1014	Patton
10016	CV-1015	Blue Hawaii
10024	CV-1016	Psycho
10003	CV-1016	Psycho
10008	CV-1017	The Longest Day
10014	CV-1017	The Longest Day
10001	CV-1017	The Longest Day
10020	CV-1018	To Kill a Mockingbird
10012	CV-1018	To Kill a Mockingbird
10007	CV-1019	One Flew Over the Cuckoo's Nest
10006	CV-1020	Bonnie and Clyde
10022	CV-1021	The Maltese Falcon
10005	CV-1022	The Wizard of Oz
10017	CV-1023	Rear Window
10018	CV-1024	Citizen Kane
10019	CV-1025	Ben Hur
10017	CV-1026	Hell's Angels
10018	CV-1027	Going My Way
10019	CV-1028	Band of Angels
10017	CV-1029	The Belts of St. Mary's
10007	CV-1030	Stormy Weather

AL2-C3-WebProductOrders(A2,Step4).accdb

4/22/2013

Feb2015WebSales

FirstName	LastName	WebOrdID	DateOrd	Qty
Vincent	Gale	10001	2/15/2015	1
Vincent	Gale	10001	2/15/2015	1
Anna	Behr	10002	2/15/2015	2
Terri	Lesniak	10003	2/16/2015	1
Terri	Lesniak	10003	2/16/2015	1
Terri	Lesniak	10003	2/16/2015	2
Franco	Felisatti	10004	2/22/2015	1
Nanci	Fernando	10005	2/22/2015	1
Nanci	Fernando	10005	2/22/2015	1
Bobbie	Vanderwyst	10006	2/23/2015	1
Gary	Gallagher	10007	2/26/2015	1
Gary	Gallagher	10007	2/26/2015	1

1b. Use the *Between* expression to add a criterion to select the records for sales during the month of February 2015.

1. With **AL2-C3-ViewIt.accdb** open, open the WebSalesWithTotal query in Design view, use Save As to name the new query *Feb2015SalesMakeTable*, and then modify the query as follows:
a. Delete the *SellPrice* and *TotalSale* columns from the query design grid.
b. Run the query to make sure the correct records are being selected.
c. Change the query to a make-table query, name the new table *Feb2015WebSales*, and archive it in the current database.
d. Save, run, and then close the query.
2. Open the Feb2015WebSales table. Adjust column widths as necessary and then print the datasheet. Close the table, saving the changes to the layout.

Page 1

3c. Create a calculated field with the column label *Tax* that multiplies the value in the *TotalSale* column times 0.06 (decimal equivalent of 6%). Format the calculated column by applying the *Standard* format.

3d. Create a second calculated column with the column label *TotalSaleWithTax* that adds the *TotalSale* column to the *Tax* column. Change the caption to *Total Sale With Tax*.

WebSalesWithTotalAndTax

Web Order ID	Date Ordered	Total Sale	Tax	Total Sale With Tax
10001	Feb-15-2015	$10.95	0.66	$11.61
10001	Feb-15-2015	$11.95	0.72	$12.67
10002	Feb-15-2015	$37.90	2.27	$40.17
10003	Feb-16-2015	$22.95	1.38	$24.33
10003	Feb-16-2015	$11.95	0.72	$12.67
10003	Feb-16-2015	$25.90	1.55	$27.45
10004	Feb-22-2015	$9.95	0.60	$10.55
10005	Feb-22-2015	$18.95	1.14	$20.09
10005	Feb-22-2015	$11.95	0.72	$12.67
10006	Feb-23-2015	$11.95	0.72	$12.67
10007	Feb-26-2015	$9.95	0.60	$10.55
10007	Feb-26-2015	$12.95	0.78	$13.73
10008	Mar-04-2015	$25.90	1.55	$27.45
10009	Mar-08-2015	$11.95	0.72	$12.67
10010	Mar-10-2015	$10.95	0.66	$11.61
10011	Mar-15-2015	$18.95	1.14	$20.09
10011	Mar-15-2015	$9.95	0.60	$10.55
10012	Mar-16-2015	$12.95	0.78	$13.73
10012	Mar-16-2015	$9.95	0.60	$10.55
10012	Mar-16-2015	$13.95	0.84	$14.79
10013	Mar-22-2015	$15.95	0.96	$16.91
10014	Mar-25-2015	$12.95	0.78	$13.73
10015	Mar-27-2015	$23.90	1.43	$25.33
10016	Mar-30-2015	$11.95	0.72	$12.67
10016	Mar-30-2015	$11.95	0.72	$12.67
10017	Apr-01-2015	$14.95	0.90	$15.85
10017	Apr-01-2015	$11.95	0.72	$12.67
10018	Apr-03-2015	$11.95	0.72	$12.67
10019	Apr-05-2015	$10.95	0.66	$11.61
10020	Apr-05-2015	$11.95	0.72	$12.67
10021	Apr-08-2015	$15.95	0.96	$16.91
10022	Apr-10-2015	$9.95	0.60	$10.55
10023	Apr-11-2015	$10.95	0.66	$11.61
10024	Apr-12-2015	$11.95	0.72	$12.67
10025	Apr-12-2015	$18.95	1.14	$20.09
10026	Apr-13-2015	$18.95	1.14	$20.09
10026	Apr-13-2015	$11.95	0.72	$12.67
10026	Apr-13-2015	$11.95	0.72	$12.67

3. Create a new query in Design view that calculates the total sale with tax as follows:
a. Nest the WebSalesWithTotal query in the new query.
b. Add the fields *WebOrdID*, *DateOrd*, and *TotalSale* to the query design grid.
c. Save the query and name it *WebSalesWithTotalAndTax*.
4. Run the query. Double-click the right column boundary for the last column in the query results datasheet to display the entire field heading and then print the query results datasheet with the left and right margins set to 0.5 inch. Close the query, saving the changes.

Reservation	First Name	Last Name	Dog's Name	Date In	Date Out	Days Boarded	Kennel Type	Daily Rate	Amount Due
1	Shawn	Jenkins	Abby	11/9/2015	11/12/2015	3	V.I.P. Suite	$38.50	$115.50
2	Shawn	Jenkins	Winnie	11/9/2015	11/12/2015	3	V.I.P. Suite	$38.50	$115.50
3	Sean	Gallagher	Tank	11/10/2015	11/13/2015	3	V.I.P. Suite	$38.50	$115.50
4	Sofia	Ramos	Apollo	11/11/2015	11/18/2015	7	Indoor/Outdoor Suite	$25.50	$178.50
5	Sofia	Ramos	Murphy	11/11/2015	11/18/2015	7	Indoor/Outdoor Suite	$25.50	$178.50
6	Dina	Lombardi	Niko	11/12/2015	11/16/2015	4	Indoor/Outdoor Suite	$25.50	$102.00
7	Natale	Rizzo	Dallas	11/12/2015	11/14/2015	2	Indoor/Outdoor Suite	$25.50	$51.00
8	James	Chung	Lassie	11/12/2015	11/13/2015	1	Deluxe Suite	$29.50	$29.50
9	Bernard	Jedicke	Kosmo	11/12/2015	11/13/2015	1	Day Care Boarding	$16.50	$16.50
10	Bernard	Jedicke	Sierra	11/12/2015	11/13/2015	1	Day Care Boarding	$16.50	$16.50
11	Bernard	Jedicke	Emma	11/12/2015	11/13/2015	1	Day Care Boarding	$16.50	$16.50
12	Carlotta	Sanchez	Scrappy	11/13/2015	11/19/2015	6	Deluxe Suite	$29.50	$177.00
13	Michael	Mancini	Harley	11/13/2015	11/23/2015	10	Indoor/Outdoor Suite	$25.50	$255.00
14	Glen	Waters	Barney	11/14/2015	11/29/2015	15	Indoor/Outdoor Suite	$25.50	$382.50
15	Lenora	Diaz	Zack	11/14/2015	11/17/2015	3	Indoor/Outdoor Suite	$25.50	$76.50
16	Maeve	Murphy	King	11/15/2015	11/19/2015	4	V.I.P. Suite	$38.50	$154.00
17	Valerie	McTague	Chloe	11/16/2015	11/19/2015	3	Deluxe Suite	$29.50	$88.50
18	Nadia	Costa	Bailey	11/17/2015	11/24/2015	7	Deluxe Suite	$29.50	$206.50
19	Juan	Torres	Taffy	11/17/2015	11/21/2015	4	V.I.P. Suite	$38.50	$154.00
20	Liam	Doherty	Zeus	11/18/2015	11/23/2015	5	V.I.P. Suite	$38.50	$192.50
21	Dillon	Farrell	Chico	11/18/2015	11/22/2015	4	Indoor/Outdoor Suite	$25.50	$102.00
22	Diane	Ye	Elvis	11/20/2015	11/25/2015	5	Indoor/Outdoor Suite	$25.50	$127.50
23	Lorenzo	Rivera	Fifi	11/22/2015	11/27/2015	5	V.I.P. Suite	$38.50	$192.50
24	Lorenzo	Rivera	Lucky	11/22/2015	11/27/2015	5	Indoor/Outdoor Suite	$25.50	$127.50
25	Bernard	Jedicke	Kosmo	11/26/2015	11/27/2015	1	Day Care Boarding	$16.50	$16.50
26	Bernard	Jedicke	Sierra	11/26/2015	11/27/2015	1	Day Care Boarding	$16.50	$16.50
27	Bernard	Jedicke	Emma	11/26/2015	11/27/2015	1	Day Care Boarding	$16.50	$16.50

AL2-C3-ReservationTotals(VB).accdb

First Name	Last Name	Web Order ID	Date Ordered	Quantity	Selling Price	Total Sale
Anna	Behr	10008	Mar-04-2015	2	$12.95	$25.90
Franco	Felisatti	10009	Mar-08-2015	1	$11.95	$11.95
Terri	Lesniak	10010	Mar-10-2015	1	$10.95	$10.95
Bobbie	Vanderwyst	10011	Mar-15-2015	1	$18.95	$18.95
Bobbie	Vanderwyst	10011	Mar-15-2015	1	$9.95	$9.95
Nanci	Fernando	10012	Mar-16-2015	1	$12.95	$12.95
Nanci	Fernando	10012	Mar-16-2015	1	$9.95	$9.95
Nanci	Fernando	10012	Mar-16-2015	1	$13.95	$13.95
Anna	Behr	10013	Mar-22-2015	1	$15.95	$15.95
Vincent	Gale	10014	Mar-25-2015	1	$12.95	$12.95
Gary	Gallagher	10015	Mar-27-2015	2	$11.95	$23.90
Nanci	Fernando	10016	Mar-30-2015	1	$11.95	$11.95
Nanci	Fernando	10016	Mar-30-2015	1	$11.95	$11.95
Jasmine	Patel	10017	Apr-01-2015	1	$14.95	$14.95
Jasmine	Patel	10017	Apr-01-2015	1	$11.95	$11.95
Pat	Portowski	10018	Apr-03-2015	1	$11.95	$11.95
Matthew	Siemens	10019	Apr-05-2015	1	$10.95	$10.95
Stephanie	Vuegas	10020	Apr-05-2015	1	$11.95	$11.95
Susan	O'Leary	10021	Apr-08-2015	1	$15.95	$15.95
Liam	Flannigan	10022	Apr-10-2015	1	$9.95	$9.95
Keenan	Smith	10023	Apr-11-2015	1	$10.95	$10.95
Paulina	Mykonos	10024	Apr-12-2015	1	$11.95	$11.95
Dana	Gorski	10025	Apr-12-2015	1	$18.95	$18.95
Claude	Dion	10026	Apr-13-2015	1	$18.95	$18.95
Claude	Dion	10026	Apr-13-2015	1	$11.95	$11.95
Claude	Dion	10026	Apr-13-2015	1	$11.95	$11.95

3. Open the Feb2015SalesMakeTable query in Design view, use Save As to name the new query *Feb2015SalesDelete*, and then modify the query as follows:
a. Change the query to a delete query. b. Remove the WebCustomers, WebOrderDetails, and WebProducts tables from the query.
c. Save, run the query and then close the query window.
4. Open the WebSalesWithTotal query. Print the query results datasheet in landscape orientation with left and right margins set to 0.5 inch and then close the query.

AL2-C3-WebSalesWithTotal(A4,Step4).accdb

PromptedSalesByAgent   4/24/2015

Agent ID	Agent First Name	Agent Last Name	Date Sold	Street Address	Sale Price	Commission Rate
16	Cecilia	Ortega	10/14/2015	22 E Holly Avenue	$229,900.00	4.00%
16	Cecilia	Ortega	10/31/2015	2900 E Cactus Road	$155,750.00	3.25%

Page 1

SalesByAgent   4/24/2015

Agent ID	Agent First Name	Agent Last Name	Date Sold	Street Address	Sale Price	Commission Rate
10	Kwan	Im	10/12/2015	151 E Culver Street	$325,500.00	3.00%
10	Kwan	Im	10/17/2015	341 E Detroit Street	$275,800.00	3.85%
10	Kwan	Im	10/22/2015	659 W Erie Street	$310,114.00	4.00%
10	Kwan	Im	10/23/2015	10 N 16th Avenue	$245,800.00	3.25%
11	William	Ludlow	10/25/2015	1665 E Campbell Avenue	$244,845.00	3.00%
19	Isabelle	Marshall	10/15/2015	334 W Mitchell Drive	$375,800.00	4.00%
19	Isabelle	Marshall	10/27/2015	1401 N Orlando Circle	$175,455.00	3.00%
14	Jaren	Newman	10/15/2015	202 S Hobson	$202,500.00	3.75%
16	Cecilia	Ortega	10/14/2015	22 E Holly Avenue	$229,900.00	4.00%
16	Cecilia	Ortega	10/31/2015	2900 E Cactus Road	$155,750.00	3.25%
21	Maureen	Pascual	10/30/2015	3033 E Hampton Circle	$166,500.00	3.00%
17	Robin	Rehberg	10/13/2015	23 W 7th Street	$189,900.00	3.25%
17	Robin	Rehberg	10/31/2015	11233 E Stearn Avenue	$165,750.00	3.25%
12	Catherine	Singleton	10/14/2015	126 E Buffalo Street	$349,900.00	4.00%

Page 1

4/24/2015

AgentsWithCoBrokers

Agent ID	Agent First Name	Agent Last Name	Co-Broker Agent Last Name
24	Julia	Alvarez	Newman
15	Lee	Hutchinson	Newman
20	Craig	Johnson	Rehberg
18	Andre	Kulisek	Rehberg
23	Marc	Lopez	Newman
11	William	Ludlow	Im
19	Isabelle	Marshall	Rehberg
25	Eva	Mendoza	Im
16	Cecilia	Ortega	Newman
21	Maureen	Pascual	Rehberg
22	Hector	Salazar	Im
12	Catherine	Singleton	Im
13	Maria	Vuegas	Im

Page 1

AL2-C3-CS-P1-AgentsWithCoBrokers(P1).accdb

AgentsAndClients

4/24/2015

Agent ID	Agent First Name	Agent Last Name	Client ID	First Name	Last Name
10	Kwan	Im	102	Christian	Rivera
10	Kwan	Im	107	Alonso	Romero
10	Kwan	Im	109	Jose	Perez
10	Kwan	Im	110	Tanya	Anderson
11	William	Ludlow	112	Luz	Sanchez
11	William	Ludlow	115	Yvonne	DeSanti
12	Catherine	Singleton	103	Juan	Torres
13	Maria	Vuegas			
14	Jaren	Newman	101	Rodrigo	Chavez
14	Jaren	Newman	111	Angela	Hildebrand
14	Jaren	Newman	119	Claudette	St. Pierre
15	Lee	Hutchinson	116	Manuel	Kellerman
15	Lee	Hutchinson	117	Sergio	Gomez
16	Cecilia	Ortega	105	Liliana	Garcia
16	Cecilia	Ortega	118	Yvette	Jorgenson
17	Robin	Rehberg	104	Irma	Hernandez
18	Andre	Kulisek			
19	Isabelle	Marshall	106	Carmen	Ortiz
19	Isabelle	Marshall	113	Kevin	Poste
19	Isabelle	Marshall	120	Victor	Winters
20	Craig	Johnson			
21	Maureen	Pascual	108	Cindy	Cutara
21	Maureen	Pascual	114	Ernesto	Guzman
22	Hector	Salazar			
23	Marc	Lopez			
24	Julia	Alvarez			
25	Eva	Mendoza			

Page 1

AL2-C3-CS-P1-AgentsAndClients(P1).accdb

AgentaWithCommQuotas

Agent ID	Agent First Name	Agent Last Name	Commission Quota
24	Julia	Alvarez	$172,500
15	Lee	Hutchinson	$172,500
10	Kwan	Im	$287,500
20	Craig	Johnson	$172,500
18	Andre	Kulisek	$115,000
23	Marc	Lopez	$230,000
11	William	Ludlow	$287,500
19	Isabelle	Marshall	$230,000
25	Eva	Mendoza	$172,500
14	Jaren	Newman	$172,500
16	Cecilia	Ortega	$115,000
21	Maureen	Pascual	$230,000
17	Robin	Rehberg	$115,000
22	Hector	Salazar	$172,500
12	Catherine	Singleton	$230,000
13	Maria	Vuegas	$172,500

AL2-C3-CS-P1-AgentaWithCommQuotas(P1).accdb

SalesByAgentWithCommission

Agent ID	Agent First Name	Agent Last Name	Date Sold	Street Address	Sale Price	Commission Rate	Commission Earned
10	Kwan	Im	10/12/2015	151 E Culver Street	$325,500.00	3.00%	$9,765.00
10	Kwan	Im	10/17/2015	341 E Detroit Street	$275,800.00	3.85%	$10,618.30
10	Kwan	Im	10/22/2015	659 W Erie Street	$310,114.00	4.00%	$12,404.56
10	Kwan	Im	10/23/2015	10 N 16th Avenue	$245,800.00	3.25%	$7,988.50
11	William	Ludlow	10/25/2015	1665 E Campbell Avenue	$244,845.00	3.00%	$7,345.35
19	Isabelle	Marshall	10/15/2015	334 W Mitchell Drive	$375,800.00	4.00%	$15,032.00
19	Isabelle	Marshall	10/27/2015	1401 N Orlando Circle	$175,455.00	3.00%	$5,263.65
14	Jaren	Newman	10/15/2015	202 S Hobson	$202,500.00	3.75%	$7,593.75
16	Cecilia	Ortega	10/14/2015	22 E Holly Avenue	$229,900.00	4.00%	$9,196.00
16	Cecilia	Ortega	10/31/2015	2900 E Cactus Road	$155,750.00	3.25%	$5,061.88
21	Maureen	Pascual	10/30/2015	3033 E Hampton Circle	$166,500.00	3.00%	$4,995.00
17	Robin	Rehberg	10/13/2015	23 W 7th Street	$189,900.00	3.25%	$6,171.75
17	Robin	Rehberg	10/31/2015	11233 E Stearn Avenue	$165,750.00	3.25%	$5,386.88
12	Catherine	Singleton	10/14/2015	126 E Buffalo Street	$349,900.00	4.00%	$13,996.00

AL2-C3-CS-P1-SalesByAgentWithCommission(P1).accdb

PreferencesStagingOrPreSaleInspection

4/24/2015

Listing Date	Street Address	Preferences.Preferences.Value	First Name	Last Name	Phone
10/8/2015	202 S Hobson	Staging service	Rodrigo	Chavez	(480) 555-3152
10/7/2015	126 E Buffalo Street	Pre-sale inspection	Juan	Torres	(480) 555-2667
10/15/2015	1221 W Vine Avenue	Pre-sale inspection	Juan	Torres	(480) 555-2667
10/1/2015	23 W 7th Street	Staging service	Irma	Hernandez	(480) 555-1485
10/9/2015	334 W Mitchell Drive	Pre-sale inspection	Carmen	Ortiz	(480) 555-6714
10/9/2015	334 W Mitchell Drive	Staging service	Carmen	Ortiz	(480) 555-6714
10/12/2015	341 E Detroit Street	Pre-sale inspection	Alonso	Romero	(480) 555-9686
10/12/2015	65 W Boston Street	Pre-sale inspection	Cindy	Cutara	(480) 555-3451
10/12/2015	65 W Boston Street	Staging service	Cindy	Cutara	(480) 555-3451
10/16/2015	37 W Clark Street	Pre-sale inspection	Tanya	Anderson	(480) 555-3481
10/16/2015	37 W Clark Street	Staging service	Tanya	Anderson	(480) 555-3481
10/18/2015	10 N 16th Avenue	Pre-sale inspection	Tanya	Anderson	(480) 555-3481
10/18/2015	10 N 16th Avenue	Staging service	Tanya	Anderson	(480) 555-3481
10/18/2015	33 E Lincoln Street	Pre-sale inspection	Tanya	Anderson	(480) 555-3481
10/18/2015	33 E Lincoln Street	Staging service	Tanya	Anderson	(480) 555-3481
10/19/2015	5333 W Elgin Street	Pre-sale inspection	Angela	Hildebrand	(480) 555-7682
10/21/2015	1401 N Orlando Circle	Staging service	Kevin	Poste	(480) 555-1679
10/23/2015	1501 N 91st Place	Staging service	Manuel	Kellerman	(480) 555-4763
10/24/2015	995 W Cross Street	Staging service	Sergio	Gomez	(480) 555-2685
10/24/2015	2900 E Cactus Road	Pre-sale inspection	Yvette	Jorgenson	(480) 555-4994

Page 1

AL2-C3-CS-P3-PreferencesStagingOrPreSaleInspection(P3).accdb

Top5SalePrices

4/24/2015

Agent ID	Agent First Name	Agent Last Name	Date Sold	Street Address	Sale Price	Commission Rate
19	Isabelle	Marshall	10/15/2015	334 W Mitchell Drive	$375,800.00	4.00%
12	Catherine	Singleton	10/14/2015	126 E Buffalo Street	$349,900.00	4.00%
10	Kwan	Im	10/12/2015	151 E Culver Street	$325,500.00	3.00%
10	Kwan	Im	10/22/2015	659 W Erie Street	$310,114.00	4.00%
10	Kwan	Im	10/17/2015	341 E Detroit Street	$275,800.00	3.85%

Page 1

AL2-C3-CS-P2-Top5SalePrices(P2).accdb

Access Level 2, Chapter 4 Model Answers

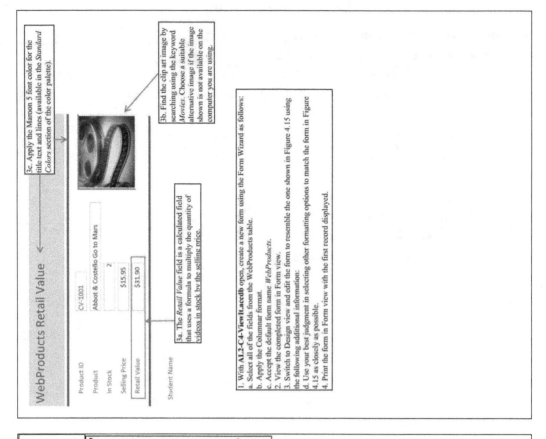

3c. Apply the Maroon 5 font color for the title text and lines (available in the *Standard Colors* section of the color palette).

3b. Find the clip art image by searching using the keyword *Movies*. Choose a suitable alternative image if the image shown is not available on the computer you are using.

WebProducts Retail Value

Product ID	CV-1001
Product	Abbot & Costello Go to Mars
In Stock	2
Selling Price	$15.95
Retail Value	$31.90

Student Name

3a. The *Retail Value* field is a calculated field that uses a formula to multiply the quantity of videos in stock by the selling price.

1. With **AL2-C4-ViewIt.accdb** open, create a new form using the Form Wizard as follows:
   a. Select all of the fields from the WebProducts table.
   b. Apply the Columnar format.
   c. Accept the default form name *WebProducts*.
2. View the completed form in Form view.
3. Switch to Design view and edit the form to resemble the one shown in Figure 4.15 using the following additional information:
   d. Use your best judgment in selecting other formatting options to match the form in Figure 4.15 as closely as possible.
4. Print the form in Form view with the first record displayed.

AL2-C4-WebProducts(A2).accdb

Web Customer Orders

Customer ID	101	Home Phone	802-555-1635
First Name	Vincent	Last Name	Gale
Street Address	350 Manhattan Drive		
City	Burlington	State	VT	ZIP Code	05401-4245

Web Order ID	Date Ordered	Quantity	Product	Selling Price
10001	Feb-15-2015	1	Blue Hawaii	$10.95
10001	Feb-15-2015	1	To Kill a Mockingbird	$11.95
10014	Mar-25-2015	1	The Longest Day	$12.95

Student Name

3b. Add a title object in the *Form Header* section and then type the text Web Customer Orders. Use the move handle that displays at the top left of the selected title control to move the title until the first letter (W) is at approximately the 1.5-inch position on the horizontal ruler.

1. Open **AL2-C4-ViewIt.accdb** and enable the content.
2. Create a query named *CustWebOrders* using the following specifications:
   a. Add the WebOrderDetails, WebOrders, and WebProducts tables to the query.
   b. Add the following fields first from the WebOrders table, then from the WebOrderDetails table, and then from the WebProducts table.
   WebOrders Table
   WebOrderDetails Table
   WebProducts Table
   WebOrdID Qty Product CustID SellPrice DateOrd
   c. Run the query and then close the query results datasheet.

3c. Add your name in a label control object centered in the *Form Footer* section.

3g. Add a tab control object below the existing fields with a height of approximately 2 inches and a width that extends to the right edge of the form.
   1) On the first page, change the caption to *Web Orders* and add all of the fields from the CustWebOrders query in a subform. Delete the subform label control object. Delete the label control object and text box control object for the *CustID* field in the subform and then move the remaining fields up to fill in the space. Move and resize the subform to fit the width of the page. Autofit column widths in Form view to view all of the columns within the page.

3. Create a new form called *WebCustOrders* using Design view and build the form using the following specifications:
   a. Expand the width of the form in the grid to the 6.5-inch position on the horizontal ruler.
   d. Apply the Retrospect theme.
   e. Connect the WebCustomers table to the form and add all of the fields to the *Detail* section in the layout shown in Figure 4.14. Adjust the widths of the control objects as shown. Remember to use the Size/Space and Align buttons to position multiple controls at the same horizontal or vertical position and adjust spacing between controls.
   f. Change the tab order of the fields so the *HPhone* field is selected after the *CustID* field.
   2) On the second page, change the caption to *Payment Information* and add all of the fields except *Cust ID* and *EmailAdd* from the WebCustPymnt table in a subform. Delete the subform label control object and move and resize the subform to fit the width of the page. Autofit column widths in Form view to view all of the columns within the page.
4. Apply bold formatting to the label control objects and Green, Accent 6, Lighter 80% (second row, last column in the *Theme* colors) background color to the text box control objects.
5. Save the form.
6. Print the form in Form view with the first record displayed and the Web Orders page active.

AL2-C4-WebCustOrders(A1).accdb

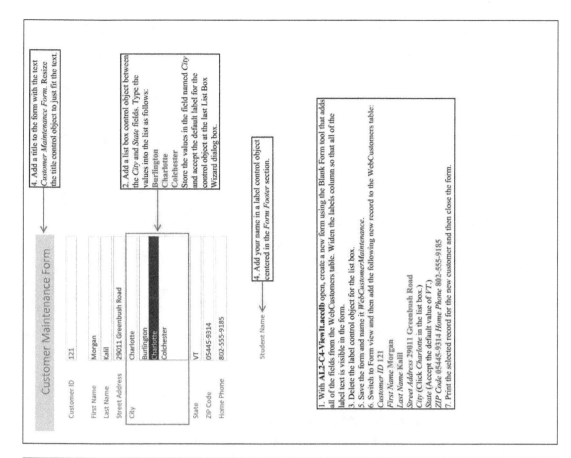

4. Add a title to the form with the text *Customer Maintenance Form*. Resize the title control object to just fit the text.

2. Add a list box control object between the *City* and *State* fields. Type the values into the list as follows:

Burlington
Charlotte
Colchester

Store the values in the field named *City* and accept the default label for the control object at the last List Box Wizard dialog box.

4. Add your name in a label control object centered in the *Form Footer* section.

1. With **AL2-C4-ViewIt.accdb** open, create a new form using the Blank Form tool that adds all of the fields from the WebCustomers table. Widen the labels column so that all of the label text is visible in the form.
3. Delete the label control object for the list box.
5. Save the form and name it *WebCustomerMaintenance*.
6. Switch to Form view and then add the following new record to the WebCustomers table:

Customer ID 121
First Name Morgan
Last Name Kalil
Street Address 29011 Greenbush Road
City (Click *Charlotte* in the list box.)
State (Accept the default value of *VT*.)
ZIP Code 05445-9314 *Home Phone* 802-555-9185
7. Print the selected record for the new customer and then close the form.

AL2-C4-WebCustomerMaintenance(A4).accdb

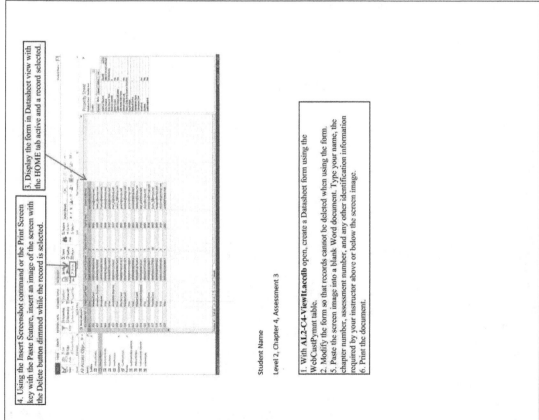

4. Using the Insert Screenshot command or the Print Screen key with the Paste feature, insert an image of the screen with the Delete button dimmed while the record is selected.

3. Display the form in Datasheet view with the HOME tab active and a record selected.

Student Name

Level 2, Chapter 4, Assessment 3

1. With **AL2-C4-ViewIt.accdb** open, create a Datasheet form using the WebCustPymnt table.
2. Modify the form so that records cannot be deleted when using the form.
5. Paste the screen image into a blank Word document. Type your name, the chapter number, assessment number, and any other identification information required by your instructor above or below the screen image.
6. Print the document.

AL2-C4-ViewItForm(A3).accdb

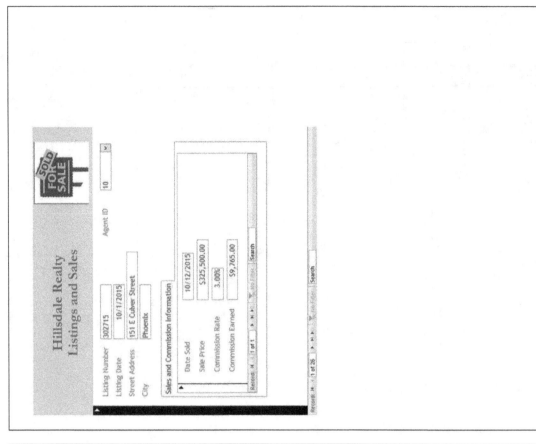

AL2-C4-CS-P1-ListingsAndSales(P1).accdb

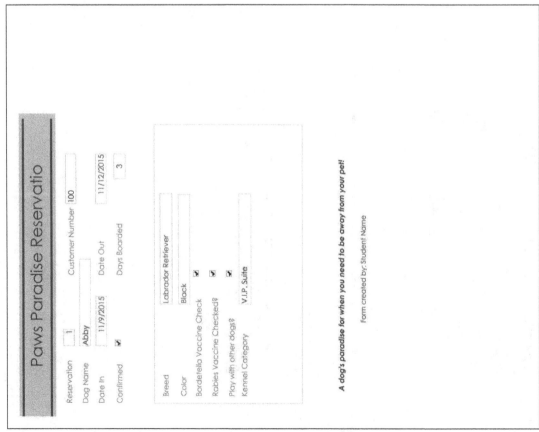

AL2-C4-Reservations(VB).accdb

Benchmark Access 2013 Level 2 Model Answers

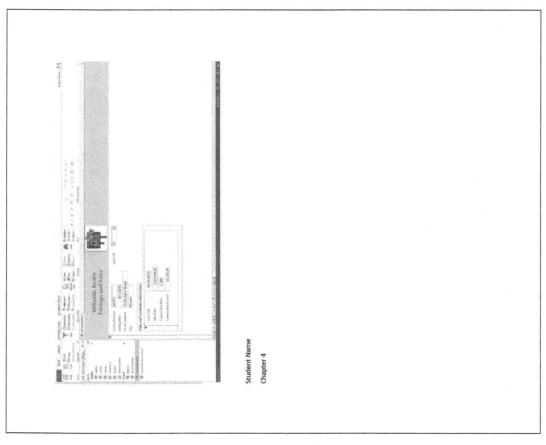

Student Name

Chapter 4

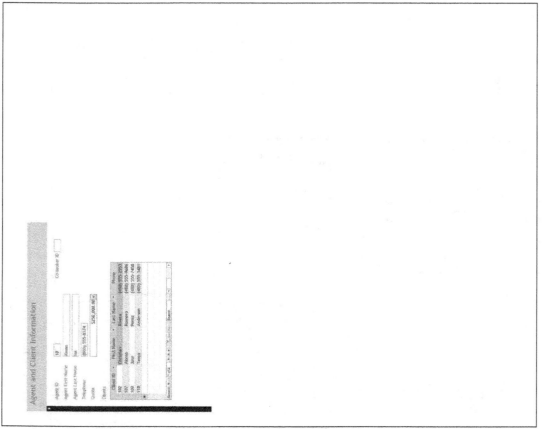

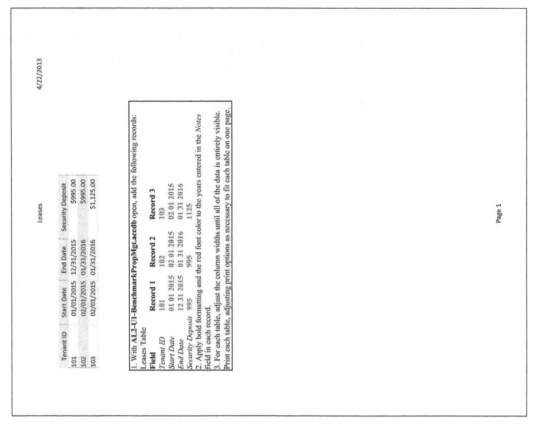

AL2-U1-Leases(A3).accdb

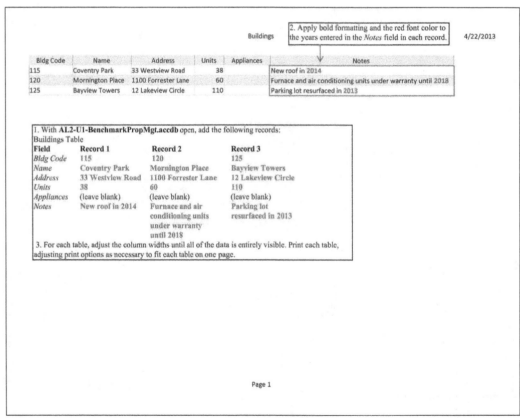

AL2-U1-Buildings(A3).accdb

Tenants — 4/22/2013

Tenant ID	Bldg Code	Unit No	Last Name	First Name	Telephone	Rent
101	115	110	Chen	Wei	519-555-8776	$995.00
102	115	215	Ayoub	Mona	519-555-2286	$995.00
103	115	320	Reiser	Helena	519-555-7668	$1,125.00

1. With **AL2-U1-BenchmarkPropMgt.accdb** open, add the following records:

Tenants Table

Field	Record 1	Record 2	Record 3
Tenant ID	101	102	103
Bldg Code	115	115	115
Unit No	110	215	320
Last Name	Chen	Ayoub	Reiser
First Name	Wei	Mona	Helena
Telephone	519 555 8776	519 555 2286	519 555 7668
Rent	995	995	1125

2. Apply bold formatting and the red font color to the years entered in the *Notes* field in each record.
3. For each table, adjust the column widths until all of the data is entirely visible. Print each table, adjusting print options as necessary to fit each table on one page.

Page 1

AL2-U1-Tenants(A3).accdb

SiteManagers — 4/22/2013

Bldg Code	Last Name	First Name	Telephone	Cell Phone	Hire Date
115	Jenkins	Blair	800-555-3485	800-555-3748	02/08/2010
120	Hernandez	Maria	800-555-8675	800-555-3996	04/23/2013
125	Doxtator	Cody	800-555-9677	800-555-7795	09/15/2014

1. With **AL2-U1-BenchmarkPropMgt.accdb** open, add the following records:

SiteManagers Table

Field	Record 1	Record 2	Record 3
Bldg Code	115	120	125
Last Name	Jenkins	Hernandez	Doxtator
First Name	Blair	Maria	Cody
Telephone	800 555 3485	800 555 8675	800 555 9677
Cell Phone	800 555 3748	800 555 3996	800 555 7795
Hire Date	02 08 2010	04 23 2013	09 15 2014

2. Apply bold formatting and the red font color to the years entered in the *Notes* field in each record.
3. For each table, adjust the column widths until all of the data is entirely visible. Print each table, adjusting print options as necessary to fit each table on one page.

Page 1

AL2-U1-SiteManagers(A3).accdb

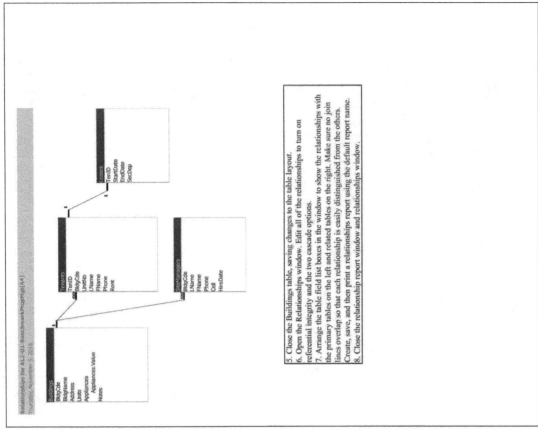

AL2-U1-Relationships for AL2-U1-BenchmarkPropMgt(A4,Step7).accdb

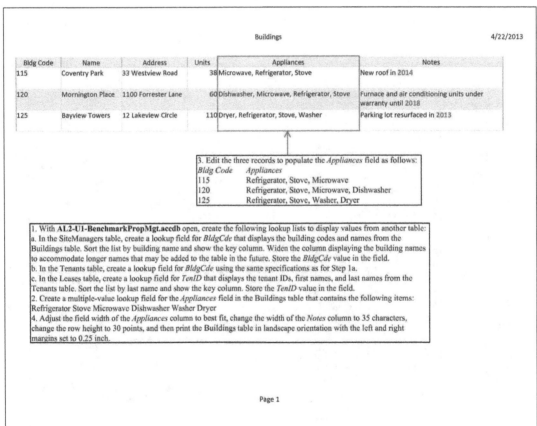

AL2-U1-Buildings(A4,Step4).accdb

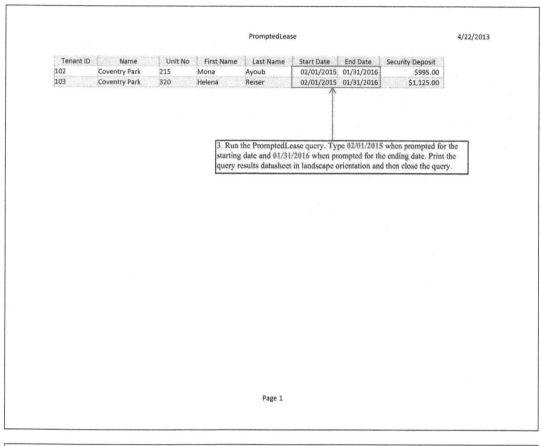

PromptedLease 4/22/2013

Tenant ID	Name	Unit No	First Name	Last Name	Start Date	End Date	Security Deposit
102	Coventry Park	215	Mona	Ayoub	02/01/2015	01/31/2016	$995.00
103	Coventry Park	320	Helena	Reiser	02/01/2015	01/31/2016	$1,125.00

3. Run the PromptedLease query. Type 02/01/2015 when prompted for the starting date and 01/31/2016 when prompted for the ending date. Print the query results datasheet in landscape orientation and then close the query.

Page 1

AL2-U1-PromptedLease(A5,Step3).accdb

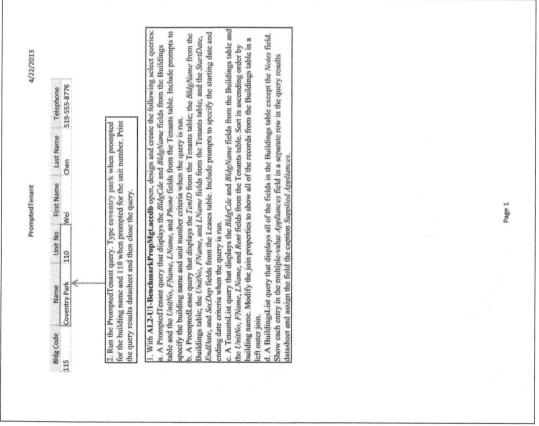

PromptedTenant 4/22/2013

Bldg Code	Name	Unit No	First Name	Last Name	Telephone
115	Coventry Park	110	Wei	Chen	519-555-8776

2. Run the PromptedTenant query. Type coventry park when prompted for the building name and 110 when prompted for the unit number. Print the query results datasheet and then close the query.

1. With AL2-U1-BenchmarkPropMgt.accdb open, design and create the following select queries:
a. A PromptedTenant query that displays the *BldgCde* and *BldgName* fields from the Buildings table and the *UnitNo*, *FName*, *LName*, and *Phone* fields from the Tenants table. Include prompts to specify the building name and unit number criteria when the query is run.
b. A PromptedLease query that displays the *TenID* from the Tenants table; the *BldgName* from the Buildings table; the *UnitNo*, *FName*, and *LName* fields from the Tenants table; and the *StartDate*, *EndDate*, and *SecDep* fields from the Leases table. Include prompts to specify the starting date and ending date criteria when the query is run.
c. A TenantsList query that displays the *BldgCde* and *BldgName* fields from the Buildings table and the *UnitNo*, *FName*, *LName*, and *Rent* fields from the Tenants table. Sort in ascending order by building name. Modify the join properties to show all of the records from the Buildings table in a left outer join.
d. A BuildingsList query that displays all of the fields in the Buildings table except the *Notes* field. Show each entry in the multiple-value *Appliances* field in a separate row in the query results datasheet and assign the field the caption *Supplied Appliances*.

Page 1

AL2-U1-PromptedTenant(A5,Step2).accdb

BuildingsList   4/22/2013

Bldg Code	Name	Address	Units	Supplied Appliances
115	Coventry Park	33 Westview Road	38	Refrigerator
115	Coventry Park	33 Westview Road	38	Stove
115	Coventry Park	33 Westview Road	38	Microwave
120	Mornington Place	1100 Forrester Lane	60	Refrigerator
120	Mornington Place	1100 Forrester Lane	60	Stove
120	Mornington Place	1100 Forrester Lane	60	Microwave
120	Mornington Place	1100 Forrester Lane	60	Dishwasher
125	Bayview Towers	12 Lakeview Circle	110	Refrigerator
125	Bayview Towers	12 Lakeview Circle	110	Stove
125	Bayview Towers	12 Lakeview Circle	110	Washer
125	Bayview Towers	12 Lakeview Circle	110	Dryer

5. Run the BuildingsList query, print the query results
datasheet in landscape orientation, and then close the query.

Page 1

AL2-U1-BuildingsList(A5,Step5).accdb

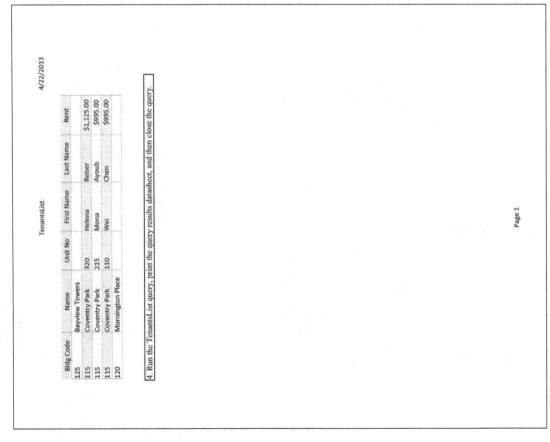

TenantsList   4/22/2013

Bldg Code	Name	Unit No	First Name	Last Name	Rent
125	Bayview Towers				
115	Coventry Park	320	Helena	Reiser	$1,125.00
115	Coventry Park	215	Mona	Ayoub	$995.00
120	Mornington Place	110	Wei	Chen	$995.00

4. Run the TenantsList query, print the query results datasheet, and then close the query.

Page 1

AL2-U1-TenantsList(A5,Step4).accdb

Bldg Code	Name	Unit No	First Name	Last Name	Rent	Annual Rent
115	Coventry Park	320	Helena	Reiser	$1,170.00	$14,040.00
115	Coventry Park	215	Mona	Ayoub	$1,034.80	$12,417.60
115	Coventry Park	110	Wei	Chen	$1,034.80	$12,417.60
Total					**$3,239.60**	**$38,875.20**

2. Create an update query named *RentIncrease* to increase all of the rents by 4%. Run the query.
3. Close the RentIncrease query.
4. Open the RentalIncome query, print the query results datasheet in landscape orientation, and then close the query.

AL2-U1-RentalIncome(A6,Step4).accdb

Bldg Code	Name	Unit No	First Name	Last Name	Rent	Annual Rent
115	Coventry Park	320	Helena	Reiser	$1,170.00	$14,040.00
115	Coventry Park	215	Mona	Ayoub	$1,034.80	$12,417.60
115	Coventry Park	110	Wei	Chen	$1,034.80	$12,417.60
Total					**$3,239.60**	**$38,875.20**

1c. Add a calculated field to the query with the column heading *AnnualRent* that calculates 12 months of rental income. Change the caption to *Annual Rent*.

1d. Run the query and add a *Total* row in the query results datasheet with a Sum function in the *Rent* and *Annual Rent* columns.

1. With **AL2-U1-BenchmarkPropMgt.accdb** open, create a query to calculate the total rental income from each unit as follows:
a. Open the TenantsList query in Design view and use Save Object As to name the query *RentalIncome*.
b. Modify the join properties to show records only when the joined fields are equal in both tables using an inner join.
c. Print the query results datasheet in landscape orientation and then close the query, saving the changes.

AL2-U1-RentalIncome(A6,Step1e).accdb

Tenant and Lease Entry Form

Tenant ID	101	Bldg Code	115	Telephone	519-555-8776
		Unit No	110		

First Name	Wei	Last Name	Chen

All new tenants must have their tenant application approved by the building manager. Submit a copy of their credit score report with their application.

Rent	$1,034.80
Annual Rent	$12,417.60

Start Date	End Date	Security Deposit
01/01/2015	12/31/2015	$995.00

Tenant ID	102	Bldg Code	115	Telephone	519-555-2286
		Unit No	215		

First Name	Mona	Last Name	Ayoub

All new tenants must have their tenant application approved by the building manager. Submit a copy of their credit score report with their application.

Rent	$1,034.80
Annual Rent	$12,417.60

Start Date	End Date	Security Deposit
02/01/2015	01/31/2016	$995.00

Tenant ID	103	Bldg Code	115	Telephone	519-555-7668
		Unit No	320		

First Name	Helena	Last Name	Reiser

AL2-U1-TenantsAndLeases(A7,Step3).accdb

Buildings and Managers

1. Include an appropriate clip art image in the form.

Bldg Code	115
Name	Coventry Park
Address	33 Westview Road
Units	38
Appliances	Microwave, Refrigerator, Stove
Notes	New roof in 2014

SiteManager	
Last Name	Jenkins
First Name	Blair
Telephone	800-555-3485
Cell Phone	800-555-3748
Hire Date	02/08/2010

Student Name

1. Add your name in the *Form Footer* section.

1. With **AL2-U1-BenchmarkPropMgt.accdb** open, design and create a form to enter data into the Buildings table as a main form with the SiteManagers table in a subform. Name the main form *BldgsAndMgrs*. You determine the form design, layout, and formatting options. Print the first record in the Buildings table displayed in Form view.

AL2-U1-BldgsAndMgrs(A7,Step1).accdb

Rent $1,170.00   *All new tenants must have their tenant application*
approved by the building manager. Submit a copy of their
Annual Rent $14,040.00   *credit score report with their application.*

Start Date	End Date	Security Deposit
02/01/2015	01/31/2016	$1,125.00

Student Name

2. Design and create a form to enter data into the Tenants table as a main form with the Leases table in a subform, similar to the one shown in Figure U1.2. Name the form *TenantsAndLeases*. Modify the tab order to move in this order: *Tenant ID, Bldg Code, Unit No, Telephone, First Name, Last Name,* and *Rent.* Remove the tab stop from *Annual Rent,* as it is a calculated control. Use your best judgment to match the color formatting with the theme colors. Add labels and graphics as shown. (Note that the subform does not show a Record Navigation bar. Refer to Case Study Part 3, on page 157 in Chapter 4, if you need help turning off the bar.)

3. Print all of the records using the TenantsAndLeases form and then close the form, saving the changes.

AL2-U1-TenantsAndLeases(A7,Step3).accdb

Access Level 2, Chapter 5 Model Answers

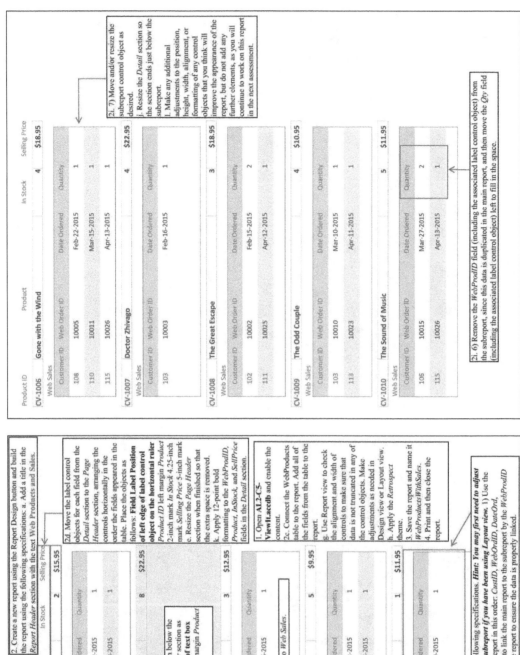

AL2-C5-WebProductsWithSales(A1).accdb (2 of 6)

AL2-C5-WebProductsWithSales(A1).accdb (1 of 6)

AL2-C5-WebProductsWithSales(A1).accdb (3 of 6)

Product ID	Product	In Stock	Selling Price
CV-1011	A Christmas Carol	4	$10.95

Web Sales

Product ID	Product	In Stock	Selling Price
CV-1012	The Bridge on the River Kwai	2	$9.95

Web Sales

Customer ID	Web Order ID	Date Ordered	Quantity
110	10011	Mar-15-2015	1

Product ID	Product	In Stock	Selling Price
CV-1013	Cool Hand Luke	5	$11.95

Web Sales

Customer ID	Web Order ID	Date Ordered	Quantity
103	10003	Feb-16-2015	1

Product ID	Product	In Stock	Selling Price
CV-1014	Patton	3	$11.95

Web Sales

Customer ID	Web Order ID	Date Ordered	Quantity
104	10009	Mar-08-2015	1
115	10026	Apr-13-2015	1

Product ID	Product	In Stock	Selling Price
CV-1015	Blue Hawaii	1	$10.95

Web Sales

Customer ID	Web Order ID	Date Ordered	Quantity
101	10001	Feb-15-2015	1

AL2-C5-WebProductsWithSales(A1).accdb (4 of 6)

Product ID	Product	In Stock	Selling Price
CV-1016	Psycho	2	$11.95

Web Sales

Customer ID	Web Order ID	Date Ordered	Quantity
108	10016	Mar-30-2015	1
119	10024	Apr-12-2015	1

Product ID	Product	In Stock	Selling Price
CV-1017	The Longest Day	5	$12.95

Web Sales

Customer ID	Web Order ID	Date Ordered	Quantity
103	10003	Feb-16-2015	2
102	10008	Mar-04-2015	2
101	10014	Mar-25-2015	1

Product ID	Product	In Stock	Selling Price
CV-1018	To Kill a Mockingbird	2	$11.95

Web Sales

Customer ID	Web Order ID	Date Ordered	Quantity
101	10001	Feb-15-2015	1
118	10020	Apr-05-2015	1

Product ID	Product	In Stock	Selling Price
CV-1019	One Flew Over the Cuckoo's Nest	3	$13.95

Web Sales

Customer ID	Web Order ID	Date Ordered	Quantity
108	10012	Mar-16-2015	1

Product ID	Product	In Stock	Selling Price
CV-1020	Bonnie and Clyde	5	$12.95

Web Sales

Product ID	Product	In Stock	Selling Price
CV-1021	The Maltese Falcon	2	$9.95

Web Sales

Customer ID	Web Order ID	Date Ordered	Quantity
106	10007	Feb-26-2015	1

Product ID	Product	In Stock	Selling Price
CV-1022	The Wizard of Oz	3	$11.95

Web Sales

Customer ID	Web Order ID	Date Ordered	Quantity
110	10006	Feb-23-2015	1

Product ID	Product	In Stock	Selling Price
CV-1023	Rear Window	2	$9.95

Web Sales

Customer ID	Web Order ID	Date Ordered	Quantity
117	10022	Apr-10-2015	1

Product ID	Product	In Stock	Selling Price
CV-1024	Citizen Kane	4	$10.95

Web Sales

Product ID	Product	In Stock	Selling Price
CV-1025	Ben Hur	3	$11.95

Web Sales

Customer ID	Web Order ID	Date Ordered	Quantity
108	10005	Feb-22-2015	1

Product ID	Product	In Stock	Selling Price
CV-1026	Hell's Angels	2	$14.95

Web Sales

Customer ID	Web Order ID	Date Ordered	Quantity
120	10017	Apr-01-2015	1

CV-1027	Going My Way	1	$11.95

Web Sales

Customer ID	Web Order ID	Date Ordered	Quantity
114	10018	Apr-03-2015	1

CV-1028	Band of Angels	2	$10.95

Web Sales

Customer ID	Web Order ID	Date Ordered	Quantity
116	10019	Apr-05-2015	1

CV-1029	The Bells of St. Mary's	2	$11.95

Web Sales

Customer ID	Web Order ID	Date Ordered	Quantity
120	10017	Apr-01-2015	1

CV-1030	Stormy Weather	2	$12.95

Web Sales

Customer ID	Web Order ID	Date Ordered	Quantity
106	10007	Feb-26-2015	1

2b. Add your name in a label control object in the center of the *Report Footer* section. ──→ Student Name

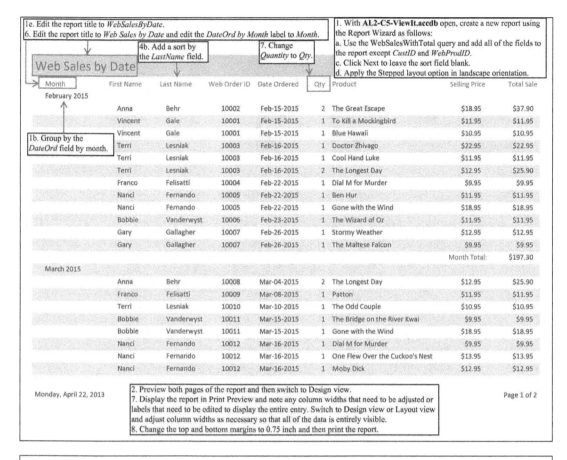

1e. Edit the report title to *WebSalesByDate*.
6. Edit the report title to *Web Sales by Date* and edit the *DateOrd by Month* label to *Month*.

4b. Add a sort by the *LastName* field.

7. Change *Quantity* to *Qty*.

1. With **AL2-C5-ViewIt.accdb** open, create a new report using the Report Wizard as follows:
a. Use the WebSalesWithTotal query and add all of the fields to the report except *CustID* and *WebProdID*.
c. Click Next to leave the sort field blank.
d. Apply the Stepped layout option in landscape orientation.

Web Sales by Date

1b. Group by the *DateOrd* field by month.

Month	First Name	Last Name	Web Order ID	Date Ordered	Qty	Product	Selling Price	Total Sale
February 2015								
	Anna	Behr	10002	Feb-15-2015	2	The Great Escape	$18.95	$37.90
	Vincent	Gale	10001	Feb-15-2015	1	To Kill a Mockingbird	$11.95	$11.95
	Vincent	Gale	10001	Feb-15-2015	1	Blue Hawaii	$10.95	$10.95
	Terri	Lesniak	10003	Feb-16-2015	1	Doctor Zhivago	$22.95	$22.95
	Terri	Lesniak	10003	Feb-16-2015	1	Cool Hand Luke	$11.95	$11.95
	Terri	Lesniak	10003	Feb-16-2015	2	The Longest Day	$12.95	$25.90
	Franco	Felisatti	10004	Feb-22-2015	1	Dial M for Murder	$9.95	$9.95
	Nanci	Fernando	10005	Feb-22-2015	1	Ben Hur	$11.95	$11.95
	Nanci	Fernando	10005	Feb-22-2015	1	Gone with the Wind	$18.95	$18.95
	Bobbie	Vanderwyst	10006	Feb-23-2015	1	The Wizard of Oz	$11.95	$11.95
	Gary	Gallagher	10007	Feb-26-2015	1	Stormy Weather	$12.95	$12.95
	Gary	Gallagher	10007	Feb-26-2015	1	The Maltese Falcon	$9.95	$9.95
							Month Total:	$197.30
March 2015								
	Anna	Behr	10008	Mar-04-2015	2	The Longest Day	$12.95	$25.90
	Franco	Felisatti	10009	Mar-08-2015	1	Patton	$11.95	$11.95
	Terri	Lesniak	10010	Mar-10-2015	1	The Odd Couple	$10.95	$10.95
	Bobbie	Vanderwyst	10011	Mar-15-2015	1	The Bridge on the River Kwai	$9.95	$9.95
	Bobbie	Vanderwyst	10011	Mar-15-2015	1	Gone with the Wind	$18.95	$18.95
	Nanci	Fernando	10012	Mar-16-2015	1	Dial M for Murder	$9.95	$9.95
	Nanci	Fernando	10012	Mar-16-2015	1	One Flew Over the Cuckoo's Nest	$13.95	$13.95
	Nanci	Fernando	10012	Mar-16-2015	1	Moby Dick	$12.95	$12.95

Monday, April 22, 2013

2. Preview both pages of the report and then switch to Design view.
7. Display the report in Print Preview and note any column widths that need to be adjusted or labels that need to be edited to display the entire entry. Switch to Design view or Layout view and adjust column widths as necessary so that all of the data is entirely visible.
8. Change the top and bottom margins to 0.75 inch and then print the report.

Page 1 of 2

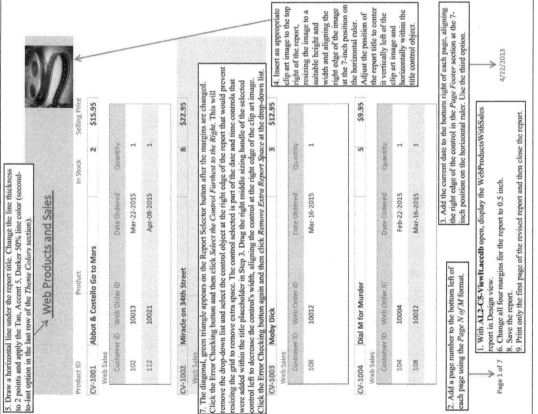

5. Draw a horizontal line under the report title. Change the line thickness to 2 points and apply the Tan, Accent 5, Darker 50% line color (second-to-last option in the last row of the *Theme Colors* section).

Web Products and Sales

Product ID	Product		In Stock	Selling Price

| CV-1001 | Abbot & Costello Go to Mars | | 2 | $15.95 |
| Web Sales | | | | |

Customer ID	Web Order ID	Date Ordered	Quantity
102	10013	Mar-22-2015	1
112	10021	Apr-08-2015	1

| CV-1002 | Miracle on 34th Street | | 8 | $22.95 |
| Web Sales | | | | |

| CV-1003 | Moby Dick | | 3 | $12.95 |
| Web Sales | | | | |

Customer ID	Web Order ID	Date Ordered	Quantity
108	10012	Mar-16-2015	1

| CV-1004 | Dial M for Murder | | 5 | $9.95 |
| Web Sales | | | | |

Customer ID	Web Order ID	Date Ordered	Quantity
104	10004	Feb-22-2015	1
108	10012	Mar-16-2015	1

4. Insert an appropriate clip art image to the top right of the report, resizing the image to a suitable height and width and aligning the right edge of the image at the 7-inch position on the horizontal ruler. Adjust the position of the report title to center it vertically left of the clip art image and horizontally within the title control object.

3. Add the current date to the bottom right of each page, aligning the right edge of the control in the *Page Footer* section at the 7-inch position on the horizontal ruler. Use the third option.

4/22/2013

7. The diagonal, green triangle appears on the Report Selector button after the margins are changed. Click the Error Checking button and then click *Select the Control Farthest to the Right*. This will remove the drop-down list and select the control object at the right edge of the report that would prevent resizing the grid to remove extra space. The control selected is part of the date and time controls that were added within the title placeholder in Step 3. Drag the right middle sizing handle of the selected control left to decrease the control's width, aligning the control at the right edge of the clip art image. Click the Error Checking button again and then click *Remove Extra Report Space* at the drop-down list.

2. Add a page number to the bottom left of each page using the *Page N of M* format.

1. With **AL2-C5-ViewIt.accdb** open, display the WebProductsWithSales report in Design view.
6. Change all four margins for the report to 0.5 inch.
8. Save the report.
9. Print only the first page of the revised report and then close the report.

Page 1 of 7

Customers with Web Sales Chart

1. With AL2-C5-ViewIt.accdb open, create a new report using the Report Wizard as follows:
a. Use the WebCustomers table and add the customer number, customer name, and home telephone fields to the report.
b. Do not group or sort the report.

1c. Apply the Columnar layout option in portrait orientation.
2. Preview the report.
3. Switch to Design view.
5. Preview the report with the bar chart and then switch to Design view.

1d. Edit the report title to *WebCustomersWithChart.*

4. Insert a chart at the right side of the page next to each customer record using the following information:
a. Use the WebSalesWithTotal query.
b. Add the *DateOrd* and *Total Sale* fields to the chart field list.
c. Select a bar chart style. You determine which bar chart style to use.
d. Accept the default chart layout that Access creates with *DateOrd by month* as the x-axis labels and *SumOfTotal Sale* as the value axis.

e. Accept *CustID* as the linked field for the report and chart. f. Edit the title for the chart to *Web Sales*.
6. Edit the chart as follows:
a. Change the chart type to a clustered column with a 3-D visual effect.
b. Change the color of the columns to dark purple (fifth column from the left, second row from the bottom).
c. Delete the legend.
7. Edit the report title to *Customers with Web Sales Chart.*

9. Make any other formatting changes you think will improve the appearance of the report.
10. Print only the first page of the report.

8. Add your name in a label control object at the bottom left of the report.

Customer ID	101
First Name	Vincent
Last Name	Gale
Home Phone	802-555-1635
Customer ID	102
First Name	Anna
Last Name	Behr
Home Phone	802-555-3486
Customer ID	103
First Name	Terri
Last Name	Lesniak
Home Phone	802-555-4986
Customer ID	104
First Name	Franco
Last Name	Felisatti
Home Phone	802-555-3487
Customer ID	105
First Name	Blaine
Last Name	Yiu
Home Phone	802-555-7544
Customer ID	106
First Name	Gary
Last Name	Gallagher
Home Phone	802-555-2766

Monday, April 22, 2013

AL2-C5-WebCustomersWithChart(A4).accdb

Month	First Name	Last Name	Web Order ID	Date Ordered	Qty	Product	Selling Price	Total Sale
	Anna	Behr	10013	Mar-22-2015	1	Abbot & Costello Go to Mars	$15.95	$15.95
	Vincent	Gale	10014	Mar-25-2015	1	The Longest Day	$12.95	$12.95
	Gary	Gallagher	10015	Mar-27-2015	2	The Sound of Music	$11.95	$23.90
	Nanci	Fernando	10016	Mar-30-2015	1	Breakfast at Tiffany's	$11.95	$11.95
	Nanci	Fernando	10016	Mar-30-2015	1	Psycho	$11.95	$11.95
							Month Total:	$191.25
April 2015								
	Jasmine	Patel	10017	Apr-01-2015	1	The Bells of St. Mary's	$11.95	$11.95
	Jasmine	Patel	10017	Apr-01-2015	1	Hell's Angels	$14.95	$14.95
	Pat	Portowski	10018	Apr-03-2015	1	Going My Way	$11.95	$11.95
	Matthew	Siemens	10019	Apr-05-2015	1	Band of Angels	$10.95	$10.95
	Stephanie	Vuegas	10020	Apr-05-2015	1	To Kill a Mockingbird	$11.95	$11.95
	Susan	O'Leary	10021	Apr-08-2015	1	Abbot & Costello Go to Mars	$15.95	$15.95
	Liam	Flannigan	10022	Apr-10-2015	1	Rear Window	$9.95	$9.95
	Keenan	Smith	10023	Apr-11-2015	1	The Odd Couple	$10.95	$10.95
	Dana	Gorski	10025	Apr-12-2015	1	The Great Escape	$18.95	$18.95
	Paulina	Mykonos	10024	Apr-12-2015	1	Psycho	$11.95	$11.95
	Claude	Dion	10026	Apr-13-2015	1	Gone with the Wind	$18.95	$18.95
	Claude	Dion	10026	Apr-13-2015	1	The Sound of Music	$11.95	$11.95
	Claude	Dion	10026	Apr-13-2015	1	Patton	$11.95	$11.95

3. Add your name in a label control object at the left edge of the *Report Footer* **section.**

Student Name

4. Open the Group, Sort, and Total pane and make the following changes:
a. Add a Sum function to each month's *Total Sale* column. Show a grand total at the end of the report and a subtotal in the group footer.

Month Total:	$172.35
Grand Total:	$560.90

Monday, April 22, 2013

Page 2 of 2

AL2-C5-WebSalesByDate(A3).accdb (2 of 2)

Dog Owners with Dogs

Customer Number	First Name	Last Name	Home Telephone	Emergency Telephone
100	Shawn	Jenkins	(814) 555-8446	(814) 555-7469

Dog's Name	Breed	Color	Bordetella Vaccine?	Rabies Vaccine?	Play with other dogs?	Kennel Category
Abby	Labrador Retriever	Black	✔	✔	✔	V.I.P. Suite
Winnie	Cocker Spaniel	Buff	✔	✔	✔	V.I.P. Suite

Customer Number	First Name	Last Name	Home Telephone	Emergency Telephone
110	Valerie	McTague	(814) 555-3456	(814) 555-1495

Dog's Name	Breed	Color	Bordetella Vaccine?	Rabies Vaccine?	Play with other dogs?	Kennel Category
Chloe	Poodle	White	✔	✔	☐	Deluxe Suite

Customer Number	First Name	Last Name	Home Telephone	Emergency Telephone
115	Glen	Waters	(814) 555-7496	(814) 555-6124

Dog's Name	Breed	Color	Bordetella Vaccine?	Rabies Vaccine?	Play with other dogs?	Kennel Category
Barney	Pug	Black	☐	☐	☐	Indoor/Outdoor Suite

Customer Number	First Name	Last Name	Home Telephone	Emergency Telephone
120	Sofia	Ramos	(814) 555-6523	(814) 555-8769

Dog's Name	Breed	Color	Bordetella Vaccine?	Rabies Vaccine?	Play with other dogs?	Kennel Category
Apollo	Greyhound	Cream	✔	✔	✔	Indoor/Outdoor Suite
Murphy	Bichon Frise	White	✔	✔	☐	Indoor/Outdoor Suite

Monday, April 22, 2013

Page 1 of 4

Customers with Payment Information

12. Insert a title at the top of the report with the text *Customers with Payment Information*.

Customer ID	101
First Name	Vincent
Last Name	Gale
Street Address	350 Manhattan Drive
City	Burlington
State	VT
ZIP Code	05401-4245
Home Phone	802-555-1635

Credit Card Type	Visa
Credit Card Number	0000156387569412
Expiry Month	6
Expiry Year	2017

5. Insert a tab control object at the right of the *Customer ID* field. Make sure you click the mouse when the pink bar displays at the right of *101*.

6. Remove the layout from the tab control column and then lengthen the tab control object to align with the bottom of the *Home Phone* field.

7. Expand the field list for the *WebCustPymnt* table and then add the following fields to the tab control object: *CCType CCNumber CCExpMonth CCExpYear*.

8. Select all of the label control objects in the tab control and widen the objects so that all of the label text is visible.

Customer ID	102
First Name	Anna
Last Name	Behr
Street Address	11 Borestone Lane
City	Burlington
State	VT
ZIP Code	05408-1841
Home Phone	802-555-3486

Credit Card Type	MasterCard
Credit Card Number	0000123785694586
Expiry Month	3
Expiry Year	2016

Customer ID	103
First Name	Terri
Last Name	Lesniak
Street Address	200 Park Street
City	Burlington
State	VT
ZIP Code	05401-5175
Home Phone	802-555-4986

Credit Card Type	American Express
Credit Card Number	000045867938456
Expiry Month	2
Expiry Year	2018

4. Widen the labels column so that *Street Address* does not wrap to a second line in the label column.

1. With **AL2-C5-ViewIt.accdb** open, create a new report using the Blank Report tool.

2. Add the first field named *CustID* from the WebCustomers table and then apply the Stacked layout to the report.

3. Add the remaining fields from the WebCustomers table below the *Customer ID* field. Make sure you release the mouse with the pink bar displayed below *101* for the first *Customer ID*.

9. Save the report and name it *CustomersWithCreditCards*.

10. Delete the second page in the tab control and then change the shape of the selected tab control object to be *Round Single Corner Rectangle*.

11. Change the caption of the page in the tab control to *Credit Card Details*.

13. Print only the first page of the report.

Customer Number	First Name	Last Name	Home Telephone	Emergency Telephone
150	Juan	Torres	(814) 555-6645	(814) 555-6465

Dog's Name	Breed	Color	Bordetella Vaccine?	Rabies Vaccine?	Play with other dogs?	Kennel Category
Taffy	Basset Hound	White and Tan	✔	✔	☐	V.I.P. Suite

Customer Number	First Name	Last Name	Home Telephone	Emergency Telephone
155	Bernard	Jedicke	(814) 555-9334	(814) 555-3734

Dog's Name	Breed	Color	Bordetella Vaccine?	Rabies Vaccine?	Play with other dogs?	Kennel Category
Kosmo	Rottweiler	Black and Ma	✔	✔	☐	Day Care Boarding
Sierra	Golden Retriever	Gold	☐	✔	✔	Day Care Boarding
Emma	Border Terrier	Tan	✔	✔	✔	Day Care Boarding

Customer Number	First Name	Last Name	Home Telephone	Emergency Telephone
160	Natale	Rizzo	(814) 555-1434	(814) 555-4341

Dog's Name	Breed	Color	Bordetella Vaccine?	Rabies Vaccine?	Play with other dogs?	Kennel Category
Dallas	Labrador Retriever	Brown	✔	✔	✔	Indoor/Outdoor Suite

Customer Number	First Name	Last Name	Home Telephone	Emergency Telephone
165	Liam	Doherty	(814) 555-6647	(814) 555-7646

Dog's Name	Breed	Color	Bordetella Vaccine?	Rabies Vaccine?	Play with other dogs?	Kennel Category
Zeus	Poodle	Black	✔	☐	✔	V.I.P. Suite

Customer Number	First Name	Last Name	Home Telephone	Emergency Telephone
170	Lenora	Diaz	(814) 555-3144	(814) 555-4111

Dog's Name	Breed	Color	Bordetella Vaccine?	Rabies Vaccine?	Play with other dogs?	Kennel Category
Zack	Beagle	Black, Tan, an	✔	✔	✔	Indoor/Outdoor Suite

Monday, April 22, 2013

Customer Number	First Name	Last Name	Home Telephone	Emergency Telephone
125	Sean	Gallagher	(814) 555-7385	(814) 555-5837

Dog's Name	Breed	Color	Bordetella Vaccine?	Rabies Vaccine?	Play with other dogs?	Kennel Category
Tank	Pug	Apricot	☐	✔	✔	V.I.P. Suite

Customer Number	First Name	Last Name	Home Telephone	Emergency Telephone
130	Nadia	Costa	(814) 555-6899	(814) 555-9986

Dog's Name	Breed	Color	Bordetella Vaccine?	Rabies Vaccine?	Play with other dogs?	Kennel Category
Bailey	Shih Tzu	White	✔	✔	✔	Deluxe Suite

Customer Number	First Name	Last Name	Home Telephone	Emergency Telephone
135	James	Chung	(814) 555-4776	(814) 555-6774

Dog's Name	Breed	Color	Bordetella Vaccine?	Rabies Vaccine?	Play with other dogs?	Kennel Category
Lassie	Collie	Sable	✔	✔	✔	Deluxe Suite

Customer Number	First Name	Last Name	Home Telephone	Emergency Telephone
140	Michael	Mancini	(814) 555-3166	(814) 555-3616

Dog's Name	Breed	Color	Bordetella Vaccine?	Rabies Vaccine?	Play with other dogs?	Kennel Category
Harley	English Foxhound	Tan and White	✔	☐	✔	Indoor/Outdoor Suite

Customer Number	First Name	Last Name	Home Telephone	Emergency Telephone
145	Dillon	Farrell	(814) 555-1633	(814) 555-3613

Dog's Name	Breed	Color	Bordetella Vaccine?	Rabies Vaccine?	Play with other dogs?	Kennel Category
Chico	Australian Shepherd	Red	✔	✔	✔	Indoor/Outdoor Suite

Monday, April 22, 2013

Benchmark Access 2013 Level 2 Model Answers

Hillsdale Realty
Agents with Sales and Commissions Earned

Agent Last Name	Agent First Name	Date Sold	Street Address	Sale Price	Commission Rate	Commission
Im	Kwan					
		10/12/2015	151 E Culver Street	$325,500.00	3.00%	$9,765.00
		10/17/2015	341 E Detroit Street	$275,800.00	3.85%	$10,618.30
		10/22/2015	659 W Erie Street	$310,114.00	4.00%	$12,404.56
		10/23/2015	10 N 16th Avenue	$245,800.00	3.25%	$7,988.50
			Agent Total:	$1,157,214.00	Agent Total:	$40,776.36
			Percent of Grand Total:	33.9%	Percent of Grand Total:	33.8%
Ludlow	William					
		10/25/2015	1665 E Campbell Avenue	$244,845.00	3.00%	$7,345.35
			Agent Total:	$244,845.00	Agent Total:	$7,345.35
			Percent of Grand Total:	7.2%	Percent of Grand Total:	6.1%
Marshall	Isabelle					
		10/15/2015	334 W Mitchell Drive	$375,800.00	4.00%	$15,032.00
		10/27/2015	1401 N Orlando Circle	$175,455.00	3.00%	$5,263.65
			Agent Total:	$551,255.00	Agent Total:	$20,295.65
			Percent of Grand Total:	16.1%	Percent of Grand Total:	16.8%
Newman	Jaren					
		10/15/2015	202 S Hobson	$202,500.00	3.75%	$7,593.75
			Agent Total:	$202,500.00	Agent Total:	$7,593.75
			Percent of Grand Total:	5.9%	Percent of Grand Total:	6.3%

Saturday, April 25, 2015

Page 1 of 2

Customer Number	First Name	Last Name	Home Telephone	Emergency Telephone
175	Diane	Ye	(814) 555-6798	(814) 555-9862

Dog's Name	Breed	Color	Bordetella Vaccine?	Rabies Vaccine?	Play with other dogs?	Kennel Category
Elvis	Irish Terrier	Red	☑	☑	☑	Indoor/Outdoor Suite

Customer Number	First Name	Last Name	Home Telephone	Emergency Telephone
180	Dina	Lombardi	(814) 555-1479	(814) 555-9527

Dog's Name	Breed	Color	Bordetella Vaccine?	Rabies Vaccine?	Play with other dogs?	Kennel Category
Nika	Maltese	White	☑	☑	☑	Indoor/Outdoor Suite

Customer Number	First Name	Last Name	Home Telephone	Emergency Telephone
185	Lorenzo	Rivera	(814) 555-1287	(814) 555-7433

Dog's Name	Breed	Color	Bordetella Vaccine?	Rabies Vaccine?	Play with other dogs?	Kennel Category
Fifi	Chihuahua	Fawn	☑	☑	☐	V.I.P. Suite
Lucky	Welsh Terrier	Black and Tan	☑	☑	☑	Indoor/Outdoor Suite

Customer Number	First Name	Last Name	Home Telephone	Emergency Telephone
190	Maeve	Murphy	(814) 555-5243	(814) 555-3285

Dog's Name	Breed	Color	Bordetella Vaccine?	Rabies Vaccine?	Play with other dogs?	Kennel Category
King	Boxer	Fawn	☑	☑	☐	V.I.P. Suite

Customer Number	First Name	Last Name	Home Telephone	Emergency Telephone
195	Carlotta	Sanchez	(814) 555-4763	(814) 555-6743

Dog's Name	Breed	Color	Bordetella Vaccine?	Rabies Vaccine?	Play with other dogs?	Kennel Category
Scrappy	Bloodhound	Red and Tan	☐	☐	☑	Deluxe Suite

Student Name

Monday, April 22, 2013

Page 4 of 4

Hillsdale Realty
Listings with Client Preferences

City	Listing Number	Street Address	Listing Date	Agent Last Name	Agent First Name	Preferences
Chandler						
	351245	126 E Buffalo Street	10/7/2015	Singleton	Catherine	MLS listing, Pre-sale inspection
	394528	341 E Detroit Street	10/12/2015	Im	Kwan	MLS listing, Pre-sale inspection
	384512	65 W Boston Street	10/12/2015	Pascual	Maureen	Exclusive listing, Pre-sale inspection, Staging service
	436851	659 W Erie Street	10/15/2015	Im	Kwan	MLS listing
	663258	5333 W Elgin Street	10/19/2015	Newman	Jaren	Exclusive listing, Pre-sale inspection
	681335	995 W Cross Street	10/24/2015	Hutchinson	Lee	MLS listing, Staging service
	693341	800 N Soho Place	10/28/2015	Pascual	Maureen	
Mesa						
	313443	23 W 7th Street	10/1/2015	Rehberg	Robin	Exclusive listing, Staging service
	362548	202 S Hobson	10/8/2015	Newman	Jaren	MLS listing, Staging service
	447856	1221 W Vine Avenue	10/15/2015	Singleton	Catherine	MLS listing, Pre-sale inspection
	496583	37 W Clark Street	10/16/2015	Im	Kwan	MLS listing, Pre-sale inspection, Staging service
	674125	1401 N Orlando Circle	10/21/2015	Marshall	Isabelle	MLS listing, Staging service
	675425	3033 E Hampton Circle	10/22/2015	Pascual	Maureen	Exclusive listing
	681235	1501 N 91st Place	10/23/2015	Hutchinson	Lee	MLS listing, Staging service
	682356	11233 E Stearn Avenue	10/24/2015	Rehberg	Robin	
	683345	11322 E Sonrisa Avenue	10/26/2015	Rehberg	Robin	

Saturday, April 25, 2015 — Page 1 of 2

Agent Last Name	Agent First Name	Date Sold	Street Address	Sale Price	Commission Rate	Commission
Ortega	Cecilia					
		10/14/2015	22 E Holly Avenue	$229,900.00	4.00%	$9,196.00
		10/31/2015	2900 E Cactus Road	$155,750.00	3.25%	$5,061.88
			Agent Total:	$385,650.00	Agent Total:	$14,257.88
			Percent of Grand Total:	11.3%	Percent of Grand Total:	11.8%
Pascual	Maureen					
		10/30/2015	3033 E Hampton Circle	$166,500.00	3.00%	$4,995.00
			Agent Total:	$166,500.00	Agent Total:	$4,995.00
			Percent of Grand Total:	4.9%	Percent of Grand Total:	4.1%
Rehberg	Robin					
		10/13/2015	23 W 7th Street	$189,900.00	3.25%	$6,171.75
		10/31/2015	11233 E Stearn Avenue	$165,750.00	3.25%	$5,386.88
			Agent Total:	$355,650.00	Agent Total:	$11,558.63
			Percent of Grand Total:	10.4%	Percent of Grand Total:	9.6%
Singleton	Catherine					
		10/14/2015	126 E Buffalo Street	$349,900.00	4.00%	$13,996.00
			Agent Total:	$349,900.00	Agent Total:	$13,996.00
			Percent of Grand Total:	10.3%	Percent of Grand Total:	11.6%
Student Name			Grand Total:	$3,413,514.00	Grand Total:	$120,818.61

Saturday, April 25, 2015 — Page 2 of 2

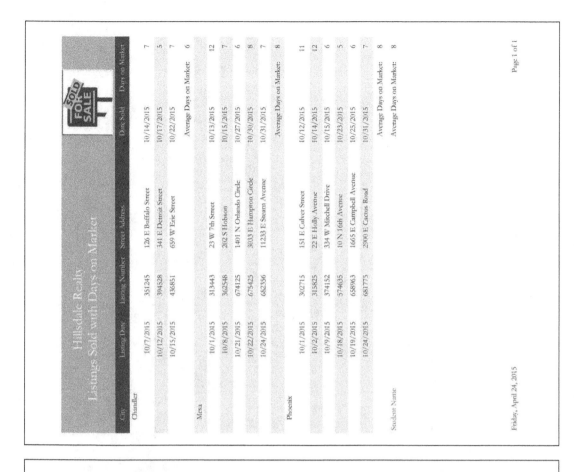

Hillsdale Realty
Listings Sold with Days on Market

City	Listing Date	Listing Number	Street Address	Date Sold	Days on Market
Chandler					
	10/7/2015	351245	126 E Buffalo Street	10/14/2015	7
	10/12/2015	394528	341 E Detroit Street	10/17/2015	5
	10/15/2015	436851	659 W Erie Street	10/22/2015	7
				Average Days on Market:	6
Mesa					
	10/1/2015	313443	23 W 7th Street	10/13/2015	12
	10/8/2015	362548	202 S Hobson	10/15/2015	7
	10/21/2015	674125	1401 N Orlando Circle	10/27/2015	6
	10/22/2015	675425	3033 E Hampton Circle	10/30/2015	8
	10/24/2015	682356	11233 E Steam Avenue	10/31/2015	7
				Average Days on Market:	8
Phoenix					
	10/1/2015	302715	151 E Culver Street	10/12/2015	11
	10/2/2015	315825	22 E Holly Avenue	10/14/2015	12
	10/9/2015	374152	334 W Mitchell Drive	10/15/2015	6
	10/18/2015	574635	10 N 16th Avenue	10/23/2015	5
	10/19/2015	658963	1665 E Campbell Avenue	10/25/2015	6
	10/24/2015	681775	2900 E Cactus Road	10/31/2015	7
				Average Days on Market:	8
				Average Days on Market:	8

Student Name

Friday, April 24, 2015

Page 1 of 1

AL2-C5-CS-P3-DaysOnMktForSales(P3).accdb

City	Listing Number	Street Address	Listing Date	Agent Last Name	Agent First Name	Preferences
Phoenix						
	302715	151 E Culver Street	10/1/2015	Im	Kwan	MLS listing
	315825	22 E Holly Avenue	10/2/2015	Ortega	Cecilia	MLS listing
	374152	334 W Mitchell Drive	10/9/2015	Marshall	Isabelle	MLS listing, Pre-sale inspection, Staging service
	655863	33 E Lincoln Street	10/18/2015	Im	Kwan	MLS listing, Pre-sale inspection, Staging service
	574635	10 N 16th Avenue	10/18/2015	Im	Kwan	MLS listing, Pre-sale inspection, Staging service
	658963	1665 E Campbell Avenue	10/19/2015	Ludlow	William	MLS listing
	677325	3209 W Bajada Drive	10/22/2015	Ludlow	William	MLS listing
	681775	2900 E Cactus Road	10/24/2015	Ortega	Cecilia	MLS listing, Pre-sale inspection
	692341	16654 S 29th Street	10/26/2015	Pascual	Maureen	
	692354	3103 E Coolidge Street	10/30/2015	Ludlow	William	

Student Name

Saturday, April 25, 2015

Page 2 of 2

AL2-C5-CS-P2-Listings(P2).accdb (2 of 2)

Hillsdale Realty
Agents with Sales and Commissions Earned

Agent Last Name	Agent First Name	Date Sold	Street Address	Sale Price	Commission Rate	Commission
Im	Kwan					
			Agent Total:	$1,157,214.00	Agent Total:	$40,776.36
			Percent of Grand Total:	33.9%	Percent of Grand Total:	33.8%
Ludlow	William					
			Agent Total:	$244,845.00	Agent Total:	$7,345.35
			Percent of Grand Total:	7.2%	Percent of Grand Total:	6.1%
Marshall	Isabelle					
			Agent Total:	$551,255.00	Agent Total:	$20,295.65
			Percent of Grand Total:	16.1%	Percent of Grand Total:	16.8%
Newman	Jaren					
			Agent Total:	$202,500.00	Agent Total:	$7,593.75
			Percent of Grand Total:	5.9%	Percent of Grand Total:	6.3%
Ortega	Cecilia					
			Agent Total:	$385,650.00	Agent Total:	$14,257.88
			Percent of Grand Total:	11.3%	Percent of Grand Total:	11.8%
Pascual	Maureen					
			Agent Total:	$166,500.00	Agent Total:	$4,995.00
			Percent of Grand Total:	4.9%	Percent of Grand Total:	4.1%
Rehberg	Robin					
			Agent Total:	$355,650.00	Agent Total:	$11,558.63
			Percent of Grand Total:	10.4%	Percent of Grand Total:	9.6%
Singleton	Catherine					
			Agent Total:	$349,900.00	Agent Total:	$13,996.00
			Percent of Grand Total:	10.3%	Percent of Grand Total:	11.6%
Student Name			Grand Total:	$3,413,514.00	Grand Total:	$120,818.61

Friday, April 24, 2015

Page 1 of 1

Access Level 2, Chapter 6 Model Answers

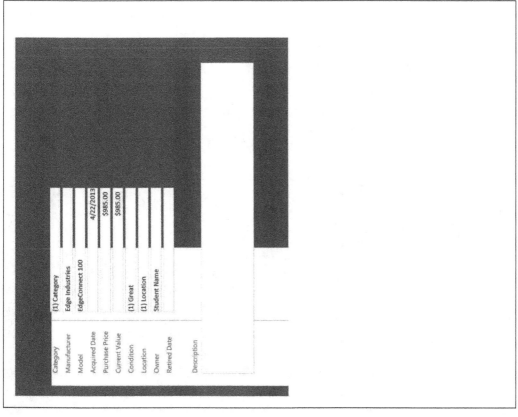

AL2-C6-Asset Details(A1).accdb (2 of 2)

AL2-C6-Asset Details(A1).accdb (1 of 2)

Task Details

WebCustPymnt   4/22/2013

CustID	Lookup to CreditCardTypes	CCNumber	CCExpMonth	CCExpYear	EmailAdd
103	American Express	0000458679938456	2	2018	terri_l@emcp.net
107	American Express	0000343441258622	2	2017	mel_b@emcp.net
114	American Express	0000238856565582	3	2016	pat_p@emcp.net
104	Discover	0000759634857615	5	2018	franco@emcp.net
102	MasterCard	0000123785694586	3	2016	anna@emcp.net
109	MasterCard	0000687944513877	9	2016	grant@emcp.net
110	MasterCard	0000334986651127	10	2016	bobbie@emcp.net
113	MasterCard	0000234518751243	7	2017	keenan@emcp.net
116	MasterCard	0000968632356112	11	2016	siemens@emcp.net
117	MasterCard	0000748412127353	10	2017	liam_f@emcp.net
101	Visa	0000156387569412	6	2017	vince@emcp.net
105	Visa	0000487613358688	3	2016	blaine@emcp.net
106	Visa	0000910087645132	7	2017	garyg@emcp.net
108	Visa	0000344698875691	7	2016	nanci_f@emcp.net
111	Visa	0000458874566852	5	2019	gorski@emcp.net
112	Visa	0000685698569852	2	2017	susan@emcp.net
115	Visa	0000326925232421	5	2016	dion@emcp.net
118	Visa	0000568695683625	6	2019	vuegas@emcp.net
119	Visa	0000135386894685	8	2019	mykonos@emcp.net
120	Visa	0000234363638547	4	2017	jpatel@emcp.net

1. With AL2-C6-Viewit.accdb open, use the Table Analyzer Wizard to analyze the WebCustPymnt table using the following information:
   a. Rename the new table that includes all of the fields except the CCType field as WebCustCreditCards.
   b. Rename the new table that includes the CCType field as CreditCardTypes.
   c. Choose an appropriate field for the primary key in the WebCustCreditCards table.
   d. If the wizard determines that the Discover card is a typographical error, choose (Leave as is) at the Correction drop-down list and then click Next.
   e. Create the query.
2. Close the Help window.
3. Delete the CCType field in the WebCustPymnt query. Adjust all of the column widths to best fit and print the query results datasheet with left and right margins of 0.25 inch.

Page 1

AL2-C6-WebCustPymnt(A3,Step3).accdb

Task Details

Task: Set up backup Web server

Status: Not Started

Priority: (1) High

Start Date: 4/22/2013   **Due Date:** 4/29/2013

% Complete: 0%

Attachments

Description: Configure hot server to be on standby in event of failover. Assigned to Student Name.

1. Open AL2-C6-Viewit.accdb and enable the content.
2. Create a new group of objects related to Tasks using the Tasks Application Part. When the Create Relationship Wizard starts, specify no relationship.
3. Using the TaskDetails form, add a record using the following information. Substitute your name for Student Name in the Description field.
   Task Set up backup Web server
   Status Not Started
   Priority (1) High
   Start Date Enter the current date
   Due Date Enter a due date that is one week from the current date
   Attachments (leave blank)
   % Complete (leave at default value of 0%)
   Description Configure hot server to be on standby in event of failover. Assigned to Student Name.
4. Click the Save and Close button.
5. Open the Tasks table to view the record added to the table using the form in Step 3. Close the table.
6. Print the selected record using the TaskDetails form.

AL2-C6-TaskDetails(A2).accdb

Groomers 4/22/2013

Groomer ID	First Name	Last Name	Street Address	City	State	ZIP Code	Home Telephone	Hourly Rate
01	Max	Lahey	715 Irish Hollow	Smethport	PA	16749-	(814) 555-6253	$28.50
02	Juan	Modesta	117 Spring Drive	Bradford	PA	16701-	(814) 555-3845	$28.50
03	Pat	O'Connor	147 Lamont Drive	Bradford	PA	16701-	(814) 555-2118	$31.50
04	Greg	Walczak	22 Foster Square	Allegheny	PA	15212-	(814) 555-7448	$35.50
05	Melissa	Cochrane	140 Congress Street	Bradford	PA	16701-	(814) 555-6489	$28.50

Page 1

AL2-C6-Groomers(VB1).accdb

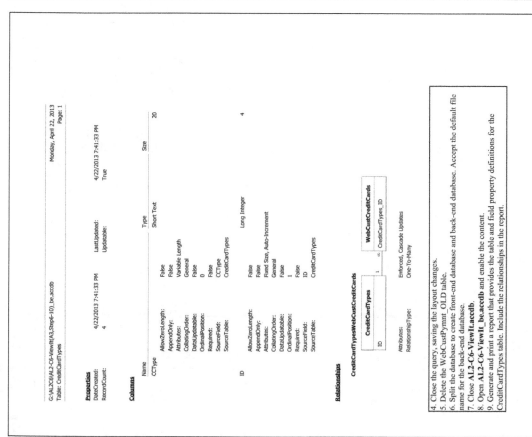

AL2-C6-doc_rptObjects(A3,Step9).accdb

4. Close the query, saving the layout changes.
5. Delete the WebCustPymnt_OLD table.
6. Split the database to create front-end database and back-end database. Accept the default file name for the back-end database.
7. Close **AL2-C6-ViewIt.accdb**.
8. Open **AL2-C6-ViewIt_be.accdb** and enable the content.
9. Generate and print a report that provides the table and field property definitions for the CreditCardTypes table. Include the relationships in the report.

AgentConferences

ID	1
Title	Window and Door Manufacturers Association Annual Conference
Start Time	11/9/2015
End Time	11/11/2015
Location	Georgia International Convention Center
Description	Three-day conference
#CompanyAttendees	5

AL2-C6-AgentConferences(P1).accdb

Groomers

Groomer ID	01
First Name	Max
Last Name	Lahey
Street Address	715 Irish Hollow
City	Smethport
State	PA
ZIP Code	16749-
Home Telephone	(814) 555-6253
Hourly Rate	$28.50

AL2-C6-Groomers(VB2).accdb

Benchmark Access 2013 Level 2 Model Answers

Event Details

Event: Homebuilders Association Trade Show

Start Time	4/14/2015	
End Time	4/16/2015	
Location	Phoenix Convention Center	
Description		
Three-day trade show		

Event: Green Home Design Conference

Start Time	10/26/2015	
End Time	10/29/2015	
Location	University of Phoenix Hohokam Campus	
Description		
Four-day design conference		

AL2-C6-Event Details(P1).accdb

Listings   4/24/2015

ListingNo	StreetAdd	Lookup to City	AgentID	ListDate
313443	23 W 7th Street	Mesa	17	10/1/2015
302715	151 E Culver Street	Phoenix	10	10/1/2015
315825	22 E Holly Avenue	Phoenix	16	10/2/2015
351245	126 E Buffalo Street	Chandler	12	10/7/2015
362548	202 S Hobson	Mesa	14	10/8/2015
374152	334 W Mitchell Drive	Phoenix	19	10/9/2015
384512	65 W Boston Street	Chandler	21	10/12/2015
394528	341 E Detroit Street	Chandler	10	10/12/2015
436851	659 W Erie Street	Chandler	10	10/15/2015
447856	1221 W Vine Avenue	Mesa	12	10/15/2015
496583	37 W Clark Street	Mesa	10	10/16/2015
655863	33 E Lincoln Street	Phoenix	10	10/18/2015
574635	10 N 16th Avenue	Phoenix	10	10/18/2015
663258	5333 W Elgin Street	Chandler	14	10/19/2015
658963	1665 E Campbell Avenue	Phoenix	11	10/19/2015
674125	1401 N Orlando Circle	Mesa	19	10/21/2015
675425	3033 E Hampton Circle	Mesa	21	10/22/2015
677325	3209 W Bajada Drive	Phoenix	11	10/22/2015
681235	1501 N 91st Place	Mesa	15	10/23/2015
681335	995 W Cross Street	Chandler	15	10/24/2015
681775	2900 E Cactus Road	Phoenix	16	10/24/2015
682356	11233 E Stearn Avenue	Mesa	17	10/24/2015
683345	11322 E Sonrisa Avenue	Mesa	17	10/26/2015
692341	16654 S 29th Street	Phoenix	21	10/26/2015
693341	800 N Soho Place	Chandler	21	10/28/2015
692354	3103 E Coolidge Street	Phoenix	11	10/30/2015

Page 1

AL2-C6-Listings(P2).accdb

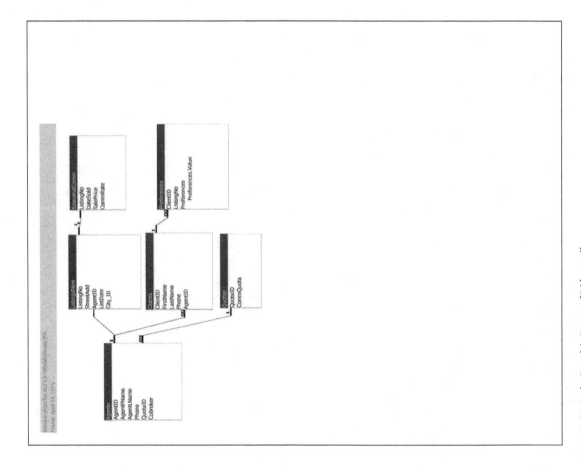

Relationships for AL2-C6-BuddsRealty(P3)
Friday, April 24, 2015

AL2-C6-RelationshipReport(P3).accdb

Access Level 2, Chapter 7 Model Answers

4. Print the FORMCustOrd macro and RPTWebSales macro by completing a step similar to Step 3.

G:\AL2C7\AL2-C7-ViewIt(A1).accdb
Macro: FORMCustOrd

Monday, April 22, 2013
Page: 1

Actions

Name	Condition	Action	Argument	Value
		OpenForm	Form Name:	WebCustOrders
			View:	Form
			Filter Name:	
			Where Condition:	
			Data Mode:	-1
			Window Mode:	Normal
		GoToControl	Control Name:	LastName
		RunCommand	Command:	30

XML: <?xml version="1.0" encoding="UTF-16" standalone="no"?>
<UserInterfaceMacro MinimumClientDesignVersion="14.0.0000.0000" xmlns="http://schemas.microsoft.com/office/accessservices/2009/11/application"><Statements><Action Name="OpenForm"><Argument Name="FormName">WebCustOrders</Argument></Action><Action Name="GoToControl"><Argument Name="ControlName">LastName</Argument></Action><Action Name="RunMenuCommand"><Argument Name="Command">Find</Argument></Action></Statements></UserInterfaceMacro>

AL2-C7-doc_rptObjects_FORMCustOrd(A1,Step4).accdb

G:\AL2C7\AL2-C7-ViewIt(A1).accdb
Macro: RptWebOrders

Monday, April 22, 2013
Page: 1

Actions

Name	Condition	Action	Argument	Value
		OpenReport	Report Name:	WebOrdersByProd
			View:	Print Preview
			Filter Name:	
			Where Condition:	
			Window Mode:	Normal

XML: <?xml version="1.0" encoding="UTF-16" standalone="no"?>
<UserInterfaceMacro MinimumClientDesignVersion="14.0.0000.0000" xmlns="http://schemas.microsoft.com/office/accessservices/2009/11/application"><Statements><Action Name="OpenReport"><Argument Name="ReportName">WebOrdersByProd</Argument><Argument Name="View">Print Preview</Argument></Action></Statements></UserInterfaceMacro>

1. Open **AL2-C7-ViewIt.accdb** and enable the content.
2. Create the following macros. Run each macro to make sure it works properly and then close it.
a. Create a macro named RPTWebOrders that opens the report named WebOrdersByProd --use the macro action *OpenReport*. In the *Action Arguments* section, change *Report* in the View Option argument option box to *Print Preview*.
b. Create a macro named RPTWebSales to open the WebSalesByDate report in Report view.
c. Create a macro named FORMCustOrd that opens the WebCustOrders form in Form view, activates the control named *LastName*, and then opens the Find dialog box. Test the macro using the customer last name *Gallagher*.
3. Open the RPTWebOrders macro in Design view. Click the File tab, click the *Print* option, and then click *Print* at the Print backstage area. At the Print Macro Definition dialog box, remove check marks as necessary until only the *Actions and Arguments* check box is checked and then click OK. Close the Macro Builder window.

AL2-C7-doc_rptObjects(A1,Step3).accdb

1. With **AL2-C7-ViewIt.accdb** open, edit the FORMCustOrd macro to remove the *OpenForm* action. Save and close the revised macro. Rename the FORMCustOrd macro in the Navigation pane as *FINDLastName*.

2. Create command buttons to run macros as follows:
a. Open the WebCustOrders form in Design view and then create a command button at the right side of the title in the *Form Header* section that runs the FINDLastName macro. You determine the appropriate text to display on the face of the button and a name for the command button. Format the button using the *Light 1 Outline, Colored Fill-Green, Accent 6* quick style. Save and close the form.

2b. Open the WebProducts form in Design view and create two command buttons as follows:
• A button at the left side of the form that runs the RPTWebOrders macro •
A button at the right side of the form that runs the RPTWebSales macro Place each button at the bottom of the *Detail* section. You determine the appropriate text to display on the face of each button as well as a name for each button. Format each button with the quick style used in Step 2a. Save and then close the form.
3. Open each form, test the button(s) to make sure the correct form or report displays, and then close each form or report.

4. Open the WebCustOrders form in Form view. Insert a screen shot of the database window showing the custom button in a new Microsoft Word document using either the Screenshot button in the Illustrations group on the INSERT tab or the Print Screen key and the Paste feature. Next, switch back to Access and open the WebProducts form in Form view. Insert a screenshot of the database window below the first image in the Microsoft Word document. Save the Microsoft Word document and name it **AL2-C7-A2-FormWindows**. Print **AL2-C7-A2-FormWindows.docx** and then exit Word.

Student Name

4. Type your name a few lines below the screen images and add any other identifying information as instructed.

AL2-C7-A2-FormWindows(A2).accdb

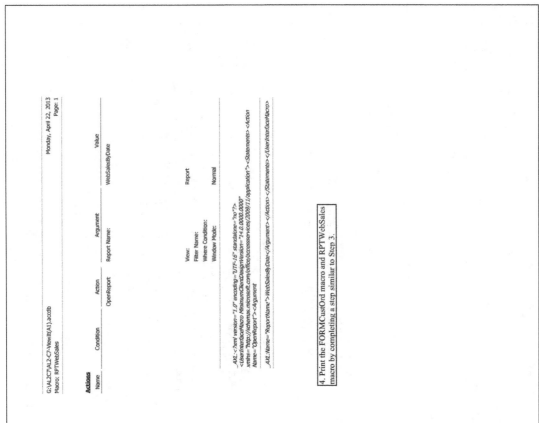

G:\AL2C7\AL2-C7-ViewIt(A1).accdb   Monday, April 22, 2013
Macro: RPTWebSales   Page: 1

Actions

Name	Condition	Action	Argument	Value
		OpenReport	Report Name:	WebSalesByDate
			View:	Report
			Filter Name:	
			Where Condition:	
			Window Mode:	Normal

Axl: <?xml version="1.0" encoding="UTF-16" standalone="no"?>
<UserInterfaceMacro MinimumClientDesignVersion="14.0.0000.0000"
xmlns="http://schemas.microsoft.com/office/accessservices/2009/11/application"><Statements><Action
Name="OpenReport"><Argument
Axl:Name="ReportName">WebSalesByDate</Argument></Action></Statements></UserInterfaceMacro>

4. Print the FORMCustOrd macro and RPTWebSales macro by completing a step similar to Step 3.

AL2-C7-doc_rptObjects_RPTWebSales(A1,Step4).accdb

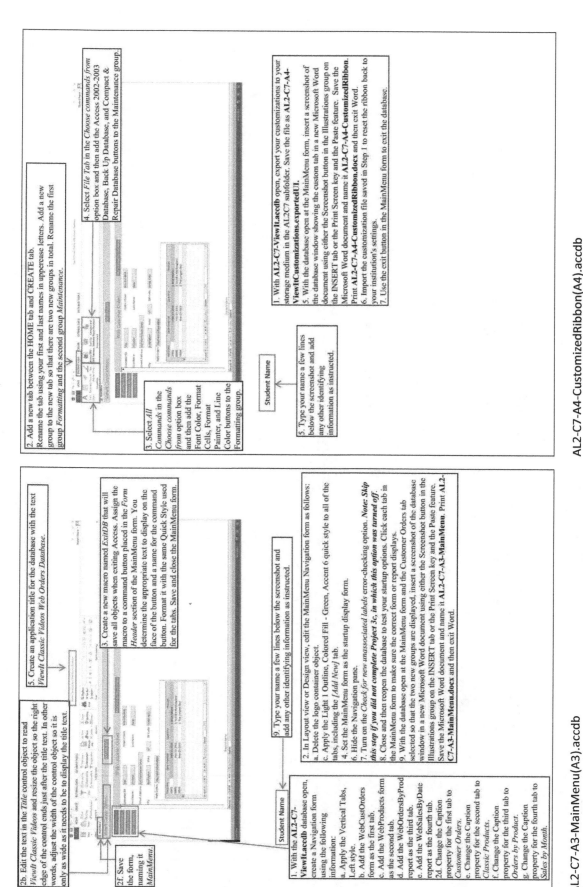

AL2-C7-A4-CustomizedRibbon(A4).accdb

2. Add a new tab between the HOME tab and CREATE tab. Rename the tab using your first and last names in uppercase letters. Add a new group to the new tab so that there are two new groups in total. Rename the first group *Formatting* and the second group *Maintenance*.

4. Select *File Tab* in the *Choose commands from* option box and then add the Access 2002-2003 Database, Back Up Database, and Compact & Repair Database buttons to the Maintenance group.

3. Select *All Commands* in the *Choose commands from* option box and then add the Font Color, Format Cells, Format Painter, and Line Color buttons to the Formatting group.

Student Name

5. Type your name a few lines below the screenshot and add any other identifying information as instructed.

1. With AL2-C7-ViewIt.accdb open, export your customizations to your storage medium in the AL2C7 subfolder. Save the file as AL2-C7-A4-ViewItCustomizations.exportedUI.

5. With the database open at the MainMenu form, insert a screenshot of the database window showing the custom tab in a new Microsoft Word document using either the Screenshot button in the Illustrations group on the INSERT tab or the Print Screen key and the Paste feature. Save the Microsoft Word document and name it AL2-C7-A4-CustomizedRibbon.docx and then exit Word. Print AL2-C7-A4-CustomizedRibbon.

6. Import the customization file saved in Step 1 to reset the ribbon back to your institution's settings.

7. Use the exit button in the MainMenu form to exit the database.

AL2-C7-A3-MainMenu(A3).accdb

2b. Edit the text in the *Title* control object to read *ViewIt Classic Videos* and resize the object so the right edge of the control ends just after the title text. In other words, adjust the width of the control object so it is only as wide as it needs to be to display the title text.

5. Create an application title for the database with the text *ViewIt Classic Videos Web Orders Database*.

3. Create a new macro named *ExitDB* that will save all objects when exiting Access. Assign the macro to a command button placed in the *Form Header* section of the MainMenu form. You determine the appropriate text to display on the face of the button and a name for the command button. Format it with the same Quick Style used for the tabs. Save and close the MainMenu form.

2f. Save the form, naming it *MainMenu*.

9. Type your name a few lines below the screenshot and add any other identifying information as instructed.

Student Name

1. With the AL2-C7-ViewIt.accdb database open, create a Navigation form using the following information:
a. Apply the Vertical Tabs, Left style.
b. Add the WebCustOrders form as the first tab.
c. Add the WebProducts form as the second tab.
d. Add the WebOrdersByProd report as the third tab.
e. Add the WebSalesByDate report as the fourth tab.
2d. Change the Caption property for the first tab to *Customer Orders*.
e. Change the Caption property for the second tab to *Classic Products*.
f. Change the Caption property for the third tab to *Orders by Product*.
g. Change the Caption property for the fourth tab to *Sales by Month*.

2. In Layout view or Design view, edit the MainMenu Navigation form as follows:
a. Delete the logo container object.
c. Apply the Light 1 Outline, Colored Fill - Green, Accent 6 quick style to all of the tabs, including the [Add New] tab.
4. Set the MainMenu form as the startup display form.
6. Hide the Navigation pane.
7. Turn on the *Check for new unassociated labels* error-checking option. *Note: Skip this step if you did not complete Project 3c, in which this option was turned off.*
8. Close and then reopen the database to test your startup options. Click each tab in the MainMenu form to make sure the correct form or report displays.
9. With the database open at the MainMenu form and the Customer Orders tab selected so that the two new groups are displayed, insert a screenshot of the database window in a new Microsoft Word document using either the Screenshot button in the Illustrations group on the INSERT tab or the Print Screen key and the Paste feature. Save the Microsoft Word document and name it AL2-C7-A3-MainMenu. Print AL2-C7-A3-MainMenu.docx and then exit Word.

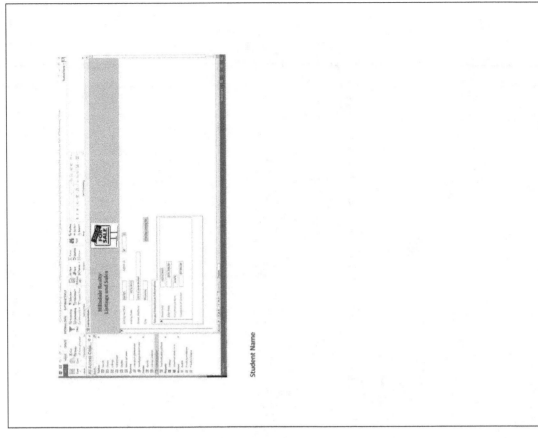

Student Name

AL2-C7-ListingsAndSalesForm(P1).accdb

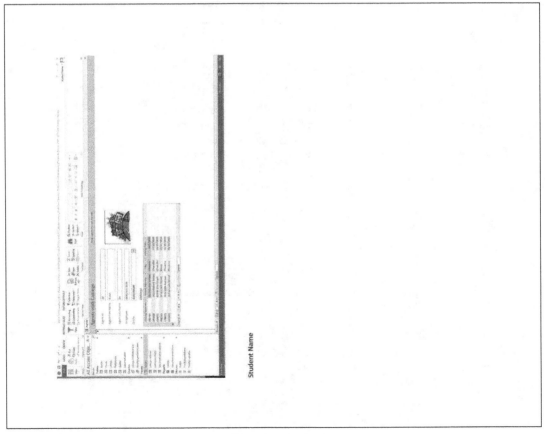

Student Name

AL2-C7-AgentsForm(P1).accdb

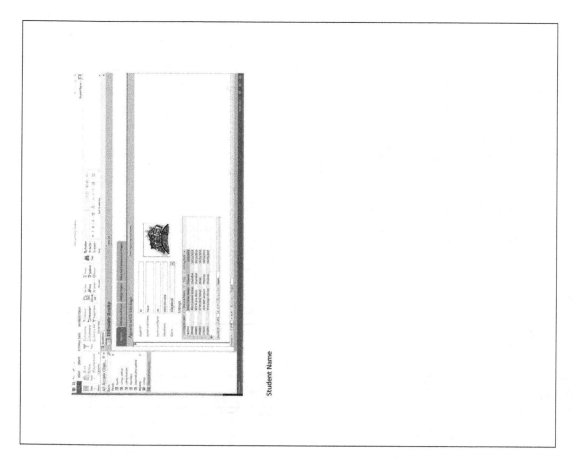

Student Name

AL2-C7-MainMenuForm(P2).accdb

Access Level 2, Chapter 8 Model Answers

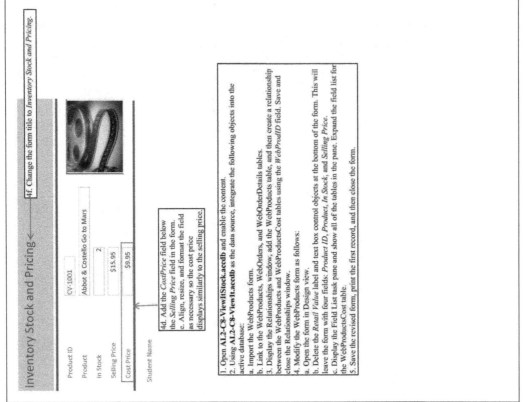

Inventory Stock and Pricing

4f. Change the form title to *Inventory Stock and Pricing*.

Product ID: CV-1001
Product: Abbot & Costello Go to Mars
In Stock: 2
Selling Price: $15.95
Cost Price: $9.95
Student Name

4d. Add the *CostPrice* field below the *Selling Price* field in the form.
e. Align, resize, and format the field as necessary so the cost price displays similarly to the selling price.

1. Open **AL2-C8-ViewItStock.accdb** and enable the content.
2. Using **AL2-C8-ViewIt.accdb** as the data source, integrate the following objects into the active database:
a. Import the WebProducts form.
b. Link to the WebProducts, WebOrders, and WebOrderDetails tables.
3. Display the Relationships window, add the WebProducts table, and then create a relationship between the WebProducts and WebProductsCost tables using the *WebProdID* field. Save and close the Relationships window.
4. Modify the WebProducts form as follows:
a. Open the form in Design view.
b. Delete the *Retail Value* label and text box control objects at the bottom of the form. This will leave the form with four fields: *Product ID, Product, In Stock,* and *Selling Price*.
c. Display the Field List task pane and show all of the tables in the pane. Expand the field list for the WebProductsCost table.
5. Save the revised form, print the first record, and then close the form.

AL2-C8-WebProducts(A1,Step5).accdb

WebProdCostsWithSupp

6c. Add a calculated column at the right of the *CostPrice* column named *GrossProfit* that subtracts the cost price from the selling price. Change the caption to *Gross Profit*.

Product ID	Company Name	Product	Selling Price	Cost Price	Gross Profit
CV-1024	Classic Videos Inc.	Citizen Kane	$10.95	$5.75	$5.20
CV-1013	Classic Videos Inc.	Cool Hand Luke	$11.95	$6.45	$5.50
CV-1006	Classic Videos Inc.	Gone with the Wind	$18.95	$12.50	$6.45
CV-1014	Classic Videos Inc.	Patton	$11.95	$7.75	$4.20
CV-1029	Classic Videos Inc.	The Bells of St. Mary's	$11.95	$6.25	$5.70
CV-1021	Classic Videos Inc.	The Maltese Falcon	$9.95	$5.25	$4.70
CV-1011	Hillman Enterprises	A Christmas Carol	$10.95	$6.25	$4.70
CV-1005	Hillman Enterprises	Breakfast at Tiffany's	$11.95	$6.95	$5.00
CV-1004	Hillman Enterprises	Dial M for Murder	$9.95	$7.95	$2.00
CV-1026	Hillman Enterprises	Hell's Angels	$14.95	$5.95	$9.00
CV-1003	Hillman Enterprises	Moby Dick	$12.95	$8.95	$4.00
CV-1019	Hillman Enterprises	One Flew Over the Cuckoo's Nest	$13.95	$7.25	$6.70
CV-1030	Hillman Enterprises	Stormy Weather	$12.95	$5.25	$7.70
CV-1012	Hillman Enterprises	The Bridge on the River Kwai	$9.95	$5.50	$4.45
CV-1008	Hillman Enterprises	The Great Escape	$18.95	$9.50	$9.45
CV-1001	KML Enterprises	Abbott & Costello Go to Mars	$15.95	$9.95	$6.00
CV-1025	KML Enterprises	Ben Hur	$11.95	$6.25	$5.70
CV-1020	KML Enterprises	Bonnie and Clyde	$12.95	$5.85	$7.10
CV-1009	KML Enterprises	The Odd Couple	$10.95	$5.95	$5.00
CV-1018	KML Enterprises	To Kill a Mockingbird	$11.95	$8.45	$3.50
CV-1015	Nostalgia Productions	Blue Hawaii	$10.95	$4.95	$6.00
CV-1007	Nostalgia Productions	Doctor Zhivago	$22.95	$8.50	$14.45
CV-1027	Nostalgia Productions	Going My Way	$11.95	$4.65	$7.30
CV-1022	Nostalgia Productions	The Wizard of Oz	$11.95	$6.50	$5.45
CV-1028	Old Tyme Distributing	Band of Angels	$10.95	$6.15	$4.80
CV-1002	Old Tyme Distributing	Miracle on 34th Street	$22.95	$9.95	$13.00
CV-1016	Old Tyme Distributing	Psycho	$11.95	$8.45	$3.50
CV-1023	Old Tyme Distributing	Rear Window	$9.95	$4.85	$5.10
CV-1017	Old Tyme Distributing	The Longest Day	$12.95	$6.75	$6.20
CV-1010	Old Tyme Distributing	The Sound of Music	$11.95	$8.25	$3.70

6. Open the WebProdCostsWithSupp query in Design view and modify it as follows:
a. Add the WebProducts table to the query.
7. Save the revised query and then run the query.
8. Print the query in landscape orientation and then close the query.

Page 1

6b. Add the *SellPrice* field to the query design grid, placing the field between the *Product* and *CostPrice* columns.

AL2-C8-WebProdCostsWithSupp(A1).accdb

WebProductsCost

Product ID	Product	Cost Price	Supplier ID
CV-1001	Abbott & Costello Go to Mars	$9.95	502
CV-1002	Miracle on 34th Street	$9.95	503
CV-1003	Moby Dick	$8.95	505
CV-1004	Dial M for Murder	$7.95	505
CV-1005	Breakfast at Tiffany's	$6.95	505
CV-1006	Gone with the Wind	$12.50	501
CV-1007	Doctor Zhivago	$8.50	504
CV-1008	The Great Escape	$9.50	505
CV-1009	The Odd Couple	$5.95	502
CV-1010	The Sound of Music	$8.25	503
CV-1011	A Christmas Carol	$6.25	505
CV-1012	The Bridge on the River Kwai	$5.50	505
CV-1013	Cool Hand Luke	$6.45	501
CV-1014	Patton	$7.75	504
CV-1015	Blue Hawaii	$4.95	503
CV-1016	Psycho	$8.45	505
CV-1017	The Longest Day	$6.75	503
CV-1018	To Kill a Mockingbird	$8.45	502
CV-1019	One Flew Over the Cuckoo's Nest	$7.25	505
CV-1020	Bonnie and Clyde	$5.85	502
CV-1021	The Maltese Falcon	$5.25	501
CV-1022	The Wizard of Oz	$6.50	504
CV-1023	Rear Window	$4.85	503
CV-1024	Citizen Kane	$5.75	501
CV-1025	Ben Hur	$6.25	502
CV-1026	Hell's Angels	$5.95	505
CV-1027	Going My Way	$4.65	504
CV-1028	Band of Angels	$6.15	503
CV-1029	The Bells of St. Mary's	$6.25	501
CV-1030	Stormy Weather	$5.25	505
CV-1031	Reds	$9.95	501
CV-1032	Cape Fear	$6.95	502
CV-1033	Casablanca	$8.95	503
CV-1034	A Streetcar Named Desire	$7.50	501
CV-1035	To Sir with Love	$8.25	504
CV-1036	West Side Story	$10.95	505
CV-1037	The Shining	$10.25	501
CV-1038	Zorba the Greek	$5.75	502
CV-1039	The French Connection	$10.25	504
CV-1040	The Outsider	$9.15	503
CV-1041	True Grit	$8.75	504

1. With **AL2-C8-ViewItStock.accdb** open, make a backup copy and then append records from a text file using the following information:
- Name the backup database file **AL2-C8-ViewItStock_yyyy-mm-dd.accdb**, where *yyyy-mm-dd* represents today's date. Save this database in your DatabaseBackUps folder, created in Project 1a.
- The data source file is named **WebProducts.csv**.
- Append a copy of the records to the end of the existing WebProductsCost table.
- Save the import steps using the following description: Import of new classic video titles from WebProducts.csv.

2. Open the WebProductsCost table and print the table datasheet.

Page 1

AL2-C8-WebProductsCost(A2,Step2).accdb

WebProdCostsWithSupp

Product ID	Company Name	Product	Selling Price	Cost Price	Gross Profit
CV-1024	Classic Videos Inc.	Citizen Kane	$10.95	$5.75	$5.20
CV-1013	Classic Videos Inc.	Cool Hand Luke	$11.95	$6.45	$5.50
CV-1006	Classic Videos Inc.	Gone with the Wind	$18.95	$12.50	$6.45
CV-1014	Classic Videos Inc.	Patton	$11.95	$7.75	$4.20
CV-1029	Classic Videos Inc.	The Bells of St. Mary's	$11.95	$6.25	$5.70
CV-1021	Classic Videos Inc.	The Maltese Falcon	$9.95	$5.25	$4.70
CV-1011	Hillman Enterprises	A Christmas Carol	$10.95	$6.25	$4.70
CV-1005	Hillman Enterprises	Breakfast at Tiffany's	$11.95	$6.95	$5.00
CV-1004	Hillman Enterprises	Dial M for Murder	$9.95	$7.95	$2.00
CV-1026	Hillman Enterprises	Hell's Angels	$14.95	$5.95	$9.00
CV-1003	Hillman Enterprises	Moby Dick	$12.95	$8.95	$4.00
CV-1019	Hillman Enterprises	One Flew Over the Cuckoo's Nest	$13.95	$7.25	$6.70
CV-1030	Hillman Enterprises	Stormy Weather	$12.95	$5.25	$7.70
CV-1012	Hillman Enterprises	The Bridge on the River Kwai	$9.95	$5.50	$4.45
CV-1008	Hillman Enterprises	The Great Escape	$18.95	$9.50	$9.45
CV-1001	KML Enterprises	Abbott & Costello Go to Mars	$15.95	$9.95	$6.00
CV-1025	KML Enterprises	Ben Hur	$11.95	$6.25	$5.70
CV-1020	KML Enterprises	Bonnie and Clyde	$12.95	$5.85	$7.10
CV-1009	KML Enterprises	The Odd Couple	$10.95	$5.95	$5.00
CV-1018	KML Enterprises	To Kill a Mockingbird	$11.95	$8.45	$3.50
CV-1015	Nostalgia Productions	Blue Hawaii	$10.95	$4.95	$6.00
CV-1007	Nostalgia Productions	Doctor Zhivago	$22.95	$8.50	$14.45
CV-1027	Nostalgia Productions	Going My Way	$11.95	$4.65	$7.30
CV-1022	Nostalgia Productions	The Wizard of Oz	$11.95	$6.50	$5.45
CV-1028	Old Tyme Distributing	Band of Angels	$10.95	$6.15	$4.80
CV-1002	Old Tyme Distributing	Miracle on 34th Street	$22.95	$9.95	$13.00
CV-1016	Old Tyme Distributing	Psycho	$11.95	$8.45	$3.50
CV-1023	Old Tyme Distributing	Rear Window	$9.95	$4.85	$5.10
CV-1017	Old Tyme Distributing	The Longest Day	$12.95	$6.75	$6.20
CV-1010	Old Tyme Distributing	The Sound of Music	$11.95	$8.25	$3.70

Page 1

WebProdCostsWithSupp(A1,Step8).accdb

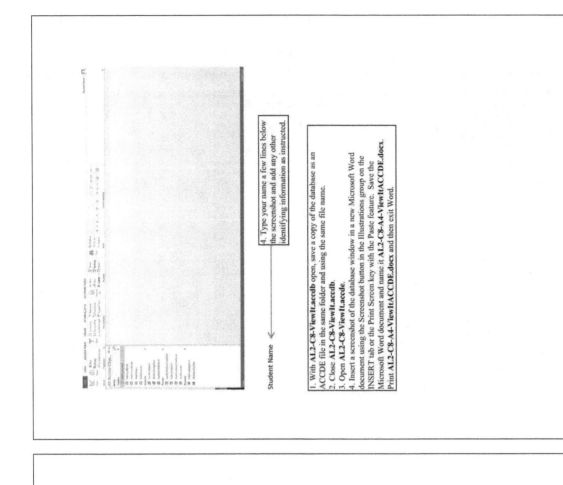

Student Name ⟵

4. Type your name a few lines below the screenshot and add any other identifying information as instructed.

1. With **AL2-C8-ViewIt.accdb** open, save a copy of the database as an ACCDE file in the same folder and using the same file name.
2. Close **AL2-C8-ViewIt.accdb**.
3. Open **AL2-C8-ViewIt.accde**.
4. Insert a screenshot of the database window in a new Microsoft Word document using the Screenshot button in the Illustrations group on the INSERT tab or the Print Screen key with the Paste feature. Save the Microsoft Word document and name it **AL2-C8-A4-ViewItACCDE.docx**. Print **AL2-C8-A4-ViewItACCDE.docx** and then exit Word.

WebOrdID,CustID,DateOrd,Qty,Product,SellPrice
10001,101,2/15/2015 0:00:00,1,Blue Hawaii,$10.95
10001,101,2/15/2015 0:00:00,1,To Kill a Mockingbird,$11.95
10002,102,2/15/2015 0:00:00,2,The Great Escape,$18.95
10003,103,2/16/2015 0:00:00,1,Doctor Zhivago,$22.95
10003,103,2/16/2015 0:00:00,1,Cool Hand Luke,$11.95
10003,103,2/16/2015 0:00:00,2,The Longest Day,$12.95
10004,104,2/22/2015 0:00:00,1,Dial M for Murder,$9.95
10005,108,2/22/2015 0:00:00,1,Gone with the Wind,$18.95
10005,108,2/22/2015 0:00:00,1,Ben Hur,$11.95
10006,110,2/23/2015 0:00:00,1,The Wizard of Oz,$11.95
10007,106,2/26/2015 0:00:00,1,The Maltese Falcon,$9.95
10007,106,2/26/2015 0:00:00,1,Stormy Weather,$12.95
10008,102,3/4/2015 0:00:00,2,The Longest Day,$12.95
10009,104,3/8/2015 0:00:00,1,Patton,$11.95
10010,103,3/10/2015 0:00:00,1,The Odd Couple,$10.95
10011,110,3/15/2015 0:00:00,1,Gone with the Wind,$18.95
10011,110,3/15/2015 0:00:00,1,The Bridge on the River Kwai,$9.95
10012,108,3/16/2015 0:00:00,1,Moby Dick,$12.95
10012,108,3/16/2015 0:00:00,1,Dial M for Murder,$9.95
10012,108,3/16/2015 0:00:00,1,One Flew Over the Cuckoo's Nest,$13.95
10013,102,3/22/2015 0:00:00,1,Abbot & Costello Go to Mars,$15.95
10014,101,3/25/2015 0:00:00,1,The Longest Day,$12.95
10015,106,3/27/2015 0:00:00,2,The Sound of Music,$11.95
10016,103,3/30/2015 0:00:00,1,Breakfast at Tiffany's,$11.95
10016,108,3/30/2015 0:00:00,1,Psycho,$11.95
10017,120,4/1/2015 0:00:00,1,Hell's Angels,$14.95
10017,120,4/1/2015 0:00:00,1,The Bells of St. Mary's,$11.95
10018,114,4/3/2015 0:00:00,1,Going My Way,$11.95
10019,116,4/5/2015 0:00:00,1,Band of Angels,$10.95
10020,118,4/5/2015 0:00:00,1,To Kill a Mockingbird,$11.95
10021,112,4/8/2015 0:00:00,1,Abbot & Costello Go to Mars,$15.95
10022,117,4/10/2015 0:00:00,1,Rear Window,$9.95
10023,113,4/11/2015 0:00:00,1,The Odd Couple,$10.95
10024,119,4/12/2015 0:00:00,1,Psycho,$11.95
10025,111,4/12/2015 0:00:00,1,The Great Escape,$18.95
10026,115,4/13/2015 0:00:00,1,Gone with the Wind,$18.95
10026,115,4/13/2015 0:00:00,1,The Sound of Music,$11.95
10026,115,4/13/2015 0:00:00,1,Patton,$11.95

1. Open **AL2-C8-ViewIt.accdb** and enable the content.
2. Export the CustWebOrders query to a comma delimited text file using the following information:
• Include the field names and remove the quotation marks.
• Save the export steps and type the following description: Export the customers' web orders to a text file.
3. Open Notepad and then open and print **CustWebOrders.txt**.

Hillsdale Realty
Agents with Sales and Commissions Earned

Agent Last Name	Agent First Name	Date Sold	Street Address	Sale Price	Commission Rate	Commission
Im	Kwan					
		10/12/2015	151 E Culver Street	$325,500.00	3.00%	$9,765.00
		10/17/2015	341 E Detroit Street	$275,800.00	3.85%	$10,618.30
		10/22/2015	659 W Erie Street	$310,114.00	4.00%	$12,404.56
		10/23/2015	10 N 16th Avenue	$245,800.00	3.25%	$7,988.50
				Agent Total: $1,157,214.00		Agent Total: $40,776.36
Ludlow	William					
		10/25/2015	1665 E Campbell Avenue	$244,845.00	3.00%	$7,345.35
				Agent Total: $244,845.00		Agent Total: $7,345.35
Marshall	Isabelle					
		10/15/2015	334 W Mitchell Drive	$375,800.00	4.00%	$15,032.00
		10/27/2015	1401 N Orlando Circle	$175,455.00	3.00%	$5,263.65
				Agent Total: $551,255.00		Agent Total: $20,295.65
Newman	Jaren					
		10/15/2015	202 S Hobson	$202,500.00	3.75%	$7,593.75
				Agent Total: $202,500.00		Agent Total: $7,593.75
Ortega	Cecilia					
		10/14/2015	22 E Holly Avenue	$229,900.00	4.00%	$9,196.00
		10/31/2015	2900 E Cactus Road	$155,750.00	3.25%	$5,061.88
				Agent Total: $385,650.00		Agent Total: $14,257.88
Pascual	Maureen					
		10/30/2015	3033 E Hampton Circle	$166,500.00	3.00%	$4,995.00
				Agent Total: $166,500.00		Agent Total: $4,995.00

Friday, June 28, 2013

Page 1 of 2

```
"ListingNo","StreetAdd","City","AgentID","ListDate"
"302715","151 E Culver Street","Phoenix","10",10/1/2015 0:00:00
"313443","23 W 7th Street","Mesa","17",10/1/2015 0:00:00
"315825","22 E Holly Avenue","Phoenix","16",10/2/2015 0:00:00
"351245","126 E Buffalo Street","Chandler","12",10/7/2015 0:00:00
"362548","202 S Hobson","Mesa","14",10/8/2015 0:00:00
"374152","334 W Mitchell Drive","Phoenix","19",10/9/2015 0:00:00
"384512","65 W Boston Street","Chandler","21",10/12/2015 0:00:00
"394528","341 E Detroit Street","Chandler","10",10/12/2015 0:00:00
"436851","659 W Erie Street","Chandler","10",10/15/2015 0:00:00
"447856","1221 W Vine Avenue","Mesa","12",10/15/2015 0:00:00
"496583","37 W Clark Street","Mesa","10",10/16/2015 0:00:00
"574635","10 N 16th Avenue","Phoenix","10",10/18/2015 0:00:00
"655863","33 E Lincoln Street","Phoenix","10",10/18/2015 0:00:00
"658963","1665 E Campbell Avenue","Phoenix","11",10/19/2015 0:00:00
"663258","5333 W Elgin Street","Chandler","14",10/19/2015 0:00:00
"674125","1401 N Orlando Circle","Mesa","19",10/21/2015 0:00:00
"675425","3033 E Hampton Circle","Mesa","21",10/22/2015 0:00:00
"677325","3209 W Bajada Drive","Phoenix","11",10/22/2015 0:00:00
"681235","1501 N 91st Place","Mesa","15",10/23/2015 0:00:00
"681335","995 W Cross Street","Chandler","15",10/24/2015 0:00:00
"681775","2900 E Cactus Road","Phoenix","16",10/24/2015 0:00:00
"682356","11233 E Stearn Avenue","Mesa","17",10/24/2015 0:00:00
"683345","11322 E Sonrisa Avenue","Mesa","17",10/26/2015 0:00:00
"692341","16654 S 29th Street","Phoenix","21",10/26/2015 0:00:00
"692354","3103 E Coolidge Street","Phoenix","11",10/30/2015 0:00:00
"693341","800 N Soho Place","Chandler","21",10/28/2015 0:00:00
```

Agent Last Name	Agent First Name	Date Sold	Street Address	Sale Price	Commission Rate	Commission
Rehberg	Robin					
		10/13/2015	23 W 7th Street	$189,900.00	3.25%	$6,171.75
		10/31/2015	11233 E Stearn Avenue	$165,750.00	3.25%	$5,386.88
			Agent Total:	$355,650.00	Agent Total:	$11,558.63
Singleton	Catherine					
		10/14/2015	126 E Buffalo Street	$349,900.00	4.00%	$13,996.00
			Agent Total:	$349,900.00	Agent Total:	$13,996.00
Student Name			Grand Total:	$3,413,514.00	Grand Total:	$120,818.61

Friday, June 28, 2013

Page 2 of 2

AL2-C8-CS-P1-SalesAndCommissions(P1).xps (2 of 2)

Access Performance Assessment Unit 2 Model Answers

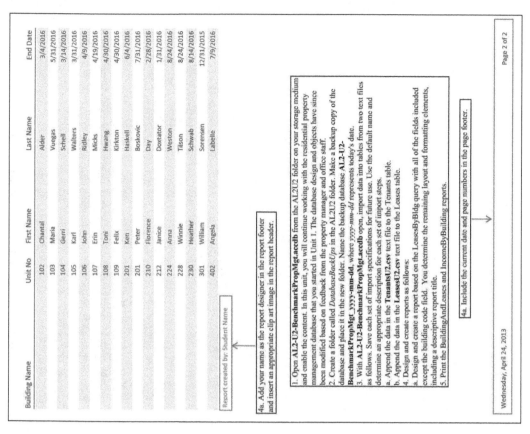

Buildings and Leases (2 of 2)

Building Name	Unit No	First Name	Last Name	End Date
	102	Chantal	Alder	3/4/2016
	103	Maria	Vuegas	5/31/2016
	104	Gerri	Schell	3/14/2016
	105	Karl	Walters	3/31/2016
	106	John	Ridley	4/9/2016
	107	Erin	Micks	4/19/2016
	108	Toni	Hwang	4/30/2016
	109	Felix	Kirkton	4/30/2016
	201	Ken	Haskell	6/4/2016
	201	Peter	Boskovic	7/31/2016
	210	Florence	Day	2/28/2016
	212	Janice	Doxtator	1/31/2016
	224	Anna	Weston	8/24/2016
	228	Winnie	Tilson	8/24/2016
	230	Heather	Schwab	8/14/2016
	301	William	Sorensen	12/31/2015
	402	Angela	Labelle	7/9/2016

Report created by: Student Name

4a. Add your name as the report designer in the report footer and insert an appropriate clip art image in the report header.

1. Open **AL2-U2-BenchmarkPropMgt.accdb** from the AL2U2 folder on your storage medium and enable the content. In this unit, you will continue working with the residential property management database that you started in Unit 1. The database design and objects have since been modified based on feedback from the property manager and office staff.

2. Create a folder called *DatabaseBackUps* in the AL2U2 folder. Make a backup copy of the database and place it in the new folder. Name the backup database **AL2-U2-BenchmarkPropMgt_yyyy-mm-dd**, where *yyyy-mm-dd* represents today's date.

3. With **AL2-U2-BenchmarkPropMgt.accdb** open, import data into tables from two text files as follows. Save each set of import specifications for future use. Use the default name and determine an appropriate description for each set of import steps.
   a. Append the data in the **TenantsU2.csv** text file to the Tenants table.
   b. Append the data in the **LeasesU2.csv** text file to the Leases table.

4. Design and create reports as follows:
   a. Design and create a report based on the LeasesByBldg query with all of the fields included except the building code field. You determine the remaining layout and formatting elements, including a descriptive report title.

5. Print the BuildingAndLeases and IncomeByBuilding reports.

4a. Include the current date and page numbers in the page footer.

Wednesday, April 24, 2013 — Page 2 of 2

AL2-U2-BuildingsAndLeases(A1,Step5).accdb (2 of 2)

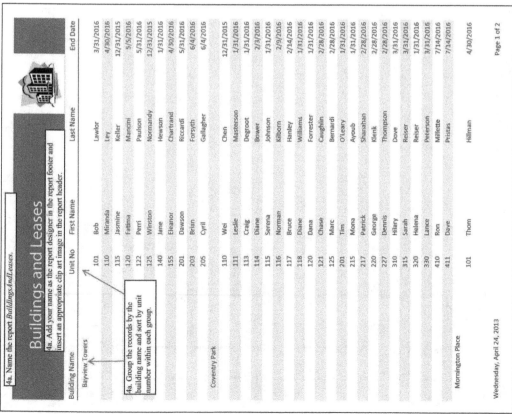

4a. Name the report *BuildingsAndLeases*.

Buildings and Leases

4a. Add your name as the report designer in the report footer and insert an appropriate clip art image in the report header.

4a. Group the records by the building name and sort by unit number within each group.

Building Name	Unit No	First Name	Last Name	End Date
Bayview Towers				
	101	Bob	Lawlor	3/31/2016
	110	Miranda	Ley	4/30/2016
	115	Jasmine	Keller	12/31/2015
	120	Fatima	Mancini	5/5/2016
	122	Perri	Paulson	5/31/2016
	125	Winston	Normandy	12/31/2015
	140	Jane	Hewson	1/31/2016
	155	Eleanor	Chartrand	4/30/2016
	201	Dawson	Riccardi	5/31/2016
	203	Brian	Forsyth	6/4/2016
	205	Cyril	Gallagher	6/4/2016
Coventry Park				
	110	Wei	Chen	12/31/2015
	111	Leslie	Masterson	1/31/2016
	113	Craig	Degroot	1/31/2016
	114	Diane	Bower	2/3/2016
	115	Serena	Johnson	1/31/2016
	116	Norman	Kilborn	2/9/2016
	117	Bruce	Hanley	2/14/2016
	118	Diane	Williams	1/31/2016
	120	Dana	Forrester	1/31/2016
	121	Chase	Caughlin	2/28/2016
	125	Marc	Bernardi	2/28/2016
	201	Tim	O'Leary	1/31/2016
	215	Mona	Ayoub	1/31/2016
	217	Patrick	Shanahan	2/28/2016
	220	George	Klenk	2/28/2016
	227	Dennis	Thompson	2/28/2016
	310	Hilary	Dove	3/31/2016
	315	Sarah	Reiser	3/31/2016
	320	Helena	Reiser	1/31/2016
	330	Lance	Peterson	3/31/2016
	410	Ron	Millette	7/14/2016
	411	Dave	Pristas	7/14/2016
Mornington Place				
	101	Thom	Hillman	4/30/2016

Wednesday, April 24, 2013 — Page 1 of 2

AL2-U2-BuildingsAndLeases(A1,Step5).accdb (1 of 2)

4b. Name the report IncomeByBuilding.

Income by Building

4b. Add your name as the report designer in the report footer and insert an appropriate clip art image in the report header.

4b. Group the records by the building name and sort by unit number within each group.

4b. Show the statistics in the group footer and as grand totals at the end of the report. Include appropriate labels to describe the statistics and format the values to a suitable numeric format, if necessary.

4a. Include the current date and page numbers in the page footer.

Building Name	Unit N	First Name	Last Name	Rent	Annual Rent
Bayview Towers					
	101	Bob	Lawlor	$1,170.00	$14,040.00
	110	Miranda	Ley	$975.00	$11,700.00
	115	Jasmine	Keller	$910.00	$10,920.00
	120	Fatima	Mancini	$975.00	$11,700.00
	122	Perri	Paulson	$975.00	$11,700.00
	125	Winston	Normandy	$1,034.80	$12,417.60
	140	Jane	Hewson	$910.00	$10,920.00
	155	Eleanor	Chartrand	$1,170.00	$14,040.00
	201	Dawson	Riccardi	$1,125.00	$13,500.00
	203	Brian	Forsyth	$975.00	$11,700.00
	205	Cyril	Gallagher	$1,125.00	$13,500.00
			Building Total:	$11,344.80	$136,137.60
Count of Units: 11					
Coventry Park					
	110	Wei	Chen	$1,034.80	$12,417.60
	111	Leslie	Masterson	$910.00	$10,920.00
	112	Pat	McCann	$1,034.80	$12,417.60
	113	Craig	Degroot	$1,034.80	$12,417.60
	114	Diane	Bower	$1,170.00	$14,040.00
	115	Serena	Johnson	$1,170.00	$14,040.00
	116	Norman	Kilborn	$1,034.80	$12,417.60
	117	Bruce	Hanley	$1,170.00	$14,040.00
	118	Diane	Williams	$1,170.00	$14,040.00
	120	Dana	Forrester	$1,034.80	$12,417.60
	121	Chase	Caughlin	$1,170.00	$14,040.00
	125	Marc	Bernardi	$1,034.80	$12,417.60
	201	Tim	O'Leary	$1,170.00	$14,040.00
	215	Mona	Ayoub	$1,034.80	$12,417.60
	217	Patrick	Shanahan	$1,034.80	$12,417.60
	220	George	Klenk	$1,034.80	$12,417.60
	227	Dennis	Thompson	$1,034.80	$12,417.60
	315	Hilary	Dove	$910.00	$10,920.00
	315	Sarah	Reiser	$910.00	$10,920.00
	320	Helena	Reiser	$1,170.00	$14,040.00
	330	Lance	Peterson	$1,034.80	$12,417.60
	410	Ron	Millette	$1,034.80	$12,417.60
	411	Dave	Pristas	$1,170.00	$14,040.00
			Building Total:	$24,507.60	$294,091.20
Count of Units: 23					

Wednesday, April 24, 2013

Page 1 of 2

Building Name	Unit N	First Name	Last Name	Rent	Annual Rent
Mornington Place					
	101	Thom	Hillman	$1,170.00	$14,040.00
	102	Chantal	Alder	$775.00	$9,300.00
	103	Maria	Vuegas	$1,034.80	$12,417.60
	104	Gerri	Schell	$775.00	$9,300.00
	105	Karl	Walters	$688.00	$8,256.00
	106	John	Ridley	$855.00	$10,260.00
	107	Erin	Micks	$775.00	$9,300.00
	108	Toni	Hwang	$688.00	$8,256.00
	109	Felix	Kirkton	$688.00	$8,256.00
	201	Ken	Haskell	$855.00	$10,260.00
	201	Peter	Boskovic	$1,034.80	$12,417.60
	210	Florence	Day	$1,034.80	$12,417.60
	212	Janice	Doxtator	$910.00	$10,920.00
	224	Anna	Weston	$775.00	$9,300.00
	228	Winnie	Tilson	$688.00	$8,256.00
	230	Heather	Schwab	$775.00	$9,300.00
	301	William	Sorensen	$1,170.00	$14,040.00
	402	Angela	Labelle	$855.00	$10,260.00
			Building Total:	$15,546.40	$186,556.80
Count of Units: 18			Grand Total:	$51,398.80	$616,785.60
Count of Units: 52					

Report created by: Student Name

4b. Add your name as the report designer in the report footer and insert an appropriate clip art image in the report header.

4b. Sum the rent and annual rent columns and count the unit numbers. Show the statistics in the group footer and as grand totals at the end of the report. Include appropriate labels to describe the statistics and format the values to a suitable numeric format, if necessary.

Wednesday, April 24, 2013

Page 2 of 2

---

1. Open **AL2-U2-BenchmarkPropMgt.accdb** from the AL2U2 folder on your storage medium and enable the content. In this unit, you will continue working with the residential property management database that you started in Unit 1. The database design and objects have since been modified based on feedback from the property manager and office staff.
2. Create a folder called *DatabaseBackUps* in the AL2U2 folder. Make a backup copy of the database and place it in the new folder. Name the backup database **AL2-U2-BenchmarkPropMgt_yyyy-mm-dd**, where *yyyy-mm-dd* represents today's date.
3. With **AL2-U2-BenchmarkPropMgt.accdb** open, import data into tables from two text files as follows. Save each set of import specifications for future use. Use the default name and determine an appropriate description for each set of import steps.
   a. Append the data in the **TenantsU2.csv** text file to the Tenants table.
   b. Append the data in the **LeasesU2.csv** text file to the Leases table.
4. Design and create reports as follows:
   b. Design and create a report based on the RentalIncome query with all of the fields included, except for the building code field. You determine the remaining layout and formatting elements including a descriptive report title.
5. Print the BuildingAndLeases and IncomeByBuilding reports.

4. Create two command buttons in the *Form Header* section: one that runs the RBldgLeases macro and another that runs the RIncome macro. You determine the placement of the buttons within the section, the text to display on the face of each button, and a name to assign each button.

5. Test each button to make sure the macro displays the correct report.

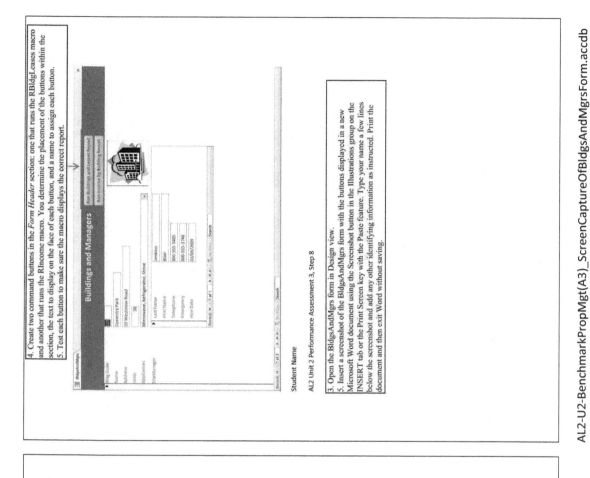

Student Name

AL2 Unit 2 Performance Assessment 3, Step 8

3. Open the BldgsAndMgrs form in Design view.

5. Insert a screenshot of the BldgsAndMgrs form with the buttons displayed in a new Microsoft Word document using the Screenshot button in the Illustrations group on the INSERT tab or the Print Screen key with the Paste feature. Type your name a few lines below the screenshot and add any other identifying information as instructed. Print the document and then exit Word without saving.

G:\AL2\AL2-U2-BenchmarkPropMgt(A2)_be.accdb   Wednesday, April 24, 2013
Table: Leases   Page: 1

Properties

AlternateBackShade:	100	AlternateBackThemeColorInd	-1
AlternateBackTint:	100	BackShade:	100
BackTint:	100	DatasheetForeThemeColorIn	-1
DatasheetGridlinesThemeCol	-1	DateCreated:	4/24/2013 7:06:17 PM
DefaultView:	2	DisplayViewsOnSharePointSit	1
FilterOnLoad:	False	HideNewField:	False
LastUpdated:	4/24/2013 7:06:17 PM	NameMap:	Long binary data
OrderByOn:	False	OrderByOnLoad:	True
Orientation:	Left-to-Right	PublishToWeb:	1
ReadOnlyWhenDisconnected	False	RecordCount:	52
ThemeFontIndex:	-1	TotalsRow:	False
Updatable:	True		

Columns

Name	Type	Size
TenID	Short Text	3
StartDate	Date With Time	8
EndDate	Date With Time	8
SecDep	Currency	8

Relationships

TenantsLeases

Tenants	Leases
TenID	TenID

Attributes: Unique, Not Enforced
RelationshipType: One-To-One

1. With **AL2-U2-BenchmarkPropMgt.accdb** open, use the Performance Analyzer feature to analyze all of the objects in the database. In the *Analysis Results* list, use the Optimize button to fix each Suggestion item. (A Suggestion item displays with a green question mark.)

2. Use the Database Splitter to split the database into two files to create a back-end database. Accept the default file name at the Create Back-end Database dialog box.

3. Close **AL2-U2-BenchmarkPropMgt.accdb**.

4. Open **AL2-U2-BenchmarkPropMgt_be.accdb** and enable the content.

5. Use the Database Documenter feature to generate a table definition report for the Leases table. Change the options as follows: Set *Include for Table* to *Properties and Relationships*; set *Include for Fields* to *Names, Data Types, and Sizes*; and set *Include for Indexes* to *Nothing*. Print and then close the report.

AL2-U2-doc_rptObjects(A2,Step5).accdb

G:\USent to EMCP\Data Files\AL2U2\Access\2U2_ModelAnswers_Final\AL2-U2-Benchmark\PropMgt(A3).accdb

Wednesday, April 24, 2013

Page: 1

Macro: QLeaseTerms

Actions

Name	Condition	Action	Argument	Value
		OpenQuery	Query Name:	LeaseTermsAndDeposits
			View:	Datasheet
			Data Mode:	Edit

XML: <?xml version="1.0" encoding="UTF-16" standalone="no"?>
<UserInterfaceMacro MinimumClientDesignVersion="14.0.0000.0000"
xmlns="http://schemas.microsoft.com/office/accessservices/2009/11/application"
xmlns:a="http://schemas.microsoft.com/office/acc

XML.a:esservices/2009/11/forms"><Statements><Action Name="OpenQuery"><Argument
Name="QueryName">LeaseTermsAndDeposits</Argument></Action></Statements></UserInterfaceMacro>

1. Open AL2-U2-Benchmark\PropMgt.accdb and, if necessary, enable the content.
2. Create the following macros. After creating each macro, print each macro's definition, and then close the macro. b.
Create a QLeaseTerms macro that opens the LeaseTermsAndDeposits query in
Datasheet view and Edit mode. Use the macro action *OpenQuery*.

AL2-U2-doc_rptObjects_QLeaseTerms(A3,Step2).accdb

G:\USent to EMCP\Data Files\AL2U2\Access\2U2_ModelAnswers_Final\AL2-U2-Benchmark\PropMgt(A3).accdb

Wednesday, April 24, 2013

Page: 1

Macro: QLeasesByTenant

Actions

Name	Condition	Action	Argument	Value
		OpenQuery	Query Name:	LeasesByTenant
			View:	Datasheet
			Data Mode:	Edit

XML: <?xml version="1.0" encoding="UTF-16" standalone="no"?>
<UserInterfaceMacro MinimumClientDesignVersion="14.0.0000.0000"
xmlns="http://schemas.microsoft.com/office/accessservices/2009/11/application"
xmlns:a="http://schemas.microsoft.com/office/acc

XML.a:esservices/2009/11/forms"><Statements><Action Name="OpenQuery"><Argument
Name="QueryName">LeasesByTenant</Argument></Action></Statements></UserInterfaceMacro>

1. Open AL2-U2-Benchmark\PropMgt.accdb and, if necessary, enable the content.
2. Create the following macros. After creating each macro, run the macro to make sure it
works properly, print each macro's definition, and then close the macro.
a. Create a QLeasesByTenant macro that opens the LeasesByTenant query in Datasheet
view and Edit mode. Use the macro action *OpenQuery*.

AL2-U2-doc_rptObjects_QLeaseByTenant(A3,Step2).accdb

Benchmark Access 2013 Level 2 Model Answers

G:\U2Sent to BMCP\Data Files\AL2U2\Access12U2_ModelAnswers_Final\AL2-U2-BenchmarkRPropMgt(A3).accdb

Macro: RIncome

Actions

Name	Condition	Action	Argument	Value
		OpenReport	Report Name:	IncomeByBuilding

View: Report
Filter Name:
Where Condition:
Window Mode: Normal

XML: <?xml version="1.0" encoding="UTF-16" standalone="no"?>
<UserInterfaceMacro MinimumClientDesignVersion="14.0.0000.0000" xmlns="http://schemas.microsoft.com/office/accessservices/2009/11/application" xmlns:a="http://schemas.microsoft.com/office/acc

XML:essservices/2009/11/forms"><Statements><Action Name="OpenReport"><Argument Name="ReportName">IncomeByBuilding</Argument></Action></Statements></UserInterfaceMacro>

1. Open **AL2-U2-BenchmarkRPropMgt.accdb** and, if necessary, enable the content.
2. Create the following macros. After creating each macro, run the macro to make sure it works properly, print each macro's definition, and then close the macro.
d. Create a RIncome macro that opens the IncomeByBuilding report in report view. Use the macro action OpenReport.

AL2-U2-doc_rptObjects_RIncome(A3,Step2).accdb

G:\U2Sent to BMCP\Data Files\AL2U2\Access12U2_ModelAnswers_Final\AL2-U2-BenchmarkRPropMgt(A3).accdb

Macro: RBldLeases

Actions

Name	Condition	Action	Argument	Value
		OpenReport	Report Name:	BuildingsAndLeases

View: Report
Filter Name:
Where Condition:
Window Mode: Normal

XML: <?xml version="1.0" encoding="UTF-16" standalone="no"?>
<UserInterfaceMacro MinimumClientDesignVersion="14.0.0000.0000" xmlns="http://schemas.microsoft.com/office/accessservices/2009/11/application" xmlns:a="http://schemas.microsoft.com/office/acc

XML:essservices/2009/11/forms"><Statements><Action Name="OpenReport"><Argument Name="ReportName">BuildingsAndLeases</Argument></Action></Statements></UserInterfaceMacro>

1. Open **AL2-U2-BenchmarkRPropMgt.accdb** and, if necessary, enable the content.
2. Create the following macros. After creating each macro, run the macro to make sure it works properly, print each macro's definition, and then close the macro.
c. Create a RBldLeases macro that opens the BuildingsAndLeases report in report view. Use the macro action OpenReport.

AL2-U2-doc_rptObjects_RBldLeases(A3,Step2).accdb

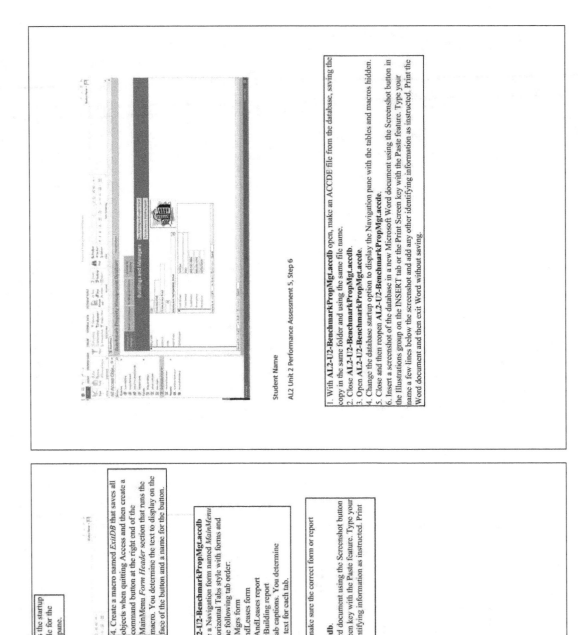

AL2-U2-BenchmarkPropMgt(A5)_ScreenCaptureACCDE.accdb

Student Name

AL2 Unit 2 Performance Assessment 5, Step 6

1. With **AL2-U2-BenchmarkPropMgt.accdb** open, make an ACCDE file from the database, saving the copy in the same folder and using the same file name.
2. Close **AL2-U2-BenchmarkPropMgt.accdb**.
3. Open **AL2-U2-BenchmarkPropMgt.accde**.
4. Change the database startup option to display the Navigation pane with the tables and macros hidden.
5. Close and then reopen **AL2-U2-BenchmarkPropMgt.accde**.
6. Insert a screenshot of the database in a new Microsoft Word document using the Screenshot button in the Illustrations group on the INSERT tab or the Print Screen key with the Paste feature. Type your name a few lines below the screenshot and add any other identifying information as instructed. Print the Word document and then exit Word without saving.

---

2. Edit the form title and delete the logo container object. You determine appropriate text to replace *Navigation Form*.

6. Set the MainMenu form to display as the startup form, add an appropriate application title for the database, and then hide the Navigation pane.

4. Create a macro named *ExitDB* that saves all objects when quitting Access and then create a command button at the right end of the MainMenu *Form Header* section that runs the macro. You determine the text to display on the face of the button and a name for the button.

1. With **AL2-U2-BenchmarkPropMgt.accdb** open, create a Navigation form named *MainMenu* using the Horizontal Tabs style with forms and reports in the following tab order:
   • BldgsAndMgrs form
   • TenantsAndLeases form
   • BuildingsAndLeases report
   • IncomeByBuilding report
3. Edit the tab captions. You determine appropriate text for each tab.

Student Name

AL2 Unit 2 Performance Assessment 4, Step 8

5. Display the form in Form view and then click each tab to make sure the correct form or report displays.
7. Close and then reopen **AL2-U2-BenchmarkPropMgt.accdb**.
8. Insert a screenshot of the database in a new Microsoft Word document using the Screenshot button in the Illustrations group on the INSERT tab or the Print Screen key with the Paste feature. Type your name a few lines below the screenshot and add any other identifying information as instructed. Print the Word document and then exit Word without saving.

AL2-U2-BenchmarkPropMgt(A4)_ScreenCaptureMainMenuForm.accdb

1. With **AL2-U2-BenchmarkPropMgt.accde** open, export the LeaseTermsAndDeposits query as a text file using the default name and making sure that the file is saved in the AL2U2 folder on your storage medium. Include the field names in the first row and remove the quotation marks. Do not save the export steps.
2. Open Notepad, open **LeaseTermsAndDeposits.txt**, and then print the text file.
3. Exit Notepad.
4. Publish the IncomeByBuilding report as an XPS document named **AL2-U2-BenchmarkRentInc.xps**, making sure the file is saved in the AL2U2 folder on your storage medium. Do not save the export steps.
5. Open **AL2-U2-BenchmarkRentInc.xps** in an XPS Viewer window and then print the report.

```
TenID,UnitNo,BldgName,FName,LName,StartDate,EndDate,SecDep
101,110,Coventry Park,Wei,Chen,1/1/2015 0:00:00,12/31/2015 0:00:00,$1034.80
102,215,Coventry Park,Mona,Ayoub,2/1/2015 0:00:00,1/31/2016 0:00:00,$1034.80
103,320,Coventry Park,Helena,Reiser,2/1/2015 0:00:00,1/31/2016 0:00:00,$1170.00
104,111,Coventry Park,Leslie,Masterson,2/1/2015 0:00:00,1/31/2016 0:00:00,$910.00
105,115,Coventry Park,Serena,Johnson,2/1/2015 0:00:00,1/31/2016 0:00:00,$1170.00
106,118,Coventry Park,Diane,Williams,2/1/2015 0:00:00,1/31/2016 0:00:00,$1170.00
107,120,Coventry Park,Dana,Forrester,2/1/2015 0:00:00,1/31/2016 0:00:00,$1034.80
108,201,Coventry Park,Tim,O'Leary,2/1/2015 0:00:00,1/31/2016 0:00:00,$1170.00
109,217,Coventry Park,Patrick,Shanahan,3/1/2015 0:00:00,2/28/2016 0:00:00,$1034.80
110,220,Coventry Park,George,Klenk,3/1/2015 0:00:00,2/28/2016 0:00:00,$1034.80
111,227,Coventry Park,Dennis,Thompson,3/1/2015 0:00:00,2/28/2016 0:00:00,$1034.80
112,310,Coventry Park,Hilary,Dove,4/1/2015 0:00:00,3/31/2016 0:00:00,$910.00
113,315,Coventry Park,Sarah,Reiser,4/1/2015 0:00:00,3/31/2016 0:00:00,$910.00
114,330,Coventry Park,Lance,Peterson,4/1/2015 0:00:00,3/31/2016 0:00:00,$1034.80
127,113,Coventry Park,Craig,Degroot,2/1/2015 0:00:00,1/31/2016 0:00:00,$1034.80
128,114,Coventry Park,Diane,Bower,2/4/2015 0:00:00,2/3/2016 0:00:00,$1034.80
129,116,Coventry Park,Norman,Kilborn,2/10/2015 0:00:00,2/9/2016 0:00:00,$1170.00
130,117,Coventry Park,Bruce,Hanley,2/15/2015 0:00:00,2/14/2016 0:00:00,$1034.80
131,121,Coventry Park,Chase,Caughlin,3/1/2015 0:00:00,2/28/2016 0:00:00,$1170.00
132,125,Coventry Park,Marc,Bernardi,3/1/2015 0:00:00,2/28/2016 0:00:00,$1170.00
148,410,Coventry Park,Ron,Millette,7/15/2015 0:00:00,7/14/2016 0:00:00,$855.00
149,411,Coventry Park,Dave,Pristas,7/15/2015 0:00:00,7/14/2016 0:00:00,$1034.80
120,101,Mornington Place,Thom,Hillman,5/1/2015 0:00:00,4/30/2016 0:00:00,$1170.00
121,103,Mornington Place,Maria,Vuegas,6/1/2015 0:00:00,5/31/2016 0:00:00,$1034.80
122,201,Mornington Place,Peter,Boskovic,8/1/2015 0:00:00,7/31/2016 0:00:00,$1034.80
123,210,Mornington Place,Florence,Day,3/1/2015 0:00:00,2/28/2016 0:00:00,$1034.80
124,212,Mornington Place,Janice,Doxtator,2/1/2015 0:00:00,1/31/2016 0:00:00,$910.00
125,301,Mornington Place,William,Sorensen,1/1/2015 0:00:00,12/31/2015 0:00:00,$1170.00
133,102,Mornington Place,Chantal,Alder,3/5/2015 0:00:00,3/4/2016 0:00:00,$1034.80
134,104,Mornington Place,Gerri,Schell,3/15/2015 0:00:00,3/14/2016 0:00:00,$775.00
135,105,Mornington Place,Karl,Walters,4/1/2015 0:00:00,3/31/2016 0:00:00,$775.00
136,106,Mornington Place,John,Ridley,4/10/2015 0:00:00,4/9/2016 0:00:00,$688.00
137,107,Mornington Place,Erin,Micks,4/20/2015 0:00:00,4/19/2016 0:00:00,$855.00
138,108,Mornington Place,Toni,Hwang,5/1/2015 0:00:00,4/30/2016 0:00:00,$775.00
139,109,Mornington Place,Felix,Kirkton,5/1/2015 0:00:00,4/30/2016 0:00:00,$688.00
146,201,Mornington Place,Ken,Haskell,6/5/2015 0:00:00,6/4/2016 0:00:00,$975.00
147,402,Mornington Place,Angela,Labelle,7/10/2015 0:00:00,7/9/2016 0:00:00,$855.00
150,230,Mornington Place,Heather,Schwab,8/15/2015 0:00:00,8/14/2016 0:00:00,$1170.00
151,228,Mornington Place,Winnie,Tilson,8/25/2015 0:00:00,8/24/2016 0:00:00,$775.00
152,224,Mornington Place,Anna,Weston,8/25/2015 0:00:00,8/24/2016 0:00:00,$688.00
115,101,Bayview Towers,Bob,Lawlor,4/1/2015 0:00:00,3/31/2016 0:00:00,$1170.00
116,115,Bayview Towers,Jasmine,Keller,1/1/2015 0:00:00,12/31/2015 0:00:00,$910.00
117,125,Bayview Towers,Winston,Normandy,1/1/2015 0:00:00,12/31/2015 0:00:00,$1034.80
118,140,Bayview Towers,Jane,Hewson,2/1/2015 0:00:00,1/31/2016 0:00:00,$910.00
119,155,Bayview Towers,Eleanor,Chartrand,5/1/2015 0:00:00,4/30/2016 0:00:00,$1170.00
140,110,Bayview Towers,Miranda,Ley,5/1/2015 0:00:00,4/30/2016 0:00:00,$688.00
141,120,Bayview Towers,Fatima,Mancini,5/6/2015 0:00:00,5/5/2016 0:00:00,$975.00
142,122,Bayview Towers,Perri,Paulson,6/1/2015 0:00:00,5/31/2016 0:00:00,$975.00
143,201,Bayview Towers,Dawson,Riccardi,6/1/2015 0:00:00,5/31/2016 0:00:00,$975.00
144,205,Bayview Towers,Cyril,Gallagher,6/5/2015 0:00:00,6/4/2016 0:00:00,$1125.00
145,203,Bayview Towers,Brian,Forsyth,6/5/2015 0:00:00,6/4/2016 0:00:00,$1125.00
```

AL2-U2-LeaseTermsAndDeposits(A6,Step2).txt

Rubrics

Note that the following are suggested rubrics. Instructors should feel free to customize the rubric to suit their grading standards and/or to adjust the point values.

Suggested Scoring Distribution: Above average = student completes 80% or more of task(s); average = student completes 70–79% of task(s); below average = student completes 69% or less of task(s)

Benchmark Access 2013 Level 1, Chapter 1

Skills Check

Assessment 1: Inserting and Deleting Rows and Columns
File: **AL1-C1-Griffin.accdb**

Steps	Tasks	Criteria	Value	Score
1-2	Organization, Accuracy	Open **AL1-C1-Griffin.accdb** from the storage medium and open the Employees table.	3	
3-6	Editing, Typing, Organization	3–4. Delete records for Scott Jorgensen (employee number 1025) and Leanne Taylor (employee number 1060). 5. Insert the following records: Emp#: **1010** Birthdate: **9/7/1976** LastName: **Harrington** AnnualSalary: **$53,350** FirstName: **Tyler** HireDate: **10/1/2010** Emp#: **1052** Birthdate: **12/4/1978** LastName: **Reeves** AnnualSalary: **$38,550** FirstName: **Carrie** HireDate: **10/1/2012** 6. Close the Employees table.	7	
7-9	Organization, Field Management, Formatting, Accuracy, Typing	7. Based on Figure 1.15, it's determined Employees table includes a *DeptID* field; open Employees table, insert new field named *DeptID*. Change field size to 2; at *Some data may be lost* message, click Yes button. Type department identification for each record as shown (see Step 7, page 37, for left-to-right listing). 8–9. Move *DeptID* column to position between *BirthDate* column and *AnnualSalary* column, then automatically adjust widths of columns.	10	
10-12	Organization, Formatting, Finishing	10. Save table. 11. Display table in Print Preview, change top margin to 1.5 inches, left margin to 1.25 inches, then print table. 12. Close table.	5	
		TOTAL POINTS	25	

Assessment 2: Create a Departments Table
File: **AL1-C1-Griffin.accdb**

Steps	Tasks	Criteria	Value	Score
1	Table and Field Management, Accuracy, Typing, Formatting	Create new table in the **AL1-C1-Griffin.accdb** database with column headings and data as shown in Figure 1.16: a. Click Create tab, then click Table button. b. Click *ID* column heading, Format as Data Type, Text. c. Limit field size to 2 and rename heading *DeptID*. d. Click *Click to Add* column heading, click *Short Text* at drop-down list, then type **Department**. e. Type data in fields as shown in Figure 1.16. f. Automatically adjust widths of columns.	12	
2-3	Organization, Finishing	Save table as *Departments*, print, then close table.	3	
		TOTAL POINTS	15	

Assessment 3: Create a Benefits Table
File: **AL1-C1-Griffin.accdb**

Steps	Tasks	Criteria	Value	Score
1	Table and Field Management, Accuracy, Typing, Formatting	Create new table in **AL1-C1-Griffin.accdb** with data shown in Figure 1.17, with the following specs: a. Name fields as shown in Benefits table in diagram in Figure 1.15, but create caption names for fields as shown in Figure 1.17 (e.g., for *LifeIns* create caption *Life Insurance*). b. For first column (EmpID) number, click *ID* column heading, then choose *Short Text* as the *Data Type*. Limit field size to 4, then rename field to *EmpID*. c–d. Apply *Yes/No* data type to second column, make default value a check mark (type **Yes** at Expression Builder dialog box), and provide the description *A check mark indicates the employee has signed up for the health plan;* apply *Yes/No* data type to third column, make default value a check mark, Type Yes at the Expression Builder, and provide the description *A check mark indicates the employee has signed up for the dental plan.* e–f. Apply *Currency* data type to fourth column, then apply the *Short Text* data type to the fifth column, field size *to 8* characters. g. Type data in each record as shown in Figure 1.17. h–i. Automatically adjust column widths, save table as *Benefits*.	20	
2-3	Finishing, Formatting, Organization	Display table in Print Preview, change top and left margins to 1.5 inches, print, then close Benefits table.	5	
		TOTAL POINTS	25	

Assessment 4: Sort Data
File: **AL1-C1-Griffin.accdb**

Steps	Tasks	Criteria	Value	Score
1	Organization, Accuracy	In **AL1-C1-Griffin.accdb**, open the Employees table.	2	
2-3, 5	Research, Editing, Accuracy	2. Experiment with the buttons in *Sort & Filter* group (Home tab) to learn how to sort columns of data in ascending and descending order. 3, 5. Sort records in Employees table in ascending order by *last name*; open the **Benefits** table, then sort records in descending order by life insurance amounts.	4	
4, 6	Organization, Finishing	4. After Step 3, save, print, then close Employees table. 6. After Step 5, save, print, then close Benefits table.	4	
		TOTAL POINTS	10	

Visual Benchmark

Create an Absences Table
File: **AL1-C1-Griffin.accdb**

Steps	Tasks	Criteria	Value	Score
1	Table and Field Mgt, Accuracy, Typing, Formatting	With **AL1-C1-Griffin.accdb** open, create Absences table shown in Figure 1.18 (using field names as shown in Figure 1.15), with the following specs: a. Use default AutoNumber data type for column 1, apply appropriate data types to other columns. b. Create an appropriate caption and description for *EmpID*, *AbsenceDate*, and *AbsenceReason* columns. c. Apply default value of *Sick Day* to the *AbsenceReason* column.	20	
2-4	Organization, Formatting, Finishing	Save the table as *Absences*, then print in landscape orientation with 1.5 inch top and left margins. Close Absences table, then close database **AL1-C1-Griffin.accdb**.	5	
		TOTAL POINTS	25	

Case Study

Part 1

File: **AL1-C1-Elite.accdb**

Steps	Tasks	Criteria	Value	Score
1	Organization, Accuracy, Table and Field Mgt, Typing	Create a new database named **AL1-C1-Elite.accdb** and in it, create **Limousines** table shown in database diagram in Figure 1.19. Include an appropriate caption and description for both fields, then change field size for *LimoID* field. Type records in the table (see Part 1, page 41).	15	
		TOTAL POINTS	15	

Part 2

File: **AL1-C1-Elite.accdb**

Steps	Tasks	Criteria	Value	Score
1	Table and Field Mgt, Accuracy, Typing, Formatting	With **AL1-C1-Elite.accdb** open, create **Drivers** table shown in database diagram in Figure 1.19. Include an appropriate caption and description for the fields, change field sizes where appropriate. Type records in the table (see Part 2, page 41).	20	
		TOTAL POINTS	20	

Part 3

File: **AL1-C1-Elite.accdb**

Steps	Tasks	Criteria	Value	Score
1	Table and Field Mgt, Accuracy, Typing, Formatting	With **AL1-C1-Elite.accdb** open, create Customers table shown in database diagram in Figure 1.19. Include an appropriate caption and description for the fields, change field sizes where appropriate. Type records in the table (see Part 3, page 42).	20	
		TOTAL POINTS	20	

Part 4

File: **AL1-C1-Elite.accdb**

Steps	Tasks	Criteria	Value	Score
1	Table and Field Mgt, Accuracy, Typing, Formatting	With **AL1-C1-Elite.accdb** open, create **Bookings** table shown in Figure 1.19; include an appropriate caption and description for the fields, change field sizes where appropriate. Type records in the table (see Part 4, page 42).	20	

Steps	Tasks	Criteria	Value	Score
2	Formatting, Finishing	Automatically adjust column widths of each table to accommodate longest entry in each column. Print each table so all records fit on one page.	5	
		TOTAL POINTS	25	

Benchmark Access 2013 Level 1, Chapter 2

Skills Check

Assessment 1: Create Relationships in an Insurance Company Database
File: **AL1-C2-CopperState.accdb**

Steps	Tasks	Criteria	Value	Score
1-2	Organization, Accuracy	Open **AL1-C2-CopperState.accdb**, enable the contents, and open the Claims table.	3	
3-7	Table and Field Management, Accuracy	3. Display table in Design view, define *ClaimID* field as primary key, click Save button on Quick Access toolbar, then close the Claims table. 4–7. Display Relationships window, then insert *Clients, Claims,* and *Coverage* tables. Create a one-to-many relationship with *ClientID* field in Clients table as the "one" and *ClientID* field in Claims table as the "many." Enforce referential integrity and cascade fields and records. Create a one-to-many relationship with *ClientID* field in Clients table as the "one" and *ClientID* field in Coverage table as the "many." Enforce referential integrity and cascade fields and records. Create a one-to-many relationship with *LicenseNo* field in Coverage table as the "one" and *LicenseNo* field in Claims table as the "many." Enforce referential integrity and cascade fields and records.	12	
8-9	Organization, Finishing	Save, then print relationships. Close relationships report without saving it, then close Relationships window.	5	
		TOTAL POINTS	20	

Assessment 2: Create a new Table and Relate the Table
File: **AL1-C2-CopperState.accdb**

Steps	Tasks	Criteria	Value	Score
1	Table and Field Mgt, Accuracy	In **AL1-C2-CopperState.accdb**, create Offices table as shown in Fig. 2.14 in the following way: Change data type of the first column to *Short Text*. The field size to 2. Change default value for *State* field to *AZ*.	6	

Steps	Tasks	Criteria	Value	Score
2-3	Typing, Formatting, Finishing	2–3. After typing records, adjust column widths to accommodate longest entry in each column, then save Offices table, print, and close.	8	
4-6	Table and Field Mgt, Accuracy	Display Relationships window, then add Offices and Assignments tables to it. Create a one-to-many relationship with *OfficeID* field in Offices table as the "one" and *OfficeID* field in Assignments table as the "many." Enforce referential integrity and cascade fields and records. Create a one-to-one relationship with *ClientID* field in Clients table and *ClientID* field in Assignments table. Enforce referential integrity and cascade fields and records.	6	
7-8	Organization, Finishing	Save, print relationships in landscape. Close relationships report without saving, then close Relationships window.	5	
		TOTAL POINTS	25	

Assessment 3: Delete and Edit Records in Tables
File: **AL1-C2-CopperState.accdb**

Steps	Tasks	Criteria	Value	Score
1-4	Organization, Editing	In **AL1-C2-CopperState.accdb**, open Clients table. 2–3. Delete record for Harold McDougal (client number 9879). (At the message about relationships, click Yes.) Delete record for Vernon Cook (client number 7335) and click Yes at relationships message. 4. Change client number for Paul Vuong from *4300* to *2560*.	5	
5-6	Finishing, Organization	Print Clients table in landscape orientation, then close. Open Claims table, print, then close.	5	
		TOTAL POINTS	10	

Assessment 4: Display and Edit Records in a Subdatasheet
File: **AL1-C2-CopperState.accdb**

Steps	Tasks	Criteria	Value	Score
1	Organization, Accuracy	In **AL1-C2-CopperState.accdb**, open Clients table.	3	

Steps	Tasks	Criteria	Value	Score
2, 4-8, 12-13	Table and Field Management, Accuracy	2, 4. Click expand indicator that displays at left side of record for Erin Hagedorn. At Insert Subdatasheet dialog box, click *Claims*, then click OK. After Step 3, click collapse indicator at left side of record for Erin Hagedorn. 5. Remove connection between Clients and Claims tables by clicking More button in Records group (Home tab), pointing to *Subdatasheet*, then clicking *Remove*. 6–8. Click More button in Records group, point to *Subdatasheet*, then click *Subdatasheet*. At Insert Subdatasheet dialog box, click *Coverage* in list box, then click OK. Expand all records by clicking More button, pointing to *Subdatasheet*, then clicking *Expand All*. 12. Click in any field heading, then collapse all records. 13. Remove the connection between the Clients and Coverage tables.	12	
3, 9-11	Editing	3. After Step 2, change amount of claim from *$1,450.00* to *$1,797.00*, change Erin's street address from *4818 Oakes Boulevard* to *763 51st Avenue*, then change her ZIP code from *85018* to *85014*. 9. After Step 8, change telephone number for Claire Azevedo (client number 1379) from *480-555-2154* to *480-555-2143*, then insert check marks in *Medical* and *UninsMotorist* fields. 10–11. Change last name of Joanne Donnelly (client number 1574) to *Marquez*, then remove check mark from *Collision* field. Display record for Brenda Lazzuri (client number 3156), then insert check marks in *UninsMotorist* and *Collision* fields for both vehicles.	10	
14-15	Organization, Finishing	Save, print, then close Clients table. (Make sure table displays in landscape orientation.) Open Coverage table, print, then close.	5	
		TOTAL POINTS	30	

Visual Benchmark

Create an Agents Table

File: **AL1-C2-CarefreeTravel.accdb**

Steps	Tasks	Criteria	Value	Score
1-2	Table and Field Mgt, Accuracy, Typing, Finishing, Organization	With **AL1-C2-CarefreeTravel.accdb** open, create Bookings table shown in Fig. 2.15. Data types and field sizes are user-determined. Create caption for each field name and description for each field (user-determined). Save, print, then close Bookings table.	15	

Steps	Tasks	Criteria	Value	Score
3-5	Table Management, Accuracy	Create a relationship between the Agents table and Bookings table. User determines the "one" and "many" Enforce referential integrity and cascade fields and records. Create a relationship between the Tours table and Bookings table. User determines what table contains the "one" and what table contains the "many". Enforce referential integrity and cascade fields and records. Save, print the relationships, close the Relationships window.	6	
6-9	Organization, Editing, Finishing	6. Open Agents table. 7–8. Change AgentID for Wayne Postovic from 137 to 115. Change Jenna Williamson's last name to Parr. 9. Print, then close Agents table.	5	
10-11	Organization, Formatting, Finishing	Open Bookings table, print, then close. Close the **AL1-C2-CarefreeTravel.accdb** database.	4	
		TOTAL POINTS	30	

Case Study

Part 1

File: **AL1-C2-GoldStar.accdb**

Steps	Tasks	Criteria	Value	Score
1	Organization, Accuracy, Table and Field Management, Typing	Create a new database named **AL1-C2-GoldStar.accdb** and in it, create Clients table shown in database diagram. Include appropriate caption and description for the fields. **Field Size**: ClientID: 3, ServiceID: 4, RateID: 1 Field sizes for the *State*, *ZIP*, and *Telephone* fields are user-determined. Set default value for *City* field to *St. Louis* and for *State* field to *MO*. Type the records in the table (see Part 1, bottom of page 74, top of page 75).	25	

Steps	Tasks	Criteria	Value	Score
2	Table and Field Management, Typing, Accuracy	Create Services table shown in database diagram. Change *ServiceID* field size to 4. Type the Services table records (see Part 1, middle of page 76). Create Rates table shown in database diagram. Change *RateID* field size to 1. Type the following records: 　　RateID: **A**　　　　　RateID: **B** 　　HrlyRate: **$75.50**　　HrlyRate: **$65.00** 　　RateID: **C**　　　　　RateID: **D** 　　HrlyRate: **$59.75**　　HrlyRate: **$50.50** Create Billing table shown in database diagram. Field Size: *BillingID:* 2, *ClientID:* 3, and *RateID:* 1. Apply appropriate data types to the fields. Type the following records in the table (see Part 1, bottom of page 76 and top of page 77). Automatically adjust column widths of each table to accommodate longest entry in each column. Print each table on one page. *Hint:* ***If necessary change to landscape orientation and change the margins.***	35	
		TOTAL POINTS	60	

Part 2
File: **AL1-C2-GoldStar.accdb**

Steps	Tasks	Criteria	Value	Score
1	Table Mgt, Accuracy, Formatting	With **AL1-C2-GoldStar.accdb** open, create one-to-many relationships required to connect the tables. (Use Fig. 2.17 as a guide.) Size of Clients table will need to be increased to view all fields.	8	
	Finishing	Print relationships report.	2	
		TOTAL POINTS	10	

Part 3
File: **AL1-C2-GoldStar.accdb**

Steps	Tasks	Criteria	Value	Score
1	Editing	Open Services table, then make following changes to field values in *ServiceID* field: 　Change *GS-1* to *GS-A* 　Change *GS-2* to *GS-B* 　Change *GS-3* to *GS-C*	6	
2	Organization, Finishing	Save, print, then close Services table.	3	

Steps	Tasks	Criteria	Value	Score
3	Organization, Editing, Typing	Open Clients table, delete record for client number 112, then insert following record: ClientID: **108** Name: **Cedar Ridge Products** Address: **6400 Olive Street** City: (default value) State: (default value ZIP: **63114** Contact: **Penny Childers** Telephone: **(314) 555-7660** ServiceID: **GS-B** RateID: **B**	10	
4	Organization, Finishing	Save, print, then close Clients table. Open Billing table, print, then close the table. Close **AL1-C2-GoldStar.accdb**.	6	
		TOTAL POINTS	25	

Benchmark Access 2013 Level 1, Chapter 3

Skills Check

Assessment 1: Design Queries in a Legal Services Database
File: **AL1-C3-WarrenLegal.accdb**

Steps	Tasks	Criteria	Value	Score
1-2	Organization, Accuracy	Open **AL1-C3-WarrenLegal.accdb**, enable the contents.	3	
3-8	Queries, Accuracy, Finishing, Organization	3. Design query that extracts information from Billing table with the following specs: a. Include fields *BillingID, ClientID, CategoryID* in query. b. Extract records with *SE* category. (Type **SE** in *Criteria* row field in *CategoryID* column.) c–d. Save query as *SECategoryBillingQuery*, then print and close query. 4. Design query that extracts information from Billing table with the following specs: a. Include fields *BillingID, ClientID, Date*. b. Extract records in *Date* field with dates between 6/08/2015 and 6/15/2015. c–d. Save query as *June8-15BillingQuery*, then print and close query. 5. Design query that extracts information from Clients table with the following specs: a. Include fields *FirstName, LastName, City*. b. Extract records with any city or than Kent in *City* field. c–d. Save query as *ClientsNotInKentQuery*, then print and close query. 6. Design query that extracts information from two tables with the following specs: a–b. Include *BillingID, ClientID, Date, Rate*ID from Billing table and field *Rate* from Rates table. c. Extract those records with rate ID's greater than 2. d–e. Save query as *RateIDGreaterthan2Query*, then print and close query. 7. Design query that extracts information from three tables with the following specs: a–c. Include *AttorneyID, FName,* and *LName* from the Attorneys table; *FirstName* and *LastName* from the Clients table; and *Date* and *Hours* from the Billing table. d. Extract records with an AttorneyID of *12*. e–f. Save as *Attorney12Query*, then print and close. 8. Design query that extracts information from four tables with the following specs: a–d. Include *AttorneyID, FName,* and *LName* from the Attorneys table; *Category* from the Categories table; *RateID* and *Rate* from the Rates table; and *Date* and *Hours* from the Billing table. e. Extract records with an *AttorneyID* of *17* and *RateID* of *4*. f. Save as *Attorney17RateID4Query*, print the query in landscape orientation, then close query.	40	

Steps	Tasks	Criteria	Value	Score
9	Queries, Editing, Accuracy, Finishing, Organization	Open the *Attorney17RateID4Query* query, click View button tab to display query in Design view, then modify query so it displays records with a *RateID* of *4* with an *AttorneyID* of *17* and also *19* by making the following changes: a–b. Click below field value *17* in *AttorneyID* column, then type **19**; click below field value *4* in *RateID* column, type **4**, and then press Enter. c. Run query. d. Save query with new name *Attorney17&19RateID4Query*. *Hint: Done at Save As dialog box. Display dialog box by clicking File tab, then clicking Save Object As.* e. Print query in landscape, then close query.	7	
		TOTAL POINTS	50	

Assessment 2: Use the Simple Query Wizard and Design Queries
File: **AL1-C3-WarrenLegal.accdb**

Steps	Tasks	Criteria	Value	Score
1–4	Queries, Accuracy, Formatting, Finishing, Organization	1. With **AL1-C3-WarrenLegal.accdb** open, use Simple Query Wizard to extract specific information from three tables with the following specs: a. At first Simple Query Wizard dialog box, include following fields: From Attorneys table: *AttorneyID, FName, LName*; from Categories table: *Category*; from Billing table: *Hours*. b. At second Simple Query Wizard dialog box, click Next. c. At third Simple Query Wizard dialog box, click *Modify the query design* option, then click Finish button. d–e. At query window, insert *14* in *Criteria* row field in *AttorneyID* column, then run query. f–g. Save query with default name, print, then close. 2. Create a query in Design view with Billing table with the following specs: a. Insert *Hours* field from Billing table to first, second, third, fourth *Field* row fields. b. Click Totals button in Show/Hide group. c–g. Insert *Sum* in first *Total* row field; *Min* in second *Total* row field; *Max* in third *Total* row field; and *Count* in fourth *Total* row field. Run query. h–j. Automatically adjust widths of columns, save as *HoursAmountQuery*, print, then close. 3. Create query in Design view with the following specs: a–e. Add Attorneys and Billing table to query window; insert *FName* field from Attorneys table to first *Field* row field; insert *LName* field from Attorneys table to second *Field* row field; insert *AttorneyID* field from Billing table to third *Field* row field; insert *Hours* field from Billing table to fourth *Field* row field. f–g. Click Totals button in Show/Hide group, then insert *Sum* in fourth *Total* row field in *Hours* column. h–j. Run query, save as *AttorneyHoursQuery*; then print and close query. 4. Create query in Design view with the following specs: a. Add Attorneys, Clients, Categories, and Billing tables to query window. b–e. Insert *AttorneyID* field from Attorneys table to first *Field* row field; *ClientID* field from Billing table to second *Field* row field; *Category* field from Categories table to third *Field* row field; and insert *Hours* field from Billing table to fourth *Field* row field. f–h. Run query, save as *AttorneyClientHours*, then print and close query.	40	
		TOTAL POINTS	40	

Assessment 3: Create a Crosstab Query and Use the Find Duplicates and Find Unmatched Query Wizards
File: **AL1-C3-WarrenLegal.accdb**

Steps	Tasks	Criteria	Value	Score
1	Queries, Accuracy, Formatting, Finishing	With **AL1-C3-WarrenLegal.accdb** database open, create crosstab query that summarizes hours by attorney by category with the following specs: a. At first Crosstab Query Wizard dialog box, click *Queries* option in *View* section, then click *Query: AttorneyClientHours* in list box. b–e. b. At second dialog box with *AttorneyID* selected in *Available Fields* list box, click One Field button; c. at third dialog box, click *Category* in list box; d. at fourth dialog box, click *Hours* in *Fields* list box, then click *Sum* in *Functions* list box; and e. at fifth dialog box, select current name in *What do you want to name your query?* text box, then type **HoursByAttorneyByCategory**. f–g. Display query in Print Preview, change to landscape orientation, change left and right margins to 0.5 inch, then print and close query.	12	
2	Queries, Accuracy, Finishing, Organization	Use Find Duplicates Query Wizard to find clients with same last name, with the following specs: a. At first wizard dialog box, click *Table: Clients* in list box; b. at second wizard dialog box, click *LastName* in *Available fields* list box, then click One Field button; c. at third wizard dialog box, click All Fields button d. at fourth wizard dialog box, name query *DuplicateLastNamesQuery*. e. Print query in *landscape* orientation, then close query.	8	
3	Queries, Accuracy, Formatting, Finishing, Organization	Use Find Unmatched Query Wizard to find all clients who do not have any billing hours, with the following specs: a. At first wizard dialog box, click *Table: Clients* in list box; b. at second wizard dialog box, click *Table: Billing* in list box; c. at third wizard dialog box, make sure *ClientID* is selected in *Fields in 'Clients'* list box in *Fields in 'Billing'* list box; d. and at fourth wizard dialog box, click All Fields button to move all fields from *Available fields* list box to *Selected fields* list box. e. At fifth wizard dialog box, click Finish. (Let wizard determine query name: *Clients Without Matching Billing*.)	8	
4	Finishing, Organization	Print query in landscape orientation, then close query.	2	
		TOTAL POINTS	30	

Assessment 4: Design and Hide Fields in a Query
File: **AL1-C3-WarrenLegal.accdb**

Steps	Tasks	Criteria	Value	Score
1	Queries, Accuracy, Organization, Finishing	In **AL1-C3-WarrenLegal.accdb**, design a query: a. At Show Table dialog box, add Clients table, Billing table, and Rates table. b. At query window, insert fields in *Field* row fields: 　　Clients table: *FirstName, LastName* 　　Billing table: *Hours* 　　Rates table: *Rate* c. Insert in the fifth *Field* row field calculated field *Total:[Hours]*[Rate]*. d. Hide the *Hours* and the *Rate* fields. e–g. Run query, save as *ClientBillingQuery*, then print and close query.	12	
2	Organization	Close **AL1-C3-WarrenLegal.accdb**.	3	
		TOTAL POINTS	15	

Visual Benchmark

Creating Relationships and Designing a Query
File: **AL1-C3-MRInvestments.accdb**

Steps	Tasks	Criteria	Value	Score
1	Organization, Accuracy	Open **AL1-C3-MRInvestments.accdb**, enable the contents.	3	
2	Table and Field Management, Accuracy	Display Relationships window, then create relationships shown in Fig. 3.7. Enforce referential integrity and cascade fields and records.	5	
3-4	Organization, Finishing	Save, then print the relationships. Close relationships report without saving, then close Relationships window.	3	
5-7	Queries, Accuracy, Organization, Finishing	Design query shown in Fig. 3.8, run it, save query with an appropriate name, then print.	7	
8	Organization	Close **AL1-C3-MRInvestments.accdb**.	2	
		TOTAL POINTS	20	

Case Study

Part 1

File: **AL1-C3-Skyline.accdb**

Steps	Tasks	Criteria	Value	Score
1	Organization, Table and Field Management, Accuracy	Open **AL1-C3-Skyline.accdb**, enable the contents, then create following relationships (enforce referential integrity and cascade fields and records): **Field Name** **"One" Table** **"Many" Table** *EmployeeID* Employees Banquets *ItemID* Inventory Orders *SupplierID* Suppliers Orders *SupplierID* Suppliers Inventory *EventID* Events Banquets	12	
2	Organization, Finishing	Save, then print the relationships.	3	
		TOTAL POINTS	15	

Part 2

File: **AL1-C3-Skyline.accdb**

Steps	Tasks	Criteria	Value	Score
1	Queries, Accuracy, Organization, Finishing	Create a separate query for each bulleted item listed below; save, name, and print queries (user-determined names). • Suppliers in Fort Myers (from Suppliers table, include supplier identification number, supplier name, city, and telephone number) • Suppliers not located in Fort Myers (from Suppliers table, include supplier identification number and supplier name, city, and telephone number) • Employees hired in 2012 (from Employees table, include employee identification number, first and last names, and hire date) • Employees that are signed up for health insurance (from Employees table, include employee first and last names, and health insurance field) • Wedding receptions (event identification WR) booked in banquet room (from Banquets table, include reservation identification number; reservation date; event identification; and first name, last name, and telephone number of person making reservation) • Banquet reservations between 6/14/2015 and 6/30/2015 and employees making the reservations (from Banquets table, include reservation identification number; reservation date; and first name, last name, and telephone number of person making reservation; from Employees table, include employee first and last names) • Banquet reservations that have not been confirmed and employees making reservations (from Banquets table, include reservation identification number; reservation date; confirmed field; and first and last names of person making reservation; from Employees table, include employee first and last names) • Banquet room reserved by someone whose last name begins with *Wie* (from Employees table, include first and last names of employee who booked reservation and from Banquets table include first and last names and telephone number of person making reservation) • A query that inserts a calculated field that multiplies number of units ordered by unit price for all orders for supplier number 2 (from Orders table, include order identification number, supplier identification number, units ordered, and unit price; from Inventory table, include item field)	40	
		TOTAL POINTS	40	

Part 3
File: **AL1-C3-Skyline.accdb**

Steps	Tasks	Criteria	Value	Score
1	Queries, Accuracy, Finishing, Organization	Use Find Duplicates Query Wizard to find duplicate items in Orders table, with the following specs: • At first wizard dialog box, specify Orders table. • At second wizard dialog box, specify *ItemID* as duplicate-value field. • At third wizard dialog, specify all fields for query. • At fourth wizard dialog box, user-determined query name. • Print, then close query.	7	
2	Queries, Accuracy, Finishing, Organization	Use Find Unmatched Query Wizard to find all employees who have not made a banquet reservation, with the following specs: • At first wizard dialog box, specify Employees table. • At second wizard dialog box, specify Banquets table. • At third wizard dialog box, specify *EmployeeID* field in both list boxes. • At fourth wizard dialog box, specify that you want all of fields in query. • At fifth wizard dialog box, user-determined query name. • Print query in landscape with 0.5-inch left and right margins, then close.	8	
3	Queries, Accuracy, Formatting, Finishing, Organization	Use Crosstab Query Wizard to create query that summarizes order amounts by supplier, with the following specs: • At first wizard dialog box, specify Orders table. • At second wizard dialog box, specify *SupplierID* field for row headings. • At third wizard dialog box, specify *ItemID* field for column headings. • At fourth wizard dialog box, click *UnitPrice* in *Fields* list box, then click *Sum* in *Functions* list box. • At fifth wizard dialog box, user-determined query name. • Automatically adjust columns in query. • Print query in landscape, then close.	15	
		TOTAL POINTS	30	

Part 4
File: **AL1-C3-CS-Queries.docx**

Steps	Tasks	Criteria	Value	Score
1	Queries, Accuracy, Organization, Finishing	Design at least three additional queries that require fields from at least two tables. Run the queries, then save and print them.	15	
2	Writing, Formatting, Organization, Finishing	In Microsoft Word, write the query information and include specific information about each query. Format the document to enhance visual appeal. Save as **AL1-C3-CS-Queries**, then print and close the document.	15	
		TOTAL POINTS	30	

Benchmark Access 2013 Level 1, Chapter 4

Skills Check

Assessment 1: Create an Employees Table with the Input Mask and Lookup Wizards

File: **AL1-C4-Hudson.accdb**

Steps	Tasks	Criteria	Value	Score
1	Database Management, Organization	Open Access, create a new database using following steps: a–b. At Access 2013 opening screen, select the Blank desktop template. Click in *File Name* text box, then type **AL1-C4-Hudson**. c–d. Click Browse button at right side of *File Name* text box, at File New Database dialog box, navigate to AL1C4 folder on storage medium, then click OK. e. Click *Create* button.	5	
2	Table and Field Management, Formatting, Controls, Accuracy	Create Employees table in Design view shown in Fig. 4.14, with the following specs: a. Limit EmpID field size to 4, FirstName and LastName fields to 20, and Address field to 30. b–c. Create default value of Pueblo for City field, then create default value of CO for State field. d. Create input mask for telephone number. e. Use Lookup Wizard to specify field choices for Status field, including the following choices: *Full-time, Part-time, Temporary, Contract*.	20	
3-5	Organization, Typing, Formatting, Finishing	3. Save table, switch to Datasheet view, then enter records as shown in Fig. 4.15. 4. Adjust the column widths. 5. Save table, then print in landscape orientation.	15	
6-9	Formatting, Typing, Organization	6. Switch to Design view, then add a row immediately above *FirstName* row. Type **Title** in *Field Name* field, limit field size to 20, type description **Enter employee job title**. 7–8. Delete *HireDate* field, then move *Status* field so it is positioned between *EmpID* row and *Title* row. 9. Save table, then switch to Datasheet view.	8	

Steps	Tasks	Criteria	Value	Score
10-13	Typing, Accuracy, Formatting, Organization, Finishing	10. Enter following information in *Title* field: **Emp#** **Title**　　　　　　**Emp#** **Title** 1466　**Design Director**　　2301　**Assistant** 1790　**Assistant**　　　　2440　**Assistant** 1947　**Resources Director**　3035　**Clerk** 1955　**Accountant**　　　3129　**Clerk** 1994　**Assistant**　　　　3239　**Assistant** 2019　**Production Director**　4002　**Contractor** 2120　**Assistant**　　　　4884　**Contractor** 11. Apply the following text formatting to the table: 　a. Change font to *Arial* and font size to *10*. 　b. Center data in *EmpID* field and *State* field columns. 　c. Apply the Aqua Blue 2 alternating row color (Standard Colors section) to the table 12. Adjust column widths. 13. Save table, then print in landscape orientation with left and right margins to 0.5 inch	14	
14-15	Editing	Find all occurrences of *Director* and replace with *Manager*; find all occurrences of *Assistant* and replace with *Associate*.	4	
16	Organization, Finishing	Save the table, print in *landscape* orientation with left and right margins of *0.5 inch*, then close table.	4	
		TOTAL POINTS	75	

Assessment 2: Create a Projects Table
File: **AL1-C4-Hudson.accdb**

Steps	Tasks	Criteria	Value	Score
1	Table and Field Management, Formatting, Accuracy	In **AL1-C4-Hudson.accdb**, create Projects table in Design view. Include following fields (make sure *ProjID* field is identified as primary key), create appropriate descriptions: **Field Name**　　**Data Type** *ProjID*　*Short* Text (field size = 4) *EmpID*　*Short* Text (field size = 4) *BegDate* Date/Time *EndDate*　　　Date/Time *EstCosts* Currency	10	
2	Typing, Accuracy	Save table, switch to Datasheet view, then type data or choose a field entry in the specified fields (see Step 2, pages 165–166 for the data).	15	
3-4	Formatting, Finishing, Organization	Adjust the column widths. Save, print, then close *Projects* table.	5	
		TOTAL POINTS	30	

Assessment 3: Create an Expenses Table with a Validation Rule and Input Mask
File: **AL1-C4-Hudson.accdb**

Steps	Tasks	Criteria	Value	Score
1	Table and Field Management, Formatting, Controls, Accuracy	In **AL1-C4-Hudson.accdb**, create Expenses table in Design view. Include following fields (make sure *ItemID* is identified as the primary key), include appropriate descriptions: **Field Name**　　**Data Type** *ItemID*　　　　AutoNumber *EmpID*　　　　*Short* Text (field size = 4) *ProjID*　　　　*Short* Text (field size = 4) *Amount*　　　　Currency (Type condition in *Validation Rule* property box that states entry must be \$500 or less. Type error message in *Validation Text* property box.) 　*DateSubmitted*　　Date/Time (Use Input Mask to control date so it is entered as a short date.)	15	
2	Organization, Typing, Accuracy	Save table, switch to Datasheet view, then type data or choose a field entry in specified fields (see Step 2, page 166 for the data).	20	
3-5	Formatting, Editing, Organization, Finishing	3. Adjust column widths. 4. Insert total row with following specs: 　a. Click Totals button in the Records group in Home tab. 　b. Click in blank field in *Amount* column in the *Total* row. 　c–d. Click down-pointing arrow at left side of field, then click 　　*Sum* at the drop-down list. Click in any other field. 5. Save, print, then close Expenses table.	8	
6-9	Table Management, Accuracy, Organization, Finishing	6–8. Create one-to-many relationship where *EmpID* in Employees table is the "one" and *EmpID* in Expenses table is the "many;" create one-to-many relationship where *EmpID* in Employees table is the "one" and *EmpID* in Projects table is the "many;" and create one-to-many relationship where *ProjID* in Projects table is the "one" and *ProjID* in the Expenses table is the "many." (Enforce referential integrity and cascade fields and records for all three relationships.) 9. Save relationships, print, then close relationships report window and relationships window.	10	

Steps	Tasks	Criteria	Value	Score
10-13	Queries, Accuracy, Organization, Finishing	10. Design and run query that displays all full-time employees, with the following specs: a. Insert Employees table in query window. b. Insert *EmpID*, *FirstName*, *LastName*, and *Status* fields. c. Click in check box in *Show* row field in *EmpID* column to remove check mark. d. Extract full-time employees. e–f. Save query as *FTEmpsQuery*, then print and close it. 11. Design and run query that displays projects managed by employee number 1947, with the following specs: a. Insert Employees and Projects tables in query window. b–c. Insert *EmpID*, *FirstName*, and *LastName* fields from Employees table, then *ProjID* field from Projects table. d. Extract projects managed by employee number 1947. e–f. Save query as ***ProjsManagedByEmp1947Query***, then print and close query. 12. Design and run query that displays expense amounts over $250.00 and the employees submitting the expense, with the following specs: a. Insert Expenses and Employees tables in query window. b–c. Insert *ItemID*, *Amount*, and *DateSubmitted* fields from Expenses table, then *FirstName* and *LastName* fields from Employees table. d. Hide *ItemID* field in query results. e. Extract expense amounts over $250. f–g. Save query as ***ExpensesOver$250Query***, then print the query and close it. 13. Design and run query that displays expenses submitted by employee number 1947, with the following specs: a. Insert Employees and Expenses tables in query window. b–c. Insert *EmpID*, *FirstName*, and *LastName* fields from Employees table, then *ProjID*, *Amount*, and *DateSubmitted* from Expenses table. d. Click in check box in the Show row field in the *EmpID* column to remove check mark. e. Extract expenses submitted by employee number 1947. f–g. Save query as ***ExpSubmittedBy1947Query***, then print the query and close.	32	
		TOTAL POINTS	85	

Assessment 4: Edit the Employees Table
File: **AL1-C4-Hudson.accdb**

Steps	Tasks	Criteria	Value	Score
1-5	Organization, Controls, Editing	1. In **AL1-C4-Hudson.accdb**, open Employees table. 2. Display table in Design view, click in *ZIP* field row *Data Type* column, then click in *Input Mask* property box in *Field Properties* section. 3. Use Input Mask Wizard to create nine-digit ZIP code input mask. 4. Save table, then switch to Datasheet view. 5. Delete record for employee number 3035 (Alia Shandra), employee number 3129 (Gloria Cushman), and employee number 4884 (Simon Banister).	14	
6	Typing, Accuracy	Insert two new records (see Step 6, page 168).	8	
7	Formatting	Adjust width of *ZIP* column. (Only the two new records will contain nine-digit ZIP code.)	2	
8-9	Organization, Formatting, Finishing	Save Employees table. Display table in Print Preview, change to *landscape*, change left and right margins to *0.5 inch*. Print, then close table. Close **Al1-C4-Hudson.accdb**	6	
		TOTAL POINTS	30	

Visual Benchmark

Design and Format a Query
File: **AL1-C4-AlpineServices.accdb**

Steps	Tasks	Criteria	Value	Score
1	Organization, Accuracy	Open **AL1-C4-AlpineServices.accdb** from the AL1C4 folder on storage medium, enable contents.	3	
2	Editing, Typing, Formatting	Design, run query that displays in Figure 4.16. Change the font for the data to *12-point Candara*, adding alternating row color, adjust column widths so query displays as in Figure 4.16	14	
3	Organization, Finishing	Save, print query in landscape, then close. Close **AL1-C4-AlpineServices.accdb**.	3	
		TOTAL POINTS	20	

Case Study

Part 1

File: **AL1-C4-BlueRidge.accdb**

Steps	Tasks	Criteria	Value	Score
1	Database Management, Table and Field Management, Controls, Organization	Create new database named **AL1-C4-BlueRidge.accdb**, then create Representatives table with following fields: • Create field for representative identification number, change data type to *Short Text*, and limit field size to 3. (This is primary key field.) • Create a field for representative's first name, limit field size *to 20*, then create field for representative's last name and limit field size to 20. • Create field for representative's telephone number and use Input Mask Wizard. • Create field for insurance plan and use Lookup Wizard to include four options: *Platinum, Premium, Standard, None.* • Create field for yearly bonus amount, then type a validation rule that states bonus must be less than $10,001; include an error message (user-determined).	25	
2	Typing, Accuracy, Formatting, Finishing, Organization	• In Datasheet view, enter six records in table. (User determined) When entering data, make sure at least two representatives will receive a yearly bonus over $5000 and at least two representatives are signed up for *Platinum* insurance plan. • Insert total row that sums yearly bonus amounts. • Change font for data in table to *Cambria*, change font size to *10,* and apply *light green alternating row color*. Center data in representative identification column. • Adjust column widths. • Save Representatives table, print in landscape, then close.	15	
		TOTAL POINTS	40	

Part 2
File: **AL1-C4-BlueRidge.accdb**

Steps	Tasks	Criteria	Value	Score
1	Table and Field Management, Controls, Accuracy	In **AL-C4-BlueRidge.accdb**, create second table named Clients (table contains info on companies doing business with Blue Ridge Enterprises) with following fields: • Create field for client identification number, limit field size to 2. (This is primary key field.) • Create field for representative identification number (use same field name you used in Part 1 in Representatives table) and limit field size to 3. • Create fields for company name, address, city, state (or province), and ZIP (or postal code). Insert student's city as default value for city field and insert student's two-letter state or province abbreviation as default value for state or province field. • Create field for client's telephone number and use an Input Mask. • Create field for client's type of business, insert *Wholesaler* as default value.	20	
2	Typing, Accuracy, Formatting, Finishing, Organization	• In Datasheet view, enter at least eight companies. (User determined) Make sure to use representative identification numbers in Clients table that match numbers in Representatives table. Identify at least one company as *Retailer* rather than *Wholesaler,* make at least one representative represent two or more companies. • Change font for data in table to *Cambria,* font size to *10,* and apply *light green alternating row color* (same color chosen in Part 1). Center data in client identification column, representative identification column, and state (or province) column. • Adjust column widths. • Save Clients table, print in landscape, then close table.	15	
		TOTAL POINTS	35	

Part 3
File: **AL1-C4-BlueRidge.accdb**

Steps	Tasks	Criteria	Value	Score
1	Table Management, Organization, Finishing	Create one-to-many relationship with representative identification number in Representatives table as the "one" and representative identification number in the Clients table as the "many." Save relationship, print report, then close without saving.	10	
		TOTAL POINTS	10	

Part 4

File: **AL1-C4-BlueRidge.docx**

Steps	Tasks	Criteria	Value	Score
1	Queries, Accuracy, Organization, Finishing	Create and print following queries: • Create query that extracts records of representatives *earning yearly bonus over $5000*. (User determines fields to insert in query window.) Save, print, then close query. • Create query to extract records of representatives signed up for *Platinum* insurance plan. (User determines fields to insert in query window.) Save, print, then close query. • Create query that extracts records of wholesale clients. (User determines fields to insert in query window.) Save, print, then close query. • Create query that extracts records of companies represented by specific representative. (Use representative identification number entered in Part 2 that represents two or more companies.) Save, print, then close query.	20	
		TOTAL POINTS	20	

Benchmark Access 2013 Level 1, Unit 1 Performance Assessment

Skills Check

Assessment 1: Create Tables in a Cornerstone Catering Database
File: **AL1-U1-Cornerstone.accdb**

Steps	Tasks	Criteria	Value	Score

1	Database Management, Organization, Table and Field Management, Controls, Accuracy	In Access, create a new database and save it as **AL1-U1-Cornerstone**.
		Create table named *Employees* that includes fields shown below. If no data type specified for a field, use *Short Text*. User-determined field size(s). Specify same field size for field contained in different tables. For example, if field size of 2 used for *EmployeeID* field in Employees table, specify field size of 2 for *EmployeeID* field in Events table. Provide descriptions for each field.
		    EmployeeID (primary key)
		    FirstName
		    LastName
		    CellPhone (Use Input Mask Wizard for this field.)
			10	

2	Typing, Accuracy	Switch to Datasheet view, then enter data in appropriate fields (see Step 2, pages 171–172).	12	

Steps	Tasks	Criteria	Value	Score
3-5	Formatting, Organization, Finishing	Change font for data in table to Cambria, font size to 10, then apply light blue alternating row color. Center-align data in the *EmployeeID* column. Adjust column widths. Save, print, then close Employees table.	8	

6	Table and Field Mgt, Accuracy	Create table named *Plans* that includes following fields:
		    PlanCode (primary key)
		    Plan
			8	

7	Typing, Accuracy	After creating table, switch to Datasheet view, then enter data in appropriate fields (Step 7, middle of page 172).	8	
8-10	Formatting, Organization, Finishing	Change font for data in table to Cambria, font size to 10, then apply light blue alternating row color. Center-align the data in *PlanCode* column. Adjust the column widths. Save, print, and then close Plans table.	8	

11	Table and Field Mgt, Accuracy	Create table named *Prices* that includes following fields:
		    PriceCode (primary key)
		    PricePerPerson (identify data type as Currency)
			8	

12	Typing, Accuracy	Switch to Datasheet view, then enter data in appropriate fields (see Step 12, top of page 173).	6	
13-15	Formatting, Organization, Finishing	Change font for data in table to Cambria, font size to 10, then apply light blue alternating row color. Center-align data in both columns. Adjust column widths. Save, print, then close Prices table.	8	

16	Table and Field Management, Accuracy	Create table named *Clients* that includes following fields:
		    ClientID (primary key)
		    ClientName
		    StreetAddress
		    City
		    State (Insert *NM* as the default value.)
		    ZIP
		    Telephone (Use Input Mask Wizard for this field.)
			10	

17	Typing, Accuracy	Switch to Datasheet view, then enter data in appropriate fields (see Step 17, pages 173–74).	15	
18-21	Formatting, Organization, Finishing	Change font for data in table to Cambria, font size to 10, then apply light blue alternating row color. Center-align data in *ClientID* column. Adjust the column widths. Save table, print in landscape, then close Clients table.	8	

22	Table and Field Management, Accuracy	Create table named *Events* that includes following fields:
		    EventID (primary key; identify as AutoNumber)
		    ClientID
		    EmployeeID
		    DateOfEvent (identify data type as Date/Time)
		    PlanCode
		    PriceCode
		    NumberOfPeople (identify data type as Number)
			12	

23	Typing, Accuracy	Switch to Datasheet view, then enter data in appropriate fields (see Step 23, pages 174–175).	12	

Steps	Tasks	Criteria	Value	Score
24-26	Formatting, Organization, Finishing	Change font for data in table to Cambria, font size to 10, then apply light blue alternating row color. Center-align in all columns except *DateOfEvent* column. Adjust column widths. Save, print, then close Events table.	12	
		TOTAL POINTS	145	

Assessment 2: Create Relationships Between Tables
File: **AL1-U1-Cornerstone.accdb**

Steps	Tasks	Criteria	Value	Score
1	Table Management	In **AL1-U1-Cornerstone.accdb**, create the following one-to-many relationships and enforce referential integrity: a. *ClientID* in Clients table is the "one" and *ClientID* in Events table is the "many." b. *EmployeeID* in Employees table is the "one" and *EmployeeID* in Events table is the "many." c. *PlanCode* in Plans table is the "one" and *PlanCode* in Events table is the "many." d. *PriceCode* in Prices table is the "one" and *PriceCode* in Events table is the "many."	12	
2	Organization, Finishing	Save, then print relationships in landscape orientation.	3	
		TOTAL POINTS	15	

Assessment 3: Modify Tables
File: **AL1-U1-Cornerstone.accdb**

Steps	Tasks	Criteria	Value	Score
1	Table and Field Mgt, Typing, Accuracy	In **AL1-U1-Cornerstone.accdb**, open Plans table in Datasheet view, then add following record at end of table: *PlanCode:* **I** *Plan:* **Hawaiian Luau Dinner Buffet**	6	
2-3	Formatting, Organization, Finishing	Adjust column widths. Save, print, then close Plans table.	4	
4	Table and Field Mgt, Typing, Accuracy	Open Events table in Datasheet view, then add following record at the end of the table: *EventID:* (AutoNumber) *PlanCode:* **I** *ClientID:* **104** *PriceCode:* **5** *EmployeeID:* **21** *NumberOfPeople:* **125** *Date:* **7/31/2015**	7	
5	Organization, Finishing	Save, print (in landscape), then close Events table.	3	
		TOTAL POINTS	20	

Assessment 4: Design Queries
File: **AL1-U1-Cornerstone.accdb**

Steps	Tasks	Criteria	Value	Score
1	Queries, Accuracy, Organization, Finishing	In **AL1-U1-Cornerstone.accdb**, create query to extract records from Events table with the following specs: a. Include fields *ClientID*, *DateOfEvent*, and *PlanCode*. b. Extract records with a PlanCode of C. c–e. Run the query. Save query as *PlanCodeCQuery*, then print and close it.	7	
2	Queries, Accuracy, Finishing, Organization	Extract records from Clients table with following specs: a. Include fields ClientName, City, and Telephone. b. Extract those records with a city of Santa Fe. c–e. Run the query, save it as *SantaFeClientsQuery*, then print and close the query.	8	
3	Queries, Accuracy, Finishing, Organization	Extract information from two tables with following specs: a–b. From Clients table, include fields ClientName and Telephone; from Events table, include fields DateOfEvent, PlanCode, and NumberOfPeople. c. Extract records with date between July 1 and July 15, 2015. d–e. Run the query, save it as *July1-15EventsQuery*, then print and close.	10	
		TOTAL POINTS	25	

Assessment 5: Design a Query with a Calculated Field
File: **AL1-U1-Cornerstone.accdb**

Steps	Tasks	Criteria	Value	Score
1-2	Queries, Accuracy, Organization	1. In **AL1-U1-Cornerstone.accdb**, create query in Design view with Events and Prices tables, inserting following fields in specified locations: a–c. Insert *EventID* from Events table to first *Field* row field; insert *DateOfEvent* from Events table to second *Field* row field; and insert *NumberOfPeople* from Events table to third *Field* row field. d. Insert *PricePerPerson* from Prices table to fourth *Field* row field. 2. Insert calculated field entry in fifth *Field* row field: *Amount: [NumberOfPeople]*[PricePerPerson]*.	12	
3-5	Accuracy, Organization, Finishing	Run query, save as *EventAmountsQuery*, then print and close query.	3	
		TOTAL POINTS	15	

Assessment 6: Design a Query with Aggregate Functions
File: **AL1-U1-Cornerstone.accdb**

Steps	Tasks	Criteria	Value	Score
1	Queries, Accuracy, Organization	In **AL1-U1-Cornerstone.accdb**, create query in Design view using EventAmountsQuery, with the following specs: a. Click Create tab, then click Query Design button. b. At Show Tables dialog box, click Queries tab. c. Double-click EventAmountsQuery in list box, then click Close button. d. Insert Amount field to first, second, third, and fourth Field text boxes. e. Click Totals button in Show/Hide group. f–i. Insert *Sum* in first *Total* row field, *Avg* in second *Total* row field, *Min* in third *Total* row field, and *Max* in fourth *Total* row field.	15	
2-5	Accuracy, Organization, Finishing	Run query, automatically adjust column widths, save as *AmountTotalsQuery*, then print and close query.	5	
		TOTAL POINTS	20	

Assessment 7: Design a Query Using Fields from Tables and a Query
File: **AL1-U1-Cornerstone.accdb**

Steps	Tasks	Criteria	Value	Score
1	Queries, Accuracy, Organization	In **AL1-U1-Cornerstone.accdb**, create query in Design view using Employees table, Clients table, Events table, and EventsAmountQuery, with following specs: b. At Show Tables dialog box, double-click Employees. c–d. Double-click Clients, then double-click Events. e. Click Queries tab, double-click EventAmountsQuery in list box, then click Close. f–i. Insert LastName field from Employees table to first Field row field; insert ClientName field from Clients table to second Field row field; insert Amount field from EventAmountsQuery to third Field row field; then insert *DateOfEvent* from Events table to fourth *Field* row field.	10	
2-4	Accuracy, Organization, Finishing	Run query, save as EmployeeEventsQuery, then close.	4	

Steps	Tasks	Criteria	Value	Score
5	Queries, Accuracy	Using Crosstab Query Wizard, create query summarizing total amount of events by employee by client using following specs: a. At first Crosstab Query Wizard dialog box, click Queries option in View section, then click Query: EmployeeEventsQuery in list box. b. At second Crosstab Query Wizard dialog box, click LastName in Available Fields list box, then click One Field. c. At third Crosstab Query Wizard dialog box, make sure ClientName is selected in list box. d. At fourth Crosstab Query Wizard dialog box, make sure Amount is selected in Fields list box, then click Sum in Functions list box. e. At fifth Crosstab Query Wizard dialog box, type **AmountsByEmployeeByClientQuery** in *What do you want to name your query?* text box.	7	
6-7	Formatting, Finishing, Organization	Automatically adjust column widths, print query in landscape orientation, then close query.	4	
		TOTAL POINTS	25	

Assessment 8: Use the Find Duplicates Query Wizard
File: **AL1-U1-Cornerstone.accdb**

Steps	Tasks	Criteria	Value	Score
1	Queries, Accuracy	In **AL1-U1-Cornerstone.accdb**, use Find Duplicates Query Wizard to find employees who are responsible for at least two events with the following specs: a. At first wizard dialog box, double-click Table: Events in list box. b. At second wizard dialog box, click EmployeeID in Available fields list box, then click One Field button. c. At third wizard dialog box, move DateOfEvent field and NumberOfPeople field from Available fields list box to Additional query fields list box. d. At fourth dialog box, name query *DuplicateEventsQuery*.	7	
2	Finishing, Organization	Print, then close query.	3	
		TOTAL POINTS	10	

Assessment 9: Use the Find Unmatched Query Wizard
File: **AL1-U1-Cornerstone.accdb**

Steps	Tasks	Criteria	Value	Score
1	Queries, Accuracy	In **AL1-U1-Cornerstone.accdb**, use Find Unmatched Query Wizard to find any employees who do not have an upcoming event scheduled, with the following specs: a–c. At first wizard dialog box, click *Table*: *Employees* in list box; at second dialog box, click *Table*: *Events* in list box; at third dialog box, make sure *EmployeeID* is selected in *Fields in 'Employees'* list box and in *Fields in 'Events'* list box. d. At the fourth wizard dialog box, click All Fields button to move all fields from *Available fields* list box to *Selected fields* list box. e. At fifth wizard dialog box, click Finish button. (Let wizard determine the query name: *Employees Without Matching Events*.)	12	
2	Finishing, Organization	Print, then close query.	3	
		TOTAL POINTS	15	

Writing Activities

Create a Payroll Table and Word Report
File: **AL1-U1-Cornerstone.accdb**, **AL1-U1-Act01-TableRpt.docx**

Steps	Tasks	Criteria	Value	Score
1	Table and Field Management, Typing, Accuracy	Create table to contain information on payroll. Table must include the fields and data (user-determined appropriate field names, data types, field sizes, and descriptions) shown on page 179.	15	
2	Finishing, Organization	Print, then close payroll table.	2	
3	Writing, Organization, Finishing	Open Word, then write report to the manager detailing how table was created. Include a title for the report, steps on how table was created, and any other pertinent information. Save completed report as **AL1-U1-Act01-TableRpt**, print, then close document.	8	
		TOTAL POINTS	25	

Internet Research

Vehicle Search
File: *User-Determined*

Steps	Tasks	Criteria	Value	Score
1	Writing, Research, Accuracy	List top five criteria to look for in a vehicle (e.g., it must be a four-door vehicle, needs to be four-wheel drive, etc.). On the Internet, using key search words, find at least two websites that list vehicle reviews. Then use search engines provided within different review sites to find vehicles that fulfill criteria listed earlier.	10	
2	Database Mgt, Table and Field Mgt, Typing	In Access, create database and table in that database that will contain results from vehicle search. Design table keeping in mind what type of data is needed to record for each vehicle that meets requirements. Include at least make, model, year, price, description, and special problems in table. Also, include ability to rate vehicle as poor, fair, good, or excellent. Rating of each vehicle depending on findings is user-determined.	15	
		TOTAL POINTS	25	

Benchmark Access 2013 Level 1, Chapter 5

Skills Check

Assessment 1: Create and Customize a Sales Form
File: **AL1-C5-PacTrek.accdb**

Steps	Tasks	Criteria	Value	Score
1-2	Organization, Accuracy	Open **AL1-C5-PakTrek.accdb** and enable the contents	3	

Steps	Tasks	Criteria	Value	Score

3-5	Forms, Typing, Editing	Use Form button in Forms group in Create tab to create a form with Suppliers table.
		Switch to Form view, then add following records:
		    SupplierID = **12**
		    SupplierName = **Seaside Suppliers**
		    StreetAddress = **4120 Shoreline Drive**
		    City = **Vancouver**
		    Prov/State = **BC**
		    PostalCode = **V2V 8K4**
		    EmailAddress = **seaside@emcp.net**
		    Telephone = **6045557945**
		    SupplierID = **34**
		    SupplierName = **Carson Company**
		    StreetAddress = **120 Plaza Center**
		    City = **Vancouver**
		    Prov/State = **BC**
		    PostalCode = **V2V 1K6**
		    EmailAddress = **carson@emcp.net**
		    Telephone = **6045551955**
		Delete record containing information on Manning, Inc.
			12	

6-7	Enhancement, Formatting	Switch to Layout view, then apply the *Organic* theme. Select and delete the logo object in the *Form Header* section, then click the Logo button in the Header/Footer group. At Insert Picture dialog box, navigate to the AL1C5 folder from the storage medium then double-click **River.jpg**.	7	

8-12	Forms, Formatting, Organization	8. Create title *Pacific Trek Suppliers* for form. Click in any field outside title, then click in title. Drag right border of title control object to left until border displays near title.
		9–10. Insert date and time in *Form Header* section, then select date and time control objects, drag in left border until border displays near date and time, then drag objects so they are positioned near title.
		11. Click text box control object containing supplier number, then drag right border to left until Lines: 1 Characters: 30 displays at the left side of the Status bar.
		12. Select Fields in the first column (Supplier ID through Telephone) an then apply the following formatting:
		  a. Apply the *bold formatting*
		  b. Apply the *Dark Blue* font color (Standard Colors)
		  c. Apply the *Align right* alignment.
		  d. Apply the *Light Blue 2 shape fill* (fifth column, third row in Standard Colors; section)
		  e. Apply the *Dark Blue shape* outline color (ninth column, bottom row in the Standard Colors section).
			28	

13	Formatting	Select the second column and then apply the following formatting:
		  a. Apply the *Light Blue 1 shape fill* (Standard Colors section)
		  b. Apply the *Dark Blue shape outline* color (Standard colors section)
			4	

Steps	Tasks	Criteria	Value	Score
14-18	Accuracy, Finishing, Organization	14. Switch to *Form* view. 15. Save the form with the name *Suppliers*. 16-17. Print only the record for supplier number 12; print only record for supplier number 34. 18. Close the Suppliers table.	6	
		TOTAL POINTS	**60**	

Assessment 2: Create and Customize an Orders Form
File: **AL1-C5-PakTrek.accdb**

Steps	Tasks	Criteria	Value	Score

1-5	Forms, Formatting	1. In **AL1-C5-PakTrek.accdb**, create form with Orders table using Form button in *Create* tab.
		2. Insert field from related table by completing following:
		  a–c. Display Field List pane; then, if necessary, click Show all tables hyperlink; expand Suppliers table in *Fields available in related tables*; drag field named *SupplierName* into form, position between *SupplierID* and *ProductID*.
		  d. Change *SupplierName* field from Lookup field to text box by clicking Options button that displays below field then clicking *Change to Text Box* at drop-down list.
		  e. Close Field List pane.
		3. Click text box control object containing text *1010,* then drag right border to left until Lines: 1 Characters: 30 displays at the left side of the Status bar.
		4. Select all objects in *Detail* section by clicking an object in *Detail* section, then clicking the table move handle. With objects selected, apply following formatting:
		  a. Change font to Cambria and font size to *12*.
		  b. Change alignment to *Align Text* Right.
		5. Select first column, then apply following formatting:
		  a–b. Apply *Green 2* shape fill; apply *bold* formatting.
			15	

6	Enhancement	Apply conditional formatting, changing font color to *blue* for any *Amount* field that contains amount greater than $999.	2	
7-8	Organization, Finishing	Save form as *Orders*, print 15th record, then close form.	3	
		TOTAL POINTS	**20**	

Assessment 3: Create a Split Form with the Products Table
File: **AL1-C5-PakTrek.accdb**

Steps	Tasks	Criteria	Value	Score
1	Forms, Accuracy	In **AL1-C5-PacTrek.accdb**, create form with Products table using *Split Form* option from the More Forms button.	3	

Assessment 3: Create a Split Form with the Products Table
File: **AL1-C5-PakTrek.accdb**

Steps	Tasks	Criteria	Value	
2-3	Formatting	2. Decrease width of second column until lines: 1 Characters: 35 displays at the left side of the status bar. 3. Select first column, then apply formatting: a–c. Apply bold, apply *Aqua Blue 1* shape fill, then change shape outline color to *Blue*.	5	
4	Enhancement	Click in text box control object containing number 0 (the *UnitsOnOrder number*), then apply conditional formatting that displays number in red in any field equal to 0 (zero).	3	

5	Accuracy, Typing	Change to Form view, create a new record, then enter following info in specified fields:
		   ProductID = **205-CS**
		   Product = **Timberline solo cook set**
		   SupplierID = **15**
		   UnitsInStock = **8**
		   UnitsOnOrder = **0**
		   ReorderLevel = **5**
			5	

6-9	Organization, Finishing	6–7. Save form as *Products*, then print current record (the record just typed). 8–9. Close Products form, then close database **AL10C5-PacTrek. accdb.**	4	
		TOTAL POINTS	20	

Assessment 4: Create and Customize an Employees Form
File: **AL1-C5-Griffin.accdb**

Steps	Tasks	Criteria	Value	Score
1	Organization, Accuracy	Open **AL1-C5-Griffin.accdb** from the AL1C5 folder, then enable the contents.	3	
2	Forms, Accuracy	Use Form Wizard to create Employees form including all fields except *AnnualSalary* field; name the form *Employees*.	3	

3-4	Enhancement, Typing	3. Switch to Form view, then type a new record with the following information in the specified fields:
		   Emp# = **1099**
		   LastName = **Williamson**
		   FirstName = **Carrie**
		   BirthDate = **6/24/1983**
		   HireDate = **8/1/2011**
		   DeptID = **RD**
		4. Switch to Layout view, then apply the Slice theme, change the theme colors to Blue Warm, change the theme fonts to Franklin Goethic.
			6	

5-6	Finishing, Organization	Print the record just typed, then close Employees form.	3	
		TOTAL POINTS	15	

Visual Benchmark

Create and Format a Properties Form

File: **AL1-C5-SunProperties.accdb**

Steps	Tasks	Criteria	Value	Score
1	Organization, Accuracy	Open **AL1-C5-SunProperties.accdb** from the AL1C5 folder, then enable the contents.	3	
2	Forms, Formatting, Accuracy, Enhancement	Create form with Properties table and format it to appear similar to Fig. 5.8, with following specs: a. Apply Facet theme, and apply the Paper theme colors. b. Insert logo, title, date, and time in *Form Header* section as shown in figure (use **SunPropLogo.jpg** for logo). Adjust size of title control object, then move date and time as shown in figure. c. Select all objects in *Detail* section, then change font color to *Maroon 5.* d. Select first column, apply bold, Light *Yellow, Background 2, Darker 10% shape fill (Theme Colors section) Apply the Maroon 5 shape outline color (Standard Colors section) and change the alignment to Align Right.* e. Decrease the size of the second column as shown in figure. f. Insert a new column to the right of the second column, merge cells in the new column to accommodate the sun image, and then insert the image **SunProp.jpg** (as a control object) Adjust the width of the third column of the image displays as shown in Figure 5.8. g. Apply conditional formatting to *MoRent* field that displays in green any rent amount greater than $999. h. Adjust the position of the control objects so that the form displays similar to what is shown in Figure 5.8.	27	
3-5	Organization, Accuracy, Editing	3. Save form with the name *Properties,* then print current record. 4. Close the form, then close database AL1-C5-SunProperties. accdb	5	
		TOTAL POINTS	35	

Case Study

Part 1

File: **AL1-C5-LewisCenter.accdb**

Steps	Tasks	Criteria	Value	Score
1	Organization, Table Management, Accuracy	Open **AL1-C5-LewisCenter.accdb**, then create the following relationships between tables: **Field Name** **"One" Table** **"Many" Table** *PatientID* Patients Billing *ServiceID* Services Billing *DoctorID* Doctors Billing	7	
2	Organization, Finishing	Save, then print the relationships.	3	

Steps	Tasks	Criteria	Value	Score
		TOTAL POINTS	10	

Part 2
File: **AL1-C5-LewisCenter.accdb**

Steps	Tasks	Criteria	Value	Score
1	Forms, Enhancement, Typing, Formatting, Finishing	Create a form for each table, then a theme (user-chosen). Enter data in the forms in order it appears in Fig. 5.10. Apply additional formatting to enhance visual appeal. After entering info, print the first record of each form.	35	
		TOTAL POINTS	35	

Part 3
File: **AL1-C5-LewisCenter.accdb**

Steps	Tasks	Criteria	Value	Score
1	Enhancement, Accuracy	Apply the following conditions to the fields in forms: • In Patients form, apply condition that city *Tulsa* displays in red, and city *Broken Arrow* displays in blue (*City* field). • In Billing form, apply condition that amounts in *Fee* field over $99 display in green.	7	
2	Finishing, Organization	Print first record of the form, close *Patients* form, then close database **AL1-C5-LewisCenter.accdb**	3	
		TOTAL POINTS	10	

Part 4
File: **AL1-C5-CS-Manual.docx**

Steps	Tasks	Criteria	Value	Score
1	Typing, Accuracy	In Word, create document for procedures manual that describes formatting and conditions applied to the forms in the **AL1-C5-LewisCenter.accdb** database.	12	
2	Finishing, Organization	Save completed document as **AL1-C5-CS-Manual**, print, then close document.	3	
		TOTAL POINTS	15	

Benchmark Access 2013 Level 1, Chapter 6

Skills Check

Assessment 1: Create and Format Reports in the Hilltop Database
File: **AL1-C6-Hilltop.accdb**

Steps	Tasks	Criteria	Value	Score
1	Organization, Accuracy	Open **AL1-C6-Hilltop.accdb** and enable the contents.	3	

2-5	Reports, Formatting, Organization, Finishing	2. Create a report with Inventory table using Report button.
		3. With report in Layout view, apply formatting:
		  a. Center data below each of following column headings: *EquipmentID, AvailableHours, ServiceHours, RepairHours.*
		  b. Select all control objects, then change font to *Constantia.*
		  c. Select money amounts below *PurchasePrice* column heading, then decrease decimal so money amounts display without a decimal point.
		  d. Click in *$473,260.00* amount, then decrease decimal so the amount displays without a decimal.
		  e. If necessary, change the height of the total amount row so the entire amount is visible.
		  f. Change title of report to *Inventory Report.*
		4–5. Print, close *InventoryReport.*
			12	

6	Queries, Organization	Create a query in Design view with following specs: a. Add *Customers, Equipment, Invoices,* and *Rates* tables to query window. b–d. Insert *Customer* field from *Customers* table in first Field row field, *Equipment* field from *Equipment* table in second Field row field, *Hours* field from *Invoices* table in third Field row field, and *Rate* field from Rates table in fourth Field row field. f. Click in fifth Field row field, type *Total: [Hours]*[Rate],* then press Enter. g–h. Run query, save as *CustomerRentals,* then close.	14	

Steps	Tasks	Criteria	Value	Score
7-8	Reports, Formatting	7. Create a report with *CustomerRentals* query using Report button. 8. With report in Layout view, apply formatting: a. *Decrease width* of columns so right border of each column displays near right side of longest entry. b. Select money amounts, then *decrease* decimal so amounts display with no decimal point. c. Click in *Total* column, then total amounts by clicking **REPORT LAYOUT TOOLS DESIGN** tab, clicking Totals button in Grouping & Totals group, then clicking *Sum*. d. Click total amount (bottom of *Total* column), click **REPORT LAYOUT TOOLS FORMAT** tab, then click *Apply Currency Format* button. e. Increase height of total amount until entire amount is visible. f. Select, then delete amount that displays at bottom of *Rate* column. g. Display Group, Sort, Total pane, group the records by *Customer*, sort by *Equipment*, then close pane. h. Apply *Integral* theme. i. Select five column headings, then *change font color* to *black*. j. Change title to *Rentals*.	18	
9-10	Organization, Finishing	Save report as *RentalReport*, then print and close.	3	
		TOTAL POINTS	50	

Assessment 2: Create Reports Using the Report Wizard
File: **AL1-C6-Hilltop.accdb**

Steps	Tasks	Criteria	Value	Score
1-2	Reports, Finishing, Organization	In **AL1-C6-Hilltop.accdb**, create a report using Report Wizard with the following specs: a. At first Report Wizard dialog box, insert following fields in Selected Fields list box: From Equipment table: Equipment; from Inventory table: PurchaseDate, PurchasePrice, and AvailableHours b–c. Do not make any changes at second or third Report Wizard dialog boxes. d. At fourth Report Wizard dialog box, choose *Columnar* option. e. At fifth last Report Wizard dialog box, click Finish. 2. Print the report, then close.	12	

Steps	Tasks	Criteria	Value	Score
3-4	Reports, Finishing, Organization	Create a report using Report Wizard with following specs: a. At first Report Wizard dialog box, insert following fields in Selected Fields list box: From Customers table: *Customer*; from Invoices table: *BillingDate* and *Hours*; from Equipment table: *Equipment*; and from Rates table: *Rate*. b–d. Do not make any changes at second, third, or fourth Report Wizard dialog boxes. e. At fifth Report Wizard dialog box, choose *Block* option. f. At sixth last Report Wizard dialog box, name report *Rentals*. 4. Print the report, then close.	13	
		TOTAL POINTS	25	

Assessment 3: Create Mailing Labels
File: **AL1-C6-PakTrek.accdb**

Steps	Tasks	Criteria	Value	Score
1	Organization, Accuracy	In **AL1-C6-Hilltop.accdb**, click *Customers* table in Navigation pane.	3	
2-4	Reports, Finishing, Organization	2. Use Label Wizard to create mailing labels (user-determined label type) with customer names and addresses, sorted by customer names. Name mailing label report *CustomerMailingLabels*. 3–4. Print the mailing labels, then close.	7	
		TOTAL POINTS	10	

Assessment 4: Add a Field to a Report
File: **AL1-C6-Hilltop.accdb**

Steps	Tasks	Criteria	Value	Score
1	Organization, Accuracy, Field Management	In **AL1-C6-Hilltop.accdb**: a. Open report named *RentalReport* (created in Assessment 1) in Layout view. b. Display Field List pane, then display all tables. c. Drag *BillingDate* field from Invoices table so field is positioned between *Equipment* column and *Hours* column. d. At message indicating Access will modify *RecordSource* property and asking if you want to continue, click Yes. e. Close the Field List pane.	7	
2-3	Organization, Finishing	Save, print, then close report and close database **AL1-C6-Hilltop.accdb.**	3	
		TOTAL POINTS	10	

Visual Benchmark

Design a Query and Create a Report with the Query
File: **AL1-C6-Skyline.accdb**

Steps	Tasks	Criteria	Value	Score
1-2	Organization, Accuracy	Open **AL1-C6-Skyline.accdb**, create and run query shown in **Fig. 6.11**, save as *Suppliers2&4Orders*, then close.	5	
3-5	Reports, Enhancement, Formatting, Editing, Organization, Finishing	3. Use Report button to create report shown in Fig. 6.12 using *Suppliers2&4Orders* query, with following specs: a. Apply *Facet* theme. b. Adjust column widths, then change alignment of data as shown in the figure. c. Change title as shown in figure. d. Select column headings, then change font color to black. e. Insert sum total of amounts in *Total* column. Format total amount as shown in figure. f. Delete sum amount at bottom of *UnitPrice* column. 4–5. Save report as *Suppliers2&4OrdersRpt*, print and then close. Close database **AL1-C6-Skyline.accdb**	10	
		TOTAL POINTS	15	

Case Study

Part 1
File: **AL1-C6-Millstone.accdb**

Steps	Tasks	Criteria	Value	Score
1	Typing, Accuracy	In the **AL1-C6-Millstone.accdb** database, enter data into appropriate tables (Part 1, bottom of page 261).	10	
		TOTAL POINTS	10	

Part 2

File: **AL1-C6-Millstone.accdb**

Steps	Tasks	Criteria	Value	Score
1	Reports, Queries, Formatting, Accuracy	Create a report with Clients table. Apply formatting to enhance the visual appeal. • Create a query that displays *client ID, first name, last name; attorney last name; billing date; fee.* Name the query *ClientBilling.* • Create a report with the ClientBilling query. Group records in report by attorney last name (*LName* field in drop-down list), and sort alphabetically in *ascending* order by client last name (*LastName* field in the drop-down list). Apply formatting to enhance the visual appeal. • Create a telephone directory by creating a report that includes client *last names, first names, and telephone numbers.* Sort records alphabetically by last name in *ascending* order. • Edit the ClientBilling query so it includes a criterion that displays only billing dates between 3/10/2015 and 3/13/2015. Save As *ClientBilling10-13.* • Create a report with *ClientBilling10-13* query. Apply formatting to enhance visual appeal of report. • Create mailing labels for clients.	20	
		TOTAL POINTS	20	

Part 3

File: **AL1-C6-Millstone.accdb**

Steps	Tasks	Criteria	Value	Score
1	Enhancement, Accuracy, Finishing	Apply the following conditions to the fields in reports, then print the reports: • In Clients report, apply condition that city *Casper* displays in *red* and *Mills* displays in *blue* in the *City* field. • In ClientBilling report, apply condition that fees over $199 display in *green* and fees less than $200 in *blue*.	10	
		TOTAL POINTS	10	

Part 4

File: **AL1-C6-CS-Manual.docx**

Steps	Tasks	Criteria	Value	Score
1	Typing, Accuracy	In Word, create document for procedures manual that describes process for creating a report using the Report button, Report Wizard, and for preparing mailing labels, using the *Label Wizard*.	12	
2	Finishing, Organization	Save completed document as **AL1-C6-CS-Manual**, print, then close document.	3	
		TOTAL POINTS	15	

Benchmark Access 2013 Level 1, Chapter 7

Skills Check

Assessment 1: Filter Records in Tables
File: **AL1-C7-WarrenLegal.accdb**

Steps	Tasks	Criteria	Value	Score
1-2	Organization, Accuracy	Open **AL1-C7-WarrenLegal.accdb** from the AL1C7 folder, and enable the contents.	3	

3-9	Editing, Accuracy, Organization, Finishing	3. Open Clients table, then filter records to display the following records:
		  a. Display only those records of clients who live in *Renton*. When records of clients in Renton display, print results in *landscape* orientation, then remove filter.
		  b. Display only those records of clients with ZIP code *98033*. When records of clients with ZIP code 98033 display, print results in *landscape* and then remove filter.
		4. Close Clients table without saving changes.
		5. Open the Billing table, then filter records by selection to display the following records:
		  a. Display only those records with a *Category of CC*. Print CC records, then remove filter.
		  b. Display only those records with an *Attorney ID of 12*. Print records, then remove the filter.
		  c. Display only those records between dates *6/1/2015 through 6/10/2015*. Print records, then remove filter.
		6. Close Billing table without saving changes.
		7. Open Clients table, then use *Filter By Form* to display clients in *Auburn* **or** *Renton*. (Use the Or tab.) Print table in landscape, then remove filter.
		8. Close Clients table without saving changes.
		9. Open Billing table, then use *Filter By Form* to display *categories G or P*. Print table, then remove filter.
			25	

10-11	Organization	Close Billing table without saving, then close database **AL1-C7-WarrenLegal.accdb**	2	
		TOTAL POINTS	30	

Assessment 2: Save a Table and Database in Different File Formats
File: **AL1-C7-Hilltop.accdb**

Steps	Tasks	Criteria	Value	Score
1	Organization, Accuracy	Open **AL1-C7-Hilltop.accdb** in Exclusive mode and enable the contents.	3	

Steps	Tasks	Criteria	Value	Score
2-7	Database Management, Accuracy, Editing, Finishing, Organization	2. Create a password for database and, with Set Database Password dialog box open, create a screen capture of screen with dialog box by completing the following: a. Press Print Screen button. b. Open Microsoft Word. c. Click Paste button. d. Click File tab, click Print option, then click *Print* option at the Print Backstage area. e. Exit Word by clicking Close button (don't save). 3–5. Click OK to close Set Database Password dialog box. At message that block cipher is incompatible with row level locking, click OK. Close database. 6. Open **AL1-C7-Hilltop.accdb** database in Exclusive mode and enter the password when prompted. 7. Remove password (Decrypt Database button).	20	
8-13	File Management, Accuracy, Finishing, Organization	8-10. Save Invoices table in PDF format. When table displays in Adobe Reader, print by clicking Print button, then clicking OK at Print dialog box. Close Adobe Reader. 11. Save **AL1-C7-Hilltop.accdb** in *Access 2002-2003 Database (*.mdb) file format. 12..With database open, make a screen capture using *Print Screen* on keyboard. Open Word, paste screen capture image, print document, then exit Word without saving. 13. Close database.	7	
		TOTAL POINTS	30	

Assessment 3: Delete and Rename Objects
File: **AL1-C7-PakTrek.accdb**

Steps	Tasks	Criteria	Value	Score
1	Organization, Accuracy	Open **AL1-C7-Hilltop.accdb**.	2	
2	Editing, File Management, Finishing, Organization	Right-click an object in Navigation pane, experiment with options in the shortcut menu, then complete steps using the shortcut menu: a. Delete Inventory form. b–c. Rename the form Equipment to *EquipForm*; rename the report InvReport to *InventoryReport*. d. Export (using the shortcut menu) *EquipmentQuery* to a Word RTF file. **Hint: Click Browse button at Export - RTF File dialog box to make Access2010L1C7 active folder.** e. Open EquipmentQuery.*rtf* file in Word, print, then exit Word.	11	
3	Organization	3. Close **AL1-C7-Hilltop.accdb** database.	2	
		TOTAL POINTS	15	

Visual Benchmark

Design a Query and Filter the Query
File: **AL1-C7-PakTrek.accdb**

Steps	Tasks	Criteria	Value	Score
1	Organization, Accuracy	Open **AL1-C7-PakTrek.accdb** and enable the contents.	3	
2-7	Queries, Accuracy, Organization, Finishing, Editing	2. Create and run query shown in Fig. 7.10. 3–4. Save query as *ProductsOnOrderQuery*, then print. 5. Filter query so records display as shown in Fig. 7.11. *Hint: Filter supplier names as shown in Figure 7.1, then UnitsOnOrder field to show records that do not equal 0.* 6–7. Print the filtered query, remove filters, then close query without saving changes.	10	
8	Organization	8. Close **AL1-C7-PacTrek.accdb** database.	2	
		TOTAL POINTS	15	

Case Study

Part 1
File: **AL1-C7-SummitView.accdb**

Steps	Tasks	Criteria	Value	Score
1	Organization, Accuracy, Table and Field Management	Open **AL1-C7-SummitView.accdb**, enable contents, then insert following additional services into appropriate table: • Edit *Doctor visit* entry the Services table so it displays as *Clinic visit*. • Add entry *X-ray* with a service identification of *X*. • Add entry *Cholesterol screening* with a service identification of *CS*.	8	
2	Typing, Accuracy	Add new patient information in database in appropriate tables (see Part 1, page 289, for information to input). Add the following information to Billing table: • Patient 109 came for cholesterol screening with Dr. Kennedy on 4/6/2015 with a $90 fee. • Patient 106 came for immunizations with Dr. Pena on 4/6/2015 with a $100 fee. • Patient 114 came for an x-ray with Dr. Kennedy on 4/6/2015 with a $75 fee.	12	
		TOTAL POINTS	20	

Part 2
File: **AL1-C7-SummitView.accdb**

Steps	Tasks	Criteria	Value	Score
1	Editing, Reports, Queries, Finishing, Organization	• Open Billing table, then filter and print records for date 04/2/2015. Clear filter, then filter and print records with doctor number of 18. Save, then close the table. • Create report that displays *patient's first name, last name, street address, city, state, and ZIP code.* Apply formatting to enhance visual appeal. Filter and print records of patients living in *Helena*, remove filter, then filter and print records of patients living in East Helena. Close the report. • Design a query that includes *doctor number, doctor last name, patient number, date of visit, and fee.* Save query as *DoctorBillingFees,* then print. Filter print records for Dr. Kennedy and Dr. Pena, remove filter, then filter and print records for dates 4/5/2015 and 4/6/2015. Save, then close query.	25	
		TOTAL POINTS	25	

Part 3
File: **AL1-C7-SummitView.accdb**

Steps	Tasks	Criteria	Value	Score
1	File Mgt, Finishing, Organization	Save Billing table in PDF format, print the table in Adobe Reader, then close Adobe Reader. Close database.	10	
		TOTAL POINTS	10	

Part 4
File: **AL1-C7-CS-Manual.docx**

Steps	Tasks	Criteria	Value	Score
1	Typing, Accuracy	In Word, create document for procedures manual that describes steps to create the *DoctorBillingFees* query and steps to create and print the two filters.	12	
2	Finishing, Organization	Save document as **AL1-C7-CS-Manual**, print, then close.	3	
		TOTAL POINTS	15	

Benchmark Access 2013 Level 1, Chapter 8

Skills Check

Assessment 1: Export a Form to Excel and a Report to Word
File: **AL1-C8-WarrenLegal.accdb**

Steps	Tasks	Criteria	Value	Score
1	Organization, Accuracy	Open **AL1-C8-WarrenLegal.accdb** from the AL1C8 folder and enable the contents.	3	

2-6	Forms, Accuracy, Exporting, Formatting, Organization	2. Create a form named *Billing* using the Form Wizard with following fields: From Billing table: *BillingID, ClientID, BillingDate, Hours;* from Rates table: *Rate*
		3–4. When form displays, close it, then create an Excel worksheet with the Billing form.
		5. Make following changes to the worksheet:
		    a. Select columns A through E, adjust column widths.
		    b. Select cells A2 through B42, Center
		    c–e. Save Billing worksheet, print and close, then exit Excel.
		6. In Access, close the Export Wizard.
			13	

7-9	Reports, Accuracy, Exporting, Formatting, Typing, Finishing	7. Create a report named *ClientBilling* using the Report Wizard (at fifth wizard dialog box, change layout to *Block*) with following fields: From Clients table: *FirstName, LastName*; from Billing table: *BillingDate, Hours*; from Rates table: *Rate*
		8. Close the report.
		9. Create a Word document with the ClientBilling report and save it to AL1C8 folder with default name. In the Word document, make following changes:
		    a. Press Ctrl + A to select entire document, change font color to black, then deselect text.
		    b–c. Insert a space between *Client* and *Billing* in title. Then position insertion point immediately right of word *Billing*, press spacebar, then type **of Legal Services**.
			20	

10-12	Organization, Finishing	Save, then print **ClientBilling.rtf**. Close the document, exit Word, and then close the wizard dialog box in Access.	4	
		TOTAL POINTS	40	

Assessment 2: Merge Table and Query Data with a Word Document
File: **AL1-C8-WarrenLegal.accdb, AL1-C8-WLLtrs.docx, AL1-C8-WLLtrMD1. docx,**
AL1-C8-WLKentLtrs.docx, and AL1-C8-WLLtrMD2.docx

Steps	Tasks	Criteria	Value	Score
1	Accuracy, Exporting	In **AL1-C8-WarrenLegal.accdb**, merge data in Clients table to a new Word document using Word merge button.	5	

Steps	Tasks	Criteria	Value	Score
2-5	Enhancement, Editing, Accuracy, Typing, Finishing, Organization	2. Maximize Word document, close Mail Merge task pane, then compose letter with following elements: a–b. Click Home tab, then click *No Spacing style*. Press Enter six times, *type current date*, and press Enter four times. c–d. Click Mailings tab, then insert «*AddressBlock*» composite field. Insert salutation **Ladies and Gentlemen**: e. Compose a letter to clients that includes the following information (see Step 2.e. for the text). f. Include an appropriate complimentary close. Use name and title *Marjorie Shaw, Senior Partner* for signature, add reference initials and document name (**AL1-C8-WLLtrs.docx**). 3. Merge to a new document, save as **AL1-C8-WLLtrs**. 4. Print first two letters in document, then close. 5. Save main document as **AL1-C8-WLLtrMD1**, close, then exit Word.	20	
6-7	Queries, Exporting, Accuracy	6. In **AL1-C8-WarrenLegal.accdb**, extract records from the Clients table of clients located in Kent, then name query *ClientsKentQuery*. (Include all fields from table in query.) 7. Merge *ClientsKentQuery* to new Word document using the Word Merge button.	6	
8-9	Enhancement, Editing, Typing, Organization	8. Maximize Word, close the Mail Merge task pane, then compose a letter with following elements: a–b. Click Home tab, then click *No Spacing style*. Press Enter six times, *type current date*, and press Enter four times. c–d. Click Mailings tab, insert the «*AddressBlock*» composite field, and then insert a proper salutation. e. Compose a letter to clients that includes text at Step 8.e. f. Include an appropriate complimentary close for letter. Use name *Thomas Zeiger* and title *Attorney* in the complimentary close and add reference initials and the document name (**AL1-C8-WLKentLtrs.docx**). 9. Merge letter to new document, then save as **AL1-C8-WLKentLtrs**.	18	
10-11	Finishing, Organization	Print first 2 letters, then close **AL1-C8-WLKentLtrs.docx**. Save main document as **AL1-C8-WLLtrMD2**, close, then exit Word.	6	
		TOTAL POINTS	55	

Assessment 3: Link an Excel Workbook
File: **AL1-C8-WarrenLegal.accdb**, and **AL1-C8-Cases.xlsx**

Steps	Tasks	Criteria	Value	Score
1-3	Importing, Accuracy, Finishing	In **AL1-C8-WarrenLegal.accdb**, link **AL1-C8-Cases.xlsx** into a new table named *Cases*. Open Cases table in Datasheet view, print, then close table.	5	

Steps	Tasks	Criteria	Value	Score
4-7	Typing, Finishing, Organization	4. Open Excel, open **AL1-C8-Cases.xlsx**, and then add the following data in the specified cells: A8 = **57-D**, B8 = **130**, C8 = **$1,100**, A9 = **42-A**, B9 = **144**, C9 = **$3,250**, A10 = **29-C**, B10 = **125**, and C10 = **$900**. 5–7. Apply the Accounting formatting with a dollar sign, no decimal places to cells *C8, C9,* and *C10.* Save, print, and close **AL1-C8-Cases.xlsx**. Exit Excel.	12	
8-10	Accuracy, Finishing, Organization	In Access, open Cases table in Datasheet view. Print, then close the table. Close database **AL1-C8-WarrenLegal.accdb**.	3	
		TOTAL POINTS	20	

Visual Benchmark

Create a Report and Export the Report to Word
File: **AL1-C8-Dearborn.accdb**

Steps	Tasks	Criteria	Value	Score
1	Organization, Accuracy	Open **AL1-C8-Dearborn.accdb** and enable the contents.	3	
2-4	Exporting, Accuracy, Organization, Finishing, Formatting	2. Use Report Wizard to create report shown in Fig. 8.3 (using Quotas and the Representatives tables). Save report as *RepQuotas,* then print. 3. Use *RepQuotas* report and export to Word. Format report in Word as Fig. 8.4. Print the document, then exit Word. 4. In Access, close database **AL1-C8-Dearborn.accdb**	12	
		TOTAL POINTS	15	

Case Study

Part 1
File: **AL1-C8-Woodland.accdb**

Steps	Tasks	Criteria	Value	Score
1	Organization, Queries, Accuracy, Exporting, Forms, Importing	Open **AL1-C8-Woodland.accdb**, then prepare the following with the data: • Create a query that displays *patient identification number, first name, last name; doctor last name; date of visit; fee.* Name query *PatientBilling.* • Export PatientBilling query to an Excel worksheet, apply formatting to enhance its appearance, then print. • Create mailing labels for patients. • Export patient labels to a Word (.rtf) document, then print document. • Import and link **AL1-C8-Payroll.xlsx** Excel worksheet to a new table named *WeeklyPayroll,* then print table.	19	

Steps	Tasks	Criteria	Value	Score
2	Accuracy, Editing, Organization, Finishing	Make the following changes to **AL1-C8-Payroll.xlsx**: Change hours for Irene Vaughn to *30*, change wage for Monica Saunders to *$10.50*, and change hours for Dale Jorgensen to *20*. After making changes, open, print, and then close table.	6	
		TOTAL POINTS	25	

Part 2
File: **AL1-C8-WLDLtr.docx**

Steps	Tasks	Criteria	Value	Score
1	Queries, Accuracy, Exporting, Typing, Organization, Finishing	In **AL1-C8-Woodland.accdb**, design a query that extracts *records of patients living in city of Altoona,* then merge query with Word. In Word document, write a letter describing new services, which include microdermabrasion, chemical peels, laser resurfacing, sclerotherapy, photorejuvenation as well as an offer for a free facial consultation. Insert appropriate fields in document, then complete merge. Save merged document as **AL1-C8-WLDLtr**, print first two letters, then close document. Close main document without saving, then exit Word.	15	
		TOTAL POINTS	15	

Part 3
File: **AL1-C8-CS-Manual.docx**

Steps	Tasks	Criteria	Value	Score
1	Research, File Management, Finishing, Organization	Use Access Help feature to learn how and when to back up a database.. Search the Access Help files using the phrase *backing up a database*. Read the hyperlinked article **Protect Your data with Backup and Restore Processes.** Create a Word document that describes how often the Woodland database should be backed up and the rationale behind the plan. Include the steps for creating a backup. Save the completed document **AL1-C8-CS-Manual**. Print and close.	10	
		TOTAL POINTS	10	

Benchmark Access 2013 Level 1, Unit 2 Performance Assessment

Skills Check

Assessment 1: Create Tables in a Clinic Database

File: **AL1-U2-LancasterClinic.accdb**

Steps	Tasks	Criteria	Value	Score

1	Organization, Table and Field Management, Accuracy	In Access, create a new database and save it as **AL1-U2-LancasterClinic**.Create a table named *Clients* that includes fields shown below (user-determined field names, data types, field sizes, and descriptions):
		    ClientNumber (primary key)
		    ClientName
		    StreetAddress
		    City
		    State
		    ZipCode
		    Telephone
		    DateOfBirth
		    DiagnosisID
			12	

2	Typing, Accuracy	Switch to Datasheet view, then enter data in appropriate fields (see Step 2, pages 319–320).	10	
3-4	Formatting, Finishing, Organization	Automatically adjust column widths, then save, print, and close Clients table.	4	

5	Table and Field Mgt, Accuracy	5. Create table named *Diagnoses* that includes these fields:
		    DiagnosisID (primary key)
		    Diagnosis
			4	

6	Typing, Accuracy	6. After creating table, switch to Datasheet view, then enter following data in appropriate fields:
		    DiagnosisID = **AD**
		    Diagnosis = **Adjustment Disorder**
		    DiagnosisID = **MDD**
		    Diagnosis = **Manic-Depressive Disorder**
		    DiagnosisID = **OCD**
		    Diagnosis = **Obsessive-Compulsive Disorder**
		    DiagnosisID = **SC**
		    Diagnosis = **Schizophrenia**
			6	

7-8	Formatting, Finishing, Organization	Automatically adjust column widths, then save, print, and close Diagnoses table.	4	

9	Table and Field Management, Accuracy	9. Create table named *Fees* that includes following fields (user-determined field names, data types, field sizes, and descriptions):
		    FeeCode (primary key)
		    HourlyFee
			4	

Steps	Tasks	Criteria	Value	Score
10	Typing, Accuracy	After creating table, switch to Datasheet view, then enter data in appropriate fields (see Step 10, page 321).	4	
11-12	Formatting, Finishing, Organization	Automatically adjust column widths, then save, print, and close Fees table.	4	
13	Table and Field Management, Accuracy	13. Create table named *Employees* that includes following fields (user-determined field names, data types, field sizes, and descriptions): *ProviderNumber* (primary key) *ProviderName* *Title* *Extension*	4	
14	Typing, Accuracy	After creating table, switch to Datasheet view, then enter data in appropriate fields (see Step 14, page 321).	4	
15-16	Formatting, Finishing, Organization	Automatically adjust column widths, then save, print, and close Employees table.	4	
17	Table and Field Management, Accuracy	Create table named *Billing* that includes following fields (user-determined field names, data types, field sizes, and descriptions): *BillingNumber* (primary key; data type is AutoNumber) *ClientNumber* *DateOfService* (apply Date/Time data type) *Insurer* *ProviderNumber* *Hours* (Change data type to *Number*, *Field Size* option in *Field Properties* section to *Double*, and *Decimal Places* option in *Field Properties* section in Design view to *1*. Two of the records will contain a number requiring this format.) *FeeCode*	6	
18	Typing, Accuracy	After creating table, switch to Datasheet view, then enter data in appropriate fields (see Step 18, page 322).	15	
19-20	Formatting, Finishing, Organization	Automatically adjust column widths, then save, print in landscape, and close Billing table.	5	
		TOTAL POINTS	90	

Assessment 2: Relate Tables and Create Forms in a Clinic Database
File: **AL1-U2-LancasterClinic.accdb**

Steps	Tasks	Criteria	Value	Score
1	Table Management, Accuracy	In **AL1-U2-LancasterClinic.accdb**, create following one-to-many relationships, enforce referential integrity and cascade fields and records: a. *ClientNumber* in Clients table is the "one" and *ClientNumber* in Billing table is the "many." b. *DiagnosisID* in Diagnoses table is the "one" and *DiagnosisID* in Clients table is the "many." c. *ProviderNumber* in Employees table is the "one" and *ProviderNumber* in Billing table is the "many." d. *FeeCode* in Fees table is the "one" and *FeeCode* in Billing table is the "many."	10	
2	Forms	Create a form with data in Clients table.	2	
3-4	Typing, Accuracy	3. After creating form, add following record: *ClientNumber:* **1179** **Timothy Fierro** **1133 Tenth Southwest** **Philadelphia, PA 19178** **(215) 555-5594** *DateOfBirth:* **12/7/1987** *DiagnosisID:* **AD** 4. Save form, print in landscape, then close form.	4	
5	Typing, Accuracy	Add the following records to the Billing table: *ClientNumber:* **1179** *ClientNumber:* **1831** *DateOfService:* **3/6/2015** *DateOfService:* **3/6/2015** *Insurer:* **Health Plus** *Insurer:* **Self** *ProviderNumber:* **15** *ProviderNumber:* **33** *Hours:* **0.5** *Hours:* **1** *FeeCode:* **C** FeeCode: **H**	4	
6-7	Organization, Finishing	Save, print in landscape orientation, then close Billing table.	5	
		TOTAL POINTS	25	

Assessment 3: Create Forms Using the Form Wizard
File: **AL1-U2-LancasterClinic.accdb**

Steps	Tasks	Criteria	Value	Score
1		In **AL1-U2-LancasterClinic.accdb**, create form with fields from related tables using Form Wizard with these specs: a. At first Form Wizard dialog box, insert following fields in Selected Fields list box: From Clients table: From Billing table: *ClientNumber* *Insurer* *DateOfBirth* *ProviderNumber* *DiagnosisID* b–c. Do not make changes at second or third Form Wizard dialog box. d. At fourth dialog box, type name **ProviderInformation** in *Form* text box.	12	
2-3		When first record displays, print it. Close the form.	3	
		TOTAL POINTS	15	

Assessment 4: Create Labels with the Label Wizard
File: **AL1-U2-LancasterClinic.accdb**

Steps	Tasks	Criteria	Value	Score
1	Reports, Accuracy, Organization	In **AL1-U2-LancasterClinic.accdb**, use Label Wizard to create mailing labels with client names and addresses, sorted by ZIP code. Name mailing label file **ClientMailingLabels**.	7	
2	Finishing, Organization	Print mailing labels, then close mailing labels file.	3	
		TOTAL POINTS	10	

Assessment 5: Filter Records in Tables
File: **AL1-U2-LancasterClinic.accdb**

Steps	Tasks	Criteria	Value	Score
1-2	Accuracy, Finishing	1. In **AL1-U2-LancasterClinic.accdb**, open Billing table, then filter records to display following records: a–b. Display only records with Health Plus insurer. Print results, then remove filter; display only records with 4419 client number. Print results, then remove filter. 2. Filter records by selection to display following records: a–b. Display only records with a C fee code. Print results, then remove filter. Display only records between dates of 3/2/2015 and 3/4/2015, print results, and then remove the filter.	12	
3	Organization	3. Close Billing table without saving changes.	2	
4	Organization, Accuracy, Finishing	4. Open Clients table, then use *Filter By Form* to display clients in Jenkintown or Cheltenham. Print the results, then remove filter.	4	
5	Organization	5. Close Clients table without saving changes.	2	
		TOTAL POINTS	20	

Assessment 6: Export a Table to Excel
File: **AL1-U2-LancasterClinic.accdb**

Steps	Tasks	Criteria	Value	Score
1	Exporting, Accuracy	In **AL1-U2-LancasterClinic.accdb**, export Billing table to an Excel workbook.	5	
2-3	Formatting	Apply formatting to cells in workbook to enhance appearance of data, then change orientation to landscape.	6	
4-5	Organization, Finishing	Save, print, then close workbook. Exit Excel.	4	
		TOTAL POINTS	15	

Assessment 7: Merge Records to Create Letters in Word
File: **AL1-U2-LancasterClinic.accdb, AL1-U2-A7-LCLtrs.docx**, and **AL1-U2-A7-ConstLtrMD.docs**

Steps	Tasks	Criteria	Value	Score
1-2	Exporting, Accuracy, Typing	1. In **AL1-U2-LancasterClinic.accdb**, merge data in Clients table to a blank Word document (user-determined fields in the inside address and appropriate salutation). Type **March 12, 2015** as date of letter and type text in body of document (see Step 1, page 324). Include appropriate complimentary close for letter. Use name and title *Marianne Lambert, Clinic Director* for signature; add reference initials and document name (**AL1-U2-A7-LCLtrs.docx**). 2. Merge to new document, save as **AL1-U2-A7-LCLtrs**.	15	

Steps	Tasks	Criteria	Value	Score
3-5	Finishing, Organization	3. Print first two letters of document, then close. 4–5. Save main document as **AL1-U2-A7-ConstLtrMD,** then close. Exit Word.	5	
		TOTAL POINTS	20	

Assessment 8: Import and Link Excel Data to an Access Table
File: **AL1-U2-LancasterClinic.accdb** and **AL1-U2-StaffHours.xlsx**

Steps	Tasks	Criteria	Value	Score
1	Importing, Accuracy	In **AL1-U2-LancasterClinic.accdb**, import and link **AL1-U2-StaffHours.xlsx** into a new table named *StaffHours*.	4	
2-3	Accuracy, Finishing, Organization	Open StaffHours table in Datasheet view, print, then close.	3	
4-7	Accuracy, Editing, Organization	4. Open **AL1-U2-StaffHours.xlsx** in Excel. 5. Insert formula in cell D2 that multiplies B2 with C2, then copy formula down to cells D3 through D7. 6–7. Save and close **AL1-U2-StaffHours.xlsx**. Exit Excel.	5	
8-9	Accuracy, Finishing, Organization	In Access, in **AL1-U2-LancasterClinic.accdb** database, open StaffHours table, print, then close.	3	
		TOTAL POINTS	15	

Writing Activities

Add a Table to the Clinic Database
File: **AL1-U2-LancasterClinic.accdb** and **AL1-U2-Act1-LCRpt.docx**

Steps	Tasks	Criteria	Value	Score
1	Table and Field Management, Typing, Accuracy	In **AL1-U2-LancasterClinic.accdb**, create table to contain information on insurance companies. Include company name, address, city, state, and ZIP code along with telephone number and name of a representative (user-determined field names, data types, field sizes, and descriptions). Include the information in appropriate fields (see Activity 1, page 325, for the data).	12	
2	Organization, Finishing	Save, print, then close insurance table.	3	
3	Writing, Organization, Finishing	Open Word, then write report to clinic director detailing how table was created. Include a title for the report, steps on how table was created, and other pertinent information. Save completed report as **AL1-U2-Act1-LCRpt**, print, then close document.	10	
		TOTAL POINTS	25	

Merge Records to Create Letters to Insurance Companies
File: **AL1-U2-LancasterClinic.accdb**, and **AL1-U2-Act2-LCIns.docx**

Steps	Tasks	Criteria	Value	Score
1	Exporting, Accuracy	Merge data in insurance company database to a blank Word document (user-determined fields for inside address and appropriate salutation).	6	
2	Typing, Organization	Compose letter to insurance companies informing them that Lancaster Clinic is providing mental health counseling services to people with health insurance through their company. An informational brochure is being sent about Lancaster Clinic and a request for information is being made from the insurance companies on services and service limitations. Include an appropriate complimentary close. Use name and title *Marianne Lambert, Clinic Director* for signature and add reference initials. When merge is completed, name document **AL1-U2-Act2-LCIns**.	10	
3	Finishing, organization	Print first two letters in merged document, then close **AL1-U2-Act2-LCIns.docx**. Close main document without saving, then exit Word. In Access, close database.	4	
		TOTAL POINTS	20	

Internet Research

Health Information Search
File: *User-Determined*

Steps	Tasks	Criteria	Value	Score
1	Research, Accuracy	Search Internet for information on health concern or disease. Look for specific organizations, interest groups, or individuals who are connected to the topic chosen. Topic may be an organization that raises money to support research, a support group that posts information or answers questions, or find information about clinics or doctors who specialize in the topic. Try to find at least ten different groups that support the health concern being researched.	10	
2	Database Management, Table and Field Management, Writing, Finishing	Create database in Access, then create a table that includes information from the research. Design table so that name, address, phone number, and web address of the organizations found can be stored. Identify connection the group has to the topic (supports research, interest group, treats patients, etc.). Create a report to summarize findings. In Word, create a letter that can be used to write for further information about the organization. Use names and addresses in database to merge with the letter. Select, then print first two letters that result from the merge. Write a paragraph describing information learned about the health concern that was not previously known.	20	
		TOTAL POINTS	30	

Job Study

City Improvement Projects
File: *User-Determined*

Steps	Tasks	Criteria	Value	Score
1	Database Mgt, Table and Field Management,	Create database, then table stores following information for each project: a project ID number, a description of project, budgeted dollar amount to be spent, amount spent to date, amount of time allocated to project, and amount of time spent to date. Enter five city improvement projects into the table (user-created sample data).	12	
2	Queries, Accuracy, Finishing, Organization	Create a query based on table that calculates percent of budgeted dollars spent to date and percent of budgeted time spent to date. Print the table and query.	8	
		TOTAL POINTS	20	

Rubrics

Note that the following are suggested rubrics. Instructors should feel free to customize the rubric to suit their grading standards and/or to adjust the point values.

Suggested Scoring Distribution: Above average = student completes 80% or more of task(s); average = student completes 70–79% of task(s); below average = student completes 69% or less of task(s)

Benchmark Access 2013 Level 2, Chapter 1

Skills Check

Assessment 1: Create a New Database
File: **AL2-C1-BenchmarkGolf.accdb**

Steps	Tasks	Criteria	Value	Score
1	Creating Database	Create a new blank database name **AL2-C1-BenchmarkGolf.accdb**.	1	
2-3	Creating Tables	Create tables shown in Figure 1.6 to store membership records for Benchmark Golf and Country Club. Include setting primary key and assigning data types and field sizes. Close all tables.	14	
		TOTAL POINTS	15	

Assessment 2: Add Captions and Disallow Blank Values
File: **AL2-C1-BenchmarkGolf.accdb**

Steps	Tasks	Criteria	Value	Score
1	Creating Captions	With **AL2-C1-BenchmarkGolf.accdb** open, create captions for fields as shown.	1	
2-3	Making Field Required	Make the *ZIP* field a required field. Disallow zero-length strings. Save and close all tables.	14	
		TOTAL POINTS	15	

Assessment 3: Create Custom Formats and Input Masks
File: **AL2-C1-BenchmarkGolf.accdb**

Steps	Tasks	Criteria	Value	Score
1	Creating Custom Formats	With **AL2-C1-BenchmarkGolf.accdb** open, create the following custom formats: • Display state text in uppercase characters • Display all birth dates with month spelled out in abbreviated form followed by day of month (2 digits) and year (4 digits) with one space separating each section • Display monthly fee in blue with two decimal values that will show zeros if no value is entered	6	
2-3	Creating Custom Input Masks	Create the following custom input masks: • In *MemberID* field in Members table and *FamilyMemID* field in Family Members table, require all three digits and display underscore character as placeholder. • Require *ZIP* field in Members table to be entered in pattern five required digits followed by a hyphen and four required digits. Display pound symbol (#) as placeholder • Use input mask wizard to create standard input mask for two telephone fields in Members table. Edit codes in property to make three characters in area code required digits. • Create input mask for both birth date fields that will match custom format pattern created for *ZIP* field in Step 1b, except include hyphens between each section. Store display characters in field and display underscore character as placeholder. Save and close all tables.	14	
		TOTAL POINTS	20	

Assessment 4: Add Records
File: **AL2-C1-BenchmarkGolf.accdb**

Steps	Tasks	Criteria	Value	Score
1	Adding Records	With **AL2-C1-BenchmarkGolf.accdb** open, add records as shown. Type text in *State* field to test format code. Test zip codes, telephone numbers, and dates, being careful to watch placeholders and enter in required pattern.	16	
2-4	Adjusting Column Widths, Printing	Adjust all column widths to Best Fit. Print each table in landscape orientation. Close all tables. Close the **AL2-C1-BenchmarkGolf.accdb** database.	4	
		TOTAL POINTS	20	

Visual Benchmark

Create a New Database

File: **AL2-C1-PawsParadise.accdb**

Steps	Tasks	Criteria	Value	Score
1	Creating Database	Create new blank database named **AL2-C1-PawsParadise.accdb**.	1	
2	Creating Tables	Create tables shown in database diagram in Figure 1.7 for Paws Paradise Boarding Inc. to store records of dog owners, dogs, and kennel categories including setting primary key and assigning data types and field sizes.	8	
3	Analyzing Datasheets	Analyze datasheets as shown in Figure 1.8. Make necessary changes to field properties. Datasheets show captions, default values, custom formats, and rich text formatting in the records. Use the following information to set other field properties not visible in the datasheet: • Make *ZIP* a required field and then use input mask wizard to create default input mask for a ZIP code. • Use input mask wizard to create default input mask for both telephone fields; then edit masks to change area code to three required digits.	6	
4	Adding Records	Add records shown in datasheets to the tables.	8	
5-7	Adjusting Column Widths, Printing, Saving	Adjust all column widths to Best Fit. Print each table in landscape orientation. Save and close all tables. Close **AL2-C1-PawsParadise.accdb**.	2	
		TOTAL POINTS	25	

Case Study

Part 1

File: **AL2-C1-CS-P1-BestarPlumbing.docx**

Steps	Tasks	Criteria	Value	Score
1	Creating Word Document	Design tables for data using invoice and the following additional information form the owner: • Customer numbers are assigned using first three letters of customer's last name all uppercase and followed by three-digits after a hyphen character. • Some invoices include parts with a labor charge. Individual parts are not itemized on customer invoice. Service technician shows a single line on invoice for all parts used. • Bestar has two labor rates: $41.75 for senior service technician and $28.00 for apprentice technician. Using Word, create a document that diagrams the tables including table names, field names, data types, and field sizes. Use asterisk to denote the primary key field in teach table. Instructor will instruct if required format of diagram in text boxes or tables in Word, or if handwritten diagram is acceptable.	8	
2	Saving, Printing	Save As **AL2-C1-CS-P1-BestarPlumbing**. Save, print, and close **AL2-C1-CS-P1-BestarPlumbing.docx**.	2	
		TOTAL POINTS	10	

Part 2

File: **AL2-C1-BestarPlumbing.accdb**

Steps	Tasks	Criteria	Value	Score
1	Creating Database	Based on table diagram created in Part 1, create a new database named **AL2-C1-BestarPlumbing.accdb**.	2	
2	Creating Tables	Create tables including setting the primary key in each table.	18	
		TOTAL POINTS	20	

Part 3

File: **AL2-C1-BestarPlumbing.accdb**

Steps	Tasks	Criteria	Value	Score
1	Modifying Field	Based on field properties learned in the chapter that can be used to ensure data integrity and consistency, modify field properties in tables that can be used to restrict data accepted into the field and display the data after it has been accepted. Enter sample record in each table to test field properties.	8	
2	Adjusting Column Widths, Printing	Adjust all column widths to Best Fit. Print each. Save and close all tables. Close **AL2-C1-BestarPlumbing.accdb**	2	
		TOTAL POINTS	10	

Benchmark Access 2013 Level 2, Chapter 2

Skills Check

Assessment 1: Create a Lookup List
File: **AL2-C2-ViewIt.accdb**

Steps	Tasks	Criteria	Value	Score
1-3	Opening Database, Reviewing	Open database named **AL2-C2-ViewIt** and enable content. Open each table in Datasheet view and review table's fields and records. Close all tables. Open Relationships window and close Show Table dialog box. Close Relationships windows.	1	
4	Creating Lookup List	Open the WebOrders in Design view, make *CustID* the active field, and create lookup list to display values from another table using the following information: • Display *CustID*, *FirstName*, and *LastName* fields from WebCustomers table • Sort list in ascending order by *LastName* field • Clear *Hide key column* check box • Store *CustID* value • Accept default label for column of *CustID*	8	
5	Modifying Property	Modify Lookup property for *CustID* field that will ensure only items within list are allowed to be entered into the field.	4	
6-8	Saving, Testing, Printing	Save table. Switch to Datasheet view. Enter record shown to test lookup list. Print datasheet. Close WebOrders table.	2	
		TOTAL POINTS	15	

Assessment 2: Create a Table with a Multiple-Field Primary Key and Lookup Lists
File: **AL2-C2-ViewIt.accdb**

Steps	Tasks	Criteria	Value	Score
1	Creating Table	With **AL2-C2-ViewIt.accdb** open, create a new table to track videos ordered by customer using the information shown.	2	
2-3	Assigning Multiple-Field Primary Key, Saving	Assign a multiple-field primary key using both *WebOrdID* and *WebProdID* fields. Save table and name it *WebOrderDetails*.	2	
4	Creating Lookup List	Create lookup list for *WebOrdID* field that connects to *WebOrdID* field in WebOrders table. Add all three fields in WebOrders table to lookup list, do not specify a sort field, clear the *Hide key column*, store *WebOrdID* in field, and accept the default field name. Modify Lookup property to ensure only items within list are allowed to be entered into the field.	5	

Steps	Tasks	Criteria	Value	Score
5	Creating Lookup List	Create lookup list for *WebProdID* field that connects to *WebProdID* field in WebProducts table. Display *Product* field sorted in ascending order, make sure column width is wide enough to display entire video title in list, hide key column, and accept default field name. Modify Lookup property to ensure only items within list are allowed to be entered into the field.	5	
6	Saving Table, Testing Lookup Lists	Save table and switch to datasheet view. Add records to the WebOrderDetails datasheet to test lookup lists.	4	
7-8	Adjusting Column Widths, Saving Changes	Adjust all column widths to Best Fit. Print the datasheet. Close WebOrderDetails table. Save changes to the layout.	2	
		TOTAL POINTS	20	

Assessment 3: Edit Relationships
File: **AL2-C2-ViewIt.accdb**

Steps	Tasks	Criteria	Value	Score
1-2	Resizing, Moving	With **AL2-C2-ViewIt.accdb** open the Relationships window to view relationships created by Access when lookup lists were created. Resize and move table field list boxes to approximate size and location shown in Figure 2.11.	2	
3	Editing Relationships	Edit the relationships as follows: • Edit one-to-many relationship between WebCustomers and WebOrders to turn on referential integrity and the two cascade options. • Edit one-to-many relationship between WebOrders and WebOrderDetails to turn on referential integrity and the two cascade options. • Edit one-to-many relationship between WebProducts and WebOrderDetails to turn on referential integrity and the two cascade options.	6	
4-7	Creating Report, Printing	Create and print a relationship report. Write on printout the type of relationship that exists between WebOrders and WebProducts. Close the Relationships for **AL2-C2-ViewIt** report. Save report and accept default name in Save As box. Close Relationships window.	2	
		TOTAL POINTS	10	

Assessment 4: Create a Table with a One-To-One Relationship
File: **AL2-C2-ViewIt.accdb**

Steps	Tasks	Criteria	Value	Score
1-3	Creating Table, Assigning Primary Key	With **AL2-C2-ViewIt.accdb** open, create a new table using Design view to store a customer's credit card information using the information shown. Assign primary key to *CustID* field. Save table and name in *WebCustPymnt*.	4	
4	Creating Lookup List	Create lookup list for *CustID* field that connects to *CustID* field in WebCustomers table by following steps similar to those in Assessment 1, Step 4.(include FirstName, LastName, and HPhone fields). Sort the list by LastName and then by FirstName. Modify Lookup property to ensure only items within list are allowed to be entered into the field.	5	
5	Saving, Entering Record	Save the table. Switch to Datasheet view and enter the record shown.	3	
6-7	Adjusting Column Widths, Printing	Adjust all column widths to Best Fit. Print datasheet in landscape orientation. Close WebCustPymnt table. Save changes to layout.	2	
8-10	Editing Relationship	Open Relationships window and open Show Table dialog box. Add WebCustPymnt table to window. Edit the one-to-one relationship between WebCustomers and WebCustPymnt to turn on referential integrity and two cascade options. If necessary, rearrange table field list boxes in Relationship window to better see join line between WebCustPymnt and WebCustomers table.	4	
11-13	Printing, Closing	Printing relationship report changing page layout options as needed to fit report on one page. Close Relationships report. Save report and name report **Relationships-Assessment4**. Close Relationships window. Close **AL2-C2-VantageVideos** database.	2	
		TOTAL POINTS	20	

Visual Benchmark

Create Lookup Lists and Edit Relationships

File: **AL2-C2-PawsParadise.accdb**

Steps	Tasks	Criteria	Value	Score
1-3	Opening, Viewing, Creating Lookup Lists	Open **AL2-C2-PawsParadise.accdb**. *Note: This database is similar to the one created in Chapter 1. An additional table was created and several records added. Students should spend some time reviewing the tables and records.* Create the following lookup lists, making sure field value saved is always the primary key field: • In Dogs table, look up Kennel Category in KennelCategories table. Hide key column in this list. • In Dogs table, look up Customer Number in DogOwners table. Clear *Hide key column* in this list. • In Reservations table, look up Customer Number in DogOwners table. Clear *Hide key column* in this list.	6	
4	Editing Relationships	Open Relationships window and edit relationships to enforce referential integrity and turn on both cascade options for each relationship.	2	
5	Rearranging Table Field List Boxes	Rearrange and move table field list boxes as needed so Relationship window appears similar to one shown in Figure 2.12	2	
6	Creating Report, Printing	Create a relationships report. Print relationships report.	4	
7-8	Saving, Closing	Save relationships report using default name. Close report and Relationships window. Close **AL2-C2-PawsParadise.accdb** database.	1	
		TOTAL POINTS	15	

Case Study

Part 1

File: **AL2-C2-HillsdaleRealty.accdb**

Steps	Tasks	Criteria	Value	Score
1	Editing	Open **AL2-C2-HillsdaleRealty.accdb** and enable content. Edit the following: • Agents table is not in first normal form. • Field named *AgentName* contains both first and last names of each sales agent. Improve table design and modify table with two separate fields for representative names. • Add captions to name fields. • Correct data so names are correctly split into two columns.	14	
2	Adjusting Column Widths, Printing	Adjust all column widths to Best Fit. Print revised Agents table datasheet. Close table.	1	
		TOTAL POINTS	15	

Part 2
File: **AL2-C2-HillsdaleRealty.accdb**

Steps	Tasks	Criteria	Value	Score
1	Creating Lookup Lists	Create lookup lists as follows: • Listings table: need to be able to select correct Agent ID by viewing agent names in a sorted drop-down list. Display *AgentID* as value in the field. • Agents table: need to be able to select quota code by viewing all of the quota codes and amounts in a drop-down list. Display Commission Quote in datasheet but store *QuotaID* as field value. Edit caption for field to read *Quota* (instead of *Quota Code*). • SalesAndComm table: need to be able to select correct Listing Number by viewing listing numbers and address from Listings table. Column width is wide enough to display all street address information. Display *ListingNo* as value in field.	9	
2	Editing	Open Relationships window. If necessary, add all tables to window. Resize and arrange boxes so join lines between tables are easy to follow and understand. Edit each relationship to turn on referential integrity and two cascade options.	4	
3	Creating Report, Printing	Create, print, save a relationships report. Close relationships report. Close relationships window.	2	
		TOTAL POINTS	15	

Part 3
File: **AL2-C2-HillsdaleRealty.accdb**

Steps	Tasks	Criteria	Value	Score
1	Creating Table	Create table named *Preferences* to database. Create table using information provided. Student determines appropriate data types and other field properties.	4	
2	Assigning Primary Key	Assign primary key as combination of two fields: *ClientID* and *ListingNo*.	2	
3	Testing Lookup Lists	Add sample record to table to test lookup lists and multiple-value field.	2	
4	Adjusting Column Width, Printing	Adjust all column widths to Best Fit. Print datasheet. Close table saving the layout.	2	
5	Adding Table	Open relationships window, add the new table, and arrange layout so join lines are not overlapping.	4	
6	Editing	Edit relationships between Preferences and Listings and Agents to turn on referential integrity and two cascade options.	4	

Steps	Tasks	Criteria	Value	Score
7	Creating Report, Printing	Create a new relationships report named *Relationships-Part3*. Print and save report.	2	
		TOTAL POINTS	20	

Benchmark Access 2013 Level 2, Chapter 3

Skills Check

Assessment 1: Extract Records Using a Filter and Prompted Queries
File: **AL2-C3-ViewIt.accdb**

Steps	Tasks	Criteria	Value	Score
1-7	Opening Using Filter by Form Printing	Open database named **AL2-C3-ViewIt.accdb** and enable content. Open table name WebCustomers. Using Filter By Form, display only those customers who reside in Burlington with a ZIP code that begins with 05401. Save filter as a query named *CustBurlington05401*. Close Filter By Format datasheet, and close table. Click No when prompted to save changes to table design. Open the CustBurlington05401 query. Print query results datasheet in landscape orientation and close query.	5	
8-9	Creating, Printing Query	Create new query in Design view using the following specifications: • Add tables WebOrderDetails, WebOrders, and WebProducts to query. • Add fields *WebOrderID*, *DateOrd*, *Qty*, and *Product* to query design grid. (Note: WebOrderID from WebOrders table). • Create parameter query to prompt user to type the title of video in *Product* column. *Prompt should read: Type the movie title.* • Save query, name it *PromptedVideo*, and close query. Run PromptedVideo query. Type **The Longest Day** at Enter Parameter Value dialog box. Print query results datasheet and close query.	9	
10-11	Creating Parameter Query, Printing	Open PromptedVideo query. Delete prompt message in *Product* column. Create parameter query to prompt user to type beginning and ending date to view Web orders in the *DateOrd* column. Use SaveAs to name revised query *PromptedOrderDates* and close query. Run PromptedOrderDates query. Type **February 1, 2015** as beginning date and **February 28, 2015** as ending date. Print query results datasheet and then close the query.	6	
		TOTAL POINTS	20	

Assessment 2: Modify Join Properties
File: **AL2-C3-ViewIt.accdb**

Steps	Tasks	Criteria	Value	Score
1-2	Creating Query, Printing	With **AL2-C3-ViewIt.accdb** open, create a new query in Design view using the following specifications: • Add tables WebCustomers and WebOrders to query. • Add fields *CustID, FirstName, LastName,* and *WebOrderID* to query design grid. • Modify join type between WebCustomers table and WebOrders table to a left outer join. • Save query and name it *CustWebOrders*. Run query and print query results datasheet. Close query.	10	
3-4	Creating Query, Printing	Create new query in Design view using the following specifications: • Add tables WebOrderDetails and WebProducts to the query. • Add fields *WebOrdID, WebProdID,* and *Product* to query design grid. (*Note: WebProdID field from WebProducts table.*) • Modify the join type between the WebProducts table and the WebOrderDetails table to a left outer join. • Save the query and name it WebProductsOrders query. Print query results datasheet. Close query.	10	
		TOTAL POINTS	20	

Assessment 3: Add a Table to a Query and Create and Use a Subquery to Perform Calculations
File: **AL2-C3-ViewIt.accdb**

Steps	Tasks	Criteria	Value	Score
1-2	Modifying Query, Printing	With **AL2-C3-ViewIt.accdb** open, open the CustWebOrders query in Design view and modify query as follows: • Modify join type between WebCustomers table and WebOrders table to an inner join. • Add WebOrderDetails table and WebProducts table to query. • Add fields named *DataOrd, Qty, Product,* and *SellPrice* to query design grid. • Delete the CustID field from the query. • Create a calculated field with the column labeled TotalSale that multiplies the quantity ordered times the selling price. • Change the caption to Total Sale. Use Save As to name the query as *WebSalesWithTotal*. Run query. Print query results datasheet in landscape orientation with a left and right margin set to 0.5 inch. Close query.	8	

Steps	Tasks	Criteria	Value	Score
3-4	Creating Query, Printing	Create new query in Design view that calculates the total sale with tax as follows: • Nest the WebSalesWithTotal query in new query. • Add fields *WebOrdID, DateOrd,* and *Total Sale* to query design grid. • Create calculated field with column label *Tax* that multiplies the value in the *Total Sale* column times .06 (decimal equivalent to 6%). Format the calculated column to *Standard*. • *Create a second calculated column with the column label TotalSaleWithTax that adds the TotalSale column to the Tax column. Change the caption to Total Sale with Tax.* • Save query and name it *WebSalesWithTotalAndTax*. Run query. Display entire field heading of last column in query results datasheet. Print query results datasheet. Close query, saving changes.	12	
		TOTAL POINTS	20	

Assessment 4: Use Action Queries to Archive Records and Update Selling Prices
File: **AL2-C3-ViewIt.accdb**

Steps	Tasks	Criteria	Value	Score
1	Modifying Query	With **AL2-C3-ViewIt.accdb** open, open the WebSalesWithTotal query in Design view and modify query as follows: • Delete *SellPrice* and *Total Sale* columns from the query design grid. • Add criterion to select the records for sales during the month of February 2015. • Run query to make sure correct records are being selected. • Change query to a make-table query, name new table *Feb2015WebSales*, and archive it in the current database. • Use Save As and name revised query *Feb2015SalesMakeTable*. • Run and then close the query.	8	
2	Adjusting Column Widths, Printing	Open **Feb2015WebSales table.** Adjust column widths as necessary. Print datasheet. Close table saving changes to layout.	2	
3	Modifying Query	Open **Feb2015SalesMakeTable** query in Design View and modify as follows: • Change query to a delete query. • Remove WebCustomers, WebOrderDetails, and WebProducts tables from query. • Use Save As and name revised query *Feb2015SalesDelete*. • Run query and close query window.	8	
4	Printing	Open WebSalesWithTotal query. Print query results datasheet in landscape orientation with left and right margins of 0.5 inch. Close query.	2	

Steps	Tasks	Criteria	Value	Score
5	Creating Query	Create new query in Design view to update the selling prices of all movies with Web product IDs between CV-1026 and CV-1029 as follows: • Add WebProducts table to query. • Add *WebProdID* and *SellPrice* fields to query design grid. • Change query to an update query and add formula that will add $1.05 to selling price of each movie that has a Web product ID between CV-1026 and CV-1029. • Save query and name it *PriceUpdate*. • Run query and close query window.	8	
6-7	Printing, Closing	Open WebProducts table. Print datasheet. Close table. Close **AL2-C3-ViewIt.accdb**.	2	
		TOTAL POINTS	30	

Visual Benchmark

Calculate Days Boarded and Amount Due Using Nested Queries
File: **AL2-C3-PawsParadise.accdb**

Steps	Tasks	Criteria	Value	Score
1-2	Creating Calculations	Open **AL2-C3-PawsParadise.accdb**. After reviewing query results datasheets shown in Figure 3.13, create the calculations as follows: • Create first query to calculate number of days a dog is boarded in the kennel. Show in query results the reservation ID, customer's name, dog's name, and two date fields. Calculate the days the dog was boarded. Save query and name it *DaysBoarded*. • Nest DaysBoarded in new query. Add the Dogs and the KennelCategories tables to the query. Join the DaysBoarded query to the Dogs table on the common *DogName* field. Add fields to query design grid as shown in Figure 3.13 and calculate the amount due for each reservation. • Sort and format the query results as shown in Figure 3.13. Font is Cambria 11-point. The alternate row color used is Maroon 1 in *Standard Colors* section of color palette. Save query and name it ReservationTotals.	18	
3-5	Printing, Closing	Print ReservationsTotals query results datasheet in landscape orientation with left and right margins set at 0.5 inch. Close query. Close **AL2-C3-PawsParadise.accdb**.	2	
		TOTAL POINTS	20	

Case Study

Part 1

File: **AL2-C3-HillsdaleRealty.accdb**

Steps	Tasks	Criteria	Value	Score
1	Editing	Open **AL2-C3-HillsdaleRealty.accdb** and enable content. Design, create, save, run, and print query results to provide the required information. Student determines appropriate descriptive names for each query. Use the following information: • A list of sales by agent that includes date of sale, address, sale price, and commission rate. Sort query results by agent's last name and then by date of sale with both fields sorted in ascending order. • Modify first query to allow office manager to type agent's name when running query so that the office manager can view individual sales reports by agent. Test query by running query using agent name *Cecilia Ortega*. Save revised query with new name. • A list that shows all agents and each agent's clients. Show client ID, client first name, and client last name next to each agent's name. Make sure query results show all agents so that the manager can see agents that have not yet signed a client. • A list of agents that show his/her co-broker agent. The Agents table contains a field named *CoBroker*. This field is the agent ID for person assigned to co-broker listings. The office manager wants to see the agent's last name instead of his/her ID number in the *CoBroker* field. Sort list in ascending order by AgentLName. • Modify first query to add a column to calculate the amount of commission that will be owed on sale by multiplying the sale price times the commission rate. Save revised query using a new name. • Use a query to update all commission quota values to add 15% to the existing quotas. After updating the values, create a new query to show each agent and his/her respective commission quote. Sort the list in ascending order by agent last name.	18	
2	Printing	Print all query results.	2	
		TOTAL POINTS	20	

Part 2

File: **AL2-C3HillsdaleRealty.accdb**

Steps	Tasks	Criteria	Value	Score
1	Modifying Query	Use Help to find how to create a top values query. Using the information, modify the first query created in Part 1 to produce the top 5 list.	8	
2	Saving, Printing	Save revise query with a new name. Print query results.	2	
		TOTAL POINTS	10	

Part 3

File: **AL2-C3-HillsdaleRealty.accdb**

Steps	Tasks	Criteria	Value	Score
1	Creating Query	The office manager wants to review client preferences for each listing with each preference on a separate line. Include in the list: date of listing, street address, client's name, client's telephone number. Add criteria to select only those records where client has request a pre-sale inspection or staging service for his/her listing.	4	
2	Saving, Printing	Save query. Print query.	2	
		TOTAL POINTS	10	

Benchmark Access 2013 Level 2, Chapter 4

Skills Check

Assessment 1: Create A Custom Form Using Design View

File: **AL2-C4-ViewIt.accdb**

Steps	Tasks	Criteria	Value	Score
1-2	Creating Query	Open database named **AL2-C4-ViewIt** and enable content. Create a query named **CustWebOrders** using the following specifications: • Add WebOrderDetails, WebOrders, and WebProducts table to the query. Add the following fields in order: • **WebOrders Table**: *WebOrderID, CustID, DateOrd* • **WebOrderDetails Table** *Qty* • **WebProducts Table**: *Product, SellPrice* Run query and close query results datasheet.	6	

Steps	Tasks	Criteria	Value	Score

3	Creating New Form	Create new form using Design view and build the form using the following specifications:
		• Expand width of form in grid to 6.5-inch position in horizontal ruler.
		• Add title in *Form Header* section with text *Web Customer Orders*. Move title until first letter in title text (W) is at approximately 1.5-inch position in horizontal ruler.
		• Add student name in label control object centered in *Form Footer* section.
		• Apply Retrospect theme.
		• Connect WebCustomers table to form and all of the fields to *Detail* section in layout shown in Figure 4.14. Adjust width of control objects as shown. Use Size/Space and Align button to assist in positioning multiple controls at same horizontal or vertical position and adjust spacing between controls.
		• Change tab order of fields: *HPhone* field selected after *CustID*.
		• Add tab control object below existing fields approximately two inches in height and width extended to right edge of form. Use the following:
		  ◦ On first page, change caption to *Web Orders* and add all fields from CustWebOrders query in subform. Delete subform label control object. Delete label control object and text box control object for CustID field in subform and move remaining fields up to fill in the space. Move and resize subform to fit width of page. Adjust column widths in Form view as needed to view all columns within the page.
		  ◦ On second page, change caption to *Payment Information* and add all fields except *CustID and EmailAdd* from WebCustPymnt table in subform. Delete subform label control object and move and resize the subform to fit width of the page. Adjust column widths in Form view as needed to view all of the columns within the page.
			14	

4	Formatting	Apply bold formatting to the label control objects and Green, Accent 6, Lighter 80% background color to the text box control objects.	4	
5-7	Saving, Printing	Save form and name in *WebCustOrders*. Print form in Form view with first record displayed and Web Orders page active. Close form.	1	
		TOTAL POINTS	25	

Assessment 2: Create a Form Using the Form Wizard; Add a Calculation and Graphics
File: **AL2-C4-ViewIt.accdb**

Steps	Tasks	Criteria	Value	Score
1-2	Creating Form	With **AL2-C4-ViewIt.accdb** open, create a new form using Form Wizard as follows: • Select all fields from WebProducts table. • Select Columnar style. • Accept default form named *WebProducts*. View completed form in Form view.	5	
3	Editing Form	Switch to Design view and edit the form similar to form shown in Figure 4.15 using the following: • *Retail Value* is a calculated field that uses a formula to multiply quantity of videos in stock times selling price. • Clip art image can be found by searching using keyword *Movies*. (Select suitable alternative image if image not available.) • Font color for title text and line is Maroon 5 in *Standard Colors*. • Format options to match as closely as possible to form in Figure 4.15.	14	
4-5	Printing, Saving	Print form in Form view with first record displayed. Save and close form.	1	
		TOTAL POINTS	20	

Assessment 3: Create a Restricted-Use Form
File: **AL2-C4-ViewIt.accdb**

Steps	Tasks	Criteria	Value	Score
1-2	Creating, Modifying Form	With **AL2-C4-ViewIt.accdb** open, create a datasheet using the WebCustPymnt table. Modify form so records cannot be deleted when using the form.	7	
3-9	Capturing Image, Creating Document, Printing, Saving	In Datasheet view, select a record and complete the following: • Use PrintScreen or Insert Screenshot command to capture image of screen with Delete button dimmed while record is selected. • Paste screen image into a blank Word document. Type student name, chapter number and assessment number, and additional identification required by instructor. • Print document. • Save As: **AL2-C4-ViewItForm.docx**. • Exit Word Save form with default form name *WebCustPymnt* and close form.	3	
		TOTAL POINTS	10	

Assessment 4: Create a Custom Form Using the Blank Form Too; Add a List Box
File: **AL2-C4-ViewIt.accdb**

Steps	Tasks	Criteria	Value	Score
1	Creating Form	With **AL2-C4-ViewIt.accdb** open, create a new form using the Blank Form tool that adds all fields from the WebCustomers table. Widen label columns so all of the label text is visible in the form.	4	
2-5	Adding, Deleting List Box Control Object	Add a list box control object between *City* and *State* fields. Type the values into list as follows: **Burlington** **Charlotte** **Colchester** Store values in field named *City*. Accept default label for control object. Delete label control object for list box. Add title *Customer Maintenance Form* to form. Save form and name it *WebCustomerMaintenance*.	8	
6-8	Adding Record, Printing	Switch to Form view. Add the following new record to the WebCustomers table: *Customer ID* **121** *First Name* **Morgan** *Last Name* **Kalil** *Street Address* **29011 Greenbush Road** *City* **Charlotte** *State* **VT** *ZIP Code* **05445-9314** Home Phone **802-555-9185** Print record and close form. Close **AL2-C4-ViewIt.accdb**.	3	
		TOTAL POINTS	15	

Visual Benchmark

Create Custom Reservations Form
File: **AL2-C4-PawsParadise.accdb**

Steps	Tasks	Criteria	Value	Score
1-3	Creating Form, Saving	Open **AL2-C4-PawsParadise.accdb**. After reviewing form shown in Figures 4.16 and 4.17, create form using their best judgment for alignment, spacing, sizing, and position of controls. Include the following information: • Connect Reservations table to main form. • Apply Ion Boardroom theme. • Line color is *Dark Blue* with thickness set at *3 pt*. • Days Boarded value is calculated by subtracting two date fields. • Each subform's Default View property changed to *Single Form*. *This view display fields one below the other*. Save form with name *Reservations*.	12	

Steps	Tasks	Criteria	Value	Score
4-5	Printing, Closing	Print form in Form view. Print first record only. Close form. Close **AL2-C4-PawsParadise.accdb**.	3	
		TOTAL POINTS	15	

Case Study

Part 1

File: **AL2-C4-HillsdaleRealty.accdb**

Steps	Tasks	Criteria	Value	Score
1	Creating Form	Open **AL2-C4-HillsdaleRealty.accdb** and enable content. Design and create form similar to Figure 4.18 using Listings and SalesAndComm tables. Include the following: • Apply Organic theme and Orange colors. • Include calculated field at bottom of subform. • Modify tab order of fields to match arrangement of fields in Figure 4.18.	14	
2	Saving, Printing	Save form with appropriate name. Print first record in form.	1	
		TOTAL POINTS	15	

Part 2

File: **AL2-C4-HillsdaleRealty.accdb**

Steps	Tasks	Criteria	Value	Score
1	Creating Form	Design and create form that display information from Agents table along with clients related to each agent. Student determines form design, layout, and formatting options.	14	
2	Saving, Printing	Save form with appropriate name. Print form with first record displayed in main form.	1	
		TOTAL POINTS	15	

Part 3

File: **AL2-C4-CS-P3-HillsdaleRealty.docx**

Steps	Tasks	Criteria	Value	Score
1	Revising Form	Open main form created in Part I. Remove Record Navigation bar in subform. Close Property sheet and display form in Form view. Save revised form.	3	

Steps	Tasks	Criteria	Value	Score
2	Capturing Image	Capture a screen image of revised form using PrintScreen or Insert Screenshot command. Paste screen image in new Word document. Type student's name, chapter number, and other identifying information required by instructor.	5	
3	Printing, Saving	Print Word document. Save Word document as **AL2-C4-CS-P3-HillsdaleRealty**. Exit Word.	2	
		TOTAL POINTS	10	

Benchmark Access 2013 Level 2
Unit 1 Performance Assessment

Skills Check

Assessment 1: Create Tables for a Property Management Database
File: **AL2-U1-BenchmarkPropMgt.accdb**

Steps	Tasks	Criteria	Value	Score
1	Creating Database	Create database **AL2-U1-BenchmarkPropMgt.accdb**.	2	
2-3	Creating Tables	Create four tables shown in Figure U1.1. Set primary key, assign data types, and field sizes. Use default setting for fields that do not have field size specified in Figure U1.1. Close all tables.	12	
4-5	Compacting	At Access Options box, set *Compact on Close*. Close **AL2-U1-BenchmarkPropMgt.accdb**.	1	
		TOTAL POINTS	15	

Assessment 2: Add Captions and Modify Field Properties
File: **AL2-U1-BenchmarkPropMgt.accdb**

Steps	Tasks	Criteria	Value	Score
1	Creating Captions	Open **AL2-U1-BenchmarkPropMgt.accdb**. Create captions for fields as instructed in assessment.	4	
2	Changing Settings	Make *UnitNo* in Tenants table a required field including disallowing zero-length strings.	2	
3	Creating Custom Format	Create a custom format for all date fields that displays dates in the short date format with leading zeroes for months and days. Use a slash to separate each section: *0105/2015*.	4	

Steps	Tasks	Criteria	Value	Score
4	Creating Custom Input Masks	Create the following custom input masks: • In *BldgCde* in Buildings table, require three digits and display underscore character as placeholder. • In *TenID* in Tenants table, require three digits and display underscore character as placeholder. • In all date fields, create an input mask that requires dates to be entered using short date format created in Step 3 with all digits required. • Require all telephone numbers to include area code with hyphens between each section of the number. Display pound symbol as the placeholder character.	8	
5-7	Editing, Saving	Enable rich text formatting in the *Notes* field in the Buildings table. Make 995.00 the default value in the *Rent* field in the Tenants table. Save and close all tables.	2	
		TOTAL POINTS	20	

Assessment 3: Add Records
File: **AL2-U1-BenchmarkPropMgt.accdb**

Steps	Tasks	Criteria	Value	Score
1	Adding Records	With **AL2-U1-BenchmarkPropMgt.accdb** open, add the records as instructed in assessment.	9	
2	Formatting	Apply bold and red font color to years entered in *Notes* field in each record.	3	
3-4	Adjusting Column Widths, Printing, Saving	Adjust column widths in each table until all data is entirely visible. Print table, adjusting print options to fit table on one page. Save and close all tables.	3	
		TOTAL POINTS	15	

Assessment 4: Create Lookup Lists and Edit Relationships
File: **AL2-U1-BenchmarkPropMgt.accdb**

Steps	Tasks	Criteria	Value	Score
1	Creating Form	With **AL2-U1-BenchmarkPropMgt.accdb** open, create the following lookup lists to display values from another table: • In the SiteManagers table, create lookup list for *BldgCde* that displays building codes and names from the Building table. Sort list by building names and show key column. Widen the column displaying building names to accommodate longer names. Store *BldgCde* value in the field. • In the Tenants table, create a lookup list for *BldgCde* using the same specifications as completed in previous step. • In the Leases table, create a lookup list for *TenID* that displays the tenant IDs, first names, and last names from Tenants table. Sort list by last names and show key column. Store *TenID* value in the field.	6	

Steps	Tasks	Criteria	Value	Score
2	Creating Multiple-Value Drop-Down List	Create a multiple-value drop-down list for the *Appliances* field in the Buildings table with the following items: **Refrigerator**　　**Dishwasher** **Stove**　　**Washer** **Microwave**　　**Dryer**	3	
3	Editing	Edit the three records to populate *Appliances* field as follows: 　*Bldg Code*　　*Appliances* 　115　　　　Refrigerator, Stove, Microwave 　120　　　　Refrigerator, Stove, Microwave, Dishwasher 　125　　　　Refrigerator, Stove, Washer, Dryer	3	
4-5	Adjusting Field Widths, Printing	Adjust field width of *Appliances* column to Best Fit. Change field width of *Notes* column to 35 and row height to 30. Print Buildings table in landscape orientation with left and right margin set to 0.25 inch. Close Buildings table and save changes to table layout.	5	
6-8	Editing Relationships, Creating and Printing Report	In Relationships window, edit all relationships to turn on referential integrity and the two cascade options. Arrange table field list boxes to show relationships with primary tables on the left and related tables on the right. Be sure no join lines overlap each other. Create, save, and print a relationships report using default report name. Close relationship report window and relationships window.	8	
		TOTAL POINTS	25	

Assessment 5: Create Select Queries
File: **AL2-U1-BenchmarkPropMgt.accdb**

Steps	Tasks	Criteria	Value	Score
1	Adding Records	With **AL2-U1-BenchmarkPropMgt.accdb** open, design, and create the following select queries: • A query named *PromptedTenant* that displays *BldgCde* and *BldgName* fields from Buildings table and *UnitNo, FName, LName,* and *Phone* fields from Tenants table. Include prompts to specify building name and unit number criteria when running query. • A query name *PromptedLease* that displays *TenID* from Tenants table, *BldgName* from the Buildings table, *UnitNo, FName,* and *LName* fields from Tenants table, and *StartDate, EndDate,* and *SecDep* fields from Leases table. Include prompts to specify starting date and ending date criteria when running queries. • A query named *TenantsList* that displays *BldCde* and *BldgName* fields from Buildings table and *UnitNo, FName, LName* and *Rent* fields from Tenants table. Sort in ascending order by building names. Modify join properties to show all records from Buildings table in left outer join. • A query names *BuildingsList* that displays all of the fields in Buildings table except the *Notes* field. Show each query in multiple-value *Appliances* field in a separate row in query results datasheet and assign the field the caption *Supplied Appliances*.	12	

Steps	Tasks	Criteria	Value	Score
2	Running Query, Printing	Run the PromptedTenant query. Type **coventry park** for building name and **110** for unit number. Print query results datasheet and close query.	2	
3	Running Query, Printing	Run PromptedLease query. Type **02/01/2015** for started date and **01/31/2016** for ending date. Print query results datasheet in landscape orientation and close query.	2	
4	Running Query, Printing	Run TenantsList query, print query results datasheets, and close query.	2	
5	Running Query, Printing	Run BuildingsList query, print query results datasheet, and close query.	2	
		TOTAL POINTS	20	

Assessment 6: Calculate in a Query and Use an Update Query to Increase Rents
File: **AL2-U1-BenchmarkPropMgt.accdb**

Steps	Tasks	Criteria	Value	Score
1	Creating Queries, Printing	With **AL2-U1-BenchmarkPropMgt.accdb** open, create query to calculate total rental income from each unit as follows: • Open TenantsList query in Design view and use Save Object As to name query *RentalIncome*. • Modify join properties to show records only when joined fields are equal in both tables using an inner join. • Add calculated field to query with column heading *Annual Rent* that calculates twelve of rental income. • Change the caption to Annual Rent. • Run query and add total row in query results datasheet with sum function in *Rent* and *Annual Rent* columns. • Print query results datasheet in landscape orientation and close query saving changes.	10	
2-3	Creating Update Query	Create an update query named *RentIncome* to increase all rents by 4 percent. Run query. Close RentIncrease query.	4	
4	Printing	Open RentalIncome query. Print query results datasheets in landscape orientation. Close query.	1	
		TOTAL POINTS	15	

Assessment 7: Design and Create Forms
File: **AL2-U1-BenchmarkPropMgt.accdb**

Steps	Tasks	Criteria	Value	Score
1	Creating Form	With **AL2-U1-BenchmarkPropMgt.accdb** open, complete the following: • Design and create a form to enter data into the Buildings table as a main form with Site Managers table in a subform. Name the main form *BldgsAndMgrs*. • Determine form design, layout, and formatting options. • Include an appropriate clip art image in the form. • Type student's name in *Form Footer* section. • Print first record in Buildings table displayed in Form view.	10	
2	Creating Form	Complete the following: • Design and create form to enter data into Tenants table as a main form with the Leases table in a subform similar to the form shown in Figure U1.2. • Name the form *TenantsAndLeases*. • Modify tab order to move in the order: • *Tenant ID, Bldg Code, Unit No, Telephone, First Name, Last Name*, and *Rent* • *Annual Rent* is a calculated control. • Match the color formatting as closely as possible within the theme colors. • Add labels and graphics as shown in assessment.	14	
3-4	Printing	Print all records using TenantsAndLeases form. Close the form saving changes. Close **AL2-U1-BenchmarkPropMgt.accdb**.	1	
		TOTAL POINTS	25	

Writing Activities

Activity 1: Design Tables for Parking Information in the Property Management Database
File: **AL2-U1-BenchmarkPropMgt.accdb; AL2-U1-Act1-BenchmarkPropMgt.docx**

Steps	Tasks	Criteria	Value	Score
1	Creating Table	With **AL2-U1-BenchmarkPropMgt.accdb** open, complete the following: • Design and create a table to store parking rates. • Design and create a table to track rental information for each parking spot using the information provided. • Create two lookup lists in the assigned parking table, on to look up the correct parking rate in the rates table and another to look up the tenant's ID in the Tenants table. • Add at least three records to test tables.	15	
2	Creating Word Document	In Microsoft Word, document table design by including each table's name and fields created in each table including data type and field properties that student set such as field size, caption, input mask, etc. Indicate primary key(s) in each type with an asterisk preceding the field name. Save As **AL2-U1-Act1-BenchmarkPropMgt.docx**. Print document and exit Word.	10	
		TOTAL POINTS	25	

Activity 2: Design Tables for a Soccer League Database
File: **AL2-U1-SoccerRegn.accdb**

Steps	Tasks	Criteria	Value	Score
1	Creating Database	Create a new database named **AL2-U1-SoccerRegn.accdb**.	1	
2	Creating Tables	Design and create tables based on the sample form shown in Figure U1.3.	6	
3	Creating Form, Printing	Create one data entry form to enter information into tables. Add at least five records to test table and form design. Print all records using form.	3	
4	Creating Queries	Design and create the following: • Prompted query that will print a list of players selecting records by age category. • Query that will print soccer players registered for current season including registration fee paid. • Add total row in query results datasheet to show total registration fees collected. • Run each query to test query design. • Print query results datasheets.	10	
5	Creating Word Document	In Microsoft Word, create a one-page quick reference guide that provides instructions on how to open the database and use the data entry form, the prompted query, and the registration fee query. Include how to print objects in database, including how to print a selected form.	9	
6	Saving, Printing	Save Word document as **AL2-U1-Act2-SoccerRegistration**. Print document and exit Word.	1	
		TOTAL POINTS	30	

Internet Research

Activity: Plan Your Volunteer Work

File: **AL2-U1-VolunteerOrg.accdb; AL2-U1-VolunteerInfo.docx**

Steps	Tasks	Criteria	Value	Score
1	Researching, Creating Tables	Using the Internet, research five to eight organizations in local area that need volunteers on a regular basis. Select a variety of organizations. Create a database **AL2-U1-VolunteerOrg.accdb**. Design and create tables to store the organization name, address, telephone number, and volunteer coordinator (if applicable). Include a field with notes about the organization's mission. Include an Events table related to the organization.	15	
2	Creating a Form, Printing	Design and create a form for data entry. Use the form to input records for the organizations researched. Print all records using the form.	4	
3	Creating Word Document	Using Microsoft Word, create a brief document with instructions for friends and relatives on how to open the database, browse records using the form, and print information.	5	
4	Saving, Printing Document	Save As **AL2-U1-VolunteerInfo**. Print document.	1	
		TOTAL POINTS	25	

Benchmark Access 2013 Level 2, Chapter 5

Skills Check

Assessment 1: Create A Custom Report Using Design View

File: **AL2-C5-ViewIt.accdb**

Steps	Tasks	Criteria	Value	Score

1-2	Creating Report	Open database named **AL2-C5-ViewIt** and enable content.
		• Create a new report using Report Design and build the report using the following specifications:
		• Add title in *Report Header* section with text **Web Products and Sales**.
		• Add student name in label control object in center of *Report Footer* section.
		• Connect WebProducts table to report. Add all fields from table to report.
		• Move label control objects for each field from *Detail* section to *Page Header* section arrange controls horizontally in order fields appear in table. Place the objects Field Label to position left edge of label control object on the horizontal ruler:
		• Field Label Product ID: left margin, Product: 2-in mark, In Stock: 4.25 inch mark and Selling Price as 5-inch mark
		• Resize *Page Header* section so extra space is removed
		• Align each text box control object in *Detail* section below object's associated label control object in *Page Header* section as specified: WebProdID: left margin, Product: 1-inch mark, Instock: 4-inch mark and SellPrice: 5-inch mark.
		• Be sure data is not truncated. Make adjustments as needed.
		• Apply Retrospect theme. Bold the title.
		• Insert subreport into *Detail* section using the following specifications:
		  ◦ Use WebSaleswithTotal query and add fields in subreport with the order of *CustID, WebOrdID, DateOrd, WebProdID,* and *Qty*.
		  ◦ Accept default subreport name.
		  ◦ Edit text in subreport label control object to *Web Sales*.
		  ◦ Be sure data is properly linked.
		  ◦ Remove *WebProdID* field from subreport and move *Qty* field left to fill in the space.
		  ◦ Move and/or resize subreport control object.
		• Resize *Detail* section so section ends below subreport.
		• Format *WebProdID, Product, InStock,* and *SellPrice* fields in *Detail* section to 12-point bold.
		• Make adjustments to position, height, width, alignment, or formatting of any control objects. Do not add further elements.
			24	

3-4	Saving, Printing	Save report as *WebProductsWithSales.* Print and close report.	1	
		TOTAL POINTS	25	

Assessment 2: Enhance the Report
File: **AL2-C5-ViewIt.accdb**

Steps	Tasks	Criteria	Value	Score
1-7	Formatting	With **AL2-C5-ViewIt.accdb** open, display WebProductsWithSales report in Design view. Make the following changes: • Add page numbering using *Page N of M* format at bottom left of each page. • Add current date to bottom right of each page aligning right edge of control in *Page Footer* section at 7-inch position in horizontal ruler. • Insert appropriate clip art image to top right of report resized with right edge of image aligned at 7-inch position in horizontal ruler. Adjust report title to center it vertically left of clip art image and horizontally within title control object. • Draw horizontal line under report title. Change line thickness to 2 points and apply the Tan, Accent 5, Darker 50% line color. • Change all margins for report to 0.5 inch. Click *Select Control Farthest to the Right* in Error Checking. Click *Remove Extra Report Space* at drop-down list in Error Checking.	9	
8-9	Saving, Printing	Save report. Print page 1 only of revise report and close report.	1	
		TOTAL POINTS	10	

Assessment 3: Create a New Report with Grouping and Totals
File: **AL2-C5-ViewIt.accdb**

Steps	Tasks	Criteria	Value	Score
1	Creating Report	With **AL2-C5-ViewIt.accdb** open, create a Report using Report Wizard as follows: • Use WebSalesWithTotal query and add all fields to report except *CustID* and *WebProdID*. • Group by *DateOrd* field by month. • Leave sort field blank. • Used *Stepped* layout in *Landscape* orientation. • Edit report title to *WebSalesByDate*.	5	
2-3	Adding Text	Preview both pages of report and switch to Design view. Add student name in label control object at left edge of *Report Footer* section.	2	
4-6	Editing	Open Group, Sort, and Total pane and make the following changes: • Add Sum function to each month's *Total Sale* column. Show grand total at end of report as well as subtotal in group footer. • Add sort by *LastName* field. Add appropriate label next to Sum function in *DateOrd Footer* section and next to Sum function in *Report Footer* section. Edit report title to *Web Sales by Date* and edit *DateOrd by Month* label to *Month*.	5	
7-9	Formatting, Printing	After viewing report in Print Preview, adjust column widths as necessary so that all data is entirely visible. Abbreviate long column labels if necessary. Change top and bottom margin to 0.75 inch. Print report. Save and close report.	3	
		TOTAL POINTS	15	

Assessment 4: Create and Format a New Report with a Chart
File: **AL2-C5-ViewIt.accdb**

Steps	Tasks	Criteria	Value	Score
1-2	Creating Report	With **AL2-C5-VantageVideos.accdb** open, create a new report using Report Wizard as follows: • Use WebCustomers table and add customer number, customer name, and home telephone fields to report. • Do not group or sort report. • Use *Columnar* layout in *Portrait* orientation. • Edit report title to *WebCustomersWithChart*. Preview report.	6	
3-4	Inserting Chart	Switch to Design view. Insert chart at right side of page next to each customer record using the following information: • Use WebSalesWithTotal query. • Add *DateOrd* and *Total Sale* fields to chart field list. • Select bar chart style. Student determines chart field list. • Accept default chart layout with *DateOrd by month* as *x*-axis labels and *SumOfTotal Sale* as value axis. • Accept *CustID* as linked field for report and chart. • Edit title for chart to *Web Sales*.	8	
5-6	Editing Chart	Preview report with bar chart and switch to Design view. Edit chart as follows: • Change chart type to clustered column chart with 3-D visual effect. • Delete legend. • Change color of bar to dark purple.	3	
7-11	Editing Report, Printing	Edit report title to *Customers with Web Sales Chart*. Add student name in label control object at bottom left of report. Make formatting changes to improve appearance of report. Print Page 1 only of report. Save and close report.	3	
		TOTAL POINTS	20	

Assessment 5: Create a Custom Report Using the Blank Report Tool
File: **AL2-C5-ViewIt.accdb**

Steps	Tasks	Criteria	Value	Score
1-3	Creating Report	With **AL2-C5-ViewIt.accdb** open, create a new report using Blank Report tool. Add first field named *CustID* from WebCustomers table. Change layout of report to *Stacked*. Add remaining fields from WebCustomers table below *Customer ID* field.	8	
4-6	Formatting	Widen label columns so that *Street Address* does not wrap to second line in label column. Insert tab control object at right of *Customer ID* field. Remove layout from tab control column and lengthen tab control object to align with bottom of *Home Phone* field.	4	

Steps	Tasks	Criteria	Value	Score
7-9	Adding Fields	Expand field list for *WebCustPymnt* table and add the following fields to the tab control object: *CCType* *CCNumber* *CCExpMonth* *CCExpYear* Select all label control objects and widen objects so that all label text is visible. Save report and name it *CustomersWithCreditCards*.	4	
10-14	Editing Report, Printing	Delete second page in tab control and change shape of selected tab control object to Round Single Corner Rectangle. Change caption of page to *Credit Card Details*. Insert title at top of report with text *Customers with Payment Information*. Print first page only of report. Save and close report. Close **AL2-C5-ViewIt.accdb**.	4	
		TOTAL POINTS	20	

Visual Benchmark

Create Custom Reservations Report with Totals

File: **AL2-C5-PawsParadise.accdb**

Steps	Tasks	Criteria	Value	Score
1-3	Creating Report, Saving	Open **AL2-C5-PawsParadise.accdb** and enable content. After reviewing the partial report shown in Figure 5.15, create a report with subreport with the following specifications: • Apply Ion Boardroom theme. • Substitute another suitable clip art image if necessary. • Add current date and page numbering to bottom of each page. • Edit labels in subreport as shown in Figure 5.15. • Add student name in *Report Footer* section. Save report with name *DogOwnersWithDogs*.	12	
4-5	Printing, Closing	Preview report. Make necessary adjustments. Save and print report. Close **AL2-C5-PawsParadise.accdb**.	3	
		TOTAL POINTS	15	

Case Study

Part 1

File: **AL2-C5-HillsdaleRealty.accdb**

Steps	Tasks	Criteria	Value	Score
1	Creating Reports	Open **AL2-C5-HillsdaleRealty.accdb** and enable content. Add student name in a label control object in *Report Footer* in each report created. Organize report with each individual agent's sales together showing total value of sales and commissions earned for that agent and sorted by date the listing sold. Include grand totals and percentage of grand total each agent has achieved for sale prices and commissions earned. Design and create report including features such as page numbering, date and time controls, and graphics.	12	
2	Saving, Printing	Save report with appropriate name. Print report with top and bottom margins set to 0.5 inch and entire group kept together on same page.	3	
		TOTAL POINTS	15	

Part 2

File: **AL2-C5-HillsdaleRealty.accdb**

Steps	Tasks	Criteria	Value	Score
1	Creating Report	Design and create a report. Information needed includes client's preferences and the agent attached to the listing grouped by city. Determine appropriate sort order within each city's group of records.	12	
2	Saving, Printing	Save report with appropriate name. Print report with top margin set to 0.75 inch and entire group kept together on same page.	3	
		TOTAL POINTS	15	

Part 3

File: **AL2-C5-HillsdaleRealty.accdb**

Steps	Tasks	Criteria	Value	Score
1	Creating Report	Design and create a report. Create a report showing number of days a listing that sold was on the market. Include the average number of days it took to sell a listing by city.	12	
3	Saving, Printing	Save report with appropriate name. Print report with top and bottom margins set to 0.75 inch.	3	
		TOTAL POINTS	15	

Part 4

File: **AL2-C5-HillsdaleRealty.accdb**

Steps	Tasks	Criteria	Value	Score
1	Using Help, Opening Report, Creating Copy of Report	Use Help and research how to create a summary report. Open report created in Part 1. Use *Save Object As* to create a copy of the report. Student determines appropriate name.	2	
2	Creating Compacted Report	Modify the design of the new copy of the report. The report shows the totals only for each agent.	6	
3	Printing, Saving	Print new report and changing page setup to fit entire report on one page. Save and close report. Close **AL2-C5-HillsdaleRealty.accdb**.	2	
		TOTAL POINTS	10	

Benchmark Access 2013 Level 2, Chapter 6

Skills Check

Assessment 1: Create A New Database Using a Template
File: **AL2-C6-Assets.accdb**

Steps	Tasks	Criteria	Value	Score
1-2	Creating Database	Using the Desktop asset tracking template, create new database named **AL2-C6-Assets.accdb**. Close the Getting Started with Assets form and enable the content. Close all objects including the Asset List form..	4	
3	Adding Records	Open the Contact Details form and add the record specified on page 263, using the form. Substitute student names in the *First Name* and *Last Name* fields. Leave the fields blank after the Business Phone.	2	
4	Adding Records	Open AssetDetails form and add records shown in assessment.	8	
5-6	Printing, Closing	Print two records as displayed in the AssetDetails form. Close form. Close **AL2-C6-Assets.accdb**.	1	
		TOTAL POINTS	15	

Assessment 2: Create a Table Using an Applications Parts Template
File: **AL2-C6-ViewIt.accdb**

Steps	Tasks	Criteria	Value	Score
1-2	Creating New Group of Objects	Open **AL2-C6-ViewIt.accdb** and enable content. Create new group of objects related to Tasks using Tasks Application Part. Specify no relationship at Create Relationship Wizard.	5	
3	Adding Record	Using TaskDetails form, add a record using the information specified.	3	
4-7	Printing Record	Save and Close. Open Tasks table to view record added to table using the form in Step 3. Close the table. Print selected record using TaskDetails form. Close form.	2	
		TOTAL POINTS	10	

Assessment 3: Use Access Tools to Improve Design and Performance
File: **AL2-C6-ViewIt.accdb**

Steps	Tasks	Criteria	Value	Score
1-2	Analyzing Table	With **AL2-C6-ViewIt.accdb** open, use the Table Analyzer Wizard to analyze WebCustPymnt table using the following information: • Rename new table with all fields except *CCType* field to *WebCustCreditCards*. • Rename new table with *CCType* field to *CreditCardTypes*. • Choose appropriate field for primary key in WebCustCreditCards table. • If wizard determines Discover card is a typographical error, select *Leave as is*. • Create the query. Close Help window.	6	
3-5	Deleting, Printing	Delete *CCType* field in WebCustPymnt query. Adjust all column widths to Best Fit. Print query results datasheet using left and right margins of 0.25 inch. Close query without saving layout changes. Delete WebCustPymnt_OLD table.	4	
6-7	Splitting Database	Split database to create front-end database and back-end database file. Accept default file name for back-end database. Close **AL2-C6-ViewIt.accdb**.	3	
8-10	Printing	Open **AL2-C6-ViewIt_be.accdb** and enable content. Generate and print report with table and field property definitions for CreditCardTypes table. Include relationships in report. Close **AL2-C6-ViewIt_be.accdb**	2	
		TOTAL POINTS	15	

Visual Benchmark

1: Create a Table to Store Groomers' Information
File: **AL2-C6-PawsParadise.accdb**

Steps	Tasks	Criteria	Value	Score
1-2	Creating Table, Copying	Open **AL2-C6-PawsParadise.accdb** and enable content. After reviewing table shown in Figure 6.10, create a new table in database by copying structure of the DogOwners table.	2	
3-5	Modifying, Adding Records, Printing	Modify table design as needed. Add records shown in Figure 6.10. Rename table as shown in Figure 6.10 Adjust all column widths. Print table. Close table.	8	
		TOTAL POINTS	10	

2: Create a Form Template
File: **AL2-C6-PawsParadise.accdb**

Steps	Tasks	Criteria	Value	Score
1-2	Creating Normal Form	With **AL2-C6-PawsParadise.accdb** open, examine control objects in form named Normal in Figure 6.11. Create Normal form to be used as template with three control objects as shown. Use font color Lavender, Accent 5, Darker 50%, bold font formatting and background color Lavender, Accent 5, Lighter 80% for formatting.	8	
2-4	Creating Form, Printing, Saving	Create new form for Groomers table. Decrease width of form title and text box control objects in form so one form will fit on one page. Print first form only. Save Groomers form accepting default name *Groomers*. Close form and close **AL2-C6-PawsParadise.accdb**.	7	
		TOTAL POINTS	15	

Case Study

Part 1
File: **AL2-C6-HillsdaleRealty.accdb**

Steps	Tasks	Criteria	Value	Score
1	Creating Database	Use Events sample template to create new database **AL2-C6-HillsdaleShows.accdb** and enable content. Add the following two trade show events using the Event List form: • Three-day Homebuilders Association Trade Show beginning April 14, 2015, at Phoenix Convention Center. • Four-day Green Home Design Conference beginning October 26, 2015, at University of Phoenix Hohokam Campus.	6	

Steps	Tasks	Criteria	Value	Score
2	Creating New Table	Close Event List form and display Navigation pane. Change Navigation pane view to display objects by *Object Type*. Copy structure of Events table to create new table named *AgentConferences*.	3	
3	Modifying Tables	Delete *Attachments* field in AgentConferences table. Add new field to store number of people the company will send to show.	2	
4	Creating Form	Create form for AgentConferences table using Form button. Add the following record: • Five employees attending three-day Window and Door Manufacturers Association Annual Conference beginning November 9, 2015, at Georgia International Convention Center.	4	
5	Adjusting Fit, Printing	Preview AgentConferences form in Print Preview. Make adjustments to fit form on one page. Print AgentConferences form with first record displayed. Save and close form.	3	
6	Opening, Printing	Open Event Details report. Print and close report. Close **AL2-C6-HillsdaleShows.accdb**.	2	
		TOTAL POINTS	20	

Part 2
File: **AL2-C6-HillsdaleRealty.accdb**

Steps	Tasks	Criteria	Value	Score
1	Analyzing Table	Open **AL2-C6-HillsdaleRealty.accdb** and enable content. Use the Table Analyzer Wizard to analyze Listings table. Accept proposed table split, create appropriate table names, assign primary key fields, and create query.	3	
2	Modifying, Sorting, Printing	Modify query as need to remove duplicate columns. Sort query in ascending order by *ListDate* field. Print query results datasheet with all column widths adjust to Best Fit.	4	
3	Deleting Table	Delete original table with *_OLD* in name.	2	
4	Deleting Control Object	Open ListingsAndSales form. Delete *City* control object.	2	
5	Adding Field, Sizing	Display Field List task pane. Add appropriate field to form. Size and align controls as needed. Save and close form.	4	
		TOTAL POINTS	15	

Part 3

File: AL2-C6-HillsdaleRealty.accdb and AL2-C6-HillsdaleDBAnalysisMemo.docx

Steps	Tasks	Criteria	Value	Score
1	Using Help, Composing Memo	Use Help to find out the difference between assignment a field the Text data type and the Number data type. Using Microsoft Word, compose a memo to instructor with the following information: • An explanation of the use of Text data type. • An explanation of the use of Number data type. • Student recommendation and explanation of which data type should be used for *four ID* fields in database.	12	
3	Saving, Printing	Save memo as **AL2-C6-HillsdaleDBAnalysisMemo.docx**. Print memo and exit Word.	2	
4	Deleting, Rearranging Field List Boxes	Delete original Listings table from window. Display new Listings table name to show relationships created. Rearrange table field list boxes so join lines are easy to follow.	4	
5	Generating Report, Printing	Generate relationship report. Print relationships report. Save and close relationships report. Close **AL2-C6-HillsdaleRealty.accdb**.	2	
		TOTAL POINTS	20	

Benchmark Access 2013 Level 2, Chapter 7

Skills Check

Assessment 1: Create and Run Macros
File: **AL2-C7-ViewIt.accdb**

Steps	Tasks	Criteria	Value	Score
1-3	Creating Macros, Editing	Open **AL2-C7-ViewIt.accdb** and enable content. Create the following macros: • A macro named RPTWebOrders that opens report named WebOrdersByProd. Use macro action *OpenReport*. In *Action Arguments* section, change *View* argument to *Print Preview*. • A macro named RPTWebSales to open WebSalesByDate report in Report view. • A macro named FORMCustOrd that opens WebCustOrders form in Form view, activates control named *LastName*, and then opens the Find dialog box. Test macro using customer last name *Gallagher*. Open RPTWebOrders macro. At Print Macro Definition dialog box, clear check marks until only *Actions and Arguments* check box is checked.	4	
4	Printing	Print FORMCustOrd macro and RPTWebSales macro using step similar in step 3.	2	
		TOTAL POINTS	15	

Assessment 2: Edit a Macro and Assign Macros to Command Buttons
File: **AL2-C7-ViewIt.accdb** and **AL2-C7-A2-FormWindows.docx**

Steps	Tasks	Criteria	Value	Score
1	Editing Macro	With **AL2-C7-ViewIt.accdb** database open, edit FORMCustOrd macro to remove *OpenForm* action. Save and close revise macro. Rename FORMCustOrd macro in Navigation pane to FINDLastName.	5	
2-3	Creating Command Buttons	Create command buttons to run macros as follows: • Open WebCustOrders form in Design view and create a command button at right side of *Form Header* section that runs FINDLastName macro. Format the button using the *Light 1 Outline, Colored Fill-Green, Accent 6* quick style. Determine appropriate text to display on fact of button and name for command button. Save and close form. • Open WebProducts form in Design view and create two commands as follows. Place each button at bottom of *Detail* section. Determine appropriate text to display on face of button and name for command button. Format each button with the quick style used in Step above. Save and close form. 　○ A button at left side of form that runs the RPTWebOrders macro. 　○ A button at right side of form that runs the RPTWebSales Macro. Open each form, test button(s).	12	
4-5	Inserting Screen Images in Word, Printing	Open WebCustOrders form in Form view. Insert screen image of database window in new Microsoft Word document. Open WebProducts form. Insert screen image of database window below first image. Type student name a few lines below screen images. Add other identifying information as instructed. Save document as **AL2-C7-A2-FormWindows.docx**. Print document and exit Word. Close both forms.	3	
		TOTAL POINTS	15	

Assessment 3: Create a Navigation Form and Configure Database Options
File: **AL2-C7-ViewIt.accdb** and **AL2-C7-A3-MainMenu.docx**

Steps	Tasks	Criteria	Value	Score
1	Creating Navigation Form	With **AL2-C7-ViewIt.accdb** open, create a Navigation form using the following information: • Use *Vertical Tabs, Left style*. • Add WebCustOrders form as first tab. • Add WebProducts form as second tab. • Add WebOrdersByProd report as third tab. • Add WebSalesByDate report as fourth tab. • Save form, naming it *MainMenu*.	8	

Steps	Tasks	Criteria	Value	Score
2	Editing Form	Edit the MainMenu Navigation form as follows: • Delete logo container object. • Edit text in Title control object to *ViewIt Classic Videos* and resize object so right edge of control ends just after title text. • Apply the Light 1 Outline, Colored Fill – Green, Accent 6 quick style to all of the tables include the [Add New] tab. • Change Caption property for first tab to *Customer Orders*. • Change Caption property for second tab to *Classic Products*. • Change Caption property for third tab to *Orders by Product*. • Change Caption property for fourth tab to *Sales by Month*.	6	
3-4	Creating Macro	Create new macro named *ExitDB* that will exit Access saving all objects. Assign macro to a command button positioned in the *Form Header* section of Main Menu form. Determine appropriate text to display on face of button and name for command button. Format it with the same Quick Style used for the tabs. Save and close MainMenu form. Set MainMenu form as startup display form.	7	
5-6	Creating Application Title	Create application title for database with text *ViewIt Classic Videos Web Orders Database*. Hide Navigation pane.	1	
7-8	Testing Startup Options	Turn on *Check for new unassociated labels* error checking option. Close and reopen database to test startup options.	1	
9	Inserting Images in Word, Saving, Printing	Open MainMenu form, create screen image, and insert image in new Word document. Type student name a few lines below screen image. Add additional identifying information as instructed. Save Word document as **AL2-C7-A3-MainMenu.docx**. Print document. Exit Word	2	
		TOTAL POINTS	25	

Assessment 4: Customize the Ribbon
File: **AL2-C7-ViewIt.accdb** and **AL2-C7-A4-CustomizedRibbon.docx**

Steps	Tasks	Criteria	Value	Score
1	Creating Navigation Form	With **AL2-C7-ViewIt.accdb** open, export customizations to your storage medium in the **AL2C7** subfolder. Save as **AL2-C7-A4-ViewItCustomizations.exportedUI**.	2	
2-5	Inserting Image in Word, Saving, Printing	Add a new tab between the HOME tab and the CREATE tab. Rename the tab using your first and last names in uppercase. Add a new group to the new tab, making it two new groups Rename the first group to *Formatting* and the second group *Maintenance*.	5	

Steps	Tasks	Criteria	Value	Score
3-4	Formatting	Select *All Commands* in the *Choose commands from* option box and then add the Font Color Format Cells Format Painter, and Line color button to the Formatting group. Add the Access 2002-2003 Database, Back Up Database, and Compact & Repair Database button to the *Maintenance* group.	3	
5	Screenshots, Saving and printing	Insert a screenshot of the database window showing the custom tab in a Microsoft Word document. Type your name a few lines below the screenshot adding any identifying information as instructed. Save and name it **AL2-C7-A4-CustomizedRibbon.** Print and then exit Word.	3	
6-7	Customization, Importing, Exiting	Import the customization file saved previously and reset ribbon back to the default. Exit from the MainMenu and exit the database.	2	
		TOTAL POINTS	15	

Visual Benchmark

Automate and Customize a Reservation Database

File: **AL2-C7-PawsParadise.accdb**

Steps	Tasks	Criteria	Value	Score
1-2	Creating Navigation Form, Reviewing	Open **AL2-C7-PawsParadise.accdb** and enable content. After reviewing table shown in Figure 7.11, create the Navigation form including command buttons and required macros assigned to command buttons. Set required startup and Navigation pane options	8	
3	Printing	Check with instructor about printing macros and screen image of database window.	2	
		TOTAL POINTS	10	

Case Study

Part 1

File: **AL2-C7-HillsdaleRealty.accdb**

Steps	Tasks	Criteria	Value	Score
1	Creating Macros	Open **AL2-C7-HillsdaleRealty.accdb** and enable content. Create three macros and determine macro names to complete the following: • Move to *AgentLName* and open Find dialog box. • Move *ListingNo* control and open Find dialog box. • Exit database saving all objects.	6	

Steps	Tasks	Criteria	Value	Score
2	Assigning Macros as Command Buttons	Assign the first macro as a command button in the Agents form. Assign the second macro as a command button in the ListingsAndSales form. In both forms, student determines position of button, text to display on button, and button name. Check with instructor about printing macros and screen image of database window.	4	
		TOTAL POINTS	10	

Part 2

File: **AL2-C7-HillsdaleRealty.accdb**

Steps	Tasks	Criteria	Value	Score
1	Creating Navigation Form	With **AL2-C7-HillsdaleRealty.accdb** create a navigation form to be used as a main menu to display Agents form, the ListingsAndSales form, and the two reports. Add appropriate application title for database. Hide tables, queries, and macros in Navigation pane.	8	
2	Assigning Macro	Assign macro to exit database as a button in the main menu form.	3	
3	Editing, Testing	Edit main menu form as needed to show descriptive labels in tabs. Apply other formatting enhancements as necessary. Close and reopen database to test startup options. Test each menu tab. Check with instructor about printing macros and screen image of database window.	4	
		TOTAL POINTS	15	

Part 3

File: **AL2-C7-CS-P3-PackageMemo.docx**

Steps	Tasks	Criteria	Value	Score
1	Using Help, Composing Memo	Use Help and search for options available to customize Access in the *Current Database* section. Using Word, compose a memo, addressed to the instructor that provides three options not discussed in the chapter. Save and name the memo **AL2-C7-CS-P3-PackageMemo.docx**. Print the memo, exit Word.	10	
		TOTAL POINTS	10	

Benchmark Access 2013 Level 2, Chapter 8

Skills Check

Assessment 1: Import and Link Objects from Another Access Database
File: **AL2-C8-ViewItStock.accdb**

Steps	Tasks	Criteria	Value	Score
1-2	Integrating Objects	Open **AL2-C8-ViewItStock.accdb** and enable content. Using **AL2-C8-ViewIt.accdb** as the data source, integrate the following objects into the active database: • Import the form named WebProducts. • Link to the tables named WebProducts, WebOrders, and WebOrderDetails.	4	
3	Creating Relationship	Create a relationship between the WebProducts and WebProductsCost tables using the field named *WebProdID*. Save and close the Relationship window.	3	
4	Modifying Form	Modify WebProducts form as follows: • Open form in Design view. • Delete *Retail Value* label and text box control objects at bottom of form. Four fields remain in form: *ProductID, Product, In Stock*, and *Selling Price*. • Show all tables in pane. Expand field list for WebProductsCost table. • Add field named *CostPrice* below *Selling Price* field. • Align, resize, and format field so that cost price displays similarly to selling price. • Modify form title to *Inventory Stock and Pricing*.	6	
5	Saving, Printing	Save revised form. Print form for first record only. Close form.	1	
6	Modifying Query	Open WebProdCostsWithSupp query in Design view. Modify query as follows: • Add WebProducts table to query. • Add *SellPrice* field to query design grid, placed between *Product* and *CostPrice* columns. • Add a calculated column at right of *CostPrice* column that subtracts cost price from selling price. Display column heading *Gross Profit*.	4	
7-8	Running Query, Saving, Printing	Save revised query and run query. Print query in landscape orientation and close query.	2	
		TOTAL POINTS	20	

Assessment 2: Import a Text File
File: **AL2-C8-ViewItStock.accdb**

Steps	Tasks	Criteria	Value	Score
1	Appending Records	With **AL2-C8-ViewItStock.accdb** database open, make a back up copy, and append records from text file using the following information: • Name the backup file **as AL2-C8-ViewItStock_yyyy-mm-dd.accdb.** Save database in DatabaseBackUps folder created in Project 1a. • Data source file named **WebProducts.csv**. • Append copy of records to end of existing WebProductsCost table. • Save import steps using the default name and type the description: *Import of new classic video titles from WebProducts.csv.*	9	
2-4	Opening, Printing	Open WebProductsCost table. Print table datasheet. Close datasheet. Close **AL2-C8-ViewItStock.accdb**.	1	
		TOTAL POINTS	10	

Assessment 3: Export and Publish Access Data
File: **CustWebOrders.txt**

Steps	Tasks	Criteria	Value	Score
1-2	Opening, Exporting Query	Open **AL2-C8-ViewIt.accdb** and enable content. Export query named CustWebOrders to a comma delimited text file using the following information: • Include field names and remove quotation marks. • Save export steps and type the description: *Export the customers' web orders to a text file.*	8	
3-4	Opening Notepad, Printing	Open Notepad. Open **CustWebOrders.txt** file. Print document. Exit Notepad.	2	
		TOTAL POINTS	10	

Assessment 4: Secure the Database
File: **AL2-C8-ViewIt.accdb**

Steps	Tasks	Criteria	Value	Score
1-3	Opening, Saving	With **AL2-C8-ViewIt.accdb** open, save a copy of the database as an ACCDE file in the same folder and using the same file name. Close **AL2-C8-ViewIt.accdb**. Open **AL2-C8-ViewIt.accde**.	2	

Steps	Tasks	Criteria	Value	Score
4-5	Screenshot, saving and printing	Insert a screenshot in a Word document. Type name a few lines below the screenshot and add any required additional information. Save the Word document as **AL2-C8-A4-ViewItACCDE.docx.** Print and exit Word. Close **AL2-C8-ViewIt.accde** database.	3	
		TOTAL POINTS	5	

Visual Benchmark

Analyze Reservation Database
File: **AL2-C7-PawsParadise.accdb**

Steps	Tasks	Criteria	Value	Score
1-5	Integrating, Linking, Saving	Open **AL2-C8-PawsParadise.accdb** and enable content. Using **AL2-C8-PawsGroomers.accd**b as the data source, integrate the objects into the active database: Importing the Groomers form and linking the Groomers table. Modify the Groomers form shown in Figure 8.12. Save a copy of the database as an ACCDE database. Close **AL2-C8-PawsParadise.accdb.**	5	
6-7	Creating PivotChart, Saving, Printing	Open **AL2-C8-PawsParadise.accde** and with instructor's instructions, print a screen image of the database window. Close **AL2-C8-PawsParadise.accde.**	5	
		TOTAL POINTS	10	

Case Study

Part 1
File: **SalesAndCommissions.xps**

Steps	Tasks	Criteria	Value	Score
1	Creating Text File	Open **AL2-C8-HillsdaleRealty.accdb** and enable content. Create a text file including the field names and quotations marks as text qualifiers. Save the export steps, and print the text file.	8	
2	Saving, Printing	Open the SalesAndCommissions report and save as an XPS document using the default name and send the file to your instructor as an email attachment. Do not save the export steps. .	2	
		TOTAL POINTS	10	

Part 2

File: **AL2-C8-HillsdaleRealty_yyyy-mm-dd.accdb**

Steps	Tasks	Criteria	Value	Score
1	Creating Backups	Create a backup copy of **AL2-C8-HillsdaleRealty_yyyy-mm-dd.accdb** and place it in the *DatabaseBackUps folder* created in Project 1a. Using **AL2-C8-HillsdaleRealty.accdb**, create an ACCDE file as **AL2-C8-HillsdaleRealty.accde**.	5	
		TOTAL POINTS	5	

Part 3

File: **AL2-C8-CS-P3-DiscontinuedMemo.docx**

Steps	Tasks	Criteria	Value	Score
1	Using Help, Composing Memo	Use Help and search discontinued features. Selecting the Discontinued features and modified functionality in Access hyperlink, read the information and compose a memo using Microsoft Word that provides the following information: • Why can you no longer open an Access 97 database in Access 2013? • What do you have to do to an Access 97n database to be able to open it in Access 2013? • Why is there no longer an option to create PivotCharts and PivotTables in Access 2013?	14	
2	Saving, Printing	Save memo as **AL2-C8-CS-P3-DiscontinuedMemo.docx**. Print memo and exit Word.	1	
		TOTAL POINTS	15	

Benchmark Access 2013 Level 2
Unit 2 Performance Assessment

Skills Check

Assessment 1: Import Data from Text Files and Create Reports for a Property Management Database

File: **AL2-U2-BenchmarkPropMgt.accdb**

Steps	Tasks	Criteria	Value	Score
1-3	Opening, Importing Data	Open **AL2-U2-BenchmarkPropMgt.accdb** and enable content. Import data into tables from two text files as follows: • Append data in text file named **TenantsU2.csv** to Tenants table. • Append data in text file named **LeasesU2.csv** to Leases table. Save each set of import specifications for future use. Determine appropriate description for each set of import steps.	4	

Steps	Tasks	Criteria	Value	Score
4	Designing, Creating Report	Design and create report as follows: • A report based on LeasesByBldg query with all fields included except building code field. • Group records by building name and sort by Unit No within each group. • Name report *BuildingsAndLeases*. • Include current date and page numbering in page footer. • Add student name as report designer in report footer. • Insert appropriate clip art image in report header. • Student determines remaining layout and formatting elements including a descriptive report title.	9	
4	Designing, Creating Report	Design and create report as follows: • A report based on RentalIncome query with all fields except building code field. • Group records by building name and sort by Unit No within each group. • Name report *IncomeByBuilding*. • Sum rent and annual rent columns and count unit numbers. • Show statistics in group footer and as grand totals at end of report. • Include appropriate labels to describe statistics and format values to a suitable numeric format. • Add student name as report designer in report footer. • Insert appropriate clip art image in report header. • Determine remaining layout and formatting elements including a descriptive report title.	10	
5	Printing	Print BuildingAndLeases and IncomeByBuilding reports.	2	
		TOTAL POINTS	25	

Assessment 2: Use Access Tools to Improve the Property Management Database Design
File: **AL2-U2-BenchmarkPropMgt.accdb** and
AL2-U2-BenchmarkPropMgt_be.accdb

Steps	Tasks	Criteria	Value	Score
1	Analyzing Objects	With **AL2-U2-BenchmarkPropMgt.accdb** open, use Performance Analyzer feature to analyze all objects in database. Fix each *Suggestion* item.	4	
2-3	Creating Back-end Database	Split database into two files to create a back-end database. Accept default file name. Close **AL2-U2-BenchmarkPropMgt.accdb**.	2	
3-6	Opening, Generating Table Definition Report, Printing	Open **AL2-U2-BenchmarkPropMgt_be.accdb** and enable content. Use Database Documenter feature to generate a table definition report for Leases table with the following options: *Include for Table* set to *Properties and Relationships*, *Include for Fields* set to *Names, Data Types, and Sizes* and *Include for Indexes* set to *Nothing*. Print and close report. Close **AL2-U2-BenchmarkPropMgt_be.accdb**.	9	
		TOTAL POINTS	15	

Assessment 3: Automate the Property Management Database with Macros and Command Buttons

File: **AL2-U2-BenchmarkPropMgt.accdb**

Steps	Tasks	Criteria	Value	Score
1-2	Opening, Creating Macros	Open **AL2-U2-BenchmarkPropMgt.accdb** and enable content. Create the following macros: • A macro named *QLeasesByTenant* that opens the LeasesByTenant query. Use macro action *OpenQuery*. • A macro named *QLeaseTerms* that opens the LeaseTermsAndDeposits query. Use macro action *OpenQuery*. • A macro named *RBldgLeases* that opens the BuildingsAndLeases report in report view. Use the macro action OpenReport. • A macro named *RIncome* that opens the IncomeByBuilding report in report view. Use the macro OpenReport.	8	
3-4	Opening, Creating Command Buttons	Open BldgsAndMgrs form in Design view. Create two command buttons in Form Header section as follows: • A button that runs RBldgLeases macro. • A button that runs RIncome macro. Determine placement of button within section, text to display on face of each button, and a name to assign each button.	8	
5-6	Testing Macros, Placing Screen Capture Image in Word, Printing	Test each button to be sure macros display correct report. Make screen capture of BldgsAndMgrs from with buttons displayed and past image into blank Word document. Student's name should be typed below the screenshot and any other identifying information as instructed. Print Word document. Exit Word without saving. Close all objects.	4	
		TOTAL POINTS	20	

Assessment 4: Create a Navigation Form and Configure Startup Options for the Property Management Database

File: **AL2-U2-BenchmarkPropMgt.accdb**

Steps	Tasks	Criteria	Value	Score
1	Creating Form	With **AL2-U2-BenchmarkPropMgt.accdb** open, create a Navigation form named MainMenu using Horizontal Tabs style with form and reports in the following tab order: • BldgsAndMgrs form • TenantsAndLeases form • BuildingsAndLeases report • IncomeByBuilding report	8	
2-3	Editing	Edit form title and delete logo container object. Determine appropriate text to replace *Navigation Form*. Edit tab captions. Determine appropriate text for each tab.	3	

Steps	Tasks	Criteria	Value	Score
4-5	Creating Macro	Create macro named *ExitDB* that quits Access saving all objects. Create command button placed at right end of MainMenu form header section that runs the macro. Determine text to display on face of button and name for button. Be sure correct form or report displays.	4	
6-7	Setting Form, Closing, Reopening	Set MainMenu form to display as startup form, add appropriate titles as application title for database, and hide Navigation pane. Close and then reopen **AL2-U2-BenchmarkPropMgt.accdb**.	4	
8	Capturing Image, Pasting, Printing	Capture an image of the database window. Paste into Word document. Student name typed below screenshot and any additional identifying information as instructed. Print Word document and exit Word without saving.	1	
		TOTAL POINTS	20	

Assessment 5: Configure Security for the Property Management Database
File: **AL2-U2-BenchmarkPropMgt.accdb** and **AL2-U2-BenchmarkPropMgt.accde**

Steps	Tasks	Criteria	Value	Score
1-2	Saving ACCDE File	With **AL2-U2-BenchmarkPropMgt.accdb** open, make an ACCDE file from the database saving in the same folder and using same file name. Close **AL2-U2-BenchmarkPropMgt.accdb**.	2	
3-4	Opening, Changing Startup Option	Open **AL2-U2-BenchmarkPropMgt.accde**. Change database startup option to display Navigation pane with Tables and Macros hidden.	6	
5-6	Closing, Opening, Capturing Image, Pasting, Printing	Close and then reopen **AL2-U2-BenchmarkPropMgt.accde**. Capture image of database window. Paste image into Word document. Print Word document and exit Word without saving.	2	
		TOTAL POINTS	10	

Assessment 6: Export and Publish Data from the Property Management Database
File: **AL2-U2-BenchmarkPropMgt.accde**

Steps	Tasks	Criteria	Value	Score
1	Exporting Query	With **AL2-U2-BenchmarkPropMgt.accde** open, export LeaseTermsAndDeposits query as text file using default name. Save file in AL2U2 folder. Include field names in first row and remove quotation symbols. Do not save export steps.	5	

Steps	Tasks	Criteria	Value	Score
2-3	Opening Notepad, Printing	Open Notepad, open **LeaseTermsAndDeposits.txt** file. Print document. Exit Notepad.	2	
4	Publishing	Publish IncomeByBuilding report as XPS document named **AL2-U2-BenchmarkRentInc.xps**. Do not save export steps.	2	
5-6	Opening, Printing	Open **AL2-U2-BenchmarkRentInc.xps** in XPS window or Internet Explorer window. Print report. Exit XPS or Internet Explorer window using the button that was created	1	
		TOTAL POINTS	10	

Writing Activities

Activity 1: Create a New Database for Renovation Contracts by Importing Data
File: **AL2-U2-DavisRenos.accdb; AL2-U2-Act1-DavisRenos.docx**

Steps	Tasks	Criteria	Value	Score
1	Creating Database	Create a new Access database named **AL2-U2-DavisRenos.accdb**. Import data from the **DavisRenos.txt**.	2	
2	Modifying Table Design	Modify table design after importing to change the *Amount* field to Currency.	4	
3	Creating Form	Design and create form based on table for entering new records.	4	
4	Creating Report	Design and create report to print records including a total of the invoice amount column.	4	
5	Creating Navigation Form	Create menu using a Navigation form and configure startup options so that menu is the only object displayed in the work area when database is opened. Test menu.	4	
6	Composing Instruction Page	Using Microsoft Word, compose a quick reference instruction page on how to open the database, add a new record, view and print the report, and exit the database.	6	
7	Saving, Printing	Save the Word document as **AL2-U2-Act1DavisRenos**. Print document.	1	
		TOTAL POINTS	25	

Activity 2: Design and Publish a Report for a Painting Franchise
File: **AL2-U2-StudentPainters.accdb** and **AL2-US-PaintingContracts.xps**

Steps	Tasks	Criteria	Value	Score
1	Creating Database	Create a new database named **AL2-U2-StudentPainters.accdb**.	1	
2	Creating Tables	Design and create tables to store records for painting contract jobs that include the date the job is completed, the invoice number, the homeowner name, address, and telephone number, and the contract price. Enter at least ten records into the tables.	9	
3	Creating Report	Design a report to print the records in ascending order by date completed. Include statistics at bottom of report with maximum, minimum, average, and total of contract price field. Include appropriate titles and other report elements. Add student name in footer as report designer.	8	
6	Publishing, Printing	Publish report as **AL2-U2-PaintingContracts.xps**. Print report.	2	
		TOTAL POINTS	20	

Internet Research

Activity: Buying a Home

File: **AL2-U2-Homes4Sale.accdb; AL2-U2-AvgHousePrices.xps**

Steps	Tasks	Criteria	Value	Score
1	Creating Database, Tables, and Relationships	Create a new database named **AL2-U2-Homes4Sale**. Design and create tables and relationships. Include fields to store data such as: address, asking price, style of home (condominium, ranch, two stories, semi-detached, etc.), number of bedrooms, number of bathrooms, type of heating/cooling system, property taxes, basement, and garage.	10	
2	Creating a Form	Design and create a form to enter the information into the tables.	4	
3	Researching, Entering Data	Research on the Internet at least five listings. Use the form to enter records for each listing.	5	
4	Creating Report	Design and create a report that groups records by style of home. Calculate the average list price at end of each group and at end of report. Include five hyperlink control objects that will link to the Web page from for each listing. Include appropriate titles and other report elements. Add student name in footer as report designer.	5	
5	Publishing, Printing	Publish report as **AL2-U2-AvgHousePrices.xps**. Print report.	1	
		TOTAL POINTS	25	

Job Study

Activity: Meals on Wheels Database
File: **AL2-U2-MealsOnWheels.accdb**

Steps	Tasks	Criteria	Value	Score
1	Creating Database, Tables, and Relationships	Create a new database named **AL2-U2-MealsOnWheels**. Design and create tables and relationships with the following: • Client name, address, telephone, gender, age, reason for requiring meals (senior, convalescent, or disability), meals required (breakfast, lunch, dinner), date service started, and estimated length of service required. • Volunteer name, address, telephone, gender, age, date started, availability by day and by meal (breakfast, lunch, dinner), and receipt of police check clearance. • Incorporate in design an assignment for both the client and the volunteer to the quadrant of the city or town in which he or she is located. City is divided by north, south, east, and west and tries to match drivers with clients in the same quadrants. • Add additional information that would be important to coordinator of the service.	9	
2	Creating Forms	Create a user-defined form template so that each form has a consistent look. Design and create forms to enter information into tables. Use the forms to enter at least eight client records and five volunteer records. Enter records for both clients and volunteers in all four quadrants and for all three meals (breakfast, lunch, dinner).	5	
3	Creating Queries	Design and create queries to extract records of clients and volunteers within the same quadrant. Include in query results datasheet useful information to set up route schedules.	5	
4	Creating Report, Printing	Design and create reports based on queries. Print reports.	5	
5	Creating Main Menu, Closing, Open	Create main menu for database to provide access to forms and reports. Configure startup options to display an application title, main menu form, and hide tables in Navigation pane when database is opened. Close database and reopen it.	5	
6	Capturing Image, Printing Image	Capture image of the Access window. Print image from Word. Exit Word without saving.	1	
		TOTAL POINTS	30	

Benchmark Access 2013 Level 1, Unit 1
Supplemental Assessment

Instructions

Part 1 – Tables

During this assessment, always replace *StudentName* with your last name followed by your first name, for example, *SmithSarahSalesRep*.

1. You have been asked by the owner of a pre-owned car dealership named *Meridian Sales* to set up a database for tracking inventory. Create a new Access database named **AL1-U1-SA-Meridian.accdb**. Create a table named *StudentNameSalesRep* using the following information:

RepID	LName	FName	Address	City	State	Zip	Phone
1AC	Perry	Jim	3453 E. State St.	Jacksonville	FL	32231	(904) 555-4353
2AF	Bauer	Evan	53 W. Grand Rd.	Jacksonville	FL	32232	(904) 555-3423
3AG	Dickens	Billy	2351 Fergus St.	Jacksonville	FL	32232	(904) 555-5632

    a. Identify the *RepID* field as the primary key.
    b. Add appropriate data types, descriptions, captions, and field sizes.
    c. Create an input mask for the phone field.
    d. Set a default value for the city and the state.
2. Input the data.
3. Adjust the column widths to display all records.
4. Print the StudentNameSalesRep table in landscape orientation. Save the table.
5. Create a new table named StudentNameInventory table with the data shown below using the following guidelines:
    a. Do not identify a primary key.
    b. Add appropriate data types, descriptions, captions, and field sizes.
    c. Use a drop-down list to enter the make of the automobile (Ford, Honda, and Pontiac).
    d. Use a drop-down list to enter the condition (Excellent, Good, Fair, and Poor).
    e. Create an input mask for the two date fields. Choose the short date option.

Make	Model	Year Built	Description	Condition	Cost	Selling Price	Date Arrived	Date Sold	Rep#
Ford	Taurus	2008	4-Door, Red	Excellent	$8,000	$9,990	5/5/2015	5/11/2015	1AC
Ford	Fusion	2009	2-Door, White	Good	$5,500	$5,995	4/15/2015	4/20/2015	3AG
Honda	Accord	2010	4-Door, Blue	Excellent	$7,000	$7,900	5/15/2015	6/15/2015	3AG
Pontiac	Firebird	2011	2-Door, Black	Fair	$4,000		5/1/2015		
Ford	Tempo	2013	2-Door, Red	Poor	$3,000	$4,000	5/5/2015	5/6/2015	2AF
Honda	Civic	2005	2-Door, White	Excellent	$8,500		5/12/2015		
Honda	CRV	2008	5-Door, Black	Good	$6,500	$7,000	4/20/2015	4/30/2015	1AC
Ford	Mustang	2010	2-Door, White	Excellent	$8,500	$10,210	5/3/2015	5/10/2015	2AF
Ford	Fiesta	2011	2-Door, Blue	Good	$6,500		5/1/2015		

6. Input the data.
7. Change the font to Cambria. Center the data in *RepID* field.
8. Adjust column widths to display all records.
9. Print the StudentNameInventory table in landscape orientation with 0.5 inch left and right margins. Save the table.

Part 2 – Relationships
1. Create a one-to-many relationship between the *RepID* field in the StudentNameSalesRep table as the "one" and the *RepID* field in StudentNameInventory table as the "many." Enforce referential integrity and turn on both cascade options.
2. Expand the field list boxes to display all fields, create a relationship report, and then print the report.

Part 3 – Queries
1. Create, save, and print the following queries:
   a. Create a query named *StudentNameFords* that lists all of the Fords in the StudentNameInventory table. Include from the StudentNameInventory table the make, model, year built, and condition.
   b. Create a query that includes all of the "2-door" models. Include from the StudentNameInventory table the make, model, and description. Save the query as *StudentName2-Door*.
   c. Create a query named *StudentNameFordsOver$6500* that lists all of the Fords with a purchase cost of $6,500 and highest. Include from the StudentNameInventory table the make, model, year built, condition, and cost.
   d. Create a query named *StudentNameDateSales* that lists all of the automobiles sold between 04/15/2015 and 05/01/2015. Include from the StudentNameInventory table the make, model, date sold, and selling price and include from the StudentNameSalesRep table the first name and last name. Sort the list in descending order by selling price.
   e. Create a query based on the query created in 1d. Use Save As and name the query *StudentNameDateProfit*. Create a calculated field called *Profit* where Profit is SellingPrice minus Cost.

f. Create the crosstab query located below. The <> indicates the vehicles that have not been sold. Add the *Total* row after the query has been created.

Make	Total Of SellingPrice	<>	1AC	2AF	3AG
Ford	$30,195.00		$9,990.00	$14,210.00	$5,995.00
Honda	$14,900.00		$7,000.00		$7,900.00
Pontiac					
Total			$16,990.00		$13,895.00

StudentNameInventory_Crosstab

Part 4

1. Submit all electronic copies of files to your instructor, along with any printouts.

Note that the following are suggested rubrics. Instructors should feel free to customize the rubrics to suit your grading standards and/or to adjust the point values.

Suggested Scoring Distribution: Above average: student completes 80% or more of task(s); average = student completes 70-79% of task(s); below average = student completes 69% or less of task(s)

Benchmark Access 2013 Level 1, Unit 1
Supplemental Assessment Rubric

Supplemental Assessment

File: **AL1-U1-SA-Meridian.accdb**

Steps	Tasks	Criteria				Value	Score
Part 1 1	Feature	Create database AL1-U1-SA-Meridian.accdb				2	
		Create table StudentNameSalesRep					
a	Feature	*RepID* field as primary key				2	
b	Feature	**Field Name**	**Data Type**	**Field Size**	**Caption**		
		RepID	Text	3	Rep Number	2	
		LName	Text	20	Last Name	2	
		FName	Text	20	First Name	2	
		Address	Text	30	N/A	2	
		City	Text	20	N/A	2	
		State	Text	2	N/A	2	
		Zip	Text	5	N/A	2	
		Phone	Text	14	N/A	2	
		Descriptions in each field (Descriptions and field sizes may vary.)				2	
c	Feature	Phone Number – input mask				2	

Steps	Tasks	Criteria				Value	Score
d	Feature	Default value for city and state				2	
2	Typing/ Accuracy	Input data				2	
3	Format	Adjust column widths to display all records				1	
4	Finishing	Print table on one page				1	
5	Feature	Create table StudentNameInventory				1	
a	Feature	No primary key				1	
b	Feature	**Field Name**	**Data Type**	**Field Size**	**Caption**		
		Make	Text	7	N/A	2	
		Model	Text	20	N/A	2	
		YearBuilt	Number	N/A	Year Built	2	
		Description	Text	20	N/A	2	
		Condition	Text	9	N/A	2	
		Cost	Currency	N/A	N/A	2	
		SellingPrice	Currency	N/A	Selling Price	2	
		DateArrived	Date/Time	N/A	Date Arrived	2	
		DateSold	Date/Time	N/A	Date Sold	2	
		RepID	Text	3	Rep Number	2	
		Descriptions in each field (Descriptions and field sizes may vary.)				2	
c	Feature	Automobile – Look up				2	
d	Feature	Condition – Look up				2	
e	Feature	DateArrived, DateSold – input mask – short date				2	
6	Typing/ Accuracy	Input data				5	
7	Format	Change font; enter data				2	
8	Format	Adjust column widths to display all records				1	
8	Finishing	Print table on one page with 0.5 inch left and right margins				1	
Part 2 1	Feature	Create relationship – Enforce RI and cascade				3	
2	Feature	Create relationship report and print				3	
Part 3 1a	Feature	Create query: *Ford* in Make criteria				1	
b	Feature	Create query: *2-door* in Description criteria				2	
c	Feature	Create query: *>=6500* in Cost criteria and *Ford* in model criteria				3	

Steps	Tasks	Criteria	Value	Score
d	**Feature**	Create query: Between 04/15/2015 and 05/01/2015 in DateSold criteria. Sort in descending order by Selling Price.	**3**	
e	**Feature**	Create query from 1d above. Create a calculated field Profit:[SellingPrice]-[Cost]	**3**	
f	**Feature**	Create a crosstab query as shown	**3**	
Part 4	**Finishing**	Print all queries	**2**	
		TOTAL POINTS	**60**	

StudentNameSalesRep   4/9/2015

Rep Number	Last Name	First Name	Address	City	State	Zip	Phone
1AC	Perry	Jim	2453 E. State. St.	Jacksonville	FL	32231	(904) 555-4353
2AF	Bauer	Evan	53 W. Grand Rd.	Jacksonville	FL	32232	(904) 555-3423
3AG	Dickens	Billy	2351 Fergus St.	Jacksonville	FL	32232	(904) 555-5632

Page 1

Part1,Step4-StudentNameSalesRep.accdb

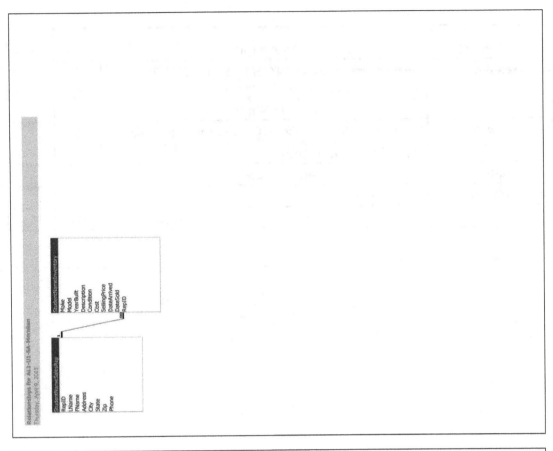

Part2,Step2-RelationshipsforAL1-U1-SA-Meridian.accdb

Relationships for AL1-U1-SA-Meridian
Thursday, June 9, 2015

StudentNameInventory
Make
Model
YearBuilt
Description
Condition
Cost
SellingPrice
DateArrived
DateSold
RepID

StudentNameSalesRep
RepID
LName
FName
Address
City
State
Zip
Phone

StudentNameInventory   4/9/2015

Make	Model	Year Built	Description	Condition	Cost	Selling Price	Date Arrived	Date Sold	Rep Number
Ford	Taurus	2008	4-Door, Red	Excellent	$8,000.00	$9,990.00	5/5/2015	5/11/2015	1AC
Ford	Fusion	2009	2-Door, White	Good	$5,500.00	$5,995.00	4/15/2015	4/20/2015	3AG
Honda	Accord	2010	4-Door, Blue	Excellent	$7,000.00	$7,900.00	5/15/2015	6/15/2015	3AG
Pontiac	Firebird	2011	2-Door, Black	Fair	$4,000.00		5/1/2015		
Ford	Tempo	2013	2-Door, Red	Poor	$3,000.00	$4,000.00	5/5/2015	5/6/2015	2AF
Honda	Civic	2005	2-Door, White	Excellent	$8,500.00		5/12/2015		
Honda	CRV	2008	5-Door, Black	Good	$6,500.00	$7,000.00	4/20/2015	4/30/2015	1AC
Ford	Mustang	2010	2-Door, White	Excellent	$8,500.00	$10,210.00	5/3/2015	5/10/2015	2AF
Ford	Fiesta	2011	2-Door, Blue	Good	$6,500.00		5/1/2015		

Page 1

Part1,Step9-StudentNameInventoryTable.accdb

StudentNameFords   4/9/2015

Make	Model	Year Built	Condition
Ford	Taurus	2008	Excellent
Ford	Fusion	2009	Good
Ford	Tempo	2013	Poor
Ford	Mustang	2010	Excellent
Ford	Fiesta	2011	Good

Page 1

Part3,Step1a-StudentNameFordsQuery.accdb

StudentName2-Door   4/9/2015

Make	Model	Description
Ford	Fusion	2-Door, White
Pontiac	Firebird	2-Door, Black
Ford	Tempo	2-Door, Red
Honda	Civic	2-Door, White
Ford	Mustang	2-Door, White
Ford	Fiesta	2-Door, Blue

Page 1

Part3,Step1b-StudentName2-DoorQuery.accdb

StudentNameDateSales

4/9/2015

Make	Model	Date Sold	Selling Price	First Name	Last Name
Ford	Fusion	4/20/2015	$5,995.00	Billy	Dickens
Honda	CRV	4/30/2015	$7,000.00	Jim	Perry

Page 1

Part3,Step1d-StudentNameDateSales.accdb

StudentNameFordsOver$6500

4/9/2015

Make	Model	Year Built	Condition	Cost
Ford	Taurus	2008	Excellent	$8,000.00
Ford	Mustang	2010	Excellent	$8,500.00
Ford	Fiesta	2011	Good	$6,500.00

Page 1

Part3,Step1c-StudentNameFordsOver$6500.accdb

Make	Total Of SellingPrice	<>	1AC	2AF	3AG
Ford	$30,195.00		$9,990.00	$14,210.00	
Honda	$14,900.00		$7,000.00		$5,995.00
Pontiac					$7,900.00
Total			$16,990.00		$13,8895.00

Part3,Step1f-StudentNameInventory_Crosstab.accdb

Make	Model	Date Sold	Selling Price	First Name	Last Name	Profit
Ford	Fusion	4/20/2015	$5,995.00	Billy	Dickens	$495.00
Honda	CRV	4/30/2015	$7,000.00	Jim	Perry	$500.00

Part3,Step1e-StudentNameDateProfit.accdb

Benchmark Access 2013 Level 1, Unit 2
Supplemental Assessment

Instructions

Part 1

You have been temporarily hired by Extreme Ski Rentals and More to convert its current customer information from Excel to Access. You will need the following data files to complete this project:

> **AL1-U2-SA-ExtremeSkiRentals-DataFile.accdb**
> **AL1-U2-SA-CustomerInformation-DataFile.xlsx**
> **AL1-U2-SA-Rentals-DataFile.xlsx**
> **AL1-U2-SA-Mountain-DataFile.jpg**

Part 2 – Tables

1. Open the database, **AL1-U2-SA-ExtremeSkiRentals-DataFile.accdb**. Enable the content and save the file as **AL1-U2-SA-ExtremeSkiRentals**.

2. Open the Employee table and enter your personal information for EmployeeID 23. Use your name for the Employee First Name and Last Name, but make up the data for the rest of the fields so that it fits, i.e., give yourself a zip code not a postal code if appropriate.
   a. Set the appropriate field sizes.
   b. Add appropriate captions. You may remove the word *employee* from the captions. **Note: Do not remove the word from the field name.**
   c. Set the default value for the *EmployeeCity* field to be *Denver*.
   d. Set the default value for the *EmployeeState* field to be *CO*.
   e. Apply appropriate input masks using the wizard for the *ZipCode* and *PhoneNumber* fields.

3. Import the Excel file **AL1-U2-CustomerInformation-DataFile.xlsx** as a new table named *CustomerInformation*.
   a. Set the primary key by choosing the appropriate field. **Note: It is one of the existing fields.**
   b. Set appropriate data types, field sizes, and captions.
   c. Apply appropriate input masks using the wizard for the *ZipCode* and *PhoneNumber* fields.

4. Import the Excel file called **AL1-U2-SA-Rentals-DataFile.xlsx** as a new table named *Rentals*.
   a. Do **NOT** set a primary key.
   b. Set appropriate data types, field sizes, and captions. **Note: The rental length is in days. It is neither a date nor text and will be used in formulas. Since rentals are done in full days, no places pas the decimal points are needed.**
   c. Make the type of rental a lookup field using *Skis*, *Snowmobile*, and *Snowboard* as the choices.

Part 3 – Relationships

1. Establish relationships and enforce referential integrity among all of the tables and enable the cascade options. There should be one-to-many relationships between the primary key in the Employee table and the foreign key in the Rentals table, and between the primary key in the CustomerInformation table and the foreign key in the Rentals table. Create a relationships report and print the report.

Part 4 – Forms

1. Create a form (including all fields) based on the Rentals table. Save the form as *Rentals*.
   a. Adjust the width of the text box control objects to be about half of their original size.
   b. Add a title to the form, using your name along with the type of form (i.e., Rentals). Insert a logo using the **AL1-U2-SA-Mountain-DataFile.jpg** image found in the data files.
   c. Insert two additional fields into the Rentals form from the CustomerInformation table. From the Field List choose *CustFirstName* and *CustLastName*. Place them directly under the *CustomerID* field. Change the two new fields to be text boxes.
   d. Add the date and time using the middle options for both at the Date and Time dialog box. Adjust the title and the date so that when it prints, it will print horizontally on one page.
   e. Apply the Integral theme.
   f. Format the field labels in the Constantia font face. Apply bold formatting.
   g. Apply conditional formatting that changes the Fill/Back color to a gray color when the rental amount is more than $500.
   h. Save the form as Rentals.
   i. Display the record for the highest rental. Print this record. Make sure this record prints on one page and print **only** this record.

Part 5 – Reports

1. Create the following report. ***Note: A query should be run first. Name the query*** **StudentNameRentalAmount.** ***Do not use a wizard to create the report.***
   a. For the query, include all of the tables. Include the fields *CustFirstName* and *CustLastName*, *LengthOfRental*, *TypeOfRental*, *RentalAmount*, and *EmployeeLastName*. Create a calculated field that calculates the daily fee by taking the rental amount and dividing it by the length of rental. Call this new field *DailyFee*. Format the new field using currency formatting.
   b. Create the report and call it *StudentNameRentalSummary*. (Use your first and last name.)
   c. Group the report by data in the *EmployeeLastName* field and sort by the data in the *CustLastName* field.
   d. Apply the Office theme. Make sure all of the records can be seen (including the total in the *Rental Amount* column).

e. Add your first and last name to the report title.

f. Center the data in the *Length of Rental* column.

g. Apply bold formatting to the column headings.

h. Adjust the column widths so that the report can be kept in portrait orientation. Print this report on one page.

i. Export the report to Word. Save the file as **AL1-U2-SA-RentalSummary.rtf**.

j. Print the document on one page.

2. Create the following report. ***Note: A query should be run first. Name the query StudentNameTotalSales. Do not use a wizard to create the report.***

a. For the query, include the CustomerInformation and Rentals tables. Include the fields *CustFirstName* and *CustLastName*, *TypeOfRental*, and *RentalAmount*.

b. In the query, create two calculated fields that calculate a 6% tax and the total. Tax is 6% of the rental amount. Total is tax plus the rental amount. Make sure the new fields are formatted as currency.

c. Create the report based on the new query and call it *StudentNameTotalSales*. (Use your first and last name.)

d. Adjust the column widths so that it will print on one page.

e. Add sums to the bottom of the *Tax* and *Total* columns. This should be done before you group and sort.

f. Group the report by data in the *CustLastName* field and sort by data in the *Total* field.

g. Apply conditional formatting that changes the Fill/Back color to a light green when the total is less than $100.

h. Make sure all of the records and totals can be seen. Delete the page numbering at the bottom.

i. Make sure that the sums at the bottom of the page are formatted to currency.

j. Add your name (first and last) as well as any necessary spaces to the report title.

k. Keep the report in portrait orientation and print the report on one page.

3. You need to send out a new brochure and mailing labels need to be made.

a. Create mailing labels in Access that can be used for this mailing. Remember your employer likes a comma after the city.

b. Use Avery C2160 labels.

c. Change the font to 11-point Cambria.

d. Sort by the customer's last name.

e. Save the mailing labels as *CustomerMailingLabels*.

Part 6

1. Close the database. Submit the folder including the database and the rtf file. Hand in this test paper. Your printouts will be matched with your paper. Check to ensure that your database and rtf document have been submitted.

Benchmark Access 2013 Level 1, Unit 2
Supplemental Assessment Rubric

Supplemental Assessment

Files: **AL1-U2-SA-ExtremeSkiRentals.accdb**

   AL1-U2-SA-RentalSummary.rtf

Steps	Tasks	Criteria				Value	Score
Part 2	**Tables**					1	
1	**Feature**	Rename database				1	
2	**Typing/Accuracy**	Enter the student's name and other information in Employees table				2	
a,b	**Feature**	**Field Name**	**Field Size**		**Caption**	0	
		EmployeeID	4		Employee ID	1	
		FirstName	20		First Name	1	
		LastName	20		Last Name	1	
		Address	30		N/A	1	
		City	20		N/A	1	
		State	2		N/A	1	
		Zip	10		N/A	1	
		Phone	14		N/A	1	
c,d	**Feature**	Default value for city and state				2	
e	**Feature**	Input mask for *ZipCode* and *PhoneNumber*				2	
3,3a	**Feature**	Import data for Customer Information Table and set primary key				2	
b	**Feature**	**Field Name**	**Data Type**	**Field Size**	**Caption**	0	
		CustomerID	Text	4	Customer ID	1	
		CustFirstName	Text	20	Cust First Name	1	
		CustLastName	Text	20	First Last Name	1	
		Address	Text	30	N/A	1	
		City	Text	20	N/A	1	
		State	Text	2	N/A	1	
		Zip	Text	10	N/A	1	
		Phone	Text	14	N/A	1	

Steps	Tasks	Criteria				Value	Score
c	Feature	Input mask for *ZipCode* and *PhoneNumber*				2	
4,4a	Feature	Import data for Rentals table – No primary key				2	
b	Feature	**Field Name**	**Data Type**	**Field Size**	**Caption**	0	
		CustomerID	Text	4	Customer ID	1	
		LengthOfRental	Number or Double	N/A	Length Of Rental	2	
		TypeOfRental	Text	9	Type of Rental	1	
		RentalAmount	Currency	N/A	Rental Amount	2	
		EmployeeID	Text	2	Employee ID	1	
c	Feature	Type of Rental – lookup – *Skis, Snowmobile, Snowboard*				3	
Part 3	Relationships					0	
1	Feature	Create relationships – Enforce RI and cascade				2	
1	Feature/Finishing	Create relationship report and print				1	
Part 4	Forms					0	
1	Feature	Create form based on Rentals table				2	
a	Format	Adjust text box control object width				1	
b	Feature	Add title to form – to include student's name				1	
c	Feature	Insert two fields in form. Change to be text boxes.				3	
d	Feature/Format	Add date and time and reposition				2	
e	Format	Apply Integral theme				2	
f	Format	Label formatting – Constantia; bold				2	
g	Feature	Conditional formatting - RentalAmount >$500 to be gray fill				2	
i	Finishing	Print only highest rental form on one page.				2	
Part 5	Reports and Exporting					0	
1a	Feature	Create a query and add calculated field				3	
b	Feature	Create report based on new query				2	
c	Feature	Group report by *EmployeeLastName* and sort by *CustLastName*				3	
d	Format	Format – Office theme				2	
e	Format	Add name to title of report				1	
f	Format	Center data in *Length of Rental* column				1	
g	Format	Apply bold formatting to column headings				1	
h	Format/Finishing	Adjust column widths and print report on one page				2	

Steps	Tasks	Criteria	Value	Score
i	Feature	Export to Word.	2	
j	Finishing	Print the rtf file.	1	
2a,b	Feature	Create a query and add calculated fields. Fields formatted to currency.	3	
c	Feature	Create report based on new query	2	
d	Format	Adjust column widths	1	
e	Feature/Format	Add sums to Tax and Total columns. Make sure they are formatted to currency.	2	
f	Feature	Group report by *CustLastName* and sort by *Total*	2	
g	Feature	Conditional formatting – Total <$100 – light green fill	2	
h	Format	Make sure report totals can be seen and delete page numbering	2	
i	Format	Make sure sums at bottom are formatted to currency	1	
j	Format	Report title – students name and spaces	1	
k	Finishing	Print portrait on one page	1	
3a,b	Feature	Create mailing labels. Use Avery C2160. Include appropriate information and ensure proper spacing	3	
c	Format	11-point Cambria font	2	
d	Feature	Sort by customer's last name	1	
		TOTAL POINTS	100	

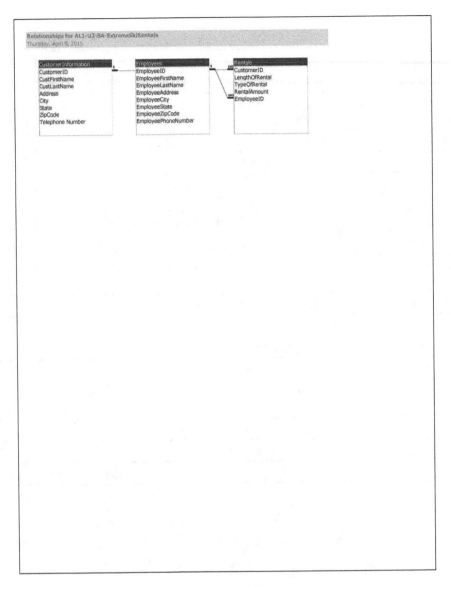

Part3-RelationshipReport.accdb

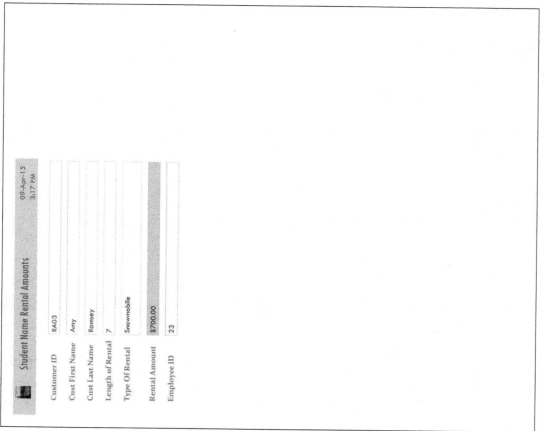

Student Name Rental Amount

Thursday, April 9, 2015
3:32:04 PM

Last Name	Cust First Name	Cust Last Name	Length of Rental	Type Of Rental	Rental Amount	DailyFee
Johnson						
	Jon	Armstrong	3	Skis	$90.00	$30.00
	Jon	Armstrong	1	Snowmobile	$100.00	$100.00
	Tyler	Jacobson	5	Skis	$108.00	$21.60
	Tyler	Jacobson	7	Skis	$125.00	$17.86
	Mark	Keller	5	Skis	$108.00	$21.60
	Mark	Keller	5	Skis	$100.00	$20.00
	Keenan	Kleaver	7	Skis	$125.00	$17.86
	Laura	Tinman	1	Skis	$40.00	$40.00
	Jesse	Winters	2	Skis	$65.00	$32.50
Name						
	Jon	Armstrong	2	Snowboard	$123.00	$61.50
	Abi	Longfellow	4	Skis	$100.00	$25.00
	Jordan	Parker	3	Snowboard	$65.00	$21.67
	Jordan	Parker	1	Snowmobile	$125.00	$125.00
	Amy	Ramsey	7	Snowmobile	$700.00	$100.00
	Anna	Voegal	2	Snowmobile	$200.00	$100.00
Smith						
	Jon	Armstrong	3	Snowboard	$75.00	$25.00
	Keenan	Kleaver	3	Snowmobile	$350.00	$116.67
	Abi	Longfellow	7	Skis	$125.00	$17.86
	Laura	Tinman	5	Skis	$108.00	$21.60
	Anna	Voegal	6	Snowmobile	$650.00	$108.33
					$3,482.00	

Student Name Rental Amounts

09-Apr-15
3:17 PM

Customer ID	RA03
Cust First Name	Amy
Cust Last Name	Ramsey
Length of Rental	7
Type Of Rental	Snowmobile
Rental Amount	$700.00
Employee ID	23

Student Name Rental Amount

Last Name	Cust First Name	Cust Last Name	Length of Rental	Type Of Rental	Rental Amount	DailyFee
Johnson						
	Jon	Armstrong	3	Skis	$90.00	$30.00
	Jon	Armstrong	1	Snowmobile	$100.00	$100.00
	Tyler	Jacobson	5	Skis	$108.00	$21.60
	Tyler	Jacobson	7	Skis	$125.00	$17.86
	Mark	Keller	5	Skis	$108.00	$21.60
	Mark	Keller	5	Skis	$100.00	$20.00
	Keenan	Kleaver	7	Skis	$125.00	$17.86
	Laura	Tinman	1	Skis	$40.00	$40.00
	Jesse	Winters	2	Skis	$65.00	$32.50
Name						
	Jon	Armstrong	2	Snowboard	$123.00	$61.50
	Abi	Longfellow	4	Skis	$100.00	$25.00
	Jordan	Parker	3	Snowboard	$65.00	$21.67
	Jordan	Parker	1	Snowmobile	$125.00	$125.00
	Amy	Ramsey	7	Snowmobile	$700.00	$100.00
	Anna	Voegal	2	Snowmobile	$200.00	$100.00
Smith						
	Jon	Armstrong	3	Snowboard	$75.00	$25.00
	Keenan	Kleaver	3	Snowmobile	$350.00	$116.67
	Abi	Longfellow	7	Skis	$125.00	$17.86
	Laura	Tinman	5	Skis	$108.00	$21.60
	Anna	Voegal	6	Snowmobile	$650.00	$108.33
					$ 3,482.00	

Part5,Step1-StudentNameRentalSummary.accdb

Student Name Total Sales

Cust Last Name	Cust First Name	Type Of Rental	Rental Amount	Tax	Total
Armstrong					
	Jon	Snowboard	$75.00	$4.50	$79.50
	Jon	Skis	$90.00	$5.40	$95.40
	Jon	Snowmobile	$100.00	$6.00	$106.00
	Jon	Snowboard	$123.00	$7.38	$130.38
Jacobson					
	Tyler	Skis	$108.00	$6.48	$114.48
	Tyler	Skis	$125.00	$7.50	$132.50
Keller					
	Mark	Skis	$100.00	$6.00	$106.00
	Mark	Skis	$108.00	$6.48	$114.48
Kleaver					
	Keenan	Skis	$125.00	$7.50	$132.50
	Keenan	Snowmobile	$350.00	$21.00	$371.00
Longfellow					
	Abi	Skis	$100.00	$6.00	$106.00
	Abi	Skis	$125.00	$7.50	$132.50
Parker					
	Jordan	Snowboard	$65.00	$3.90	$68.90
	Jordan	Snowmobile	$125.00	$7.50	$132.50
Ramsey					
	Amy	Snowmobile	$700.00	$42.00	$742.00
Tinman					
	Laura	Skis	$40.00	$2.40	$42.40
	Laura	Skis	$108.00	$6.48	$114.48
Voegal					
	Anna	Snowmobile	$200.00	$12.00	$212.00
	Anna	Snowmobile	$650.00	$39.00	$689.00
Winters					
	Jesse	Skis	$65.00	$3.90	$68.90
			$3,482.00	$208.92	$3,690.92

Part5,Step2-StudentNameTotalSales.accdb

Jon Armstrong
91 Asbury Street
New York, NY 10012-6582

Tyler Jacobson
P.O. Box 1999
Grayville, IL 62844-5845

Mark Keller
3999 East Second Street
Somerset, IN 46984-3325

Keenan Kleaver
933 Sooner Drive
North Metro, GA 30026-9564

Abi Longfellow
P.O. Box 9000
Cypress, CA 90630-3256

Jordan Parker
2049 Eagle Valley Road
Longmont, CO 80501-6658

Amy Ramsey
800 North Oregon Street
Port Saint Lucie, FL 34986-9854

Laura Tinman
P.O. Box 12
Taylors Falls, MN 55084-5873

Anna Voegal
11556 Tiner Road
Bellingham, WA 98225-9537

Jesse Winters
200 North Overton Drive
Alton, KS 67623-1145

Part5,Step3-CustomerMailingLabels.accdb

Benchmark Access 2013, Level 2, Unit 1
Supplemental Assessments

Supplemental Assessment 1

Part I

1. Family Eye Care is a locally owned eye care facility specializing in fitting glasses and contacts and in performing laser eye surgery. You have been hired to maintain their records through the use of the Access database named **AL2-U1-SA1-FamilyEyeCare-DataFile.accdb**. Copy the database to your work area and rename it **AL2-U1-FamilyEyeCare**. Currently there are three tables in the database.
   a. Review each of the tables and optimize data entry by modifying the data types and field sizes where necessary.
   b. Add captions to the fields.
   c. Create a custom format for the *DateofAppointment* field (Appointment Information table) to display like the following example: Fri, *Apr 24, 2015*.
   d. Make *ReasonforAppointment* in the Appointment Information table a multiple-value lookup list. The list should contain Contacts Fitting, Eye Exam, Follow-up Visit, Glasses Fitting, and Laser Surgery. Add eye exam to patient 101 for March 22, 2015.
   e. Add input masks to anywhere you find any *PatientID*, *DoctorID*, or *PostalCode* fields as well as any fields containing phone numbers.
   f. You will be extracting information from the various tables, so be sure to create appropriate relationships between the tables. Enforce referential integrity where applicable.
   g. In Design view, create attractive-looking forms for each of the tables. Add information about yourself to the Patient form. Your patient ID is 106. Assume that you have an appointment for laser surgery on March 24, 2015 with Dr. Denney. The charge is $1,500.

2. When a patient is charged for an office visit, assume that insurance pays 80 percent and the patient pays 20 percent. On the form with appointment information, create and appropriately place two calculated controls. One control should display the insurance coverage and the other control should display the patient balance. Add a graphic to the form if not already done in Step 1g above. Add additional formatting where appropriate. Save the form again.

3. Create another form that includes the patient's first and last name in the main form and the patient's corresponding appointment information in a subform. Include a title. Format the form so that it is easy to understand. Save the main form as **PatientAppointmentInformation**. Add a graphic to the form. Use the default name for the subform. Print the last record in the form.

4. Create a query based on the Appointment Information table that prompts the user to enter the doctor's ID. Include all fields. Save the query as **DoctorAndPatientAppointmentInformation**. Print the appointment information for Dr. Denney.

5. The doctors would like to move appointment information to a new table for all appointments between March 23 to the March 27. Make a new table query based on all of the fields from the Appointment Information table **except** the *ReasonforAppointment* field. Name the new table **Mar23to27AptInfo.** Run the query, open the table and then print it. Save the query as **Make-TableDateAppointments**.

6. Create a query that shows all Family Eye Care patients. Include information on why and when they were last in. There will be some patients who have not been in at all. Sort the list so that it shows the patients who have not been in at the top. Save the query as **AllPatients**.

Part II

The doctors are considering an increase in the price of their eye exams; however, they are interested in their competition. They have asked you to use the Internet to research other eye care facilities to determine the price of their eye exams. Locate at least three other facilities and create and print a memo that summarizes your findings. (Save the memo as a Word document with the file name **AL2-U1-SA1-EyeExamComparison.**)

Supplemental Assessment 2

Part I

1. You are the office manager for South County Premium Spas and Pools. You maintain the database named **AL2-U1-SA2-SouthCountyPSP-DataFile.** Copy the database to your work area and rename it **AL2-U1-SA2-SouthCountyPSP.** Currently, there are four tables in the database.
   a. Review each of the tables and optimize data entry by defining appropriate data types, field sizes, formats, input masks, and captions.
   b. You will be extracting information from the various tables, so be sure to create appropriate relationships between the tables.
   c. Create attractive-looking forms for the Customer Information and Customer Purchases tables. Add a graphic to the forms. Use the forms to add information about yourself. Assume you are from Newburgh, IN. Your customer ID is CA205. Assume that you purchased a spa on June 3, 2015. Julia Howell provided information about the spa and helped you with the purchase.

2. The manager would like to know the total value of inventory in stock. Create a query that summarizes this information. Save the query as **TotalInventoryValue2.** (*Note: you may have to make two queries.*)

3. Filter out the customers who are from Newburgh, IN. Save the query as **NotNewburghCustomers.** Print the results.

4. Due to a distributor price increase in spas, the manager is forced to increase the price of each item he sells by 5 percent. Use an update query to quickly make these changes. Save the update query as **5%PriceIncrease.**

5. The **CustomerPurchases** form created in Step 1d needs to be modified to include tabbed pages. One tab should be labeled *Customer Information* and show the customer ID and their first name and last name. The second tab should be called *Inventory* and should include the inventory ID, item name, and price. Format it appropriately.

6. Sort the Customer Purchases form by price in descending order. Print only the first record.

Part II

The manager is a little concerned about the increase in prices that he had to impose on his products. He is especially concerned with the price of the spa and how it compares to his competitors. He would like you to search the Internet for potential competitors to see what prices they are offering for spas. Research at least three different competitors and report back to him (your professor) via email with your findings.

Note that the following are suggested rubrics. Instructors should feel free to customize the rubrics to suit your grading standards and/or to adjust the point values.

Benchmark Access 2013 Level 2, Unit 1
Supplemental Assessments Rubrics

Note: Answers will vary.

Supplemental Assessment 1

Files: **AL2-U1-SA1-FamilyEyeCare.accdb**
      AL2-U1-SA1-EyeExamComparison.docx

Steps	Tasks	Criteria	Value	Score*
Part I	Feature	Rename database and folder	1	
1 a, b	Feature	*Appointment Information table* Add captions, datay types, field sizes	3	
	Feature	*Doctor Information table* Add captions, datay types, field sizes	3	
	Feature	*Patient Information table* Add captions, datay types, field sizes	3	
c	Feature	*Appointment Information table* *DateofAppointment* field - Custom format as follows: Thu, Apr 24, 2015 - ddd, mmm dd, yyyy	2	
d	Feature	*Appointment Information table* Lookup values – *DoctorID* field – use the doctor's names and possibly specialty	2	
	Feature	*Appointment Information table* *ReasonforAppointment* field – Make a multiple-value lookup field listing all appointment types	3	
e	Feature	Add input masks to all PatientID, DoctorID, PostalCode fields and any phone number fields.	6	
f	Feature	Create relationships and enforce referential integrity Two one-to-many relationships	2	

Steps	Tasks	Criteria	Value	Score*
g	Feature	Create three forms – one for each table Format appropriately • Control box alignment • Are control boxes wide enough to see data? • Apply theme or format *For Appointment Information form see 2 below.*	9	
	Editing	Add 1 record Patient 106 – Student information	1	
2	Feature	Add two calculated controls to the Appointment Information form: • 80% of the service charge = Insurance Coverage • 20% of the service charge = Patient Balance	4	
	Editing	*Appointment Information form* Add a graphic to the form	2	
3	Feature	Create a form to include • Patient's first and last names • Subform – appointment information • Add a graphic • Apply theme or format	4	
	Finishing	Print the last record	1	
4	Feature/Finishing	Prompted query Test with B102 (Denney) Print – 3 records showing B102	2	
5	Feature	Make new table query Contains all fields from Appointment Information table except *ReasonforAppointment* field *Note: The reason this field was deleted from the query is that it will not work with a multiple-valued lookup field.* New Table - May12to16thAptInfo New Query - Make-TableDateAppointments	5	
6	Feature	Query – shows all patients Relationship join changed to 2. Sort to show patients with no appointments on top. **AllPatients**	3	
Part II	Research/Writing/Finishing	Create a memo Summarize findings from Internet research List three prices of eye exams	5	
		TOTAL POINTS	61	

Supplemental Assessment 2

File: **AL2-U1-SA2-SouthCountyPSP.accdb**, email

Steps	Tasks	Criterion / Criteria	Value	Score*
Part I	**Feature**	Rename database file	1	
1 a, b	**Feature**	*Custome Information table* Add captions, input masks, and change field sizes.	3	
	Feature	*CustomerPurchases table* Add captions, input masks, and change field sizes.	3	
	Feature	*Inventory table* Add captions, input masks, and change field sizes.	3	
	Feature	*SalesRepInformation table* Add captions, input masks, and change field sizes.	3	
c	**Feature**	Create relationships and enforce referential integrity Three one-to-many relationships	3	
d	**Feature/Editing**	Create two forms for CustomerInformation and CustomerPurchases tables Add a graphic to each form Format appropriately • Control box alignment • Are control boxes wide enough to see data • Apply theme or format *For CustomerInformation form ,see 5 below.*	8	
	Editing	Add 1 record in *CustomerInformation* and *CustomerPurchases* tables Patient SC-205 – Student information Purchased spa on June 3, 2012 from Julia Howell (SC501)	1	
2	**Feature**	Query – Summarizes total value of inventory in stock Two queries need to be created – one nested in the other **TotalInventoryValue1** **TotalInventoryValue2**	4	
3	**Feature**	Query or Filter – Customers who are not from Newburgh **NotNewburghCustomers**	2	
	Finishing	Print the query	1	
4	**Feature**	Update query to increase price by 5% Check the increased prices in the Inventory table Inventory ID 10000 = $3.68 (previously $3.50)	2	

Steps	Tasks	Criterion / Criteria	Value	Score*
5	**Feature**	*CustomerPurchases* form Add tabbed page with two subforms • Customer Information – Customer ID, First Name, and Last Name • Inventory - Inventory Name, Inventory ID, and Price.	4	
6	**Feature/Finishing**	Sort the form by Price in descending order Print first record (Transaction #6)	2	
Part II	**Research/ Writing/ Finishing**	Create and send an email Summarize findings from Internet research List three competitors	5	
		TOTAL POINTS	45	

DoctorAndPatientAppointmentInformation   7/16/2013

Patient ID	Date of Appointment	Reason for Appointment	Service Charge	Doctor ID
102	Mon, Mar 23, 2015	Laser Surgery	$1,500.00	B102
104	Mon, Mar 23, 2015	Laser Surgery	$1,500.00	B102
102	Fri, Mar 27, 2015	Follow-up Visit	$20.00	B102
102	Fri, Mar 27, 2015	Follow-up Visit	$20.00	B102
098	Fri, Mar 27, 2015	Laser Surgery	$1,500.00	B102
098	Mon, Mar 30, 2015	Follow-up Visit	$20.00	B102

Page 1

AL2-U1-SA1-DoctorAndPatientAppointmentInformation(Step4).accdb

AL2-U1-SA1-PatientAppointmentForm(Step3).accdb

Memo

To: Professor's Name

From: Student Name

Date: July 16, 2013

Re: Eye Exam Comparison

Students will research other eye care facilities via the internet and will summarize their findings in a memo to the Professor.

AL2-U1-SA1-EyeExamComparison(PartII).docx

March23to27AptInfo

7/16/2013

PatientID	DateofAppointm	ServiceCharge	DoctorID
100	3/24/2015	$125.00	B101
101	3/23/2015	$20.00	B102
102	3/23/2015	$1,500.00	B100
103	3/23/2015	$175.00	B101
100	3/23/2015	$20.00	B101
104	3/23/2015	$1,500.00	B102
105	3/24/2015	$125.00	B101
102	3/27/2015	$20.00	B102
102	3/27/2015	$20.00	B102
099	3/27/2015	$175.00	B100
098	3/27/2015	$1,500.00	B102
095	3/27/2015	$125.00	B101
100	3/24/2015	$30.00	B101
103	3/23/2015	$20.00	B100
105	3/24/2015	$30.00	B101
099	3/27/2015	$20.00	B100
106	3/24/2015	$1,500.00	

Page 1

AL2-U1-SA1-March23to27AptInfo(Step5).accdb

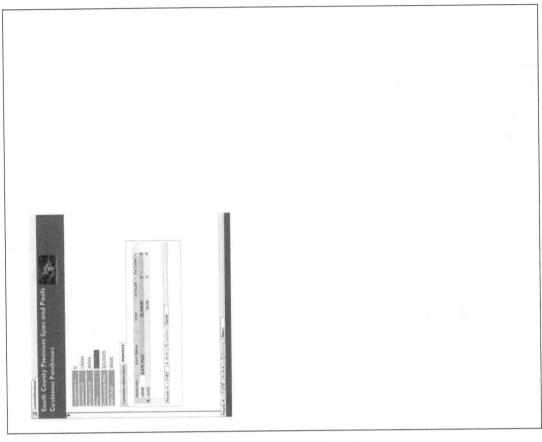

AL2-U1-SA2-CustomerPurchasesForm(Step6).accdb

AL2-U1-SA2-NotNewburghCustomers(Step3).accdb

Benchmark Access 2013, Level 2, Unit 2
Supplemental Assessments

Supplemental Assessment 1

Part I

1. Family Eye Care is a locally owned eye care facility specializing in fitting glasses and contacts and in performing laser eye surgery. You have been hired recently to maintain their records through the use of the Access database named **AL2-U2-SA1-FamilyEyeCare-DataFile.accdb**. Create a folder called *YourName*, copy the database to your work area, and rename it **AL2-U2-SA1-FamilyEyeCare**. Please place any documents that you create within this folder. Open the database and review the table and relationship structure. This case study will allow you to exercise creativity and polish your Access skills. In each activity, specific step-by-step instructions may not be provided to simulate a more realistic workplace assignment. Some instructions may appear vague or not comprehensive, but they are purposefully open-ended to allow each student to do original work and showcase individual creativity in problem solving.

2. In the Patient Information table, change Patient 106 to be your name.

3. Prepare a report that calculates the total amount of each patient's service charges. First create a query to include the patient information (patient ID and names) and all appointment information (except patient ID, reason for appointment, and doctor ID). Save the query as **PatientTotals**. Create a report from this query. View the report by the *PatientInformation* field and sort the report by the *DateOfAppointment* field. Call the report **PatientTotals**.

    a. For the *ServiceCharge* field, show the sum of the Grand Total and sum of the Subtotal in the Group footer. Bold and underline these amounts.

    b. Format the report so that the data is nicely presented and easy to read.

    c. Add you name in the footer as the person who prepared the report. Print the report.

4. Analyze the tables using the database analyzer. Open Word and use the screenshot to insert a picture of the analysis. Type your name in the Word document and save the Word document as **AL2-U2-SA1-FamilyEyeCareDatabaseAnalysis.docx**. Print it. Do not incorporate any of the changes.

5. At the end of the month, Dr. Payne needs his records of appointments (date and service charges only) exported as a delimited, comma separated text file. Save the text file as **AL2-U2-SA1-PayneAppointments**. Save the export steps.

6. Create the following report including the chart. The report is based on the DoctorIncome query. The report below is shown in Report view. Export the report as a PDF and print it. Save the PDF document as **AL2-U2-SA1-DoctorIncomeReport**.

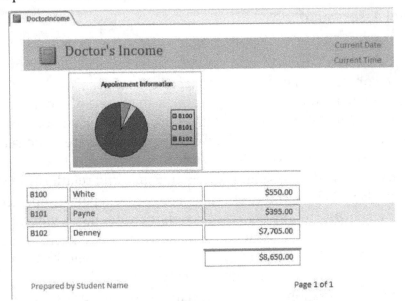

7. Create a Navigation form and save it as *MainMenu*. Include the PatientInformation, AppointmentInformation, and DoctorInformation forms as well as the PatientTotals report. Have this form open when the database opens. Create a button that will close the database. The text on the button should read *Close Family Eye Care Database*. Hide the tables in the Navigation pane.

8. One of the doctors would like to have access to the information in the **AL2-U2-SA1-FamilyEyeCare.accdb** database to generate her queries and reports. You will need to split the database into two files. Use the default options when performing this task.

Part II

To keep a competitive edge, the laser eye doctors would like to know what other practices are charging for this same type of surgery. Search the Internet for at least three businesses specializing in laser eye surgery. Report back to the doctors the name of the business and the price of the surgery in the form of a column chart created in Excel. Include in the chart the price of Family Eye Care's fees so that the doctors will see how they compare to the other businesses. Put your name in as a textbox. Save the workbook as **AL2-U2-SA1-LaserEyeSurgeryComparison**. Print the chart.

Supplemental Assessment 2

1. You are the office manager for South County Premium Spas and Pools. You maintain the database named **AL2-U2-SA2-SouthCountyPSP-DataFile.accdb**. Copy the database to your work area and rename it **AL2-U2-SA2-SouthCountyPSP**. This case study will allow you to exercise creativity and polish your Access skills. In each activity, specific step-by-step instructions may not be provided to simulate a more realistic workplace assignment. Some instructions may appear vague or not comprehensive, but they are purposefully open-ended to allow each student to do original work and showcase individual creativity in problem solving.

2. Create a macro named *FindInventory* that opens the Inventory form in Form view, activates the control named *ItemName*, and then opens the Find dialog box. Test the macro with the item *Spa*.

3. Create a macro named *CustPur* that opens the CustomerPurchases report—use the macro action *OpenReport*. In the *Action Arguments* section, change *Report* in the View Option argument option box to *Print Preview*.

4. Create command buttons to run macros as follows:

    a. On the CustomerInformation form, create a command button on the right side of the form in the *Detail* section to run the FindInventory macro. You determine the appropriate text to display on the face of the button and a name for the command button. Format the button to coordinate with the form.

    b. On the CustomerPurchases form, create a button at the right side of the form in the *Detail* section to run the CustPur macro. You determine the appropriate text to display on the face of the button and a name for the command button. Format the button to coordinate with the form.

5. Create a new macro named *ExitDB* that will close the Database. Assign the macro to a command button placed in the *Form Header* section of the Main Menu form. You determine the appropriate text to display on the face of the button and a name for the command button. Format the button to coordinate with the form.

6. Create a backup copy of the database in the same folder. Use the default file name.

7. Save the database as an ACCDE file in the same folder and using the same file name.

Benchmark Access 2013 Level 2, Unit 2
Supplemental Assessments Rubrics

Note: Answers will vary.

Supplemental Assessment 1

Files: **AL2-U2-SA1-FamilyEyeCare-BeforeSplit.accdb**
AL2-U2-SA1-FamilyEyeCare-Be.accdb
AL2-U2-SA1-DoctorIncomeReport.pdf
AL2-U2-SA1-PayneApopintments.txt
AL2-U2-SA1-FamilyEyeCareDatabaseAnalysis.docx

Steps	Tasks	Criteria	Value	Score*
Part I 1	Feature	Rename database and create folder	1	
2	Editing	Change Patient 106 to be student name	1	
3	Feature	Create report based on student-created query Query – **PatientTotals** - Patient ID, Patient First Name, Patient Last Name, Date of Appointment, and Service Charge Create a report based on this query • View report by *PatientInformation* • Sort by *DateOfAppointment*	4	
a	Feature	For *ServiceCharge* field include • Sum of Grand Total • Sum of Subtotal • Bold and underline these amounts	3	
b	Feature	Format report	2	
c	Feature	Prepared by Student Name in footer	1	
	Finishing	Print report	1	
4	Feature/Edit/ Finishing	Run Database Analyzer Insert screenshot in Word document Add name and print	3	
5	Feature	Create a query - Doctor name, date, service charges Export as a delimited, comma separated text file Save export steps	3	
6	Feature/ Finishing	Create the report based on the report shown • Use DoctorIncome query • Total • Prepared by • Format	5	

Steps	Tasks	Criteria	Value	Score*
	Feature	Create and format the chart for the report	3	
	Feature/Finishing	Export and save as PDF Print PDF	2	
7	Feature/ Finishing	Create Navigation Form – MainMenu • Patient Information form • Appointment Information form • Doctor Information form • Patient Information report • Form to open when database opens • Button to close the database • Hide the tables in Navigation pane	7	
8	Feature	Split the database	2	
Part II	Research/ Writing/ Finishing	Create a memo Summarize findings from Internet research in an Excel column chart for three businesses that perform laser surgery Print the chart	5	
		TOTAL POINTS	43	

Supplemental Assessment 2

File: **AL2-U2-SA2-SouthCountyPSP.accdb**

Steps	Tasks	Criteria	Value	Score*
1	Feature	Copy and rename database	1	
2	Feature	Create a macro named *FindInventory* Opens Inventory form in Form view. Activates control ItemName Opens Find dialog box.	5	
3	Feature	Create a macro named *CustPur* Opens Customer Purchases report (*Open Report*) Change Report to Print Preview in the View Option argument option box	5	
4a	Feature/Editing	Create a command button in the *Detail* section on the right side of the CustomerPurchases form Assign the FindInventory macro to the button Text and command name determined by student Format button to coordinate with form	5	

Steps	Tasks	Criteria	Value	Score*
b	**Feature/Editing**	Create a command button in the *Detail* section on the right side of the CustomerInformation form Assign the CustPur macro to the button Text and command name determined by student Format button to coordinate with form	5	
5	**Feature/Editing**	Create a macro to close the database Assign macro to button in *Form Header* section of the MainMenu form. Text and command name determined by student Format button to coordinate with form	5	
6	**Finishing**	Create a backup copy using default name and the same folder.	2	
7	**Finishing**	Save database as an ACCDE file using same name and folder location.	2	
		TOTAL POINTS	30	

Family Eye Care Patient Totals

Patient ID	Patient First Name	Patient Last Name	Date of Appointment	Service Charge
100	Linda	Easton	Fri, Mar 13, 2015	$125.00
			Fri, Mar 13, 2015	$20.00
			Fri, Mar 20, 2015	$1,500.00
				$1,645.00
101	Malory	Jefferson	Thu, Mar 12, 2015	$250.00
				$250.00
102	Jason	Reed	Thu, Mar 12, 2015	$1,500.00
			Fri, Mar 20, 2015	$20.00
				$1,520.00
103	Greg	Sloan	Thu, Mar 12, 2015	$175.00
				$175.00
104	Ellie	Oliver	Fri, Mar 13, 2015	$1,500.00
			Fri, Mar 20, 2015	$20.00
				$1,520.00
105	Kim	Jones	Fri, Mar 13, 2015	$125.00
			Fri, Mar 20, 2015	$20.00
				$145.00
106	Student	Name	Thu, Mar 19, 2015	$1,500.00
			Mon, Mar 23, 2015	$20.00
				$1,520.00
107	Sean	Edwards	Mon, Mar 23, 2015	$125.00
				$125.00
108	Nicholas	Williams	Mon, Mar 23, 2015	$125.00
				$125.00
109	Jan	Peterson	Mon, Mar 23, 2015	$1,500.00
			Thu, Mar 26, 2015	$1,625.00
				$8,650.00

Prepared by Student Name

Wednesday, July 17, 2013

AL2-U2-SA1-FamilyEyeCareDatabaseAnalysis(Step4).docx

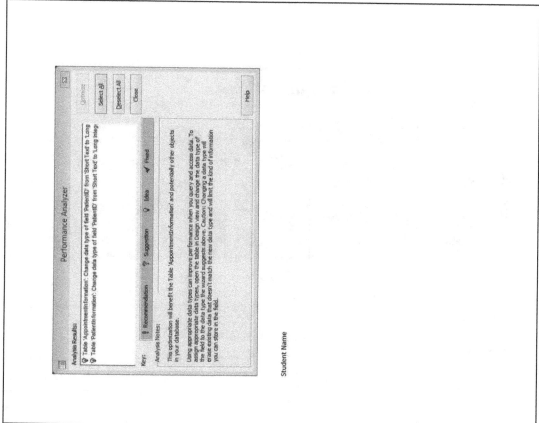

Student Name

AL2-U2-SA1-PatientTotals(Step3c).accdb

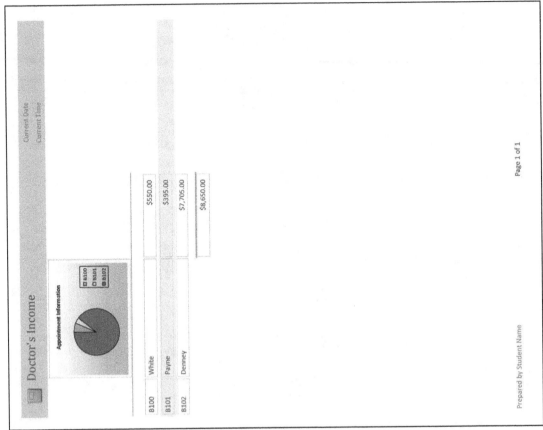

Prepared by Student Name

AL2-U2-SA1-LaserEyeSurgeryComparison-ModelAnswer(PartII).xlsx

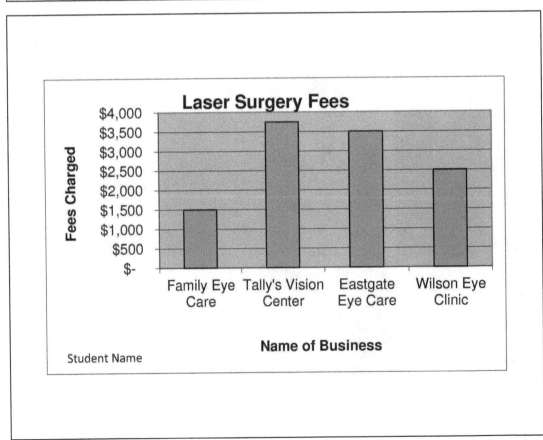

AL2-U2-SA1-DoctorIncomeReport(Step6).accdb

Benchmark Access 2013 Level 1
Final Case Study

Scenario: You are on temporary work assignment at CellOne Phones. CellOne Phones provides mobile services at competitive prices. Your expertise in Access has been requested to assist management in updating their database. As you work through each activity, additional information will be provided as needed.

This case study will allow you to exercise creativity and polish your Access skills. In each activity, specific step-by-step instructions may not be provided to simulate a more realistic workplace assignment. Some instructions may appear vague or not comprehensive, but they are purposefully open-ended to allow each student to do original work and showcase individual creativity in problem solving.

Part 1

1. Rename the database called **AL1-FCS-CellOnePhones-DataFile.accdb** as **AL1-FCS-CellOnePhones**.
2. In the database, there are two tables, one with customer information and another with a variety of cell phone plans. Open the CustomerInformation table and perform the following tasks:
   a. Add appropriate captions.
   b. Set any properties that would aid in data entry such as field formats or default values.

Part 2

1. Create a relationship between the tables and enforce referential integrity and select both cascade options. Create a relationship report and print it.

Part 3

1. Create, save, and print the following queries:
   a. A query to list all customers who are in zip code 90999. Use the *FirstName, LastName, Address, City, State,* and *ZipCode* fields. Save the query as *ZipCode90999*. Print the query in landscape orientation.
   b. Query to list all customers who are in Plan A or B. Include the *CustomerID, FirstName, LastName,* and *PlanCode* fields. Save the query as *PlanAorB*.
   c. A query to list the customers whose activation date is October 1, 2015 to October 14, 2015. Use the *FirstName, LastName, CellPhoneNumber,* and *ActivationDate* fields. Save the query as *Oct1to14*. Sort the list in ascending order by activation date.
   d. A query based on the query created in 1c to also show the customers who purchased PlanCode A during that time frame. Save the query as *Oct1to14PlanA*.
   e. A query to calculate the total bill. The tax rate is 6% of the Plan Price. Create field to calculate the actual tax and the total bill. Apply the currency formatting to the values in the tax amount column. Use all of the fields in the CustomerInformation table except the *ActivationDate* field. Save the query as *TotalBill*. Print the query in landscape orientation.

Part 4

1. Create a form based on the CustomerInformation table along with the *PlanPrice* field from a related CellPhonePlans table. Name the form *CustomerInformation*.
   a. Include a title for the form.
   b. Add conditional formatting that changes the fill color to a different color for each of the cell phone plans.
   c. Add the date and time.
   d. Apply a theme to the form.
   e. Format the form attractively so one record will print on one page.
   f. Add another record using the form with your information. Assign yourself the CustomerID 1011. Assume that you choose plan A and your activation date is October 12, 2015. Print only your record on one page.

Part 5

Create the following reports. Format appropriately and to print on one page.

1. Using information in the CustomerInformation table, create mailing labels to mail out the monthly bills.
   a. Use Avery C2160 labels.
   b. Sort by the customer's last name.
   c. Save the mailing labels as *CustomerMailingLabels*.
   d. Print the labels.
2. Use the Report Wizard to create a report that is grouped by the data in the *PlanCode* field. Include all of the fields from the CellPhonePlans table and use all of the fields in the CustomerInformation table except the plan code and activation date. In the Report Wizard, apply the Block layout style and change to landscape orientation. Adjust the columns so that all of the information can be seen. Include a title and format appropriately. Save the report as *CellPhonePlans*. Print the report.
3. Create a report based on the TotalBill query created in 1d. Sort it by the *LastName* field. Add a total to the bottom summing up the taxes and the total bills and adjust field heights as necessary so entire total amounts display. Decrease columns widths (make sure all records display) and change the report orientation to landscape. Save the report with the name *TotalBill*. Export the report to PDF and save the file as **AL1-FCS-CellPhonePlans**.
4. Create a cell phone number list (report) showing the customers whose plan code is A. Include the first and last name (sorted by last name in ascending order) and cell phone number. ***Note: Create and run a query and then create the report with the query.*** Include a title and format appropriately. Save the report as *CellPhoneListForPlanA*. Print the report.

Part 6

1. One of your coworkers would like to use some of the Excel features to analyze and possibly adjust the prices of the plans. Export the CellPhonePlans table to Excel. AutoFormat it in Excel, insert your name as a footer, save the file as **AL1-FCS-CellPhonePlans**, and print it.
2. Compact and repair the database.

Part 7

To maintain your competitive edge, you decide to research other companies that specialize in cell phone sales. Use the Internet to research at least three different companies and review the plans they offer to potential customers. Summarize your findings in a memo to the sales division. Save the memo as Word document with the file name **AL1-FCS-CompetitorsCellPhonePlans** and print it.

Part 8

Close the database. Submit the folder including the database and any other files. Hand in this test paper. Your printouts will be matched with your paper. Check to ensure that your database and other documents have been submitted.

> Note that the following are suggested rubrics. Instructors should feel free to customize the rubrics to suit your grading standards and/or to adjust the point values.

Benchmark Access 2013 Level 1
Final Case Study Rubric

Final Case Study

Files: **AL1-FCS-CellOnePhones.accdb**

   AL1-FCS-CellPhonePlans.pdf

   AL1-FCS-CellPhonePlans.xlsx

   AL1-FCS-CompetitorsCellPhonePlans.docx

Steps	Tasks	Criteria			Value	Score
Part 1						
1	Feature	Rename database and folder			1	
2	Feature	**Field Name**	**Caption**	**Special Formatting**	0	
		CustomerID	Customer ID		1	
		FirstName	First Name		1	
		LastName	Last Name		1	
		Address	N/A		0	
		City	N/A	Default Value	1	
		State	N/A	Default Value	1	
		ZipCode	Zip Code		1	
		CellPhoneNumber	Cell Phone		1	
		PlanCode	Plan Code		1	
		ActivationDate	Activation Date	Input Mask	2	
Part 2					0	
1	Feature	Create relationships – Enforce RI and cascade			2	

Steps	Tasks	Criteria	Value	Score
1	Feature/Finishing	Create relationship report and print	1	
Part 3			0	
1a	Feature	Create **ZipCode90999** query with criteria of 90999	2	
1b	Feature	Create **PlanAorB** query with criteria of A or B	2	
1c	Feature	Create **Oct1to14** query with criteria of Between 10/01/2015 and 10/14/2015 Sort Ascending by date	2	
1d	Feature	Create **Oct1to14PlanA**. Add A to criteria from query above. Use Save As to rename.	2	
1e	Feature	Create **TotalBill** query. Add two calculated fields Tax:[PlanPrice]*.06 TotalBill:[PlanPrice]+[Tax]	3	
Part 4			0	
1	Feature	Create form based on CustomerInformation table and *PlanPrice* field from CellPhonePlans table	2	
a	Feature	Add title to form	2	
b	Feature	Conditional formatting – fill color to change with each plan	3	
c	Feature	Date and time added	1	
d	Feature	Apply a theme	1	
e	Feature	Format the form 　　Adjust width of control objects 　　Change font 　　Ensure all data can be seen on one page	3	
f	Finishing	Add a record with student's own information and print just the student's record on one page	2	
Part 5			0	
1	Feature	Create mailing labels report	2	
a	Feature	Use Avery C2160 labels	1	
b	Feature	Sort by Customer's last name	1	
2	Feature	Create report Group by Plan Code	2	
	Format	Include all contact information (except activation date) Can be seen on one page	2	
	Finishing	Print the report	1	
3	Feature	Create report based on TotalBill query	2	
	Format	Sort by LastName	1	
	Feature	Add totals to bottom for taxes and total bills	1	

Steps	Tasks	Criteria	Value	Score
4	Feature	Create cell phone number report	2	
		Create query with Plan Code criteria of A		
	Feature	Sort by last name in ascending order	1	
	Format	Format title, text	1	
	Finishing	Print report	1	
Part 6			0	
1	Feature	Export CellPhonePlans table to Excel	1	
	Feature	Insert footer	1	
	Finishing	Print	1	
2	Feature	Compact and repair the database	2	
		Model answer database should be down around 1200 kb after it was compacted and repaired		
Part 7			0	
	Research/ Writing/ Finishing	Search Internet for competitor's plans and prices Create memo summarizing findings	3	
		TOTAL POINTS	65	

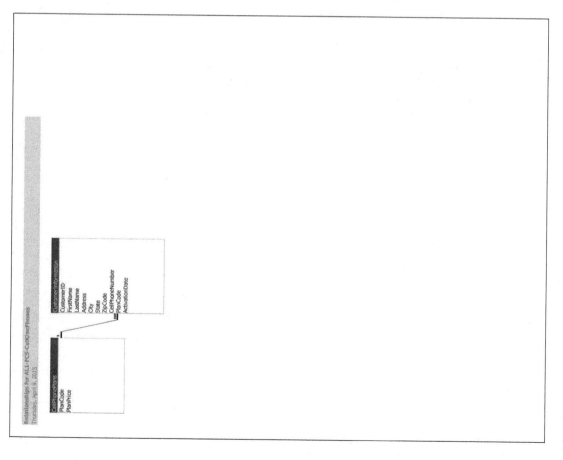

Part2Step1-RelationshipReport.accdb

PlanAorB

Customer ID	First Name	Last Name	Plan Code
1006	Sarah	Williamson	B
1007	Jan	Richards	A
1000	Kelly	Anderson	A
1002	Mike	Peterson	B
1003	Danielle	Rabers	A
1004	Sean	Reynolds	B
1005	Kaelan	Taylor	A
1010	Cathy	Clarkson	A

Part3,Step1b-PlanAorBQuery.accdb

ZipCode90999

First Name	Last Name	Address	City	State	Zip Code
Kelly	Anderson	470 East Washington Street	Florence	TX	90999
Kaelan	Taylor	45 Valley Way	Florence	TX	90999
Cathy	Clarkson	32 Ivey Walk	Florence	TX	90999

Part3,Step1a-ZipCode90999Query.accdb

Oct1to14PlanA 4/9/2015

First Name	Last Name	Cell Phone Num	Activation Date	Plan Code
Jan	Richards	(686) 555-7895	10/6/2015	A
Kelly	Anderson	(686) 555-4564	10/13/2015	A

Page 1

Part3,Step1d-Oct1to14PlanAQuery.accdb

Oct1to14 4/9/2015

First Name	Last Name	Cell Phone Num	Activation Date
Dani	Clarke	(686) 555-8889	10/4/2015
Mike	Peterson	(686) 555-4999	10/4/2015
Jan	Richards	(686) 555-7895	10/6/2015
Lynn	Daniels	(686) 555-3424	10/8/2015
Student	Name	(686) 555-9121	10/12/2015
Kelly	Anderson	(686) 555-4564	10/13/2015

Page 1

Part3,Step1c-Oct1to14Query.accdb

Plan Code	PlanPrice	Tax	TotalBill
A	$29.99	$1.80	$31.79
A	$29.99	$1.80	$31.79
A	$29.99	$1.80	$31.79
A	$29.99	$1.80	$31.79
A	$29.99	$1.80	$31.79
B	$39.99	$2.40	$42.39
B	$39.99	$2.40	$42.39
B	$39.99	$2.40	$42.39
C	$49.99	$3.00	$52.99
C	$49.99	$3.00	$52.99
C	$49.99	$3.00	$52.99

Customer ID	First Name	Last Name	Address	City	State	Zip Code	Cell Phone Num
1007	Jan	Richards	93 Magnolia Way	Florence	TX	90997	(686) 555-7895
1000	Kelly	Anderson	470 East Washington Street	Florence	TX	90999	(686) 555-4564
1003	Danielle	Rabers	404 Rueger Drive	Florence	TX	90097	(686) 555-1234
1005	Kaelan	Taylor	45 Valley Way	Florence	TX	90999	(686) 555-9876
1010	Cathy	Clarkson	32 Ivey Walk	Florence	TX	90999	(686) 555-1212
1006	Sarah	Williamson	456 First Street	Florence	TX	90995	(686) 555-8796
1002	Mike	Peterson	3000 North 3rd Street	Florence	TX	90998	(686) 555-4999
1004	Sean	Reynolds	10002 South Georgia Drive	Florence	TX	90099	(686) 555-5595
1008	Lynn	Daniels	29 Hunt Club Drive	Florence	TX	90989	(686) 555-3424
1009	Dani	Clarke	4 Richmond Street	Florence	TX	90990	(686) 555-8889
1001	Crystal	Harper	P.O. Box 1900	Florence	TX	90998	(686) 555-4965

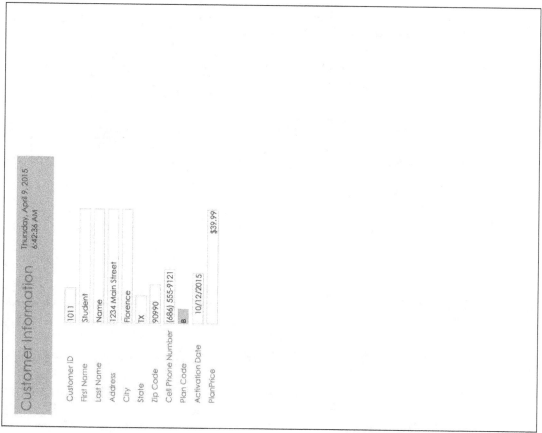

Part5,Step1-CustomerMailingLabels.accdb

Kelly Anderson
470 East Washington Street
Florence, TX 90999

Dani Clarke
4 Richmond Street
Florence, TX 90990

Cathy Clarkson
32 Ivey Walk
Florence, TX 90999

Lynn Daniels
29 Hunt Club Drive
Florence, TX 90989

Crystal Harper
P.O. Box 1900
Florence, TX 90098

Student Name
1234 Main Street
Florence, TX 90990

Mike Peterson
3000 North 3rd Street
Florence, TX 90998

Danielle Rabers
404 Rueger Drive
Florence, TX 90097

Sean Reynolds
10002 South Georgia Drive
Florence, TX 90099

Jan Richards
93 Magnolia Way
Florence, TX 90997

Kaelan Taylor
45 Valley Way
Florence, TX 90999

Sarah Williamson
456 First Street
Florence, TX 90095

Customer Information
Thursday, April 9, 2015
6:42:36 AM

Customer ID	1011
First Name	Student
Last Name	Name
Address	1234 Main Street
City	Florence
State	TX
Zip Code	90990
Cell Phone Number	(686) 555-9121
Plan Code	B
Activation Date	10/12/2015
PlanPrice	$39.99

Part4-CustomerInformationForm.accdb

TotalBill

Thursday, April 9, 2015
7:07:43 AM

Customer ID	First Name	Last Name	Address	City	State	Zip Code	Cell Phone Number
1000	Kelly	Anderson	470 East Washington Street	Florence	TX	90999	(6B6) 555-4564
1009	Dani	Clarke	4 Richmond Street	Florence	TX	90990	(686) 555-8889
1010	Cathy	Clarkson	32 Ivey Walk	Florence	TX	90999	(686) 555-1212
1008	Lynn	Daniels	29 Hunt Club Drive	Florence	TX	90989	(686) 555-3424
1001	Crystal	Harper	P.O. Box 1900	Florence	TX	90098	(686) 555-4965
1011	Student	Name	1234 Main Street	Florence	TX	90990	(686) 555-9121
1002	Mike	Peterson	3000 North 3rd Street	Florence	TX	90998	(686) 555-4999
1003	Danielle	Rabers	404 Rueger Drive	Florence	TX	90097	(686) 555-1234
1004	Sean	Reynolds	10002 South Georgia Drive	Florence	TX	90099	(686) 555-5595
1007	Jan	Richards	93 Magnolia Way	Florence	TX	90997	(686) 555-7895
1005	Kaelan	Taylor	45 Valley Way	Florence	TX	90999	(686) 555-9876
1006	Sarah	Williamson	456 First Street	Florence	TX	90995	(686) 555-8796

Cell Phone Plans

PlanCode	PlanPrice	Customer ID	First Name	Last Name	Address	City	State	Zip Code	Cell Phone Number
A	$29.99	1010	Cathy	Clarkson	32 Ivey Walk	Florence	TX	90999	(686) 555-1212
		1007	Jan	Richards	93 Magnolia Way	Florence	TX	90999	(686) 555-7895
		1005	Kaelan	Taylor	45 Valley Way	Florence	TX	90999	(686) 555-9876
		1003	Danielle	Rabers	404 Rueger Drive	Florence	TX	90097	(686) 555-1234
		1000	Kelly	Anderson	470 East Washington Street	Florence	TX	90990	(686) 555-4564
B	$39.99	1011	Student	Name	1234 Main Street	Florence	TX	90990	(686) 555-9121
		1006	Sarah	Williamson	456 First Street	Florence	TX	90995	(686) 555-8796
		1004	Sean	Reynolds	10002 South Georgia Drive	Florence	TX	90099	(686) 555-5595
		1002	Mike	Peterson	3000 North 3rd Street	Florence	TX	90998	(686) 555-4999
C	$49.99	1009	Dani	Clarke	4 Richmond Street	Florence	TX	90990	(686) 555-8889
		1008	Lynn	Daniels	29 Hunt Club Drive	Florence	TX	90989	(686) 555-3424
		1001	Crystal	Harper	P.O. Box 1900	Florence	TX	90098	(686) 555-4965

Thursday, April 9, 2015

Page 1 of 1

Cell Phone List For Plan A

First Name	Last Name	Cell Phone Number	Plan Code
Kelly	Anderson	(686) 555-4564	A
Cathy	Clarkson	(686) 555-1212	A
Danielle	Robers	(686) 555-1234	A
Jan	Richards	(686) 555-7895	A
Kaelan	Taylor	(686) 555-9876	A

Part5,Step4-CellPhoneListForPlanA.accdb

Plan Code	PlanPrice	Tax	TotalBill
A	$29.99	$1.80	$31.79
C	$49.99	$3.00	$52.99
A	$29.99	$1.80	$31.79
C	$49.99	$3.00	$52.99
C	$49.99	$3.00	$52.99
B	$39.99	$2.40	$42.39
B	$39.99	$2.40	$42.39
A	$29.99	$1.80	$31.79
B	$39.99	$2.40	$42.39
A	$29.99	$1.80	$31.79
A	$29.99	$1.80	$31.79
B	$39.99	$2.40	$42.39
	$459.88	$27.59	487.4728

Part5,Step3-AL1-FCS-CellPhonePlans.accdb (2 of 2)

Page 1 of 1

TO: Sales Division

FROM: Student Name

DATE: April 9, 2015

SUBJECT: Other Cell Phone Plans

Students will research other cell phone companies using the Internet, and then they will summarize their findings in a memo to the professor.

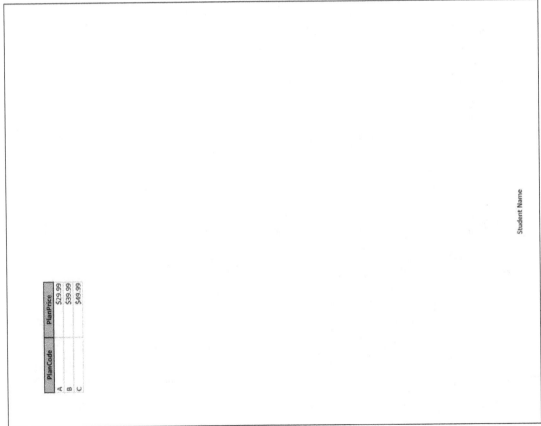

PlanCode	PlanPrice
A	$29.99
B	$39.99
C	$49.99

Student Name

Part6,Step1-AL1-FCS-CellPhonePlans.xlsx

Benchmark Access 2013 Level 2
Final Case Study

Scenario: You are an intern at Global Wholesale Enterprises, a distributor of consumer goods worldwide. As part of your duties, you have been assigned to database administration at the head office in New York. The human resources manager has asked you to review the database created by the intern who has returned to school. The previous intern was a self-taught Access user who took on the Access project in his spare time. The manager thinks your Access training will help fine-tune the database.

This case study will allow you to exercise creativity and refine your Access skills. In each activity, specific step-by-step instructions will not be provided to simulate a more realistic workplace assignment. Some instructions, if they appear vague or not comprehensive, are purposefully open-ended to allow each student to do original work and showcase individual creativity in problem-solving cases.

Activity 1

You have been hired recently by Global Wholesale Enterprises to maintain their records through the use of the Access database named **AL2-FCS-GWEEmployees-DataFile.accdb**. Before you begin this activity, copy the **AL2-FCS-GWEExpensesPaid-DataFile.txt** and **AL2-FCS-GWEEmployees-DataFile.accdb** files to your work area, renaming the database file **AL2-FCS-GWEEmployees**. Your first task is to review the existing structure.

    a. Open the database and browse each table, query, and form object within the file.

    b. The database contains three tables which currently have no relationships defined. You realize that before you can add more forms and reports to the database you will need to set up relationships between the tables. Look at each table in Design view and note the primary key field. Decide how to relate the tables and then open the Relationships window and create the relationships. For each relationship, turn on the relationship options you think are appropriate.

    c. Global Wholesale Enterprises has 2,700 employees worldwide. As the database grows when the remaining records are added, you anticipate that sorting and finding records to view or edit will become slow and reduce efficiency. Review the current index fields in the Employees and EmployeeDatesandSalaries tables. Decide whether or not additional fields should be indexed and then modify the table design to include the additional indexes. Create at least two new indexes.

    d. Create a new table to keep track of any changes you made to the indexing. The new table should include fields for *ID*, *Title*, *OpenDate*, *Status*, *Priority*, and *Description*. Name the table *Documentation*. Add a new record to the Documentation table in which you explain the reasoning for the additional indexes you created. Each change should have its own ID. The priority is *High*. **_Note: When you complete a task, change the status to_ Closed.** An example of a record is given below.

ID	Title	OpenDate	Status	Priority	Description
1	Indexing	Currents date	Open	High	Include a description of what fields were involved and what you did.

Activity 2

The EmployeeDatesandSalaries table is not well designed. Upon opening the table you notice that some data is duplicated several times within the database. Whenever data is duplicated you know this can lead to inconsistency and input errors. In addition to the data duplication, you note that some fields are repeated in this table.

a. The EmployeeDatesandSalaries table contains a design error—fields should not be repeated in multiple tables. Decide which fields should be deleted from the table and then remove them from the table design. Open the Documentation table and type a short explanation describing why the fields you deleted are not required.

b. The EmployeeDatesandSalaries table also contains duplicated information that could be split into smaller related tables. Use the Table Analyzer feature to split the EmployeeDatesandSalaries table into two tables to remove the duplication. Decide on new names for the tables and which fields should be the primary keys. Allow Access to create a query that looks like the original table. When the wizard is finished, review the query and the two new tables.

c. When the original EmployeeDatesandSalaries table was split, any existing relationships with the table were removed. Revise the relationships to incorporate the new tables.

d. Generate a table definition documentation report for the new tables created in Steps b and c above that includes properties, relationships, all field options, and no indexes. Print the report.

Activity 3

The manager of Human Resources needs a few reports to present to the Director. Format the reports attractively, including a picture and proper title for each report. Put your name in the footer to indicate that you prepared the report.

a. Create a report that sums the salaries by department. Include the department, last and first names, and annual salary. Also include the total salary expense for the company. Sort in descending order by annual salary and then in ascending order by last name. You may need to create a query. Format all numbers to currency and zero decimals. Save the report as *TotalSalaryExpense*. Print the report.

b. Create the report shown below. It shows employee vacations by department. You will see that some employees do not receive any vacation. They still need to be included in the report. *Note: A query may need to be used and the join properties changed.* Print the report.

Global Wholesale Enterprises
Vacation by Department

Department	Vacation	AnnualSalary
European Division		
		$42,238.00
		$43,659.00
	2 weeks	$44,694.00
	2 weeks	$44,387.00
	2 weeks	$42,126.00
	3 weeks	$69,725.00
		$286,829.00
North American Division		
	1 week	$43,695.00
	4 weeks	$69,725.00
	4 weeks	$44,892.00
	4 weeks	$45,558.00
	4 weeks	$45,651.00
		$249,521.00
Overseas Division		
		$44,771.00
	1 week	$42,248.00
	2 weeks	$42,857.00
	2 weeks	$42,824.00
	2 weeks	$45,395.00
	3 weeks	$69,725.00
		$287,820.00
		$824,170.00

Current Date   Prepared by Student Name   Page 1 of 1

Activity 4

The manager of Human Resources wants you to import the **AL2-FCS-GWEExpens-esPaid-DataFile.txt** file. Do not set a primary key. After you look at the imported table you realize that there are some fields that are redundant. Delete these fields. You also realize that you need to change some of the field properties to allow for ease of data entry and data integrity. Make any necessary changes. Update the relationships to incorporate this new table.

   a. Create a form for the GWEExpensesPaid table. Include all of the fields. Add the first name and last name of the employee. Set the Tab Stop property to *No*. Format to enhance the appearance.

   b. The manager would like to view expenses as shown in the report below. Don`t forget to include your name in the footer. Print the report.

GWE Expenses Paid

Current Date
8:52:10 PM

Type	Employee No	Date	Amount	Description
Administration				
	1010	7/20/2015	$874.10	Distributor's Association Fee
	1040	8/10/2015	$124.65	Outsourced photocopying
	1070	10/10/2015	$84.75	Digital picture prints
			$1,083.50	
Sales				
	1001	3/15/2015	$1,543.10	NorthWest Sales Meeting
	1001	4/10/2015	$775.12	Distributor Promotion
	1005	5/9/2015	$5,432.12	Overseas Sales Meetings
	1045	5/13/2015	$153.15	Tradeshow
	1010	6/6/2015	$6,320.15	European Sales Meetings
	1025	6/18/2015	$1,127.88	Sales Conference
	1001	6/18/2015	$2,254.16	New York Sales Meetings
	1005	7/27/2015	$2,211.10	Canadian Sales Meeting
	1025	8/3/2015	$541.22	Client Entertainment
			$20,358.00	
Shipping				
	1015	6/25/2015	$174.10	Overnight Delivery to California
	1010	9/2/2015	$34.10	Overnight Delivery to Nevada
			$208.20	
			$21,649.70	

Prepared by Student Name

Page 1 of 1

Activity 5

As your final steps to fine-tune the Human Resources database, you decide to automate some tasks, create a navigation form, and set startup options.

   a. On the EmployeesNamesandAddresses form, create a button to open the EmployeeBenefits form.

   b. Create a navigation form and add the following:

- The EmployeesNamesandAddresses form.
- The GWEExpensesPaid form.
- The TotalSalaryExpense report.
- The VacationByDepartment report.
- A button on the Navigation form to Close the database.

   c. Remove the display of the Navigation pane and have the Navigation form open up when the database is opened.

Submit the electronic copy of the **AL2-FCS-GWEEmployees.accdb** file to your instructor. Keep a copy of all files completed in this case study until you have received your grade.

Benchmark Access 2013 Level 2
Final Case Study Rubric

Note: Answers will vary.

Final Case Study

File: **AL2-FCS-GWEEmployees.accdb**

Step	Tasks	Criteria	Value	Score*
		Note: Use F11 to display all objects.		
1 b	Feature	Two relationships created as follows: - 1:1 Employees (primary) to EmployeeBenefits (related) - Referential integrity, cascade update/delete options activated - 1:1 Employees (primary) to EmployeeDatesandSalaries (related) - Referential integrity, cascade update/delete options activated	4	
c	Feature	Employees table - Multiple field index – *FirstName* and *LastName* EmployeeDatesandSalariesTable - *BirthDate* field set up as an index - There should be at least two new indexes created. Student answers may vary.	4	
d	Feature/Typing	Documentation table created with clear, logical explanations included for fields that were indexed.	5	
2a	Editing	EmployeeDatesandSalaries table - *LastName, FirstName,* and *MiddleInitial* fields should be deleted. - Documentation table contains explanation that tells why these fields are not needed	5	
b	Feature/Editing	EmployeeDatesandSalaries table split into two newly named tables (look for EmployeeDates and Salaries_OLD in table object list) - Two new tables created – logical name given to new EmployeeDatesandSalaries table and table containing divisions (model answer table names are *EmployeeDemographics* and *DepartmentList*) - Primary keys in new tables set correctly - Query created for old EmployeeDatesandSalaries table	7	

Step	Tasks	Criteria	Value	Score*
c	**Feature**	Relationship created between Employees (primary) and newly created table—new EmployeeDatesandSalaries (related) - Same relationship options set as for other similar relationships	5	
d	**Feature/Finishing**	A table definition documentation report was generated and printed. See model answers for a sample of this report.	3	
3a	**Feature/Editing/ Finishing**	A report is created that sums salaries by department. The *Department, FirstName, LastName,* and *AnnualSalary* fields were included. - Department totals should be included - Company total should be included - An appropriate picture should be added - Fields should be aligned nicely - Totals should be displayed as currency - Print the report	5	
b	**Feature/Editing Finishing**	A report is created that groups the employees by department and then by vacation as shown. - Query needs to be created and join type changed - Department totals should be included - Company total should be included - An appropriate picture should be added - Fields should be aligned nicely - Totals should be displayed as currency - Print the report	7	
4	**Feature/Editing**	Import the GWEExpensesPaid text file. Delete both of the name fields. Change the properties. - Delete extra space in any field names - There is no primary key - Input mask for Employee ID - Watch for data types, field sizes, and captions Add this table to the relationships and create a relationship. Employees (primary) to GWEExpensesPaid - Referential integrity, cascade update/delete options set	7	
a	**Feature/Editing**	Create a form for the GWEExpensesPaid table. Add *FirstName* and *LastName* fields - Set Tab Stop property to *No* Format to enhance the appearance	5	

Step	Tasks	Criteria	Value	Score*
b	Feature/Editing/Finishing	A report is created that groups the expenses by type and then sorts them by date as shown - Department totals should be included - Company total should be included - An appropriate picture should be added - Fields should be aligned nicely - Totals should be displayed as currency - Print the report	7	
5a	Feature	On EmployeeNamesandAddresses form - button to open EmployeeBenefits form	2	
b	Feature/Finishing	A Navigation form is created to - Open EmployeeNamesandAddresses form - Open GWEExpensesPaid form - Open TotalSalaryExpense report - Open VacationByDepartment report - Close the database	7	
c	Feature/Finishing	Startup options - Navigation form is shown at start up - Navigation pane is removed from view	3	
		TOTAL POINTS	76	

Properties

DateCreated:	7/16/2013 4:09:02 PM	GUID:	{guid {3283194D-B01E-46AB-8F5E-29F0B88772C3}}
LastUpdated:	7/16/2013 4:09:02 PM	RecordCount:	3
Updatable:	True		

Columns

Name	Type	Size
Department	Short Text	50

AllowZeroLength: False
AppendOnly: False
Attributes: Variable Length
CollatingOrder: General
DataUpdatable: False
GUID: {guid {81EDFEEF-6212-4940-A0FA-005979380D30}}
OrdinalPosition: 0
Required: False
SourceField: Department
SourceTable: Departments

ID	Long Integer	4

AllowZeroLength: False
AppendOnly: False
Attributes: Fixed Size, Auto-Increment
CollatingOrder: General
DataUpdatable: False
GUID: {guid {ED947111-4719-4661-B012-805846C7C56A}}
OrdinalPosition: 1
Required: False
SourceField: ID
SourceTable: Departments

Relationships

DepartmentsEmployeesDates&Salaries

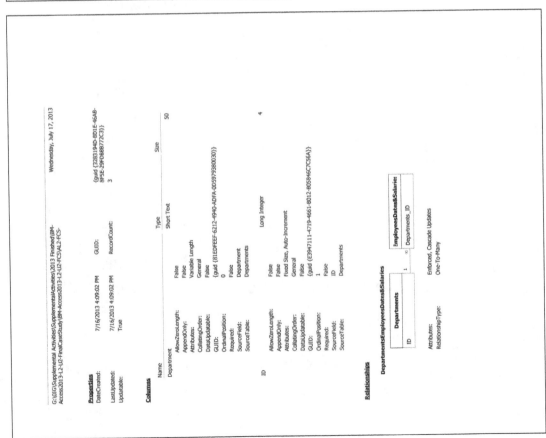

Departments		EmployeesDates&Salaries
ID		Departments_ID

Attributes: Enforced, Cascade Updates
RelationshipType: One-To-Many

AL2-U2-FCS-doc_rptObjects(Step2d).accdb (Step 1 of 3)

Properties

DateCreated:	7/16/2013 4:09:02 PM	GUID:	{guid {9380EF16-5B7E-4C1F-9B14-0CFF47B03A80}}
LastUpdated:	7/16/2013 4:10:14 PM	RecordCount:	17
Updatable:	True		

Columns

Name	Type	Size
EmpNo	Short Text	4

AllowZeroLength: False
AppendOnly: False
Attributes: Variable Length
CollatingOrder: General
DataUpdatable: False
GUID: {guid {3761AA3D-2849-4583-99A8-E12807CD9E46}}
OrdinalPosition: 1
Required: False
SourceField: EmpNo
SourceTable: EmployeesDates&Salaries

BirthDate	Date With Time	8

AllowZeroLength: False
AppendOnly: False
Attributes: Fixed Size
CollatingOrder: General
DataUpdatable: False
GUID: {guid {60FA0BD2-230C-4FA5-9186-4933010D0139C}}
OrdinalPosition: 2
Required: False
SourceField: BirthDate
SourceTable: EmployeesDates&Salaries

HireDate	Date With Time	8

AllowZeroLength: False
AppendOnly: False
Attributes: Fixed Size
CollatingOrder: General
DataUpdatable: False
GUID: {guid {89A8E428-E476-479C-944F-FD0008F341ECD}}
OrdinalPosition: 3
Required: False
SourceField: HireDate
SourceTable: EmployeesDates&Salaries

AnnualSalary	Currency	8

AllowZeroLength: False
AppendOnly: False
Attributes: Fixed Size
CollatingOrder: General
DataUpdatable: False
GUID: {guid {E4ECD68E-E650-417F-AA19-0693776B3621}}

AL2-U2-FCS-doc_rptObjects(Step2d).accdb (Step 2 of 3)

Total Salary Expense

Department	Last Name	First Name	AnnualSalary
European Division			
	Postma	Hanh	$69,725
	Fistouris	Valerie	$44,694
	Zakowski	Carl	$44,387
	Couture	Leo	$43,659
	Yiu	Terry	$42,238
	McKnight	Donald	$42,126
			$286,829
North American Division			
	Vestering	Sam	$69,725
	Besterd	Lyle	$45,651
	Doxtator	Angela	$45,558
	Biliski	Jorge	$44,892
	Liszniewski	Norm	$43,695
			$249,521
Overseas Division			
	Deptulski	Roman	$69,725
	Lafreniere	Guy	$45,395
	Jhawar	Balfor	$44,771
	Fitchett	Mike	$42,857
	Hicks	Thom	$42,824
	Thurston	Edward	$42,248
			$287,820
			824170

Page 1 of 1

AL2-U2-FCS-TotalSalaryExpense(Step3a).accdb

G:\0\G\Supplemental Activities\Supplemental Activities\2013 Finished\IBM-Access2013-L2-U2-FinalCaseStudy\IBM-Access2013-L2-U2-FCS-
Wednesday, July 17, 2013

4

OrdinalPosition:	4
Required:	False
SourceField:	AnnualSalary
SourceTable:	EmployeesDates&Salaries

Departments_ID

AllowZeroLength:	Long Integer
AppendOnly:	False
Attributes:	False
BoundColumn:	Fixed Size
Caption:	1
CollatingOrder:	Lookup to Departments
ColumnCount:	Neutral
ColumnHeads:	3
ColumnWidths:	True
DataUpdatable:	0;1;2365
DisplayControl:	False
GUID:	Combo Box
	{guid {B2C9HC14-39BD-4CA2-9780-B5E86C9C9309}}
LimitToList:	True
ListRows:	8
ListWidth:	1.8423611111111
OrdinalPosition:	6
Required:	False
RowSource:	SELECT [ID] AS xyz_ID_xyz, [Department] AS xyz_DispExpr_xyz, [Department] FROM [Departments] ORDER BY [Department]
RowSourceType:	Table/Query
SourceField:	Departments_ID
SourceTable:	EmployeesDates&Salaries

Relationships

EmployeesEmployeesDates&Salaries

Employees	EmployeesDates&Salaries
EmpNo	EmpNo

Attributes: Unique, Enforced, Cascade Updates, Cascade Deletes
RelationshipType: One-To-One

DepartmentsEmployeesDates&Salaries

Departments	EmployeesDates&Salaries
ID	Departments_ID

Attributes: Enforced, Cascade Updates
RelationshipType: One-To-Many

AL2-U2-FCS-doc_rptObjects(Step2d).accdb (Step 3 of 3)

GWE Expenses Paid

Current Date 8:52:10 PM

Type	Employee No	Date	Amount	Description
Administration				
	1010	7/20/2015	$874.10	Distributor's Association Fee
	1040	8/10/2015	$124.65	Outsourced photocopying
	1070	10/10/2015	$84.75	Digital picture prints
			$1,083.50	
Sales				
	1001	3/15/2015	$1,543.10	NorthWest Sales Meeting
	1001	4/10/2015	$775.12	Distributor Promotion
	1005	5/9/2015	$5,432.12	Overseas Sales Meetings
	1045	5/13/2015	$153.15	Tradeshow
	1010	6/6/2015	$6,320.15	European Sales Meetings
	1025	6/18/2015	$1,127.88	Sales Conference
	1001	6/18/2015	$2,254.16	New York Sales Meetings
	1005	7/27/2015	$2,211.10	Canadian Sales Meeting
	1025	8/3/2015	$541.22	Client Entertainment
			$20,358.00	
Shipping				
	1015	6/25/2015	$174.10	Overnight Delivery to California
	1010	9/2/2015	$34.10	Overnight Delivery to Nevada
			$208.20	
			$21,649.70	

Prepared by Student Name

Page 1 of 1

AL2-U2-FCS-GWEExpensesPaid(Step4b).accdb

Global Wholesale Enterprises
Vacation by Department

Department	Vacation	AnnualSalary
European Division		
		$42,238.00
		$43,659.00
	2 weeks	$44,694.00
	2 weeks	$44,387.00
	2 weeks	$42,126.00
	3 weeks	$69,725.00
		$286,829.00
North American Division		
	1 week	$43,695.00
	4 weeks	$69,725.00
	4 weeks	$44,892.00
	4 weeks	$45,558.00
	4 weeks	$45,651.00
		$249,521.00
Overseas Division		
	1 week	$44,771.00
	2 weeks	$42,248.00
	2 weeks	$42,857.00
	2 weeks	$42,824.00
	2 weeks	$45,395.00
	3 weeks	$69,725.00
		$287,820.00
		$824,170.00

Current Date   Prepared by Student Name   Page 1 of 1

AL2-U2-FCS-VacationByDepartment(Step3b).accdb

NOTES

NOTES

NOTES

NOTES

NOTES